PRAISE FOR PAUL DICKSON AND

WAR SLANG

"Paul Dickson is one of my heroes—*WAR SLANG* is both an invaluable reference and a word lover's delight."

—Charlie Elster,
author of *There Is No Zoo in Zoology*
and *Is There a Cow in Moscow?*

"Paul Dickson is a national treasure who deserves a wide audience."

—*Library Journal*

"Intriguingly, Dickson has organized his dictionary by war, matching each bit of slang to its appropriate conflict. . . ."

—Malcolm Jones, Jr., *Newsweek*

"A trivia lover's delight . . . should be of interest to anyone who was, or is, in the military. . . ."

—*Blade-Citizen Preview* (Oceanside, CA)

"There are surprises: words still in common use that are much older than most people imagine. And some of the extinct words and phrases are so colorful they deserve to be resurrected. . . ."

—Olin Chism, *Dallas Morning News*

"For many, the volume will bring back memories of the days when those in military service often made up their own colorful and down-to-earth language to describe events of dangerous days."

—*St. Joseph* (Missouri) *News-Press*

"The author's brief but carefully thought-out informal introductions to each section help define the flavor of the period."

—*Booklist*

Books by Paul Dickson

Think Tanks
The Great American Ice Cream Book
The Future of the Workplace
The Electronic Battlefield
The Mature Person's Guide to Kites, Yo-yos, Frisbees, and Other
    Childlike Diversions
Out of This World: American Space Photography
The Future File
Chow: A Cook's Tour of Military Food
The Official Rules
The Official Explanations
Toasts
Words
There Are Alligators in Our Sewers & Other American Credos
    with Joseph C. Goulden
On Our Own: A Declaration of Independence for the Self-employed
Family Words
The Library in America
The New Official Rules
The Dickson Baseball Dictionary
Slang!*
What Do You Call a Person From?
Timelines
Baseball's Greatest Quotations
On This Spot
    with Douglas E. Eveleyn
The Dickson Word Treasury
The Dickson Joke Treasury
Myth-Informed
    with Joseph C. Goulden
The Congress Dictionary
    with Paul Clancy
The Worth Book of Softball

*Published by POCKET BOOKS

WAR
S★L★A★N★G

American Fighting Words and Phrases from the Civil War to the Gulf War

PAUL DICKSON

POCKET BOOKS

New York   London   Toronto   Sydney   Tokyo   Singapore

POCKET BOOKS, a division of Simon & Schuster Inc.
1230 Avenue of the Americas, New York, NY 10020

Copyright © 1994 by Paul Dickson

Interior photos by Lee MacLeod

All rights reserved, including the right to reproduce
this book or portions thereof in any form whatsoever.
For information address Pocket Books, 1230 Avenue
of the Americas, New York, NY 10020

Dickson, Paul.
    War slang : fighting words and phrases of Americans from the
Civil War to the Gulf War / Paul Dickson
        p.   cm.
    ISBN 0-671-75024-0
    1. Soldiers—United States—Language (New words, slang, etc.)
—Dictionaries.   2. Military art and science—United States—Slang
—Dictionaries.   3. United States—History, Military—Slang
—Dictionaries.   4. English language—United States—Slang
—Dictionaries.   5. Americanisms—Dictionaries.   I. Title.
PE3727.S7D53   1993
427'.09—dc20   93-16264
                                                                    CIP

First Pocket Books trade paperback printing June 1995

10   9   8   7   6   5   4   3   2   1

POCKET and colophon are registered trademarks of
Simon & Schuster Inc.

Design: Stanley S. Drate/Folio Graphics Co. Inc.

Cover design by Camille Coticchio
Cover art by Lee MacLeod

Printed in the U.S.A.

CONTENTS

"That seems to be one of the nicer things about war—
it enriches the language so."

—Novelist Robert C. Ruark,
in his syndicated newspaper column
at the beginning of the Korean War,
July 12, 1950.

INTRODUCTION: FIRE CAKES

One of the Revolutionary War's lowest points was reached during the winter of 1777–1778 at Valley Forge, where George Washington's army teetered on the edge of starvation. Albigance Waldo, a Connecticut surgeon, wrote about the fare at the encampment:

> What have you for our Dinners, Boys? "Nothing but Fire Cake & Water, Sir." At night . . . What is your Supper, Lads? "Fire Cake & Water, Sir."
>
> What have you got for Breakfast, Lads? "Fire Cake & Water, Sir." The Lord send that our Commissary of Purchases may live on Fire Cake & Water.

Fire cakes were simple to make and terrible to eat. To prepare one, the soldier's flour ration was mixed with water to create a paste that was spread on a flat stone and stood next to the fire. When sufficiently charred on the outside, the fire cake was peeled off the stone and eaten. Invariably, these crude cakes were sooty on the outside and doughy and unappetizing on the inside.

The Americans at Valley Forge were not the first—nor would they be the last—military group to eat poorly, nor were they alone in their ability to give bad food a good name. The stalwarts who called their terrible bread "fire cakes" were just getting started. Not too many months ago troops in the Persian Gulf given M.R.E.'s (Meals Ready to Eat) turned around and renamed them "Meals Rejected by Ethiopians."

From the Revolutionary War to the 1990–1991 war in the Persian Gulf, tens of thousands of new words and phrases have been born of conflict, boredom, good humor, bad food, new technology, and the pure horror of war. These new words were heard across the lines during the Civil War, in which enemies spoke the same language; they emerged from the trenches of World War I and out of the jungles of Vietnam.

Bailouts and blackouts, bug-outs and blast-offs, G.I.'s and grunts, Yanks and Rebs, SNAFU and FUBAR, ANZAC and ARVN, Jeeps and Hueys, sidearms and sideburns, scuttlebutt and skinny, Scuds and spuds, bolo squads and boondocks, dogfaces and doughboys—these are just a few of the thousands of slang expressions created by, for, or about American fighting men and women.

The study of how soldiers spoke and what they spoke about is a fascinating one, and I have become all but obsessed by it. I hope that the reader is similarly hooked by this book. After all, these are more than "mere words," because they give us a different look at times and places when blood was spilled and many very young men died. That said, what comes through in much of this material is a sense of humor, irony, and comradeship.

This book was born of an odd impulse on my part. In 1990 I began a vigorous attempt to collect the slang of the American fighting men and women in the Persian Gulf. It was an attempt to get hold of the sound of conflict while the conflict was still going on. Paul McCarthy of Pocket Books saw a book in this urge to collect war slang, but immediately suggested that the Persian Gulf War be a chapter in a larger work that would look at war slang one war at a time. That inspired notion resulted in this book, which begins with the Civil War and takes the reader through Desert Storm, concluding with a chapter on the slang of the Cold War.

The quest was a fascinating one, leading to the unavoidable conclusion that wars create great bodies of new language that sound as different as do a musket, an M-1, and a Patriot missile. For every term that becomes part of the larger language there are three that live on only in the literature of a particular period or in the heads of those who were there. The sheer volume of war slang is sometimes overwhelming. For instance, the chapter on World War II—the largest in the book—contains approximately three thousand slang words and phrases of the American forces. Yet those three thousand terms are but a sampling, meant to give the reader only the most important terms and a feel for the vast variety and relentlessly playful nature of World War II slang.

Many people helped with this project, and they will be named later. However, three individuals were so key to the book that their influence must be acknowledged here. The first is the indefatigable linguistic researcher Charles D. Poe, who spent hundreds of hours perusing scores of books, fiction and nonfiction, for examples of war slang in context. His citations and notations—numbering in the many thousands—give this book whatever edge it may have over others of the genre.

The second individual was Randy Roberts, who, along with the staff of the Western Historical Manuscript Collection at the University of Missouri, helped me navigate through the complexities of the mother-lode source on American slang: the Peter Tamony Collection. This is the collection where, for example, those small soldiers' and sailors' glossaries from two world wars are carefully preserved. These are the very items that long ago disappeared from general library collections, if they were held in the first place. The courtesy and help of the Missouri archivists in this project and others has been nothing short of remarkable. The third has been, as always, Joseph C. Goulden.

A few quick notes on the chapters that follow. Each is organized in dictionary form for easy access. Terms are cross-referenced to the extent that seemed practicable. An attempt has been made to provide a rich sampling of word etymologies, but space and the fact that many of these terms have such elusive origins that the major dictionaries list them as "origin unknown" have limited the number of etymologies. For instance, the only way to tackle a term like "gadget," with a clearly military origin, would be purely by conjecture. Other terms—such as "bogey," meaning an unidentified or enemy aircraft—have such complicated and controversial word histories that they go beyond the scope of this book.

So much of modern military language is in the form of acronyms and initialisms. Acronyms are pronounced as words and spelled without periods ("radar," "WAVES," and "scuba," for instance), while initialisms are pronounced as sequences of letters and written with periods ("G.I." and "P.X.," for example). A few terms are seen both ways, such as the term for "absent without leave," which is pronounced either as four separate letters ("A.W.O.L.") or as a single word ("AWOL").

Note that the letter-by-letter alphabetizing system is used. For example, the following entries appear in the order shown:

> I.C.
> icebird
> ice wagon
> I.D.
> in a spin
> incendiary
> in velvet

Numbers are alphabetized as if spelled out. For example:

> about played out
> A-1
> A.W.O.L.

CIVIL AND UNCIVIL WORDS

★

War Slang Before the Great War: From the War Between the States Through the War with Spain

★

Madeline Hutchinson was a small, attractive woman with wispy white hair, an eruptive smile, and a most infectiously gleeful Yankee "down east" voice. She was born in Weld, Maine, in 1909, the year of a great forest fire, which she says was known for decades as "the year the fire came over the mountain"; she was married and moved into her home and farm in 1931, was widowed in 1974, and died in Weld in 1991.

Madeline had a lifelong fascination with language and her own "old-fashioned" vocabulary, and she and the author of this book spent many hours discussing the subject. One thing that seemed most remarkable was the fact that her language—and life—though removed by many miles and many decades from the war, was still influenced by it.

The war? The Civil War, that is. Madeline's view of history was strong and emotional, and she seldom used that name for the war. The "Great Rebellion" or "Rebellion" was her term for the Civil War, and there was still a hint of reproach in her voice as she talked of what that conflict had done to her small town. She said, "Ninety-three men went to that war and twenty-odd men didn't come back." It is clear from what Madeline said that this sacrifice was felt by that small rural community for many decades.

Words from the war—special words—still stuck with her. SKEDADDLERS was the name for those who ran away from the war, although the history books call them deserters. Madeline added that her mother-in-law, who lived to the age of ninety-six, had seen skedaddlers as they passed through town and could show you a place where they hid.

This is a direct link to those men who ran from the Army and the draft and were on their way to Canada through Maine. A verse appeared in the Canadian press in 1864 entitled "The Cowards Are Coming," which contained this stanza:

> This wretched skedaddle (I name it with pain),
> Commenced in loyal lumbering Maine:
> With instinctive cunning and recreant craft,
> They cleared at the "smell" of the purgative "draught."

There are other examples from Madeline's vocabulary, but the point is made that the words of that war of division still live in the language of Americans. In fact, there is still division as to what to call it—the Civil War, the War Between the States, or, as Madeline termed it, the Great Rebellion.

Not only are there different names for the conflict itself, but also for its various encounters, and this confusion extends to the present. The point is driven home with this sampling: Boonsboro was the southern name for what the North called South Mountain; Chickahominy was what the North called a battle that the South called Cold Harbor; Manassas (and then Second Manassas) was the southern name for what the North called Bull Run (and then Second Bull Run); Sharpsburg was how the South recalled what the Federals knew as Antietam; Elk Horn was the southern name for what the North said was Pea Ridge; Leesburg was the southern name for what the North called Ball's Bluff; and Shiloh was the southern name for what the North called—in particular, General Grant—Pittsburg Landing.

The Civil War (1861–1865)

Without question, the Civil War spawned a slang that was both identifiable and proliferating. It was also seen as a nuisance. Here is how it was typified in an 1865 article, "A Word About Slang," by R. W. McAlpine, in the *United States Service Magazine*: "The existence of a slang element in the Army cannot, of course, be prevented. It came from home, where the fault lies."

What follows is a Civil War glossary that includes some terms that existed before the war but only became important during the war. It is an interesting compilation because it serves as a baseline for American military slang and shows its many early influences: the frontier, rural America, British shipping (as the item **"A-1"** attests), and the ancient traditions of the sea. That glossary is, in turn, followed by some of the new slang of the Spanish-American War.

★ ☆ A ☆ ★

about played out. Demoralized and discouraged (said of an individual or a unit).

Agnew. A shirt worn by female nurses serving with the Union Army. The garment was worn with tails out, sleeves up, and the collar open. The name came from a Dr. Agnew, who lent one of his shirts to a nurse during the 1862 Peninsula campaign and thus set the style.

Anaconda Plan. General Winfield Scott's plan to crush the South through blockade and limited military action. It was also known as SCOTT'S GREAT SNAKE or SCOTT'S SNAKE.

A-1. Prime; the best; of the highest class; first class; first-rate in every respect. The expression did not originate in the classroom. It is derived from the classification of ships in Lloyd's Register in London, England, and first appeared as an adjective in 1837. The famous firm of underwriters described the quality of a ship's hull by a letter and that of its equipment by number. "A-1" means a ship of first-class condition as to both hull and equipment.

The use of "A-1" exemplified a trend in this war to shorten and abbreviate.

In his 1865 essay, "A Word About Slang," R. W. McAlpine commented at some length on this trend: In the army, as in the walks of civil life, our language loses much by abbreviation and contraction, "letters, like soldiers, being very apt to drop off on a long march, especially if their passage happens to lie near the confines of the enemy's country." And, "abbreviations and corruptions are always busiest with the words which are most frequently in use."

Thus it is that "bombshell" became SHELL; "Minié rifle," plain MINNIE, without the accent; "Navy cut tobacco," "navy"; "commission," COMMISH; and "secessionist," SECESH. By the same process and in obedience to the same law, "Colt's revolvers" metamorphosed into "Colts"; SPONDULIX became "spons"; and "greenbacks," GREENS. A man who reenlists is a VET; one who represents another is a SUB; and it was no uncommon thing to hear a D.B. ordered to go to the "Sut's" to get "two botts" of "Whisk" for "Cap and Lute," so strong is the inclination to do away with all vowels and consonants whose utterance impedes business or lengthens the time between drinks.

A.W.O.L. Absent without official leave. Even prior to the war this term was used in the Army. Confederate soldiers caught while A.W.O.L. were made to walk about the camp carrying a sign bearing these letters. See also under World War I and under World War II.

★ ☆ B ☆ ★

bayonet. A soldier. A statement from Abraham Lincoln quoted in Shelby Foote's *The Civil War* (1959) contains the line, "There are fifty thousand bayonets in the Union armies from the border states." See also under the Spanish-American War era.

As a dagger attached to a rifle muzzle, the bayonet has been an efficient little instrument for use in disemboweling an enemy in wartime. It took its name from the French *bayonette* ("knife"), which in turn was derived from the name of the lovely city of Bayonne, France, where it was first made or used. The Italian *baionettata*, a dagger that was whimsically called "little joker," was first manufactured in Bayonne, and the early bayonet was simply a dagger screwed to the muzzle of a rifle.

bell the cat. To encounter and cripple one of great and superior force; from the fable of the mice resolving to place a bell on the cat.

bellyache. (1) A colic. (2) To complain. This very old bit of slang has roots in the sixteenth century.

belly robber. A cook or mess sergeant. See also under World War I.

big thing. Any potentially notable event or achievement that does not come off as notable. In *A Dictionary of Soldier Talk* (1984), by John R. Elting, Dan Cragg, and Ernest Deal, "big thing" is explained as: "Something on the order of the mountain that labored and gave birth to a mouse; a big project that trips over its own feet. Big thing was sometimes howled in chorus, to the everlasting confusion of the recipient. Gen. George McClellan was a big-thing specialist."

big ticket. An honorable discharge from military service.

black gang. All the members of a ship's engineering department. A "seaman" sails on deck as a "sailor," while all crewmen "below" belong to the "black gang," so-called because of the soot, oil, and pitch that darkened their faces.

blizzard. An intense volley of musket fire.

Blue, the. The North and its army; from the color of its official uniform.

Blue and the Gray, the. The armies of the North and the South; so-called from the colors of the uniforms worn by the troops.

bluebacks. Confederate paper currency; from its color.

bluecoat. A soldier of the Union Army. After the war, the term saw increasing use as a nickname for a policeman.

blue light. A traitor; an early-American term still used during the Civil War, especially in the North. According to Robert Hendrickson, in *American Talk* (1986), it originated during the War of 1812, "when pro-British Americans flashed blue lights to British ships off the coast as a signal that Commodore Stephen Decatur's two frigates would soon be sailing from their New London, Connecticut, harbor."

blues. The blue uniform of the Union Army. According to Elbridge Colby, in *Army Talk: A Familiar Dictionary of Soldier Speech* (1943):

> The blue uniform of the army, as distinct from the khaki first introduced in Cuba and the Philippines, and the olive drab wool worn for a decade and more after 1917. It used to be standard in the service. That is why the Union Army in the Civil War was called "the boys in blue." That is why the graduating cadet at West Point sadly and gladly sang:
>
> > We'll bid farewell to 'Kaydet Gray,'
> > And don the Army Blue.

bounty jumping. That business in the North by which a man would take a cash bounty to enlist as a substitute for another who had been called to serve, then desert and enlist again as a substitute, for another bounty. In his *War Memories of an Army Chaplain* (1910), H. C. Trumbull recalled the custom:

> The dimension of this evil grew at a fearful rate. . . . I speak of what came under my own observation, when I say that substitutes enlisted and deserted three, five, and seven times over; that in single regiments one-fourth and again one-half, and yet again a larger proportion, of all the men assigned under the new call of the President for five hundred thousand more volunteers, deserted within a few weeks of being started to the front.

bowlegs. A cavalryman. Elbridge Colby writes in *Army Talk: A Familiar Dictionary of Soldier Speech* (1943): "This is a somewhat derisive term for a cavalryman, and like all true slang is descriptive and figurative in origin. Because constant riding of horses is thought to bow his legs, the cavalryman has for years been called bowlegs."

boys in blue. Union soldiers.

boys in gray. Confederate soldiers.

boys of the sod. An affectionate name for the Irish—and the all-Irish brigades—on either side. A song of an Irish unit began with the lines:

> Ye boys of the sod, to Columbia true.
> Come up, lads and fight for the Red,
> > White and Blue.

Brains Regiment. The 33rd Illinois, because of the many college students and teachers in its ranks. It was one of many units nicknamed because of a special characteristic.

brass. Courage; nerve; impudence. All are good military characteristics. In his *Concise Etymological Dictionary of the English Language* (1882), Walter W. Skeat suggests that this meaning of "brass" stems from the Icelandic verb *brasa* ("to be hardened by fire").

bridgehead. (1) A military salient in hostile country (c. 1812). (2) A defensive position dominating or covering the extremity of a bridge nearest the enemy.

briney. The sea.

Bucktails. The 13th Pennsylvania Reserves; so-called because its members ornamented their hats with deer fur.

bum. To carouse.

bummer. (1) A deserter. See also HOSPI-
TAL BUMMER. (2) An individual more interested in the spoils of war than in good
conduct; a predatory soldier. (3) A generic name for the destructive horde of
deserters, stragglers, runaway slaves, and
marauders who helped make life miserable in the war-torn South. Bummers
robbed, pillaged, and burned along with
General Sherman and his army in Georgia. These men were known far and wide
as SHERMAN'S BUMMERS. The term was not
shortened to "bum" until after the war
(c. 1870). It is almost certainly a mod-
ification of the German *Bummler*
("loafer"). (The contemporary "bummer"—as in "What a bummer"—stems
from the "bum trip" of drug usage, specifically a bad reaction to a hallucino-
genic drug such as LSD.)

bump. To kill; to die; to shell or bombard a certain position. The term dates
from c. 1849 and lives on in the twen-
tieth-century "bump off" ("to murder").

Butternuts. Confederate troops; from
the fact that some had uniforms dyed
with a home-brewed butternut dye.

by hook or by crook. By whatever
means possible.

by the numbers. How the Union Army
taught its recruits to load and fire. See
NINE TIMES, THE. See also under World
War II.

★ ☆ **C** ☆ ★

cannon fever. War weariness; a strong
desire to get away from the front lines.

cap. (1) A captain. (2) To place a percussion cap in a musket so that it can be
fired without delay.

Cape Cod turkey. Salted cod.

case / casket. A burial box. In 1863
Nathaniel Hawthorne became so upset
with the sudden spread of the word "casket," which had hithertofore signified a
jewel box, that he deemed it "a vile modern phrase which compels a person . . .
to shrink . . . from the idea of being
buried at all." In *The American Language* (1937), H. L. Mencken reports that
the term "case" shows up in a report on
the May 1864 burial of General J. E. B.
Stuart.

chap. Pal; from the archaic "chapman"
("merchant" or "trader").

Chimneyville. Jackson, Mississippi,
after it had been burned to the extent
that all that was left of many buildings
were their brick chimneys; a Union
army term.

chips. A ship's carpenter.

chow. Food; a meal. The term first appeared in print in 1856, according to
*Webster's Ninth New Collegiate Dictio-
nary.* In *The American Language* (1937),
H. L. Mencken concluded that it had
been introduced into the United States
with the first arrival of Chinese in California in 1848, and he believed it to be an
Americanized corruption of the Chinese
chia ("food"). Evidence suggests that the
word was used by civilians on the Pacific
Coast for many decades, but had pretty
well died out in civilian life in the coun-

try as a whole until it made a comeback after World War II as G.I.'s returned home. The word "chow" is still very common in the armed forces. A "chow hound" is first in line at mess; mealtime is "chowtime"; and one who eats "chows down."

coffee boiler. A malingerer; a shirker. The type is described in Morris Schaff's *The Battle of the Wilderness* (1910):

> A real adept skulker or coffee boiler is a most interesting specimen, and how well I remember the coolness with which he and his companion "for they go in pairs" would rise from their little fires upon being discovered, and ask innocently, "Lieutenant, can you tell us where the Umpteenth Regiment is?" And the answer, I am sorry to say, was too often: "Yes, right up there at the front, you damned rascal, as you well know!" Of course, they would make a show of moving, but were back at their little fires as soon as you were out of sight.

commish. A commission of any sort.

Company Q. A special detachment of the 150th Pennsylvania Regiment, composed of officers who had been broken in rank for cowardice and were being given the chance to redeem themselves as private soldiers. "Company Q turned out to be a good fighting unit, and most of the men in it ultimately regained their commissions," reports Bruce Catton in *A Stillness at Appomattox* (1954).

Confederate disease. Diarrhea.

confisticate. To confiscate; to SNATCH BALD-HEADED.

Copperhead. (1) A northerner with sympathy for the South; an antiwar northerner. Copperheads got their name from the identifying lapel emblems they wore, which were copper heads cut from pennies and mounted on pins or clasps. (2) By extension, any treacherous person.

Corn Exchange Regiment. The 118th Pennsylvania Regiment; so-called because it had been raised and equipped by the members of the Philadelphia Corn Exchange.

cotton-clads. Steamers protected by cotton bales, which temporarily broke the Union blockade at Galveston on January 1, 1863. The term was a play on IRONCLAD.

Crabtown. Annapolis, Maryland; so-called by the naval cadets. The Naval Academy was opened at Annapolis in October 1845, and the term was born during its opening or immediately following.

crack-up / crack up. (1) An accident. (2) To fail in an examination; to wreck; to cry out; to become insane. The term is believed to have originated on the western frontier.

croaker. A pessimist. In *A Stillness at Appomattox* (1954), Bruce Catton described croakers as "congenital pessimists . . . men who fought well but who always darkly prophesied ultimate Rebel victory." See also GROWLER.

crooked shoes. Footwear cut for right and left feet. Such shoes were provided to Union soldiers, many of whom, prior to enlisting, had only worn two shoes cut identically.

crow's nest. A place of observation on the foremast of a ship. At some point this term, which first appeared before the war, became a nickname for the entrance gate to an Army post, so-called because wives and sweethearts gathered there to meet their loved ones.

cumshaw. A bonus; it refers to a "boodle" or bribe, rather than a reward or present. This Chinese-based word (*from kamsia,* the traditional thank-you of street beggars) had been in use along the seaboards of America since the 1830s.

currency. Money. This new term was regarded as slang during the war. Money had many nicknames during this period, including STAMPS, SOAP, and SHINPLASTER.

★ ☆ **D** ☆ ★

damn Yankee. A southern term expressing rancor toward the politicians and soldiers of the Union. As Robert Hendrickson points out in his *Encyclopedia of Word and Phrase Origins* (1987), the term predates the war by many years, having first been applied to dishonest northern peddlers who went south to sell their goods.

Davy Jones. The spirit of the sea; the sailor's devil (c. 1751). In his *Origins of Sea Terms* (1985), John G. Rogers says the name is of uncertain origin, but, "A good guess is that West Indian sailors invented him, and that it could be a corruption of Devil Jonah, or possibly Duffy Jonah, duffy being a British West Indian word for devil."

Davy Jones's locker. The ocean, especially as the grave of all who perish at sea.

deadbeat / D.B. Anyone exempt from military action, even if in uniform.

"desecrated" vegetables. Dried vegetables offered as part of the Union Army ration. The use of the word "desecrated" to describe the Army's patented desiccated vegetables was entirely justified. One official report of the time forthrightly stated that these desiccated items were "very disagreeable to the taste." (These vegetables were very early forerunners of the dehydrated foods used so extensively during World War I.)

dog robber. A servant to an officer. According to R. W. McAlpine, in his 1865 essay on Civil War slang, "A Word About Slang," it was first used at Fort Bridges in 1861 and implies "that the man is a consumer of what daily morsels should fall," thus robbing the officer's dog of his due.

dog tent. A portable tent. It later became known as a PUP TENT.

Doodle. A Union soldier; a Confederate term, from "Yankee Doodle." A song of the Confederate army that protested the constant shortage of guns contained this stanza:

Want a weapon? Why capture one!
Every Doodle has got a gun,
Belt and bayonet, bright and new,
Kill a Doodle, and capture two!

doughboy. A foot soldier (as early as the 1850s). In *Glory Road* (1952) Bruce

Catton quotes from the diary of a disgruntled foot soldier:

> "Our cavalry had lost caste altogether with the infantry. Their reported skirmishes with the enemy, and 'driving in the rebel pickets,' were received with incredulous smiles and jeers until they became mum as oysters. When hailed for information . . . they would gaze at the infantry in stupid wonder at such questions, then would laugh among themselves at some remark of one of theirs about 'DOUGHBOYS' the laugh would then change to sullen anger as some shrill-voiced infantry veteran would inquire, loud enough to be heard a mile away, 'Did you see any dead cavalrymen out there?' This pertinent question had the effect of making every rider drive spurs into his horse and briskly move forward, while the sounds of laughter and jeers long and loud of their tormentors the 'DOUGH-BOYS' followed them."

See also under World War I.

draftee. One who has been drafted for the Army. Robert Hendrickson reports on the term in *Encyclopedia of Word and Phrase Origins* (1987):

> First recorded in an 1866 Civil War memoir, draftee was surely used before this during the war, probably as soon as the Confederate Conscription Act of 1862 and the Union Draft Law of 1863 were passed. In the North single men 20 to 45 and married men 29 to 35 were drafted, while the South conscripted all men 18 to 35. Most men volunteered, however; and only about 2 percent of the Union Army consisted of draftees. During World War II draftee and other ee-ending words (such as trainee, enlistee, escapee, and amputee) were widely used. Draft in the sense of conscription comes from the "to draw or pull" meaning of the verb to draft.

dry seaman. A sailor. In 1862, Congress took away the GROG RATION and instead began giving each sailor five cents a day.

★ ☆ E ☆ ★

elephant, the. Combat. Recruits were said to be ready to "meet the elephant," while seasoned soldiers had "seen the elephant." The term comes from the language of farmers, who tended to be bowled over on seeing an elephant at a traveling circus. The term, which predated the war dating back to the Mexican War and was used as a euphemism for the overland experience by those heading west in the 1849 gold rush to California, has been used ever since. Here is a line from Harold Coyle's 1987 novel, *Team Yankee:* "Those who hadn't seen the elephant yet didn't know how to treat him so they left him alone."

evacuation of Corinth, the. Diarrhea.

★ ☆ F ☆ ★

fight it out of this line. To adopt a course of action and thought and to continue with it to the end. The phrase was made popular by General U. S. Grant during the war.

fire eater. (1) A fire fighter. (2) A proslavery extremist in Congress before the war; a "disunionist." *The Fire-Eaters*, a book by Eric H. Walther, profiles the nine most prominent prewar fire-eaters.

fluke. (1) A fiasco; a failure. (2) A fortunate turn of events that is the result of accident rather than skill. The term came into the language just before the war and found applications aplenty during the war.

F.M.C. / F.W.C. "Free man of color" and "free woman of color." Before and during the war these initials were attached to the names of freed and escaped slaves.

follow the sea. To pursue the calling of a sailor.

foot cavalry. Fast marchers; those with the strength and endurance of a horse.

Fort Hell. The name given to Fort Sedgwick, outside of Petersburg, Virginia, by the soldiers defending it. The fort was the focal point of several lines of fire from the Petersburg defenses.

forty acres and a mule. An unkept promise made by northern politicians to divide the lands of slaveholders and give forty acres and a mule to any freed man who wanted a farm; also called TEN ACRES AND A MULE.

French fever. Syphilis; from the nineteenth-century belief that all things French are naughty.

fresh fish. Cry that went up from veterans as a new regiment showed up for training.

★ ☆ **G** ☆ ★

galley. A ship's kitchen.

galoot. An inexperienced soldier; a clumsy fool. Alfred H. Holt says of it, in his *Phrase and Word Origins* (1961): "This belongs in the same category as 'Tell it to the marines,' for it was originally (1812) applied by sailors to the de-spised marines, and has loyally kept its sense of awkward or worthless fellow." Holt was able to connect it plausibly with the Italian *galeotto* ("galley slave"), but admitted that the major dictionaries deemed its origin obscure.

galore. A great deal. The term was brought into our speech by sailors. It is from the Irish *go leor* ("in abundance").

galvanized Yankee. A southerner who took the oath to the North and served in the Union army. It comes from the galvanization process, in which something is changed by the application of an electric current.

Gibraltar of the West. Vicksburg, as seen by the South.

goat. (1) A gullible person; a fool; one who could easily become a scapegoat. (2) A junior officer.

God's country. A Union name for the North, especially in comparison with the heat and humidity of the war-torn South. By extension, the stars and stripes were called "God's flag."

go up. To be killed; to be TUMBLED OVER.

grand division. An oversized grouping of two or more divisions in the Union Army.

grapevine. News mysteriously conveyed. This term was coined during the war; it is a shortened form of "grapevine telegraph."

In *Why Do We Say Such Things? The Stories Behind the Words We Use* (1947), by Bruce Chapman, this account is given:

> In 1859 Colonel Bernard Bee constructed a telegraph line between Placerville and Virginia City by attaching the wire to trees. With time the wire "no longer taut" lay on the ground in loops that looked a lot like wild, trailing grapevine. During the Civil War similar lines were used by the troops and since the reports came in over such "grapevine telegraph" the term was used to refer to widespread rumors which had no definite source and were generally false.

Gray, the. The South and its army; from the color of its official uniform.

grayback / graycoat. A Confederate soldier.

Graybeard Regiment. The 37th Iowa Volunteer Infantry specially created by special arrangement with the War Department to show that older, "draftproof" men were welcome in the Union Army. All members of the 37th were over forty-five years of age.

greaser. A Mexican or a Spanish-American; a racist slur from the start. It first appeared in print in 1849, for "Mexican," but there is also evidence that it was California slang for a person of mixed Indian and Mexican descent. In World War II, the term took on a new meaning: "mechanic."

Great Rebellion. See WAR OF REBELLION.

Great Scott. An exclamation of surprise; an allusion to General Winfield Scott, a hero of the War of 1812 and the Mexican War. The term came from the election of 1852, when Scott was the Whig candidate and campaigned with great swagger and vanity. He was jeered as "Great Scott" during the campaign, and lost the election to Franklin Pierce.

greens. Money; from "greenbacks."

grog ration. A traditional daily ration of liquor given to sailors in the Navy until July 14, 1862, when Congress deemed that it should "forever cease." See also DRY SEAMAN.
Grog is a mixture of spirit, originally rum, and cold water, but then and now the term referred to alcoholic drink generally. "Grog" came into use in 1745 when Admiral Edward ("Old Grog") Vernon introduced it into the British navy; he was so-called from his wearing in cold weather a "grogram cloak."

growler. A pessimist. In *The Road to Richmond* (1939), Major Abner R. Small describes "growlers who on the opening of every campaign were attacked with a dyspeptic foreboding that defeat and disaster would follow us." See also CROAKER.

grub. Food (since c. 1659).

gunboats. A pair of boots; also known as "mud hooks."

★ ☆ **H** ☆ ★

hammer and tongs. Violently.

hand. A workman; a laborer. This term first appeared in print in 1658, defined as "a seaman."

hardtack. (1) A ship's biscuit; ordinary sea fare, as distinguished from food eaten or obtained ashore; coarse food. (2) A baked mixture of flour and water, often soaked in cold water overnight and fried in grease for breakfast. It was a staple in the diet of those fighting in the war.

The noted historian Charles Francis Adams spoke for all his fellow veterans of the war when he said: "I was poisoned by incessant feeding on hardtack and meat freshly killed and fried in pork-fat, and the inordinate drinking of black coffee—quarts of it each day."

Cooking at that time was done by untrained personnel. Messes consisted normally of four to eight men, each of whom took his turn in serving as cook. On the march or in contact with the enemy, men often found it more convenient to prepare their food individually.

heavy. An oversized artillery regiment. This is one of those fascinating terms with a number of military slang applications; the term has also been used in later days to refer to heavy machine guns, large aircraft, aircraft carriers, and high-ranking officers.

Here's how! A toast.

high-number regiments. New regiments, with higher numbers in their names, sent south after 1862; they were never seen to be the equals of the lower-numbered regiments, composed of men who had enlisted earlier in the war. Some regiments from New York and Pennsylvania had numbers well over one hundred.

hike. A march; from the Chinook Indian *hyak* ("to hurry").

hog and hominy. Lincoln's term for southern rations. Cutting off the Confederates from Knoxville and the West, for instance, was seen as a means of cutting off "hog and hominy." The comparable alliterative ration for the North was probably "bread and bacon," used by Major Abner R. Small in *The Road to Richmond* (1939). Both sides were provisioned by "food and forage."

hooker. Prostitute. The term did not originate during the war, as it was already in use. The war gave it a boost, however, thanks to Union General Joseph Hooker, whose name was given to a large red-light district in Washington, D.C. The area was known as "Hooker's Division" after the wild proclivities of Hooker and his men.

horse collar. A bedroll with straps. It was used in lieu of the cumbersome knapsack and worn like a huge collar.

hospital bummer. One who fakes his way out of combat and into a military hospital. See also BUMMER.

howitzer. A gun of high trajectory and low muzzle velocity. At the time of the war, there were six different types of howitzers in the Army, two of which were used in seacoast defense. Later the term was used by soldiers to refer to a large woman or girl.

The word "howitzer" is derived from the German word *Haubitze* (a sling). The same type of weapon as the howitzer is referred to in German literature as *Steilfeuergeschütze* ("steep fire gun"). Howitzers first appeared at the time of Louis XIV and were used for both field and siege work in the British and Dutch armies.

howker. A sailor with two or more sweethearts; from the Dutch *howker* (a vessel with two masts).

in the air. Unprotected; for example, the unprotected flank of an army. It is a term that survived to other wars; for instance, Joe Goulden's *Korea: The Untold Story of the War* (1982) tells of Marine companies "hanging in the air."

iron. Short for IRONCLAD.

Iron Brigade. Five midwestern regiments whose troops wore black hats and had a reputation as particularly tough fighters. Bruce Catton wrote that nobody was quite sure where the name came from but that the accepted story was that General George McClellan watched the progress of the regiments through the gap at South Mountain and exclaimed, "That brigade must be made of iron!" There was also a Confederate Iron Brigade, whose riders, writes Burke Davis in *The Long Surrender* (1985), "terrorized enemy-held areas of the Trans-Mississippi."

iron rations. U. S. Army staples of HARDTACK, salt pork, and coffee.

ironclad. (1) A man-of-war plated with thick sheets of steel. (2) Hard, strong, unyielding; a severely chaste woman.

★ ☆ **J** ☆ ★

jiffy. An instant; the shortest possible time.

Johnny Reb. A soldier in the Confederate army; also, those of the South, collectively. Sometimes it was plain "Johnny"—and hardly hostile—as in these lines from *The Personal Memoirs of U. S. Grant*, on fraternization at the siege of Vicksburg:

> During the siege there had been a good deal of friendly sparring between the soldiers of the two Armies, on picket where the lines were close together.... Often "Johnny" would call, "Well, Yank, when are you coming to town?" The reply was sometimes: "We propose to spend the Fourth of July there."

★ ☆ **K** ☆ ★

Kearny patch. A red marker—a red lozenge of flannel—worn on the caps of the men under the leadership of Phil Kearny. Because of the patches, the outfit became known as the Red Diamond Division, and new units joining the division could not wear it until they had proven themselves in combat. "Later in the war," writes Bruce Catton in *Mr. Lincoln's Army* (1951), "Kearny's device was taken up at headquarters, and a special patch was made up for each army corps. The shoulder patches worn by American soldiers in subsequent wars were direct descendants of Phil Kearny's morale builder."

keelhaul. To haul under the keel of a ship; to punish with humiliation.

kick the bucket. To die (since c. 1785, but in common use during the period of the Civil War). Harold Wentworth and Stuart Berg Flexner's *Dictionary of American Slang* (1960) states: "Now widely believed to refer to the last volitional act of one who, standing on an upturned bucket, fixes around his neck a noose suspended from the ceiling."

★ ☆ **L** ☆ ★

lamp post. A large shell (for example, the ten-inch shell fired from Union gunboats at targets ashore).

late unpleasantness, the. Term used in the postwar period to describe the American Civil War.

leg case. Abraham Lincoln's own term for a brave man cursed by cowardly legs—that is, a man who ran from combat. Lincoln often pardoned condemned "leg cases" as well as soldiers who fell asleep at their posts, to the consternation of some of his generals. One one occasion Lincoln was confronted by an angry general who accused Lincoln of destroying discipline with his pardons and demanded that he sign a death warrant. Lincoln's reply: "General, there are too many weeping widows in the United States now. For God's sake don't ask me to add to the number; for I tell you plainly that I won't do it."

lick into shape. To train; to fashion (1663). In *The Animal Things We Say* (1983), Darryl Lyman explains: "In the Middle Ages, it was widely believed that a baby bear is born as a shapeless mass and that the mother has to lick the object with her tongue until the blob is molded into the proper shape for a little bear cub."

Little Mac. General George McClellan, also known as "The Young Napoleon." There were many colorful nicknames in this war: General Edwin V. Sumner, a man with a booming voice, was known as "The Bull of the Woods"; Brigadier General William H. French was known, alternatively, as "Old Winkey" and "Old Blinky"; General Henry Halleck was known as "Old Brains"; and General Alpheus S. Williams was known simply as "Pop" by his troops. Some nicknames had interesting explanations; for example, General George Armstrong Custer was known as "Cinnamon" because of the cinnamon-flavored hair oil he used.

long swords. The Cavalry; so-called by Indians.

loyalist. A Union sympathizer in the South.

★ ☆ **M** ☆ ★

madam. A brothel keeper.

mail carrier. A spy.

mate. (1) A partner; a companion. (2) One who ranks above a chief petty officer and below a warrant officer and who is regarded as having the status of both an officer and an enlisted man (also used with a qualifying term, as in "boatswain's mate" and "gunner's mate," as a title for certain petty officers).

medico. A member of the medical department.

meet the elephant. See ELEPHANT, THE.

mess. (1) A group of sailors, Marines, or soldiers eating at the same table. In his *Origins of Sea Terms* (1985), John G. Rogers says of the term: "The word came from Middle English, *mes*, and goes back to Late Latin, *missum*, that which is put on the table. It is a military as well as a seafarer's term." (2) A difficulty; a mixture; disorder.

Melvillian Mess

The common seamen in a large frigate are divided into some thirty or forty messes, put down on the purser's books as Mess No. 1, Mess No. 2, Mess No. 3, & c. The members of each mess club their rations of provisions, and breakfast, dine, and sup together in allotted intervals between the guns on the maindeck. In undeviating rotation, the members of each mess (excepting the petty-officers) take their turn in performing the functions of cook and steward. And for the time being, all the affairs of the club are subject to their inspection and control.

—Herman Melville, *White-Jacket, or, The World in a Man-of-War* (1850)

---

middy. A midshipman (since the War of 1812).

Minnie. The Minié rifle.

Monitor. An ironclad turret-ship created by John Ericsson, who came up with the name himself. In a letter of January 2, 1862, to the naval authorities, he said that he had designed the vessel "to admonish the leaders of the Southern Revolution" and that it would "prove a severe monitor to them." He then wrote: "On these and other grounds I propose to name the new battery *Monitor*."

mosquito fleet. The Confederate workboats outfitted with one gun apiece; a derisive name. The term "mosquito" came into play again during World War II. See also under World War I.

Mozart Regiment. The 40th New York Regiment, which according to Bruce Catton in *Mr. Lincoln's Army* (1951) took this name "not because the men were devoted to music, but because the regiment had been organized with the special blessing of Mayor Wood of New York, whose personal faction in the New York Democratic party was known as the Mozart Hall Group, in opposition to Tammany."

mud hooks. A pair of boots; also known as "gunboats."

mud lark. See **slow bear.**

mudsill. A person of the lowest possible social class; a lowlife. The term came into play as a taunt; for instance, southern newspapers called Sherman's troops a "grand army of mudsills."

mugger. A prisoner who preyed on fellow prisoners. In *The Road to Richmond* (1939), Major Abner R. Small talks of a Maryland prison with desperado muggers "who seemed to have the white card to beat, rob, and kill the weaker of their fellow prisoners." By the end of the war, the term was in general use as a name for one who attacks with the intent of robbery.

muster out. To be killed in action.

★ ☆ N ☆ ★

neck decoration. The Medal of Honor, which was created by Congress on July 12, 1862. It was—and still is—the highest-ranked medal and the only "neck" decoration among U.S. military medals.

news walker. A self-appointed reporter who would wander up and down the lines after battle to exchange information. Bruce Catton says of news walkers in *A Stillness at Appomattox* (1954): "They were always welcomed, and they were always watched quite closely, because they were notoriously light-fingered and would steal any haversacks that were within their reach."

nine times, the. The nine separate and distinct operations involved in loading a Springfield muzzle loader; recruits were trained to load BY THE NUMBERS. Bruce Catton notes in *Mr. Lincoln's Army* (1951): "Drill on the target range began with the command, 'Load in nine times: load!'"

★ ☆ O ☆ ★

off the country. Foraged for (as in "food off the country").

Oh, Perdition! An oath.

old man. The commander of a unit; the father of a family; a husband; a term of cordiality or endearment. See also under World War I.

old Navy. The federal Navy of the prewar period.

old soldier. One who pretended to be sick or disabled so he could avoid drill and take life easy in a hospital tent.

old woodpecker. One who would be hard to take by surprise. In Shelby Foote's *The Civil War* (1959).

★ ☆ P ☆ ★

paper collar / paper-collar soldier. A soldier from the northeast (to westerners). In *Battle Cry of Freedom* (1988), James M. McPherson tells of western farm boys and outdoorsmen regarding themselves as much tougher than the effete and "pasty-faced" office workers, or "paper collars." McPherson goes on to say that the "clerks and mechanics of the East proved to be more immune to the diseases of camp life and more capable in combat of absorbing and inflicting punishment than Western Union soldiers."

Pathfinder of the Sea. The nickname of Confederate Matthew Fontaine Maury, who had, among other accomplishments, published the first textbook on oceanography and conducted much research on ocean currents and winds.

pea jacket. A short coat of thick woolen cloth, worn by seamen. The term has nothing to do with "pea soup" (a thick fog), as has been written on more than one occasion. The word "pea" would seem to be a corruption of the Dutch *pije*, a coat made with coarse wool.

peas on a trencher. The breakfast bugle call. All bugle calls had nicknames: the dinner call was known as "roast beef," and according to Bruce Catton in *Glory Road* (1952), "the call which summoned men to advance against the enemy was known for some reason as 'Tommy Totten.'"

pig sticker. A bayonet; a long-bladed pocketknife.

platoon. A small body of soldiers, especially a portion of a company operating as a unit.

political general. One appointed for political rather than military reasons. James M. McPherson says in *Battle Cry of Freedom* (1988) that the term became "almost a synonym for incompetency."

pond, the. The Atlantic Ocean.

powder monkey. One who carries shells or gunpowder from the magazine to the gun.

pup tent. A portable tent.

★ ☆ **Q** ☆ ★

Quaker gun. A dummy or decoy gun; so-called because of the pacifist nature of Quakers. In 1861, General Joseph Johnston, the Confederate commander at Manassas, erected Quaker guns at Centerville. Johnston's guns were nothing more than logs painted black, sawed off at one end and pointed in the right direction. The trick caused the Union to think it faced a much stronger force. See also QUAKER, under World War II.

★ ☆ **R** ☆ ★

rackansacker. A hard-bitten outdoorsman fighting for the South, who would, presumably, be quick to "wrack and sack" (ruin and pillage) in a war.

ration. The food allowance for one man for one day. Elbridge Colby wrote in *Army Talk: A Familiar Dictionary of Soldier Speech* (1943): "[T]his word is so widely understood that it would not have been included here were it not necessary to caution folk that to pronounce it to rhyme with 'nation' is the mark of a civilian and a raw recruit." He then cautions: "Old soldiers always pronounce it to rhyme with the first two syllables of 'national.' Another quirk of speech causes it almost always to be used only in the plural, and loosely so as to mean merely 'something to eat.'"

ready-finder. A civilian who followed the Army to pick up the discarded coats, blankets, and other items shed by soldiers, especially when the weather turned hot. The term was used by Union troops.

reb. A REBEL; personified as JOHNNY REB.

rebel. A southern soldier; an inhabitant of the Confederate States of America.

rebel yell. The Confederate battle cry; a prolonged, high-pitched cry issued before combat. Bruce Catton writes in *Glory Road* (1952):

> That yell—"that hellish yell," a Michigan soldier called it—appears to have been an actual power in battle, worth many regiments to the Confederacy. A federal surgeon wrote after the war: "I have never

since I was born, heard so fearful a noise as a rebel yell. It is nothing like a hurrah, but rather a regular wildcat screech."

The Union Army's equivalent was to give three cheers.

Was the term "rebel yell" used during the war? According to *Webster's Ninth New Collegiate Dictionary*, it did not appear in print until 1868. In J. A. Worsham's memoir, *One of Jackson's Foot Cavalry* (1912), the yell is referred to as a "Confederate yell."

Red Diamond Division. See **Kearny patch.**

red tape. Official formality (from the actual red tape used to bind government documents); adherence to a prescribed routine, especially when delay results. This term seemed to come into its own during the war. In *The Road to Richmond* (1939), Major Abner R. Small tells of various hurdles he encounters trying to get the remains of a dead soldier back to Maine from Virginia; he obtains the body and the money to ship it, but concedes, "Red tape was more difficult to manage." At another point he complains that "we couldn't clothe our men with reports and red tape."

red-tape-ism. Red tape as a belief system. In Bruce Catton's *Mr. Lincoln's Army* (1951), a young officer in the 57th New York Regiment is quoted as complaining about an old officer who "suffered from red-tape-ism slowness, desire for a comfortable berth, and above and beyond all, jealousy."

red-tapist. An excessively bureaucratic government official.

reign of iron. The new age dawning in naval warfare. Shortly after the first engagement of IRONCLADS, in 1862, Rear Admiral John Dahlgren said, "Now comes the reign of iron—and cased sloops are to take the place of wooden ships."

reveille. A signal, as of a drum or bugle, given about sunrise, to waken soldiers and sailors for the day's duties; from the French *réveiller* ("to awaken"). The lyrics for the wake-up bugle call are usually given as follows:

> I can't get 'em up,
> I can't get 'em up,
> I can't get 'em up in the morning;
> I can't get 'em up,
> I can't get 'em up a-tall.
> The corp'ral's worse than privates,
> The sergeant's worse than corp'rals,
> The lieutenant's worse than sergeants,
> And the captain's worst of all.

run amuck. To be in a state of murderous frenzy; to try to kill all who come in one's way. This is an old Malay term— *amok* (a murderous, frenzied state)— which entered the English language in the seventeenth century. By the time of the Civil War the phrase was being used figuratively to describe a person maddened with liquor or one who attacks others indiscriminately.

"Running amuck" has acquired a lurid history that lacks scholarly verification, but makes up for it in purple prose. Here is how it was explained in a dictionary of military slang and terminology, *Words of the Fighting Forces* (1942), by Clinton A. Sanders and Joseph W. Blackwell, Jr.: "The term is used to describe the behavior of Malays when, maddened with opium, they rush about in a frenzied state shouting, 'Amoq, Amoq!' (Kill!

Kill!) and murderously attack anyone who gets in their way. One man running amuck may kill a dozen people before he is struck down."

★ ☆ **S** ☆ ★

salt. Salt beef; an old sailor.

schooner. (1) A vessel rigged fore and aft with two masts, a foremast and a mainmast. The word, borrowed from the Scottish dialect, was first used in America by Captain Andrew Robinson, the builder of the first schooner, launched at Gloucester, Massachusetts, in 1713. The Scotch took the term from the Norse *skunna* ("to hasten"). (2) A large glass holding twice the amount contained by an ordinary glass.

Scott's Great Snake / Scott's Snake. Other names for the ANACONDA PLAN, aimed at strangling the South snake-style.

A Bogus Word History

At the Bizerte Naval Base, we got the first scuttlebutt about the coming invasion of continental Italy. "Scuttlebutt," that's Navy slang for gossip. Nobody seems to know how the word "scuttlebutt" got started unless somebody saw Crosby from the rear . . . although Crosby from the rear is definitely not rumor: that is solid fact. (Note to Compositor: Please leave the "c" in that last word even though you've seen Crosby from the rear.)

—Bob Hope, *Life* (August 7, 1944)

---

scuttlebutt. Gossip. Originally, "scuttlebutt" referred to the place from which a ship's crew got drinking water. A scuttle is a hole and a butt is a barrel. The term was first seen in print in the early nineteenth century.

secesh / sesesch. Secession (as in "secesh sympathies"). Generally, it was a northern term of derision. The term was able to hang on for many years after the war. In *Our Times: The Turn of the Century* (1936), Mark Sullivan writes of the way Americans spoke in the year 1900 and points out that despite the fact that many of the rancors of the Civil War had been buried, "Such terms as Rebel, Yank, and damn Yankee and Secesh were still occasionally used, sometimes with a touch of ancient malice."

secesher. A southerner.

see the elephant. To go into combat for the first time. See ELEPHANT, THE.

sharpshooter. One skilled in shooting, especially with a rifle; a marksman of accurate aim, especially one engaged in skirmishing and outpost duty. The term was given particular relevance in the title of an Alexander Gardner photograph, "Home of a Rebel Sharpshooter." The man lay dead between two immense bullet-scarred rocks. He had been wounded in the head and had had time to prop his rifle against one of the rocks before lying down to die.

It has been widely reported that the term "sharpshooter" was coined in connection with the demonstrated accuracy of the Sharps breechloading rifle, invented in 1848 by Christian Sharps. Plausible as that may sound—and most bogus etymologies sound plausible—the explanation is incorrect because the term "sharpshooter" was used long before the Sharps rifle was invented, to designate specially skilled riflemen selected to pick off members of a hostile force. "Mounted sharpshooters" is the phrase so used in James's *Universal Military Dictionary* (1802). The advent of the Sharps rifle no doubt contributed to the popular use of the term "sharpshooter" during the Civil War.

she. The pronoun used when referring to a ship.

Word Her-Story

There is considerable lore attached to the nautical genderfication represented by this use of "she":

- The ancient Greeks called their ships by feminine names out of respect for Athene, inventor of sailing ships and chariots.
- In the Latin language, the word for "ship" *(navis)* is feminine.
- Through the ages, ships have been endowed, in imagination, with womanly qualities, because of their beauty and grace and their hold upon the affections of seamen.
- Sailing vessels often had the head or bust of a woman at the prow as a figurehead.

---

shell. A bombshell.

Sherman necktie. An iron rail heated over a bonfire of railroad ties and twisted around a tree. This was a northern means of disabling railroads in the South. It was also known as a "Sherman hairpin."

Sherman's bummers. Desperadoes who helped Sherman burn and pillage. See BUMMER.

Sherman sentinel. Any chimney left standing after General Sherman's drive to the sea.

shinplaster. The fractional currency (worth ten cents, twenty-five cents, etc.) issued by the Union in response to coin shortages during the war. The term has been assumed to have come from the notion that the only practical use for these bills was to plaster your shins with them.

Shoddy. Noun used to describe the uniforms provided to the Union Army by unscrupulous suppliers. Shelby Foote describes it in *The Civil War* (1958):

> *Shoddy* was . . . used to designate an inferior woolen yarn made from fibers taken from worn-out fabrics and reprocessed, then later as the name of the resultant cloth. "Poor, sleazy stuff," one of Horace Greeley's *Tribune* reporters called it, "woven open enough for sieves, and then filled with shearsmen's dust"; while *Harper's Weekly* referred to it as "a villainous compound, the refuse and sweepings of the shop, —pounded, rolled, glued, and smoothed to the external form and gloss of cloth, but no more like the genuine article than the shadow is to the substance. . . . soldiers on the first day's march or in the earliest storm, found their clothes, overcoats, and blankets scattering to the wind in rags, or dissolving . . . under the pelting rain."

shrapnel. A type of artillery shell that showers pieces of metal on exploding; invented by a Briton, Henry Shrapnel (1761–1842). A single shell discharged 350 or more shots, each capable of killing or wounding within forty-four yards of the bursting point.

sideburns. The popular side-whiskers of the period; named after General Ambrose Burnside of the Army of the Potomac. The two halves of the man's name were transposed in the 1880s, after the war.

skedaddler / skedaddle. (1) A deserter. (2) To desert. In *The American Language, Supplement 1* (1945), H. L. Mencken says that this term was probably in use before the war, but did not become popular until men began to desert. Its origins have mystified etymologists. According to Stuart Berg Flexner, in *I Hear America Talking* (1976), it is from Scots and a northern England dialect, probably derived from the Greek *skedannunai* ("to split up"). R. W. McAlpine insists in his 1965 essay on Civil War slang, "A Word About Slang," that it comes from "good Hellenic stock," the Greek *skedannumi* ("to run in a crowd"), but McAlpine is at a loss to explain how or when this term from Homer and Hesiod was Americanized.

skeesicks. One's tentmate.

skillygalee. HARDTACK soaked in water, drained, and fried in pork fat. In *Mr. Lincoln's Army* (1951), by Bruce Catton, a vet is quoted as saying that the dish was "certainly indigestible enough to satisfy the cravings of the most ambitious dyspeptic."

skim, simmer, and scour. The motto of Civil War cooks. It is explained in *Camp Fires and Camp Cooking* (1862), by Captain James M. Sanderson:

Remember that beans, badly boiled, kill more than bullets; and fat is more fatal than powder. In cooking, more than anything else in this world, always make haste slowly. One hour too much is vastly better than five minutes too little, with rare exceptions. A big fire scorches your soup, burns your face, and crisps your temper. Skim, simmer, and scour, are the true secrets of good cooking.

slouch hat. A British-style widebrimmed felt hat; first introduced into the U.S. in the 1830s. Confederate troops made them popular.

slow bear. A pig. In *I Hear America Talking* (1976), Stuart Berg Flexner writes that "slow bear," along with the synonymous "mud lark," were just two of the humorous euphemisms the shortrationed, foraging troops used to refer to the farmers' pigs they killed and ate. He adds: "'Confederate beef' was a term the Union troops gave the Southern cows and horses they killed and ate but, after Grant's six-weeks siege of Vicksburg, May 19–July 4, 1963, it referred to the mules the Confederate army had been forced to eat there."

slows, the. Chronic caution and slowness. When General George McClellan was relieved of command of the Armies of the United States on March 11, 1862, it was only after President Lincoln had said on more than one occasion that "Little Mac has got the slows."

slum / slumgullion. A stew created from whatever is at hand. The term appears to be a pure Americanism that first shows up during the gold rush of 1849, when, according to H. L. Mencken in *The American Language, Supplement 1* (1945), it was used to describe a muddy residue left after sluicing gravel; but it was soon extended to food and drink,

Slum (100 servings)

Over time, slum(gullion) became a more formalized stew. The following is from *Army Recipes* (1944):

Meat, carcass	40 lb.
or	
Meat, boneless	20 lb.
Flour, sifted	1½ lb.
Salt	6 oz.
Pepper	½ oz.
Fat	1½ lb.
Water or beef stock	4 gal.
Onions, small whole	8 lb.
Carrots, sliced or cubed	8 lb.
Turnips, sliced or cubed	8 lb.
Celery, diced	5 lb.
Peas, fresh or frozen	5 lb.
Water, boiling	
Flour, sifted (for gravy)	1 lb.
Water, cold (for gravy)	
Salt	
Pepper	

Directions
1. Cut meat into one- to two-inch cubes.
2. Mix flour, salt, and pepper together. Roll meat in flour and cook in fat until brown.
3. Add water or stock. Cover and heat to boiling point. Reduce heat and simmer 2½ to 3 hours or until tender.
4. Add vegetables in the following order, allowing required time for each to cook: onions 45 minutes to 1 hour; carrots 30 minutes; turnips and celery 15 to 20 minutes. Drain, reserve liquid.
5. Barely cover peas with boiling water. Heat to boiling point. Reduce heat and simmer 30 minutes or until tender.
6. Mix flour and water. Stir until smooth. Add to hot meat and vegetable stock. Heat to boiling point. Boil 2 minutes stirring constantly. Add salt and pepper.
   Pour gravy over meat and vegetables. Add cooked peas. Reheat.

and by the time of the war was applied to campfire stews. See also under World War I.

smart money. (1) An allowance of money granted to soldiers, sailors, Marines, and others of the fighting forces of the United States who have been wounded or injured in the line of duty. (2) A sum of money paid by a person to buy himself off from the unexpired portion of his enlistment. This term was ancient at the time of the war, but nevertheless relevant.

snatch bald-headed. To confiscate; to steal with strategy rather than on impulse.

soap. Money.

son of a bitch. A term of contempt; a term of endearment; a rascal. According to H. L. Mencken in *The American Language, Supplement 1* (1945): "It rose to popularity in the United States during the decade before the Civil War, and at the start was considered extremely offensive." Its softer cousin, "son of a gun," is old slang and had its origin as a seafaring term in the British navy back in the days of square-rigged ships. Dagobert A. Runes, the editor of *Better English*, published in the 1930s, gave this version of the etymology of the term:

In those days women sometimes accompanied ships of the fleet and on voyages of extended duration it was not unusual for some of these women to become with child. When that happened the gun deck was improvised into a maternity ward, and the blasts from a cannon were employed as a crude measure to hasten labor. The offspring which resulted in such cases, usually uncertain of his paternal forebear, was nicknamed a "son-of-a-gun."

Others agree that this was the general origin, but Runes may be alone in his claim that the guns were fired to induce labor.

spondulix. Money (from the shell of the mussel *Spondylus*); suggestive of wampum. Sometimes shortened to spons.

stamps. Money.

stars and bars. The flag of the Confederate States of America; a play on the Union's "stars and stripes."

strawfoot. (1) A rural or backwoods soldier (as if he still had straw on his shoes). (2) A rookie.

Here is what Stuart Berg Flexner says of the term in *I Hear America Talking* (1976): "[L]egend has it that drill sergeants found such men didn't know their left foot from their right, so taught them to march by having them tie hay to their left foot and straw to the right, then called out the marching cadence 'hayfoot! strawfoot!' instead of the usual 'left! right!'"

sub. One who represents or serves for another.

substitute broker. An agent whose business was to secure men to enlist as substitutes for men called to serve. The brokers took a percentage of the bounty paid to the substitute by the draftee for enlisting.

swab. (1) A sailor; from "swabber" (for "mop"), a term applied to a large mop used aboard ship for cleaning decks. (2) Anything used for mopping; a cleaner for the bore of a cannon. (3) An epaulet of a naval officer. (4) An awkward fellow.

swabber. One who uses a SWAB; one of a ship's crew charged with swabbing the decks; a petty officer in charge of swabbing the decks.

swamp angel. The eight-inch Parrott gun. The gun was used in 1863 to shell Charleston with 200-pound incendiary projectiles during the Union siege of that city. Placed in the marshes of James Island, it was not terribly effective, but it was seen as an atrocity by the South because it was aimed at the old men, women, and children of a sleeping city. The gun was named for its inventor, Robert Parker Parrott, of West Point, and was America's first rifled cannon.

After the war, "swamp angel" was, according to H. L. Mencken in *The American Language, Supplement 1* (1945), "used to designate one of the bands of Ruffians associated with the Ku Klux Klan."

★ ☆ **T** ☆ ★

taps. (1) A signal on a drum, bugle, or trumpet at which all lights in the soldiers' or sailors' quarters must be extinguished. Taps was blown for the first time over the grave of Robert Elocombe in July 1865. This call or signal is now used by the English and French, too. (2) A specific bugle call of peculiar beauty and solemnity; by extension and because of its use at funerals and at the end of the day, it has come to mean the end, death.

Elbridge Colby wrote of it in *Army Talk: A Familiar Dictionary of Soldier Speech* (1943):

> It is the last call blown by buglers at night, and is always sounded at military funerals. In its present form, the call was devised during the Civil War by General Daniel Butterfield, to replace the earlier "Lights Out," or "Tattoo," which had been inaugurated at West Point in 1840 and used in some regiments during the Mexican War in connection with funerals.

In *Glory Road* (1952), Bruce Catton adds that Butterfield knew that it was not musical, but "he wanted one which would somehow express the idea of a darkening campground with tired men snugging down to a peaceful sleep, and he hoped his new call would do it."

tell it to the Marines. A phrase that expresses doubt. It is not American, as many think, but English. Its first written use was in *Samuel Pepys's Diary*, in which the seventeenth-century author reported that a colonel of the marines told King Charles II a wild tale of having seen flying fish. According to Pepys, the king then said:

> Mr. Pepys, from the very nature of their calling, no class of our subjects can have so wide a knowledge of seas and lands as the officers and men of our loyal maritime regiment. Henceforth whenever we cast doubt upon a tale that lacketh likelihood we will tell it to the Marines—if they believe it, it is safe to say it is true.

See also under World War I.

ten acres and a mule. See FORTY ACRES AND A MULE.

Tennessee quickstep. Diarrhea.

tinclad. A derisive term for **ironclad.**

toad stabber / toad sticker. A sword; a knife; a bayonet.

torpedo. A waterborne device for the destruction of a ship. Many types were devised during the war, and these inventions were responsible for destroying twenty-two Union vessels and six Confederate. It was at this time that Matthew Fontaine Maury, the man known as the PATHFINDER OF THE SEA, working at his home, at 1105 East Clay Street, Richmond, Virginia, invented the submarine torpedo. He also invented a method for planting and testing torpedoes, but the end of the war came before the value of the discovery could be realized.

The name "torpedo" was given by Robert Fulton to an enclosed mass of gunpowder designed to be exploded under a hostile vessel. This type of torpedo was invented by David Bushnell of Connecticut, who in 1776 attempted unsuccessfully to blow up the British warship *Eagle* in New York harbor with a torpedo attached to a hand-propelled submarine. In 1801 Fulton, attempting to interest Napoleon in torpedoes, blew up a sloop in a British harbor, the first vessel ever sunk with a torpedo. Although Fulton did not interest Napoleon, the U.S. Navy Department became interested in such machines for destroying shipping. On June 21, 1813, a line of defensive torpedoes was laid across the Narrows in New York harbor.

trick. (1) A turn at the helm of a ship; a spell; a watch. (2) A sexual act; a beautiful woman. (3) A round of cards.

trooper. A soldier in a troop of cavalry; a horse ridden by such a soldier.

troop ship. A ship designed to move infantry (1862).

tumbled over. To be killed; to **go up.**

turkey shoot. An ambush; an easy killing, a term that will be used in all future wars for any engagement which tests marksmanship rather than courage. Originally, in colonial times, a shoot at live turkeys for a fee in which the person hitting the bird in the head won it.

★ ☆ U ☆ ★

unborn tadpole. A term of derision aimed at the Confederacy by northerners at the beginning of the war. Shortly after war was declared, a *New York Times* editorial said: "Let us make quick work. The 'rebellion' as some people designate it, is an unborn tadpole."

Unconditional Surrender. A nickname for Ulysses S. Grant, who was the first military commander to use the term. On February 16, 1862, when Fort Donelson, in Tennessee, was about to fall, he was asked for the terms of capitulation and he replied, "No terms except unconditional surrender."

up the hawse pipe. To have worked one's way up from the enlisted ranks in the Navy. It alludes to the passage through which anchor cables pass in the bow of a ship.

★ ☆ V ☆ ★

vet. One who reenlists; one on his way to becoming an old soldier. The official U.S. name for those who re-enlisted was "veteran-volunteer" and indicated by a special chevron worn on the sleeve.

veteranize. To get out of the Army; to enjoy veteran status outside the Army.

★ ☆ W ☆ ★

War of Rebellion. Name commonly used in the North during, and for many years after, the war to describe it. Acts of Congress directing the compilation of official records in 1874 and 1880 referred to it by this name.

war widow. A woman whose husband is away at war.

war will be over by Christmas, the. According to Stuart Berg Flexner in *I Hear America Talking* (1976), this was a popular 1861 expression. Flexner adds: "Since then several generals and politicians have used the phrase or variations on it, in World War I, World War II, and the Korean War—and none of the wars was over by Christmas."

we'uns. Us; used in the South. See also YOU'UNS.

worm castle. A HARDTACK biscuit.

★ ☆ Y ☆ ★

Yank. (1) A YANKEE (applied by the Confederates to the soldiers of the Union Army); personified in the name "Billy Yank" (which had been used as early as the Revolutionary War), who was the counterpart of JOHNNY REB. By World War I, the name was being applied to Americans in general. (2) To cheat; to trick.

Yankee. (1) A Union soldier; used with varying degrees of disparagement by the Confederates. Here was how the Yankees were regarded in a popular song of the South written after the Battle of Bull Run, when many in the South felt the war was all but over:

> I come from old Manassas with a pocket full of fun—
> I killed forty Yankees with a single-barrelled gun;
> It don't make a niff-a-stifference to neither you or I,
> Big Yankee, little Yankee, all run or die.

(2) A native or inhabitant of New England; by extension, a native or inhabitant of any of the northern states. (3) Of, pertaining to, or characteristic of Yankees (as in "Yankee shrewdness").

The term is of disputed origin; it is commonly referred to as a term of unknown origin in major dictionaries.

Young Napoleon. General George McClellan, also known as LITTLE MAC.

you'uns. You all (before people said "you all" in the South). In M. Schele de Vere's *Americanisms* (1872), a Confederate soldier captured by Sheridan's troops during the charge through Rockfish Gap is credited with this line: "We didn't know *you-uns* was around us all, and *we-uns* reckoned we was all safe, till *you-uns* came ridin' down like mad through the gap and scooped up *we-uns* jest like so many herrin'."

★ ☆ Z ☆ ★

Zouave. A member of any of a number of dashing volunteer regiments from the North whose troops dressed in the colorful and romantic red, baggy-panted uniform of the French Zouaves.

The Spanish-American War Era

The Spanish-American War itself lasted for only four months in 1898, but it had an extended aftermath—including the American occupation of the Philippines and Cuba—and the period saw the creation of some fascinating new slang. The era was linguistically prophetic because it marked the first time that American troops had a chance to absorb foreign languages. As author Elbridge Colby wrote in *Army Talk: A Familiar Dictionary of Soldier Speech* (1943): "[Tell me w]here has the army been, and I'll tell you what some of the origins of its speech will be." For starters, this Army was in the Philippines, from which it brought back terms in both Spanish and Tagalog, such as BOLO SQUAD, PADRE (a chaplain), BOONDOCKS, and that nasty and longtime term of derogation, GOOK. In his *The American Language* (1937), H. L. Mencken pointed out that American English borrowed a fistful of foreign words from the Spanish-American War, including: "INSURRECTO, **trocha, junta, ladrone, incommunicado, ley fuga, machete, mañana,** and **rurale**." In *The American Language, Supplement 1* (1945), Mencken noted that some of these words had been used in English before, but that it was the war that had made them popular.

★ ☆ A ☆ ★

Asiatic. An odd person; one who acts abnormally. Originally it meant a soldier or sailor who had gone crazy from too much service in the Far East (probably the Philippines), but later was applied to anyone appearing slightly deranged. Asian-Americans and others have long regarded this term as a racial slur.

★ ☆ B ☆ ★

backbone. Courage. Theodore Roosevelt used the term often and quotably. Goading President William McKinley on his reluctance to go to war with Spain, Assistant Secretary of the Navy Roosevelt said, "McKinley has no more backbone than a chocolate éclair."

big stick. Military power. President Theodore Roosevelt was responsible for coining and/or popularizing this term; beginning in 1900, he advocated that the nation speak softly and carry a big stick. It is believed that the first time he uttered the phrase in public was at the Minnesota State Fair on September 2, 1901, when he said, "There is a homely adage which runs, 'Speak softly and carry a big stick; you will go far.'" It is worth noting that among the many other words and phrases coined by Roosevelt was "preparedness" (as in "military preparedness"), which he debuted in 1915.

bolo squad. Bad shots. Soldiers who at first show lack of aptitude at rifle marksmanship are put in a special group for extra training. In *Army Talk: A Familiar Dictionary of Soldier Speech* (1943), by Elbridge Colby, this explanation is given for the term's origin: "[O]ver in the Philippines, in the days of the empire, the soldiers had rifles and knew how to use them well, but the Filipinos were short on rifles, only their best shots had them; the others swung bolos. They were 'bolomen' and so a soldier who was not a good shot with a rifle was dubbed as no better than a mere native boloman."

See also BOLO, under the Vietnam War.

boodle. Candy, cake, ice cream, etc.; originally a term used by West Point cadets. When it first appeared in America, it referred to illegal gain or profit, and was long associated with corrupt politics. See also under World War II.

boondocks. A distant, unpopulated place; the sticks. The term was first used by Marines fighting against Filipino guerrillas (during 1899–1902), to refer to isolated or outlying mountain country. It stems from the Philippine Tagalog *bundok* ("mountain").

American troops shortened "boondocks" to BOONIES during the Vietnam War; combat boots have long been nicknamed "boondockers."

boot. A Navy or Marine recruit. The term is thought to come from the leggings that newly recruited sailors used to wear during training, which were called "boots." (Since colonial days, Americans had used "boot" to mean footwear reaching to the knee.) See also under World War I.

boot camp. Training camp for new recruits. This term was first heard during the war and was all but universally accepted by World War I.

bull's eye. To make a hit; to score a success. To make a bull's-eye is to score a hit in the center spot of a target. The term first appeared in print with this meaning in the New York *Herald*, on August 1, 1888; but earlier meanings of "bull's-eye" included a small piece of hard candy and a small piece of glass inserted in a wall or a ship's deck to let in light.

bust. To reduce in rank; to break.

★ ☆ **C** ☆ ★

canteen. A liquor store on a military base. Congress banned canteens on January 9, 1901, but Secretary of War Elihu Root opposed the ban and suggested that young men should be allowed to consume liquor in a friendly and benign environment lest they be driven "out into the horrible and demoralizing and damning surroundings that cluster around the outside of the camps." This meaning of the word, from the French *cantine* ("bottle case"), followed the British use of the term to refer to a flask for carrying liquids.

Cuban War, the. One of the popular names for the war while it was being fought. It was also known as the "War with Spain."

★ ☆ **D** ☆ ★

destroyer. A type of warship. It was a new American term, first used in 1898 in reference to the *Farragut*.

dog. A HARDTACK dish (see under the Civil War) described and explored in an article by W. J. Henderson in the September 1899 *Scribner's Magazine*:

> The United States Navy allows 30 cents a day for the rations of each man, and it is the problem of the paymaster and cook to keep him alive and well on this allowance. It seems liberal, however, relatively at least, when compared with the merchant-service allowance of only 10 cents a day. The merchantman's cook has a simple menu card displaying only the composition known as "dog." "Dog" is most largely hard-tack, put to soak overnight until it becomes sort of a pulp, mixed with molasses into a mush, and then fried. The man-of-war's man is saved from the necessity of eating "dog" some thirty days out of the month, but there are some analogies to it which must be achieved by the cook in order to eke out on this 30 cents a day.

★ ☆ **E** ☆ ★

embalmed beef. Pickled beef. Teddy Roosevelt testified to its nastiness when he stated that only one tenth of the beef arriving in Cuba for American troops was fit for human consumption. Many soldiers became sick because of embalmed beef, which led to a major court of inquiry that, despite graphic and often disgusting testimony, was unable to prove anyone guilty. In summarizing the case, *Medical Record* strongly suggested that the inquiry showed evidence of a whitewash.

One of the more interesting moments in the proceedings of the court of inquiry came when a regimental commissary sergeant testified that he had attempted to turn down a beef shipment that both looked and smelled bad. The packer's agent told him not to worry, that the meat had been treated with "preservatine," a special chemical that preserved but did not hurt the beef.

★ ☆ **F** ☆ ★

Filipino. (1) A native of the Philippines. (2) Someone running against a regularly nominated candidate for office. The term came into use during the time when the Filipinos, as H. L. Mencken put it in *The American Language* (1937), "were in armed revolt against their first salvation by the United States."

★ ☆ **G** ☆ ★

gain ground. To make progress; to gain headway; to secure the advantage.

goo-goo / gu-gu. A Filipino. The term is probably the basis—certainly part of the basis—for GOOK.

gook. A derogatory term for certain foreigners encountered by American troops. It was first used in reference to Filipinos, but it has survived to show up in other wars, especially those in Korea and Vietnam. In *The American Language, Supplement 1* (1945), H. L. Mencken reports: "The Marines who occupied Nicaragua in 1912 took to calling the natives gooks, one of their names for Filipinos."

In *Encyclopedia of Word and Phrase Origins* (1987), Robert Hendrickson holds that the evolution of the term was aided by the Korean *kuk* ("nationality";

pronounced "kook") and by the slang term "gook" (rhymes with "book"), meaning "slime" or "dirt," which, Hendrickson points out, is a blend term ("goo" + "muck").

★ ☆ **H** ☆ ★

hard as the hobs of hell. Said of HARDTACK biscuits (see under the Civil War). The hob alluded to in this expression is the projection inside a fireplace on which food can be rested to keep warm.

★ ☆ **I** ☆ ★

insurrecto. An insurrectionist. Stuart Berg Flexner wrote of this term in *I Hear America Talking* (1976):

Soon after the U.S. occupation of the Philippines began, the Filipino guerrillas who had fought Spain for independence began to fight us, with each side using about 70,000 men. We now called the "ungrateful" Filipino guerrillas under Emilio Aguinaldo insurrectos and put many Filipinos in relocation camps (which were somewhat more humane than the Cuban reconcentration camps that had helped start the Spanish-American War in the first place).

★ ☆ **K** ☆ ★

khaki. The color of and name for the summer uniform of American soldiers; from the Hindi *khaki* ("dust-colored"). Like so many terms of this war, this one was tied to Theodore Roosevelt. His ROUGH RIDERS, officially the 1st U.S. Volunteer Cavalry regiments in the war in 1898, are credited with having introduced the dust-colored cotton cloth into our Army, while the regulars, as Roosevelt said, were "dressed in heavy blue woolen uniforms and catapulted into a midsummer campaign in the tropics." The term was new only to America at this point. It was reported during the Indian Mutiny, says Elbridge Colby in *Army Talk: A Familiar Dictionary of Soldier Speech* (1943):

A provisional force of volunteer civilians and unattached officers, formed at Mirath, was called "the Khaki Force" from the color of the uniform they adopted, "khaki" being in Persian actually "dusty." The first British regiment to wear clothing of this color is said to have been the 52nd Infantry who dyed their white uniforms a mud color before leaving for the front where they went into battle at Trimmu Ghat, on July 12, 1857. It was first used generally by British troops who went out from India for the Boer War.

★ ☆ **L** ☆ ★

little brown brother. A term used by William Howard Taft, governor-general of the Philippines, to invoke America's obligation to the people of the Philippines and other occupied areas. It was America's version of Rudyard Kipling's poetic injunction to "Take up the White Man's burden" (see WHITE MAN'S BURDEN). Not all Americans occupying the Philippines were quite as enthusiastic about the idea as Taft. The common line among the troops was:

He may be a brother of Big Bill Taft;
But he ain't no brother of mine.

★ ☆ P ☆ ★

padre. A chaplain. In the Philippines, troops began calling the regimental chaplain "padre"—Spanish for "father" —because that was the way the Spanish-speaking natives spoke of their village priests.

police. To clean up an area. First recorded in 1893, the verb may be a corruption of "polish." By the time of World War I it had become part of the construction KITCHEN POLICE, or K.P.

puttee. A long strip of cloth wound spirally around the leg from ankle to knee by soldiers and sailors, as a protection or support. The term and the object came into being in 1886.

Clinton A. Sanders and Joseph W. Blackwell, Jr., in *Words of the Fighting Forces* (1942), wrote:

> Many readers, and esp. enlisted men of World War I, who used to struggle at every reveille to encase their shanks in regulation spiral *puttees*, will find it hard to believe that the pronunciation "put-TEE" has no sanction. The accent, says the dictionaries, should be placed on the first syllable, not the second. *Puttee* is the Anglicized form of the Hindu word "patti," meaning "bandage." *Puttee* should be pronounced exactly like the word putty, say: PUTT-ee. Also recalled as "wrapped leggings," or "wrapped leggin's."

★ ☆ R ☆ ★

Remember the Maine. A slogan of the Spanish-American War, prompted by the sinking of the *Maine* in Havana harbor. Stuart Berg Flexner pointed out that the *real* motto, uttered by the red-blooded,

was, "Remember the *Maine*—the hell with Spain!"

The slogan would be echoed in "Remember Pearl Harbor!" of World War II.

Rough Rider. A member of a volunteer regiment of cavalry, composed partly of western cowboys, organized by Theodore Roosevelt and Leonard Wood for service in the war. The term is a synonym for "cowboy" and was coined in an 1888 article by Roosevelt in *The Century Magazine*. The notion of the cowboy-soldier exemplified by "Rough Rider" is an old American tradition. Elbridge Colby wrote in *Army Talk: A Familiar Dictionary of Soldier Speech* (1943):

> The use of the word "cowboys" started among fighting men, drifted into civil life, and has come back home again in a new sense. During the Revolution, it was the title given to a group of Tory guerillas who roamed the region between the lines in Westchester County, and you can find it in many writings of that time and books about that time.

★ ☆ S ☆ ★

sharpshooter. An expert marksman. The term acquired a new meaning at this time, which differed from its general Civil War meaning of one skilled with a rifle. According to Elbridge Colby in *Army Talk: A Familiar Dictionary of Soldier Speech* (1943), it was: "A rating, just above that of 'marksman' and just below that of 'expert,' secured by a soldier who demonstrates a prescribed accuracy with the rifle by actual performance on the range."

This system was established as a formal qualification in the Army by General

Order 12, dated February 20, 1884, and was in place by the time of the war.

shavetail. A newly commissioned lieutenant or an inexperienced officer, beginning with this war. Here is how the term was discussed in the official *Words of the Fighting Forces* (1942), by Clinton A. Sanders and Joseph W. Blackwell, Jr.:

> The green second lieutenant emerging out of West Point in his well-pressed uniform has been given this colorful name by the privates in the rank and file. Ironically enough, the term can trace its origin back to the army mule. The word was first used to designate the green, unbroken mules purchased by the Army. Since the mule-dealer shaved the animal's tail, leaving only a tuft of hair hanging at the end, the mule was called a "shavetail." It was no great tax on the private's imagination to call a young, green officer a "shavetail." The use of the word has been extended lately, however, to include young officials in the industrial world.

See also under World War I.

Soapsuds Row. Married quarters (by the time of the war and thereafter). The term was sometimes applied with a degree of irony. In Leonard Mosley's *Marshall: A Hero for Our Times* (1982), a slummy married quarters in the Oklahoma Territory in 1903 is described as an area of filth and unkempt streets: "The quarter was known as Soapsuds Row, but soap was the last thing that was used around it."

★ ☆ **W** ☆ ★

War with Spain, the. A popular name for the war while it was being fought; also called "the Cuban War."

white man's burden. A term created by British writer Rudyard Kipling in a 1899 poem that began:

> Take up the White Man's burden,
> Send forth the best ye breed . . .
> To wait in heavy harness,
> On fluttering folk and wild—
> Your new-caught sullen peoples,
> Half devil and half child.

According to Mark Sullivan in *Our Times: The Turn of the Century* (1936), the poem was "taken as being addressed partly to America in its adventures in the Philippines, and partly to Kipling's own country and its attempt to master the Boers." The phrase "white man's burden" became common shorthand for American imperialism.

W.M.B. Impaled

Not every American was willing to take up Kipling's charge. When politician Richard Croker was asked for his definition of the term, he said, "My idea of anti-imperialism is opposition to the fashion of shooting everybody who doesn't speak English."

The following bit of counter-poetry showed up in *The New York Times*, which recast Kipling from the point of view of those being taken on as a burden:

> Take up the White Man's burden,
> Send forth your sturdy sons,
> And load them down with whiskey
> And Testaments and guns.
> Throw in a few diseases
> To spread in tropic climes . . .

★ ☆ **Y** ☆ ★

yellow. In 1898, this word appeared in a new context: the press. It showed up in such terms as "yellow journalism" and "the yellow press." It was used to deplore those newspapers—specifically, the New York *Journal*, owned by William Randolph Hearst, and the New York *World*, owned by Joseph Pulitzer—which were sensationalizing Spanish actions in Cuba, calling them atrocities and fanning the flames of war. As several leading etymologists have shown (Stuart Berg Flexner and Robert Hendrickson, for example), the word "yellow" had been associated with sensationalism for many years and had nothing to do with Richard Outcault's pioneering comic strip, "The Yellow Kid," which appeared in both newspapers during the period.

yellow jack. Yellow fever.

Sources

★

Catton, Bruce. *Glory Road*. New York: Dolphin, 1952.
———. *Mr. Lincoln's Army*. New York: Dolphin, 1951.
———. *Stillness at Appomattox*. New York: Doubleday and Co., 1954.
Catton, William, and Bruce Catton. *Two Roads to Sumter*. New York: McGraw-Hill, 1963.
Chapman, Bruce. *Why Do We Say Such Things? The Stories Behind the Words We Use*. New York: Miles-Emmett, 1947.
Colby, Elbridge. *Army Talk: A Familiar Dictionary of Soldier Speech*. Princeton, N.J.: Princeton University Press, 1943.
Davis, Burke. *The Long Surrender*. New York: Random House, 1985.
Elting, John R., and Cragg and Ernest Deal. *A Dictionary of Soldier Talk*. New York: Scribners, 1984.
Flexner, Stuart Berg. *I Hear America Talking*. New York: Van Nostrand Reinhold, 1976.
Foote, Shelby. *The Civil War*. New York: Vintage, 1958
Hendrickson, Robert. *Encyclopedia of World and Phrase Origin*. New York: Facts on File, 1987.
Holt, Alfred H. *Phrase and Word Origins*. New York: Dover, 1961.
Leech, Margaret. *In the Days of McKinley*. New York: Harper and Brothers, 1959.
Lyman, Darryl. *The Animal Things We Say*. New York: Jonathan David Publishers, 1983.
McAlpine, R. W. "A Word about Slang." *United States Service Magazine* (June 1865).
McPherson, James M. *Battle Cry of Freedom*. New York: Oxford University Press, 1988.
Melville, Herman. *White-Jacket, or, The World in a Man-of-War*. New York: 1850.
Mencken, H. L. *The American Language*. New York: Alfred A. Knopf, 1937.
———. *The American Language, Supplement 1*. New York: Alfred A. Knopf, 1945.
———. *The American Language, Supplement 2*. New York: Alfred A. Knopf, 1948.
Rogers, John G. *Origins of Sea Terms*. Mystic, Conn.: Mystic Seaport Museum, 1985.

Sanders, Clinton A., and Joseph W. Blackwell, Jr. *Words of the Fighting Forces*. New York Military Intelligence Service, 1942.

Schemmer, Benjamin. *Almanac of Liberty*. New York: Macmillan, 1974.

Small, Maj. Abner R. *The Road to Richmond*. University of California, 1939.

Sullivan, Mark. *Our Times: The Turn of the Century*. New York: Scribner's, 1936.

Trumbull, H. Clay. *War Memories of an Army Chaplin*. New York: Charles Scribner's Sons, 1898.

Wood, William, and Ralph Henry Gabriel. *In Defense of Liberty*. New Haven, Conn.: Yale University Press, 1928.

Worsham, John H. *One of Jackson's Foot Cavalry*. New York: Neale Publishing Co., 1912.

WORLD WAR I: OVER THERE AND OVER THE TOP

★

Terms That Came Up from the Trenches; Down from the Dogfight

★

World War I: Doughboys Over There

The Army meant another way of life, and a new language arose to express and picture it. By reviving old terms, by borrowing or inventing new ones, the soldier formed a special and racy vocabulary which he spoke with a professional flair.

—Mark Sullivan, *Our Times: The United States, 1900–1925,*
Vol. V, Over Here, 1914–1918 (1933)

American war slang came into its own during World War I, with terms growing like mushrooms in the dank trenches from the linguistic spores of earlier wars. It mocked German and—KAPUT!—rendered it ERSATZ. It grabbed hold of French and turned it into the language of comic opera. *Esprit de corps* became **ESPRITT DE CORPSE;** *je ne sais pas* came out as **JENNY'S PA** or **JENNY SASS PASS;** and the town of Doingt, France, was renamed **DOING IT** for the duration.

The American slang of World War I was also very much tied to British war slang, as it had been during the American Revolution. The two armies fought together in World War I, and it was the American SAMMY who joined the war after the British—in the person of TOMMY ATKINS, the British every-private—were well entrenched in their trenches.

Some claims were made that American trench lingo was supplanting the British, but the claims were not convincing. Here is one journalist's attempt to report on the emerging American slang:

> With the American Armies in France, September 17—"Zero hour" and "over the top" are expressions which have passed from the American Army after long popularity with the British.
>
> America's attack in the Lorraine sector has brought out typical American expressions.
>
> "Over the top" is now "the jump off" and "zero hour" has changed to "H hour."
>
> —Baltimore *Star* (September 17, 1918)

American linguistic innovation was significant enough to have a major impact on the way the British soldier spoke, but not enough to overwhelm it. Americans said OVER THE TOP for the duration, and they did send the British home with a headful of Americanisms.

Aviation was a new and important factor in the war, and aviators from the two English-speaking nations seemed to vie with each other to see who could come up with the most colorful way of minimizing the risks of the business they were in.

There were linguistic changes and ironies everywhere, even in the business of numbers. The following appeared in an Associated Press dispatch of March 11, 1919:

> The consideration of reparations has introduced the word "trillion" in recognizing money, probably for the first time in any single financial operation, for, although millions and billions often have been used in war finance, no sum has yet been reached touching a trillion. In estimating the war losses of all the powers the first figures of one of the great powers aggregated a trillion francs and those of another power were slightly above a half trillion francs, namely, six hundred billion francs.

Many of the terms had staying power, surviving to World War II and beyond. In his book *Up Front* (1945), Bill Mauldin compares a German and an American soldier in World War II, in a line that could easily have come from World War I: "Both had cooties, both had trench foot, and each had an intense dislike for the other."

Here then is a large helping of the American slang of the DOUGHBOY.

★ ☆ A ☆ ★

A.B.C. powers, the. The South American republics of Argentina, Brazil, and Chile, which entered into a peace treaty with each other in 1915.

ace. A combatant aviator who has brought down five or more enemy aircraft, or as James R. McConnell put it in *Flying for France* (1916): "When a pilot has accounted for five Boches he is mentioned by name in the official communication, and is spoken of as an 'Ace,' which in French aerial slang means a super-pilot. Papers are allowed to call an 'ace' by name, print his picture, and give him a write-up. The successful aviator becomes a national hero."

ace of aces. An ACE who brought down or killed twenty-five or more enemy aircraft. Here is a newspaper account of one such ace of aces:

> Paris, November 16—Six new victories over German airplanes were gained during the late fighting in the Aisne region by Lieut. Rene Fonck, ace of aces of all the belligerent powers, with 75 airplanes officially destroyed, plus 40 probable victories.
> —Paul Ayres Rockwell, the Baltimore *Evening Sun* (November 16, 1918)

Ace of Diamonds Division. The U.S. 5th Division; its insignia was a red ace of diamonds. See also **RED DIAMOND DIVISION.**

aces up. A squadron of expert fighter pilots.

Acorn Division. The 87th Division, composed of men from Arkansas, Mississippi, and Louisiana; its insignia was a brown acorn on a green disk.

acting jack. A temporary sergeant.

A.E.F. American Expeditionary Forces. It was said by many Americans to have stood for "after England failed."

aggie. The adjutant general; primarily officer slang.

ah-ah treatment. An examination for a sore throat, from the noise made after a tongue depressor went into a soldier's mouth.

airnat. An airman. The word is said to have been formed from "aeronaut" and to have been adopted by balloting of the flying corps of the U.S. Army. According to Eugene S. McCartney in *Slang and Idioms of the World War* (1929): "The word was utterly lacking in spontaneity and does not seem to have obtained any vogue."

Alamo Division. The 90th Division, composed of Texas and Oklahoma troops. The name is very appropriate, since the division trained at Camp Travis, just outside San Antonio. Its insignia was a red monogrammed TO.

All-American Division. The 82nd Division, composed largely of troops from Georgia, Alabama, and Tennessee. It was said to owe its name to the fact that nearly every state in the Union was represented in its membership. Its insignia was the letters AA in gold on a blue field, which in turn was set upon a red square.

allo. (1) A radio notice that a U-boat has been seen. (2) A rendering of "hello."

all's quiet on the western front. Tranquillity prevails, save for the normal daily attrition in the trenches. A phrase coined by an unknown, ingenious newspaper man "somewhere in France" in 1915. With irony and bitterness, Erich Maria Remarque titled his 1929 war novel *All Quiet on the Western Front* because men were still dying while the clichéd quietness was in effect.

amalgam. A section of front where American and French troops mingled.

America first. A motto alluding to American glory and America's place in the world; proclaimed by Woodrow Wilson in a speech on April 20, 1915.

American pony. A Missouri mule; named with a tip of the hat to the Shetland pony.

ammo. Ammunition.

ammunition. Pies and pastry, as doled out by the Salvation Army.

A.M.T. landing. An expression used at Kelly Field, Texas, to designate an airplane landing of such a character that the airman needed the services of an ambulance, motorcycle, or truck (hence A.M.T.) to convey him to a hospital.

Anzac. Australian and New Zealand Army Corps. It was reportedly first used in a telegram sent by General William Birdwood from the Gallipoli Peninsula during the summer of 1915. One account says that publicity was given to the word by Major Oliver Hogue of Sydney, who used it as a code word in dispatches to the Sydney *Morning Herald*. The term continued to be used in World War II.

Acronyms

One of the earliest recorded acronyms, if not the earliest, is VAMP. It was rediscovered by William and Mary Morris and reported in their *Morris Dictionary of Word and Phrase Origins* (1977). It dates back to the midnineteenth century, when it was used in fire-fighting circles to refer to the Voluntary Association of Master Pumpers. Prior to the Morrises' revelation, it had been broadly concluded that the earliest English acronym was ANZAC. In any event, Anzac had at least one other World War I antecedent in the British FANY (First Aid Nursing Yeomanry).

---

apartment. A DUGOUT.

aprons. Wire obstacles against airplanes. They were described in *The London Illustrated News* of December 14, 1918:

Wires suspended from balloons at such intervals as to prevent big airplanes from getting through; nets formed by kite-balloons, each a certain distance from the next, each connected to the next by a horizontal wire-cable, and each horizontal cable carrying suspended from it at intervals some thousands of feet of fine wire, each with a plumb-bob at the end.

Archie. An antiaircraft gun.

argue the toss. To argue a point; from the practice of flipping (or tossing) a coin to settle an argument.

Army game. This term was defined by Mark Sullivan in *Our Times*, Vol. V, *Over Here* (1933): "The 'old Army Game,' hoary with age and tradition, is to 'pass the buck.'"

arrival. The sound made by an approaching shell. This term was defined by E. F. Wood in *The Note-Book of an Intelligence Officer* (1917): "One first dimly hears the far-off rush of the shell as it approaches, rising in crescendo to a scream and finally terminating by the roar of the burst. This is called an 'arrival.'"

artillery. Beans.

ash can. A large German shell.

assault ration. A tablespoonful of rum given to the men in the early morning just before an assault.

attaboy. (1) An American soldier. The term stems from a cry of approval of the time—"That's the boy!" or "That's the stuff, boy"—and was applied to soldiers, especially by the British. (2) A cry of encouragement for Americans. The French used it approvingly in cheering General John J. ("Black Jack") Pershing and his stalwarts.

Attaboy Special. The train that ran between Chaumont and Tours.

A.W.O.L. Absent without official leave. Journalist Mark Sullivan marks this war as the debut of this term, in *Our Times*, Vol. V, *Over Here* (1933), with this definition: "Said of a man who believes that nine days at home is worth six months pay." Many others saw the term as a verbal novelty, especially since it was a set of initials that could be pronounced "a-wall"—but it is clearly a term that had been used by both sides in the U.S. Civil War and was common in World War I. What apears to have been new was saying a-wall rather than A.W.O.L.

axle grease. Butter.

★ ☆ **B** ☆ ★

baby elephant. A small corrugated-iron shelter.

balmy. Nervous; afraid. This word was used in thieves' cant of more than a generation before, in the sense of "mad."

bantam. A short or small man, affectionately. The British actually boasted of their Bantam Division, composed of men under the minimum army height of five feet three inches.

bantam doughboy. An American who fell under the regulation height but was nonetheless allowed to enter the service.

baptism of fire. An individual's or a unit's first engagement with the enemy.

barbed-wire disease. A nervous breakdown brought about by imprisonment. According to *The New York Times* of May 27, 1918:

> Turkish officials that have heard the expression translate it literally. Wherefore the Turkish government, in ratifying an agreement with the British for an exchange of prisoners, stipulated that plain wire should be substituted for barbed wire around prison camps for Turks in English territory.

barbwire garters. A mythical award for those who got no special honors or decorations; perhaps a play on the British Order of the Garter.

barndook. A gun; a rifle. The rifle was called also "bundook" and "bondook." These are apparently intermediate stages between "barndook" and *banduc,* a Hindi word for "gun" that was familiar to the British soldier in India. The nickname "barndook" was used in both British and American armies before the war and by both armies in the trenches. In 1991, during the Persian Gulf War, it was used by the British troops and reported widely as a Briticism.

barn door. Hello; good day. The term is a play on the French *bonjour.*

baron. An Army commander.

barrel. A stunt of the airman, which consists of rolling the airplane over and over like a barrel. A scientific explanation is given in *The Scientific American* of September 7, 1918:

> This is usually started by slightly reducing the speed of the engine, pulling the control stick well towards the pilot, and giving a very quick push at the rudder—to the full extent, in fact—and at once replacing all controls in the center. The machine starts to mount suddenly, but the full effect of the rudder swings the machine up on one wing, over completely sideways, which follows with a wing slip and a flattening sidewise.

bashed in. Smashed in by a shell.

basket case. A soldier who had lost all four limbs and was brought home as a living head and torso in a basket. There were countless unofficial reports of such cases—and many soldiers were of the opinion that there were many of them—but their existence was denied by the government. In 1939, Dalton Trumbo's harrowing novel about a basket case, *Johnny Got His Gun,* kept the idea alive. Today it is used to describe mental distress—"I was falling apart . . . A real basket case."

Basket Cases—The Official Word

The War Department authorizes the following statement from the office of the Surgeon General:

The Surgeon General of the Army, Maj. Gen. Merritte W. Ireland, denies emphatically that there is any foundation for the stories that have been circulated in all parts of the country of the existence of "basket cases" in our hospitals. A basket case is a soldier who has lost both legs and both arms and therefore cannot be carried on a stretcher.

Gen. Ireland says: "I have personally examined the records and am able to say that there is not a single basket case either on this side of the water or among the soldiers of the A.E.F. Further, I wish to emphasize that there has been no instance of an American soldier so wounded during the whole period of the war."

—*Official U.S. Bulletin,* Washington, D.C. (March 28, 1919)

---

bayonet. A soldier. Soldiers were also sometimes called "thinking bayonets." See also under the Civil War.

beachcomber. A tramp or bum who hung around saloons and begged sailors for money or drinks.

beak cover. Gas mask.

beans. (1) A commissary sergeant. (2) Ammunition.

bean shooter. A commissary officer.

bean tote. Soon; from the French *bientôt*.

Beef Villas. Biefvillers, France.

belly robber. A Navy commissary steward or paymaster whom the crew believed to be robbing them of decent vittles. It is an old term, dating back at least to the Civil War.

Bertha. See **Big Bertha.**

Bertha pill. A large German shell, such as that fired by **Big Bertha.**

Best of luck and God bless you. A parting salutation to men going OVER THE TOP.

Betsy the Sniper. A nickname for the 155-mm cannon manned by the Americans. According to the May 13, 1919, issue of *Literary Digest:* "She won her first fame in the Toul sector by being the forward gun of our lines. Not merely was she farthest north, but she scorned the steady brand of firing that most guns of her class indulged in. She went in for emergency sharp-shooting. It was thus that she won the sobriquet of 'sniper.'"

Bevo officer. A new officer; an officer who has not gone through West Point. Bevo was one of the new drinks, a near-beer.

Big Bertha. (1) A large siege gun used by the German army in shelling Paris. It was a mammoth rifle-cannon with which the Germans shelled the city from a distance of up to nine miles. (2) By extension, a big or fat woman.

The name alludes to Bertha Antoinette Krupp von Bohlen und Halbach, at whose factory the gun was manufactured. She was sole heir to the Krupp armaments empire.

Big Bill / Big Willie. Kaiser Wilhelm II of Germany, who was seen as the person most responsible for the war and the resulting sacrifice of millions of lives.

big bow-wow. A regimental sergeant-major.

big boy. A large gun, generally of an eight-inch bore or more.

Big Five, the. The leading nations at the Paris peace conference of 1919: Great Britain, France, Italy, Japan, and the United States.

Big Lizzie. The ocean liner *Queen Elizabeth;* so-called by the Anzac troops at Gallipoli.

Big Push, the / Big Show, the. Any major engagement, but usually used to refer to the battle of the Somme (1916).

big stuff. Large shells (eight inches or over).

big ticket. An honorable discharge; a Navy term. A SMALL TICKET was a dishonorable discharge.

Bill. See BIG BILL.

Billard. No-man's-land.

Bing boy. A Canadian soldier; in recognition of Sir Julian Byng, who took command of the Canadian forces, and after the popular musical comedy *The Bing Boys*.

binged. Vaccinated. A "bing spot" was a vaccination mark.

bite and hold. A strategy by which the enemy is forced to consolidate its defenses and required to undertake costly counterattacks.

bitter ender. One who was opposed to any terms of peace other than the total defeat of the Central Powers. The term came into wide use in this war, but it was used as early as the Civil War (to describe those who wanted to fight the South to the bitter end) and as late as the Vietnam War (to describe those who carried the conflict to the bitter end).

black boat. A destroyer or a torpedo-boat destroyer.

blackey. A blacksmith.

black gang. A ship's engineers' division, whose work covered its members with grease, oil, and grime. According to Logan E. Ruggles in *The Navy Explained* (1910): "Men of the firerooms, engine rooms, ice machine, evaporators, and every man in the department are members of the gang." See also under the Civil War.

Black Hawk Division. The 86th Division, composed of troops recruited from northern Illinois. "So named," according to Eugene S. McCartney in *Slang and Idioms of the World War* (1929), "because its forces mobilized on the 'Black Hawk Trail' at Camp Grant, near Rockford, Ill., and adopted as their battle-cry the war-whoop 'Ki-a-ki-ak' of a Black Hawk chief." Its insignia was a small monogrammed b.h. on a red shield superimposed on a black hawk, and the whole superimposed on a red shield.

black jack. (1) A strong physic, generally jollop. (2) Coffee. (3) The nickname for General John ("Black Jack") Pershing, the American commander in chief, 1917–1919.

black Maria. A high-explosive shell; from the slang name for English police-patrol wagons. The following theory appeared in the Detroit *Free Press* on June 14, 1925: "One explanation is that a negress called Maria formerly kept a sailors' boarding house in Boston. She was a bit of a terror, and ruled her lodgers with an iron hand. Finally she became so famous that in moments of stress the Boston police gasped: 'Send for Black Maria!'"

black pill. A German shell that emitted black smoke on exploding.

black strap. Coffee.

blimp. A dirigible balloon from which a cabin shaped like an airplane fuselage is suspended. Blimps were developed by the British. The word was applied to small airships and large women as well.

Blimp—A Disputed Word History

There was much speculation as to where the term "blimp" came from. For instance: *"blimp.* The captive observation balloon rejoices in the above appellation for reasons known only to the lads who use them over there" (from the Baltimore *Sun,* September 29, 1918). The following passage from *Words of the Fighting Forces* (1942), by Clinton A. Sanders and Joseph W. Blackwell, Jr., offers a plausible explanation: "During World War I the British non-rigid airship was known as the type B-limp airship. The British soldier dropped the hyphen and christened the ship 'blimp' and the term was later adopted by the United States Armed Forces."

Doubt is cast on this and other theories by Robert Hendrickson, in his *Encyclopedia of Word and Phrase Origins* (1987). He starts by shooting down a theory advanced by H. L. Mencken, which held that the term was created by two Britishers while they were having "blunch" (or "brunch," as it is called in America) at an airport. Hendrickson states:

Nor was the nonrigid dirigible airship so named by its manufacturer, the Goodyear Company in the early years of World War I. It is often reported that Goodyear's first model, the "A limp" (nonrigid), hadn't worked and that their second model, the "B limp," succeeded and kept its name, but Goodyear has denied that they or anyone else had airships with "limp" or type "B" designations.

Hendrickson's belief is that all of this leaves us with the possibility that the word is onomatopoeic, possibly coined by a Lieutenant Cunningham of the British Royal Navy Air Service in 1915. "Cunningham, according to this story," writes Hendrickson, "flicked his thumb at one of the airships while on an inspection tour and 'an odd noise echoed off the taut fabric. . . . [He] orally imitated the sound his thumb had drummed out of the airship bag: 'Blimp!' Those nearby saw and heard this unusual interlude in the inspection, and its account quickly spread."

blind. (1) Sentenced by court-martial to forfeiture of pay without confinement. (2) A DUD (a shell that fails to explode).

blind pig. A huge shell from a trench mortar.

blister-skin. A broad shelf at the waterline of a British monitor, rendering the vessel torpedo-proof. The device was illustrated in *Collier's* (April 5, 1919, page 15).

blooded. Describing an individual or unit that had seen combat.

Blue and Gray Division. The 29th National Guard Division, composed of men from Delaware, the District of Columbia, Maryland, New Jersey, and Virginia. As explained by Eugene S. McCartney, in his *Slang and Idioms of the World War* (1929): "[O]bviously so named because the men came from states that fought on different sides in the Civil War." Its insignia was a blue and gray pierced disk, symbolizing the union of North and South. The insignia is said to have been taken from the Korean symbol meaning "good luck."

blue boy. A French soldier; so-called because of the color of the dashing blue uniform.

blue funk squad. A firing squad, the duty of which was to execute those guilty of cowardice. The term "blue funk" has long been slang for a state of depression.

Blue Ridge Division. The 80th Division, composed of men from Pennsylvania, Virginia, and West Virginia; also called the LEE DIVISION. Its insignia was three blue mountains on a shield edged with white, each mountain representing a state.

blue triangle. The nickname for the symbol of the Young Men's Christian Association (Y.M.C.A.).

boat-tailing. Describing the shape of shells. The term was explained in *Everybody's* magazine (July 1919):

> Modern long-range shells are cigar-shaped. They taper both at the front and at the rear. This tapering of the rear is called "boat-tailing." You have noticed that racing automobiles have torpedo-shaped sterns. A square-tailed shell or automobile is actually held back at high speeds because of the vacuum created behind it by the velocity of its movement. Tapering the tail leads the air gently and easily into the hole that the shell or the racing car bores in the atmosphere and thus lessens vacuum's impending grip on the flying object.

bobtailed. Dishonorably discharged; from the practice of removing ("bobbing") the portion of discharge papers that confers honor.

boche. A German, but usually a German soldier; from the French slang *ce boche* ("that chump"), according to a study of the term that appeared in the April 7, 1916, *New York Times*. In *Words of the Fighting Forces* (1942), by Clinton A. Sanders and Joseph W. Blackwell, Jr., it is pointed out that a number of constructions were based on "boche," including "boche army" (the German army), "bocheland" (Germany), "boche navy" (the German navy), and "boche stabber" (bayonet). See also BUSHER.

boche aspirin. A hand grenade used by the German army.

body snatcher. (1) A sniper at the front. (2) A stretcher bearer.

bokoo. An abundance of anything; from the French *beaucoup*. "Bokoo soused" is a term meaning "very drunk."

bone jar / bone jaw. Hello; from the French *bonjour*.

bonswar / bonswart. Farewell; from the French *bonsoir*.

boot. A Navy recruit. The term is defined in Logan E. Ruggles's *The Navy Explained* (1918): "A young sailor who has recently enlisted in the navy; a man who is exceedingly wooden in the performance of his duties and who is uncouth in his habits." The term was also in use during the Spanish-American War.

boot lace. An airman's term used to describe a sort of combined spin and roll.

bosom chums. Vermin.

bounce. A bad landing, causing the airplane to jump. A bounce was often the cause of a crash.

bouquet. A group or cluster of shells or bombs.

bowlegs. A Cavalryman. See under the Civil War.

B.P. A BUCK PRIVATE. Mark Sullivan defines the term in *Our Times*, Vol. V, *Over Here* (1933): "A government employee of the next grade above civilian who usually believes that it is his function to avoid all responsibility and to do as little work as possible."

brains. An intelligence officer.

brain trust. The general staff.

brass hat. A staff officer. This term was borrowed from the British, whose staff officers wear gilt on their hats.

brass looie. A lieutenant.

brig. A prison; also called a "cage," "jug," and "cooler." It is a traditional Navy term for a ship's jail, but is now used by other branches of the armed services.

Broad Arrow Division. The 32nd Division, composed of troops from Michigan and Wisconsin. Its insignia was a red arrow, because "they shot through every line."

Says *The New York Times* (May 18, 1919): "To the army in general it is the Thirty-second, to the people of Michigan and Wisconsin, it is the Broad Arrow Division, while the French will always remember it by the name given to it by the poilu [the privates at the front], Les Terribles."

The division was also called the Iron Jaw Division, because it was employed on both flanks of the Marne salient, and as LES TERRIBLES.

broomstick. The control lever of an airplane.

bubbly. Champagne.

buck. A private; a common soldier.

bucked. Proud or pleased. The term is a rare piece of American slang and appears to have existed only in this war.

Buckeye Division. The 37th Division, made up exclusively of men from Ohio. The nickname was adopted in November 1917. Its insignia was a red circle superimposed on a white circle, a design adapted from the Ohio flag.

buck private. A term sometimes used in speaking of a private. See also B.P.

buckshee. Free; faked; done surreptitiously, as in "buckshee pass"; extra; surplus, as in "buckshee helping"; smart; superfine (for example, as regards clothes). According to the journal *Notes and Queries* (December 1918): "Buckshee is an Atkinized [Briticized] form of an Indian word. Bakhsh is a gift; bakhshi is the giver, paymaster; bakhshish is a gift, a tip. All these ideas seem to have had a hand in making 'buckshee' mean something extra."

buddy. A companion in arms; a chum; a nickname given to the American fighting man during the war. Mark Sullivan, in *Our Times*, Vol. V, *Over Here* (1933), notes that after the war the term was "taken over into civilian use by hitchhikers and panhandlers." The vets, however, held the term in high esteem; the name they gave to a paper replica of a Flanders poppy on Memorial Day, sold to benefit disabled soldiers, was "Buddy poppy."

buddy seat. A motorcycle sidecar.

Buffalo. A Sopwith airplane designed for reconnaissance and contact patrols.

Buffaloes. Members of the 92nd Division, composed of African-American troops from various sections of the country. Its insignia was a black buffalo. According to Eugene S. McCartney in *Slang and Idioms of the World War* (1929):

> It is said that the name goes back to pioneer days when Negro soldiers were called upon to aid in suppressing Indian uprisings. The redskins, learning to respect them as soldiers, nicknamed them "Buffaloes." The title is inherited from the 367th Regiment of the 15th New York (colored) Infantry, which was incorporated in the division.

The color of the buffalo varied according to the arm of the service.

bull. Small talk; "a mean brand of chatter." This "bull" was euphemistic for "bullshit," and it became general slang after the war.

bullets. Beans.

bull ring. (1) A training school. The term is defined in *With Our Soldiers in France*, by S. Eddy (1917):

> Just before going into the trenches the British, French and American troops take a final course for a few weeks in a training school, where the expert drill masters put them through a rigorous discipline, and the finishing touches are given to each regiment. . . . The men commonly call this training school, or specially prepared final drill ground, the "Bull Ring."

(2) A "hanging-out" place on many large cruisers and battleships. According to Logan E. Ruggles, in *The Navy Explained* (1918): "It is situated on the main deck forward just under the conning tower and at the base of the cage mast."

Bull's-eye Division. The 37th Division, composed of troops from Arkansas, Louisiana, and Mississippi. In *Slang and Idioms of the World War* (1929), Eugene S. McCartney explains the symbolism of its insignia:

> On February 23, 1919, The New York Times described the insignia as an inner circle of red, a middle one of white, and an outer circle of black. The National Geographic Magazine for December, 1919, p. 513, gives the insignia as a delta enclosing three small deltas, but says, p. 518, that it was never approved by the A.E.F. The insignia was due, of course, to the fact that the personnel came from the vicinity of the delta of the Mississippi.

bully beef. Canned corned beef. It is described by Arthur Guy Empey in *Over the Top* (1917): "A kind of corned beef with tin round it. The unopened cans make excellent walls for dugouts." The word "bully" meant "fine" or "first-rate" and had been borrowed by Americans from British slang before the war.

bumboat. A hawker or peddler aboard a Navy ship. The term originally was used to describe the scavengers' boats that plied the Thames River in London in the seventeenth century.

bumped off. Killed.

bunk. (1) A bed. (2) To sleep with someone. The term had long been used to refer to a wooden case or berth. Walter W. Skeat, in his *Concise Etymological Dictionary of the English Language* (1908), says it is from the old Swedish *bunke*, for the planking of a ship forming a shelter for merchandise.

bunker plates. Hotcakes, flapjacks, and pancakes; a Navy term. They were so-called because of their resemblance to the heavy lids of coal chutes, which were also known as bunker plates.

bunk fatigue. Illness requiring a patient to stay in bed.

bunkie. A sleeping companion.

bunk lizard. A chronic sleeper.

Burleson magazines. Periodicals contributed by the public to the Army and Navy and forwarded to the services by the Post Office Department. The name was derived from the fact that Postmaster General Burleson authorized the postal force to forward these magazines and periodicals under a one-cent stamp.

busher. A German; from BOCHE. In *The Doughboys* (1963), Laurence Stallings says: "Many of the baseball players among the French Doughboys simply referred to the enemy as 'them bushers.'"

bust. To reduce a noncommissioned officer to the rank of private.

butcher. A company barber.

butcher shop. An operating room; a surgical department.

butt. That part of an enlistment still to be served; usually, a fraction of a year.

buzzers. Members of the Army Signal Corps; also known as "iddy-umpties."

buzz wire. A telephone or telegraph line.

by Joe. A jewel; from the French *bijou* (a finger ring or other small item of value).

★ ☆ **C** ☆ ★

Cactus Division. The 18th Division, which was organized at Camp Travis, Texas, in August 1918. Its insignia was a cactus, with the Latin motto *Noli me tangere* ("Don't touch me").

cadge. To borrow.

camel. Nickname for the British Sopworth scout airplane because of its shape.

camel corps. The Infantry.

camel flags. Camouflage, in a popular pronunciation.

camouflage. The art of concealment. A French slang dictionary says that *se camoufler* is thieves' cant, meaning "to disguise one's self." The word was employed by soldiers and civilians alike to indicate any form of concealment.

Word History—Camouflage's American Debut

Popular writer Will Irwin, reporting in the *Saturday Evening Post* of September 29, 1917, told Americans about a new word and something about the slang of the war:

There's a new word in the English language, and by that I mean the corrupt dialect of our mother tongue used in the British Isles, not the pure and yet improved variety current in North America. As soon as this war is over and Tommy resumes his civilian activities, the British will be getting out new editions of those dictionaries wherein, they vainly believe, is embalmed the standard English language of the world.

And in the C section, probably without the comment of "argot" or "slang" or "colloquial," or any other mark of disreputability, will appear camouflage. Doubtless it will make its way, though more slowly, into those purer repositories of the tongue published in Boston or New York; for we are sending an army over to France just now, and the first new word they will learn at the Front will be camouflage. The term was pretty nearly unknown, even to the French, three years ago; and the thing it represents was absolutely unknown. It is pronounced, at present, French fashion, like this—"cam-oo-flazh," the first a being short, as in cat; the second a broader, as in harm.

It had laboured along for centuries, a rare and obscure French word, having several meanings, mostly slang. But in the theatrical business it signified makeup. The scene painters of the Parisian theaters carried it with them to the war and fixed it in army slang; for just about that time the armies of Europe began to introduce a new branch of tactics into warfare. By the first winter of the war both sides were at it. The British, as they worked up to efficiency, adopted the method and learned the word.

This word—having none other for the process—they added to the vocabulary of the British Army; it was new, and it was susceptible to a great variety of metaphorical uses. At latest accounts the British soldiers were working it to death. They use it as a noun, verb and adjective. They use it for any variety of concealment—moral, spiritual, or intellectual.

can. An airplane.

Canada. A Canadian name for no-man's-land.

Canary cruisers. German submarines that used the Canary Islands as a supply base. The name was used by Navy personnel on ships engaged in escort duty at the Azores.

candidate for gold bars. An aspirant for a second lieutenancy.

canned horse. Canned beef.

canned Willie. Canned corned beef hash. The term is described and defined by Elbridge Colby in *Army Talk: A Familiar Dictionary of Soldier Speech* (1943):

> This name for corned beef hash has a long and honorable history in the speech of the American Army. The A.E.F. took it to France with them and brought it back, and then distributed it over the country in the ranks of the American Legion. If it can be said to be general slang, it was specially military in origin and remains military. It was immediately taken up by the drafted men of 1940.

cannon fodder. Soldiers, regarded as food for cannon. The Germans were fond of this expression at the beginning of the war, when their superior equipment gave them a tremendous advantage, but it was quickly adopted by U.S. and British troops. It came to refer to infantry units sent into combat situations in which they will almost certainly suffer heavy casualties. The term has remained in use.

Can the Kaiser. A popular slogan of the American Army. One of the soldiers' songs runs as follows:

We're off to can the Kaiser,
Hooray! Hooray! In Kaiserland we'll take our stand
Until we can the Kaiser.
Let's go, let's go, let's go and can the Kaiser!
Let's go, let's go, let's go and can the Kaiser!

carry on. To resume what you were doing; to continue firmly and steadily; to persist. The term is clearly a Briticism, dating back to the early eighteenth century; it was picked up by American troops and used with mocking good nature.

cartwheel. A kind of acrobatic stunt of an airman.

Casey. Knights of Columbus; when abbreviated to "K.C.," the pronunciation suggested "Casey."

caterpillar. An engine or tractor that draws big guns.

cat stabber. A bayonet.

ceiling work. The protection by an airman at high altitude of planes below.

Charlie. An infantryman's pack.

Charlie Chaplin's Army Corps. A clearinghouse for Canadian casualties. One can only assume that this irreverent nickname alluded to the film comedian's odd way of walking, which some of the casualties may have been forced to mimic because of their wounds.

chase prisoners. To guard prisoners employed at labor.

chats. Lice.

cheese toaster. A bayonet; a sword.

cherched. To scrounge; to obtain. The term is given close scrutiny in Captain Carroll J. Swann's *My Company* (1918): "cherched"—a much-used expression among the soldiers, meaning "to get" something. The American soldier uses his head in obtaining something necessary to complete his equipment, to satisfy the inner man, to make his pal's or someone else's life brighter. He doesn't steal it. He may buy it, or borrow it, or find it,—but he gets it, and no questions asked. That's "cherched."

chief. The chief musician of a band.

chow. (1) Food. (2) To eat.
Several writers, including Eugene S. McCartney in *Slang and Idioms of the World War* (1929), held that it had a canine history, but this idea is almost certainly bogus. To quote McCartney: "The soldier and sailor use of this word has been laid at the door of the Chinese chow dog, which has a reputation for insatiable hunger." Most evidence indicates that the American history of this term began with Chinese railroad workers in the West and their use of the Chinese word for food, *chia*. See also under the Civil War.

chuck a dummy. To be absent; to feign a fainting fit to get out of duty or gain sympathy.

cits. Civilian (citizen) clothes.

civvies. Civilian clothes. Although commonly seen as pure World War II slang, it was in use as early as 1915 by the British and then by the A.E.F.

clicked it. Got killed; was wounded. The term comes from the slight, sharp noise made by a gun fired from a hostile position.

clink. A guardhouse. The first clink was probably British. In *Notes and Queries*, December 1918, W. C. Forman writes: "Lock-up or gaol was always 'clink' in the vernacular in South Devon when I was a boy nearly 70 years ago. 'I'll 'ave 'ee put in clink' is a threat I often had shouted at me when a small boy bent on mischief."

clobber. Clothing. This was British street slang adopted by the Yanks. (It would not be until the war in Korea that this term became a verb meaning "to smash" or "to overwhelm.")

clock. One's face.

Cloverleaf Division. The 88th Division, composed of troops from Iowa, Illinois, Minnesota, and North Dakota. Its insignia was a black four-leaf clover, with a loop for each state. The insignia comes from placing two 8's at right angles.

C.M. Court-martial.

c'mon you sonsabitches, do you want to live forever? Oft-quoted words of encouragement to Marines; first heard in this war and still heard in Korea. Many earlier references replaced "sonsabitches" with "Leathernecks."

C.O. (1) Commanding officer. (2) Conscientious objector.

C.O. and Other Initialisms

World War I slang never reflected the mania for initialisms and acronyms of the next war, but it signaled the beginning of a trend toward shortening words and phrases so they could be quickly uttered or written. Hundreds of these terms emerged, such as the following small sample that helped the readers of the postwar novel *Aces Up* understand the dialogue:

C.O. Commanding Officer.
E.A. Enemy Aircraft.
G.H.Q. Great Headquarters.
G.O. General Order.
O.D. Olive Drab.
P.C. Post of Command.
R.F.C. Royal Flying Corps.

—From *Aces Up*, by Covington Clarke (1929)

---

coal box. A German shell that gave off large amounts of smoke.

cockpit. The observatory area of an airplane, usually fitted with machine gun, AMMO, and a pistol. The term was adapted from its nautical use, to refer to the area from which a small ship is steered. Originally, it meant the confined pit or enclosure used for cockfights.

coffin nail. A cigarette, especially a cheap one.

cognaceyed. Drunk; from the American taste for cognac, the best of the brandies.

cognacked. Drunk. See also COGNACEYED.

cold feet. Nervousness; cowardice. In *Soldier and Sailor Words and Phrases* (1925), Edward Fraser and John Gibbons say that this term originally came from the Air Force; however, it clearly predates military aviation (*Webster's Ninth New Collegiate Dictionary* cites its first appearance in print as dating from 1893).

collarbone camp. A French training area; so-called by Americans serving with the French because so many were hurt doing the intense exercises prescribed by the French, with a common injury being a broken collarbone.

come-along. A strand of barbed wire about three feet long made into a noose. Come-alongs were used by raiding parties to induce enemy prisoners to "come along."

commissaries. Groceries; things obtained in a military grocery store or commissary.

compray. An Anglicization of the French *comprenez?* ("do you understand?"). Arthur Guy Empey, in *Over the Top* (1917), says that the term was "universally used in the trenches." American troops were still using the term during World War II.

concertina. A collapsible wire entanglement, resembling the shape of a concertina.

conchie / conchy. A conscientious objector. This term was more British than American in World War I, but was common in both British and American slang during World War II.

conked. Said of an airplane engine failing to operate while in flight. According to E. M. Roberts, in *A Flying Fighter* (1918), the term is: "A new word which is taken from the Russian language and which means stopped or killed."

cootie. A flea or louse. The term inspired a special verse to an Army standard:

You're in the Army now,
You're not behind a plow.
You'll never get rich,
You've got the itch,
You're in the Army now.

This term, which first showed up in print in 1917, is probably British in origin, deriving from the much older slang term "coot" (an old or stupid fellow). As Americans were introduced to the body louse, the term was eagerly adopted and brought back home. See also the "cootie" entries under World War II.

cootie bills. Franc and half-franc notes.

cootie carnival. A search for cooties; better known as a SHIRT HUNT.

cootie explorer. One who conducts a **shirt hunt.**

cootie garage. Earmuffs.

cop it. (1) To be struck by a bullet or shell. (2) To be picked out for some duty.

corkscrew. A kind of spiral dive by an airplane.

corn Willy / corned Willy. (1) Canned beef. (2) Specifically, corned beef; corned beef hash, also known as "corned Bill."

corpse. Corps.

corpse tag. Any marker used to identify a dead body.

cosmoline soldiers. Heavy artillery; so-called from the oil used on the guns.

cow. Milk.

crasher. The violent landing of an airplane brought down by antiaircraft fire.

crate. A military aircraft. Alfred H. Holt writes of the term in *Phrase and Word Origins* (1961):

> The old biplane with the maze of struts and wires certainly justified the nickname of "crate" more than the slick flying fish of today's air lines. It used to be said, you know, that the mechanics would release a pigeon between the wings of one of the early planes; if the bird succeeded in escaping, they would know there was a wire broken. Applied to such a plane, or to an old car, the term derives from the ricketiness of a crate, its sides being open for ventilation. It comes ultimately from Latin *cratis*, a wicker framework, and is related to *grate* and to Dutch *krat*, basket.

crawl. (1) To admonish. (2) To buy favors.

cream puffs. Spherical clouds of white smoke created by bursting shells; an airman's term.

creeping Jimmy. A high-velocity shell that gives no audible warning of its approach.

crow. A rating. The term is defined by Logan E. Ruggles in *The Navy Explained* (1918): "The rating badges of the service have an eagle spread over the designated insignia of the wearer and when a man gets rated, it is said that he got the crow—buzzard, bird or hawk."

crump. A shell that burst with a *cr-r-r-rump*, which is to say a shell filled with high explosives.

crumper. A large shell.

cubby hole / cubby hutch. A small dugout in the trenches. Edward Fraser and John Gibbons, in *Soldier and Sailor Words and Phrases* (1925), suggest that America got this term from the British, specifically the Royal Navy, which had long used it to describe a pigeonhole or other small compartment.

cuckoo. (1) A Sopwith airplane. (2) A torpedo plane, so-called, according to the London *Daily Mail* of December 27, 1918, "because of its weakness for laying eggs in other people's nests." (3) An airman who does his fighting with his mouth. (4) COOTIE.

cuff leggins. Puttees. See also PUTTEE, under the Spanish-American War.

cum-sah. What's its name? What is it? The term is from the French *comme-ça*; it also appears as "u-jah."

cumshaw / cum shaw. Something extra; something gratis. In the Navy, the expression is also used to indicate the receipt of a bribe or graft.

It has been suggested that the term comes from the Chinese merchant's pidgin rendering of "come ashore." In *Soldier and Sailor Words and Phrases* (1925), Edward Fraser and John Gibbons say that it is a pidgin rendering of the Chinese *kamsia* (*kam* ["grateful"] + *sia* ["thanks"]) and go on to say that it shows up as early as c. 1775 in Chinese ports.

curtain fire / curtain of fire. A wall of fire; a barrage; shells falling in a vertical plane, designed to prevent the enemy from escaping or from bringing up men or supplies.

cushy. Comfortable; at ease. There are many theories about the etymology of this term. Some maintain that it came from "cushion," others say that it was a play on the Anglo-Indian *khushi* ("pleasant"), while still others insist that it comes from the French *coucher* ("to lay down") or *couché* ("laid down") or from the town of La Cauchie, near Arras. A fascinating comment on the term and its possible relationship to the French word for bed (*couche*) appeared in the *Atlantic Monthly* for February 1917: "Since uncertain French is mixed with English, a 'couchy' wound—no doubt from the French 'coucher'—stands for an injury necessitating a short layoff in the hospital."

Custer Division. The 85th Division. Here is the explanation for its name from *The New York Times* (December 29, 1918):

> When the 85th Division was stationed at Camp Custer, Michigan, there was a long discussion over a suitable nickname for the outfit. Such names as Wolf, Badger, Buck, Lynx, Grizzly, Eagle, Wolverine, Brown Devils, Invincibles, Iron Ore, Lightning and Great Lakes were suggested and discarded on the ground that they were not distinctive. It was finally christened the "Custer Division." At first this division was made up solely of men from Michigan and Wisconsin, but later troops from Kentucky, Indiana and Illinois were transferred to it.

Its insignia was the letters C.D. in red on a white background.

Cyclone Division. The 38th Division, composed of troops from Indiana and Kentucky. Its insignia was CY on a blue and red shield.

★ ☆ **D** ☆ ★

daily news. Latrine rumors.

Eugene S. McCartney explains in his *Slang and Idioms of the World War* (1929): "In very cold weather the latrine was the warmest place to be found, since it contained a large boiler to heat water for the showers. The warm spots near the boiler were the center of camp gossip."

day, the. A specified time or period. In the German army and navy before and at the beginning of the war, *Der Tag!* ("The day!") was a toast given with an eye toward the day when the British and German fleets would clash. It was adopted, with a hint of irony, by the British and Americans.

dazzle painting. Camouflage, in the Navy. It was described in the annual report of the secretary of the Navy for 1918:

> There has been developed, however, particularly during the last year a system of so-called "dazzle painting"—the vessel being painted in an apparently grotesque and bizarre manner for the purpose, not of rendering it invisible, but rendering it difficult for the submarine commander, peering through his periscope for a few seconds at a time, to determine the course of the vessel.

dead-leaf fall. An airman's stunt, resembling the free fall of a leaf from a tree.

dead soldier. An empty beer bottle; also a "dead dog," especially in the Navy.

death bomb. Depth charge.

decks. The wings of an airplane; one of many adaptations of terms of the sea to the air.

deedonc / didonk. A French soldier; from the French term of address *dis donc,* equivalent to the American "say" (as in "say, can you tell me . . .").

deep-sea turkey. A salmon.

defeatist. Anyone who doubted the allied ability to defeat the German war machine.

dekko. A look at; a view of.

demob. To demobilize.

departure. This term was defined by E. F. Wood in *The Note-Book of an Intelligence Officer* (1917): "When a shell starts from one of our own guns, one hears first the crash of the discharge, followed in diminuendo by the noise of the shell progressing farther and farther towards the enemy. This is called a 'departure.'"

depth bomb. An egg.

der uffs. Two eggs; from the French *deux oeufs.*

desk hooks. Spurs; an expression employed in the air service, because the only use an officer had for spurs was to keep his feet from sliding off his desk.

Devil Dogs. U.S. Marines; from the German *Teufelshunde,* a German nickname for the Marines, given because of the Marines' fierce behavior in combat. Here is a quote from *Army Boys on the Firing Line* (1919), by Homer Randall, which underscores the regard in which this term was held: "'They thought our marines would run too,' laughed Frank, 'but do you see what they're calling them now? *Teufelhunden.* They're devil-hounds all right and the dachshund yelps when he sees them coming.'"

The Marines have long treasured the nickname. Here is the dateline and first sentence of an Associated Press dispatch that appeared in the February 20, 1991, Houston *Chronicle:* "WITH THE 2ND MARINE DIVISION IN NORTHEASTERN SAUDI ARABIA— They call each other Devil Dog and let out rousing barks to boot."

devil egg. A land mine.

dial. One's face. See also **clock.**

didonk. See **deedonc.**

digger. An Australian, and a term of affection and comradeship. In *The New York Times* (February 23, 1919), Captain Edward M. Kent wrote: "And when we called them diggers to their faces they'd have gone sheer to—oh, almost any place for us. . . . Sort of made them pals with us."

dig-in. A small excavation.

dipped. An expressive word for being torpedoed at sea. In the British navy the term means also "to receive a setback" and "to get ditched."

dirty neck. A French prostitute or woman of easy virtue.

dirty puss. A young Frenchwoman.

dishy billy. A state of undress or careless dress; from the French *déshabillé,* for the same state.

division that fought the battle of Paris, the. Those units stationed at Paris in 1917–1918. See also FOUGHT THE BATTLE OF PARIS.

dixie. A cooking pot. This term was described by R. Derby Holmes, in *A Yankee in the Trenches* (1918), as: "An iron box or pot, oblong in shape, capacity about four or five gallons. It fits into the field kitchen and is used for roasts, stews, char, or anything else. The cover serves to cook bacon in."

In *Slang and Idioms of the World War* (1929), Eugene S. McCartney adds: "Strictly speaking, this is not slang. The cooking-pots issued by the Army Ordnance Corps are officially designated as Dixies, though no one seems to know why. The term was also used by the British for the same object."

Dixie Division. The 31st Division, composed of men from Alabama, Florida, and Georgia. Its insignia was DD in red, enclosed in a red rim on a white background.

dizzies. Islandlike pieces of ground surrounded by communicating trenches.

dock. A hospital; perhaps a combined play on "dock" (a berth in a harbor) and "doc" (a doctor).

dodge the column. To shirk; to avoid work.

dogey-dog. A guardhouse.

dogfight. A battle between aircraft. This term has a very strong association with World War II, but it seems to have appeared late in this war or just after it;

the *Oxford English Dictionary* lists it as first appearing in 1919.

dogs. Feet. (Marines.)

dog tag. An identification disk; also known as a **meal ticket.** See also under World War II.

dog tag on file. Dead and buried.

dog tent. A small shelter tent.

Doing It. Doingt, France.

doing one's bit. Performing military service. As the late John Ciardi commented in his *Second Browser's Dictionary*, "a coy euphemism when that service involved rotting and dying in the trenches of the forever ungrateful French."

dollar-a-year man. Someone who serves the federal government for patriotic rather than financial reasons. The term came into use during the war when such volunteers were paid that sum because one dollar was the "valuable consideration" needed to make their contracts binding.

donk. An Army mule; a shortened form of "donkey."

doss. (1) To sleep. (2) Sleep. The term predated the war as hobo or vagabond slang for "sleep."

dough boy. A baker.

doughboy. An infantryman. The term was universally accepted then as now (Laurence Stallings's 1963 book on America in World War I was called *The*

Doughboys). In July 1941 a writer for *The New York Times* observed that there was no term to replace the "doughboy" of World War I; however, at about the same time, others began to comment on the increasing use of the term "G.I." as a name that soldiers applied to themselves.

The term "doughboy" was exclusively applied to the Infantry and was taken as a name to be proud of:

The cavalry and artillery
And the lousy engineers,
They couldn't lick the doughboys
In a hundred thousand years.

Word History—Many Theories

One of the few things that are certain about this term is that it is old. The following are the two earliest uses of the word, as given in the *Oxford English Dictionary.* (1) From 1685: "These . . . men had each of them three or four Cakes of bread (called by the English *Doughboy's*) for their provision and Victuals." (2) From 1697: "This Oil served instead of Butter, to eat with Dough-boys or Dumplins."

But as for its use to describe a soldier, the proposed etymologies are as numerous as the authorities who claim to have the answer. In *The American Language* (1937), H. L. Mencken held that the term originated in the Continental Army, whose troops wore white piping on their uniforms and applied pipe clay—the kind used to make clay pipes for smoking tobacco—to keep it white. When they were caught in the rain, the clay ran and smeared, covering the men with doughy blobs, whence came the then-derisive "doughboys." Here are a half dozen other "authoritative" explanations:

(1) A correspondent of *The New York Times* writes (October 13, 1918): "I have known of the term 'doughboy' as applied to infantry soldiers for 70 years; it did not originate in the civil war, but was in use long before in the British Army."

(2) In *The Doughboys* (1963), Laurence Stallings says: "There can be little dispute as to the derivation of the name. In Texas, U.S. Infantry along the Rio Grande were powdered white with the dust of adobe soil, and hence were called 'adobes' by mounted troops. It was a short step to 'dobies' and then by metathesis, the word was Doughboys."

There have been British subscribers to this theory. For example, quoting a Colonel Repington in the *Morning Post* of October 5, 1918, the following lines appeared in *Notes and Queries* of October 1918: "I believe that the name comes from a Spanish word, and was given by the American cavalry to the infantry during the old war in Mexico, because the infantry were usually covered with dust."

(3) Heywood Broun, in *The A.E.F.* (1918), writes:

Another story has it that during some maneuvers in Texas an artilleryman, comfortably perched on a gun, saw a soldier hiking in the thick sticky Texas mud. The mud was up to the shoetops of the infantryman and the upper part which had dried looked almost white. "Say," shouted the artilleryman, "what've you been doing? Walking in dough?" And so the men who march have been doughboys ever since.

(4) The following appeared in *Notes and Queries* (November 1918): "Fifty or sixty years ago Richard Bedford Poulden, late of the 56th Regiment, distinguished himself in Australia by the capture of a powerful aboriginal murderer named Doughboy. Probably the name was given to that individual in the days of his innocence, and from his own, and not his buttons', resemblance to a dumpling." The connection between an Australian criminal and the soldier is elusive; but it shows the term in use.

(5) The following paragraph is from Richard H. Thornton, *An American Glossary* (1912), quoting the wife of General George Armstrong Custer in her 1888

book, *Tenting on the Plains:* "A doughboy is a small round doughnut served to sailors on shipboard, generally with hash. Early in the civil war, the term was applied to the large globular brass buttons of the infantry uniform, from which it passed by natural transition to the infantrymen themselves."

(6) A letter to *The New York Times* (July 19, 1944), signed by "Major," says: "In the Peninsular Campaign, an infantry outfit acquired a large supply of wheat and ground its own flour. The site of the flour mill came to be called Doughboy Hill and the soldiers got the name of 'doughboys.'"

The letter also contains three other theories, which is about par for the course; for example, four popular explanations of the origin of the word are quoted by George H. McKnight in *English Words and Their Background* (1923).

doughfoot. An infantryman. The term was not nearly as common as DOUGHBOY. See also under World War II.

doughgirl. A Y.M.C.A. or Red Cross girl (i.e., one who bakes and gives out doughnuts).

doughnut army. The Salvation Army.

dough puncher. A baker. (Army or Navy.)

dovetail. A soldier who has completed training in officers' training school and is awaiting a commission. One such was quoted in the *Literary Digest* (April 19, 1919):

We were attending the Artillery School at Saumur, France, when the armistice was signed. An order was received from Washington to the effect that no more commissions would be granted. But we had to finish the course of training. We were sure

S.O.L. ["strictly out of luck"]. Later the order was modified to the effect that we would be commissioned in the U.S.R. [United States Reserves] upon discharge in the States. But between graduation in France and discharge in the States, we have no standing. We are supposed to fit in some place between a buck private and a "Shavetail," so some bright bird christened us "Dovetails" or "Third Lieutenants," and the name has stuck, and as such we are known around our outfits.

down for a shoot. Having to appear at the mast before the captain; same as "down for a chance" and "up for a shoot."

dozey. Dull; slow; as if dozing.

dream sack. A hammock; a Navy term.

drum fire. Artillery fire so intense that the successive shots merge into one another, suggesting the roll of a drum.

dry canteen. An Army store selling food and beverages, but no liquor.

duck. A bed urinal; also known as a "submarine" or a "sub." All of these names derive from its long, ducklike shape.

duckwalk. A slatted wooden walk built to prevent soldiers from sinking into the mud.

dud. An unexploded shell (also called a "blind"). The term was extended to apply to anything bad or unfavorable, even to persons (to refer to someone lacking energy or initiative). Eugene S. McCartney writes in *Slang and Idioms of the World War* (1929): "This idea was doubtless suggested by the use of the word to mean ragged and worthless clothes. The word was employed occasionally, however, before the war in speaking contemptuously of a person."

Dud in Action

Some ready witted Tommy addressed himself one day to a huge German shell that had fallen near him but failed to explode. "You dead old dud," beamed the Tommy. Since then all harmless shells, bombs or cartridges have been known as "duds."

From explosives that do not explode, the word soon extended itself in fighters' vocabularies to describe idle parts of the front as "dud sectors," war weary Boches as "dud Fritzes," and battles that fail to develop into expected big actions as "dud shows."

—*Stars and Stripes* (February 15, 1918)

---

dugout. (1) A protected place in the trenches. (2) Elderly officers returning to temporary service; used familiarly. Edward Fraser and John Gibbons wrote in *Soldier and Sailor Words and Phrases* (1925):

It first came in apparently during the South African War of 1899–1902 for pensioned or retired officers who came back to service in consequence of the depleting of the active establishment through casualties in the field. In the War hundreds came forward as volunteers and served in every capacity both naval and military, in most cases filling subordinate posts, regardless of former rank. Retired admirals and captains did duty in auxiliary craft of all kinds, or trained and disciplined ashore the men of all callings who came forward to serve at sea. On the Army side, retired Generals and Colonels rendered equally invaluable service in training units and recruits for the New Armies.

The term first appeared in print in 1818 in America to refer to a canoe made from a hollowed-out log.

dum-dum. (1) A soft-nosed bullet that "mushrooms" (expands) when it hits. (2) A silly or stupid person. The following etymology is given in *Soldier and Sailor Words and Phrases* (1925), by Edward Fraser and John Gibbons:

An unofficial name, originally used for the Mark IV Lee-Metford bullet with a cavity in the head, introduced after the Chitral Campaign of 1895 in consequence of the lack of stopping power in the small-bore bullet hitherto in use. The Hague Tribunal, at the insistence of Germany, interdicted its employment in European warfare, but in the Great War allegations were made on both sides that the other side was using such bullets, the term being used loosely for any bullet so tampered with as to increase its wounding power. The name comes from the Indian Arsenal at Dum-Dum, a few miles from Calcutta, where the small-arms ammunition of the Indian Army is principally made.

dumdums. Beans.

dupan. Bread; from the French *du pain* ("some bread").

dust disturber. An infantryman.

Dutch. A German; from the German *deutsch* ("German").

Dutchland. Germany; from *Deutschland*, which is what Germans call their country.

★ ☆ E ☆ ★

Eagle boat. Any of a class of large, quickly built, oil-burning ships used in antisubmarine warfare. The first Eagles were built in the Ford plant at River Rouge, Michigan, near Detroit.

Easter Egg flotilla. The small boats of the patrol squadron; the name was doubtless suggested by the nestful of EGGS, or depth charges, that each of these little boats carried, ready to be dropped over the stern.

easterner. One who maintained that the war could be won if more attention were paid to the eastern front (or Turkey), rather than the western front. See also **westerner.**

Eatables. Étaples, France; also called "eat-apples." This is one of many place names that were rendered American (for example, Sailly-la-Bourse became "Sally Booze").

eelight. Elite; best; choice; select.

effectives. Those military men able to fight. During this war some National Guard officers were deemed not combat effective.

egg. (1) A bomb; a mine; a depth charge. (2) A new member of a unit.

egg basket. An arrangement of metal struts in which bombs were carried in an airplane.

eighteen-pounder. An underage recruit (under eighteen years old); used affectionately.

elephant dugout. A safe and roomy dugout braced by heavy steel girders.

Elsie. A fine inflicted by a summary court-martial (for example, "a five-dollar Elsie").

emma gee. A machine gun or a machine gunner. The term came from the British communications code for "M" and "G" and saw use among the Americans. In the same way, "M.P." became "emma pip."

embuss and debuss. To get in and out of an omnibus.

Empire Division. The 27th Division, composed of men from New York, the Empire State; also called "New York's Own." Its insignia was the letters NY monogrammed in red on a black field with the constellation of Orion; the constellation is a pun on the name of the division's commander, Major General John F. O'Ryan. See also **HOBNAIL EXPRESS.**

enemy's delight. Mustard gas.

erf. Egg, the French *oeuf* comically pronounced.

ersatz. False; substandard (as in "ersatz butter"). The term is from the German term for reserves or substitutes, as in *Ersatztruppen* ("reserve units"). See also under World War II.

espritt de corpse. Brotherhood; comradeship. The term derives from the French *esprit de corps* (group enthusiasm or spirit).

evening hate. A German cannonade, which at one time was a regular evening performance.

exemption. An ailment, real or simulated (generally simulated), by which a man hoped to be exempted from duty. Confirmed "invalids" of this type were greeted in the morning with the salutation, "Full of exemption again?"

eye. A periscope.

eye-wash. Activities performed in getting ready for inspection (i.e., making things outwardly presentable). This term is first cousin to "hogwash," for that which is insincere or misleading.
    Notes and Queries (January 1919) reported: "It is apparently used to denote anything that is exaggerated or calculated to deceive or mislead. Any portion of an official document, or a list of regulations which is not of vital importance, is designated 'eyewash.' So also are complimentary remarks, either true or otherwise."
    According to Eugene McCartney in Slang and Idioms of the World War (1929), others have suggested that the term was "applied to most circular memoranda received, particularly about wearing of slacks or Sam Brownes, saluting, or economization of petrol; something to be winked at."

★ ☆ **F** ☆ ★

fag. A cigarette; from British street slang.

fag issue. A cigarette ration.

fast freight. A heavy shell.

fatal pill. A cannonball.

father rheumatism. A constant complaint of men in the trenches.

fatigew. A man detailed for fatigue duty, or routine drudgery. The term is an exaggerated pronunciation of "fatigue."

feather. The wake or ripple left by a protruding periscope. The feather was often visible when the periscope was not.

fed up. Sated; disgusted; having had enough. A contributor to Notes and Queries for March 1919 states very guardedly that he thinks the expression was picked up from the Australian troops in the Boer War of 1899–1902.

fedupness. Satiation; disgust.

feeneesch. All gone; too late. Writing in Scribner's Monthly for November 1918, Roy S. Durstine says, "It is a combination of finis and finish. Literally it means all gone."

festoon. A wire entanglement.

field day. A day or a number of hours set aside for cleaning decks in the Navy. According to John G. Rogers in Origins of Sea Terms (1985), "the term appeared during or shortly after World War I."

fighting on the cognac front. Intoxicated with strong drink.

finance. One's finances.

fineesh. See FEENEESCH.

fireworks. A night bombardment.

first hitch. A first enlistment. See HITCH.

first-to-fight boys. The Marines; so-called because of their "first to fight" motto.

fish. (1) A torpedo. (2) A dirigible balloon, because of its shape. (3) A submarine. (4) A man who is afraid to fly in an airplane.

fish tail. A grenade. The term was used for everything from the small "pineapple" fired from a rifle to monstrous aerial torpedoes. The name derived from a kind of vane or rudder that served to guide the projectile in its flight.

five nine. The standard German shell, which was 5.9 inches in diameter.

fix. The location or position of a submarine as established by listening devices. The object of many an antisubmarine chase during this war was to get a fix.

fizz-bang. A shell.

F.L. The front line.

flags. A semaphore signaler.

flag-wagger. A semaphore signaler.

flaming coffin. (1) An airplane falling in flames. (2) A nickname for certain aircraft, such as the De Havilland 4.

flap. A state of excitement or alarm. The term was used mostly by the British navy in World War I. See also under World War II.

flare. A rocket fired at night from a pistol to light up NO-MAN'S-LAND; the blaze of light from STAR SHELLS (target-illumination devices). Arthur Guy Empey, in *Over the Top* (1917), defines the term from the perspective of the man in the trenches: "A rocket fired from a pistol which, at night, lights up the ground in front of your trench."

fleabag. An officer's sleeping bag.

flipper. A hand.

flivver. A small destroyer. The term is discussed by James B. Connolly in *The U-Boat Hunters* (1918):

> There was another young officer—Chisholm call him—who played poker occasionally. He commanded a flivver, which is the service name for the smaller class of destroyers, the 750-ton ones. In our navy there are plenty of . . . officers who will tell you that they never built destroyers which keep the sea better than that same little flivver class. Young Captain Chisholm on the 323 was one.

At about the same time, this term became general slang for a dilapidated automobile.

fluid war. The period before the four-year war of trenches and barbed wire.

flying ace. See ACE.

Flying Circus. Nickname of German Baron von Richtofen's elite aerial pursuit squadron.

flying fish. (1) A rifle grenade. (2) An airplane (in the naval air service).

flying fish hooks. Hooks attached to fireballs by the Germans to make sure of burning up planes in case contact was made.

flying tank. An armor-plated scout plane.

flying turtle. A French observation balloon. See also SAUSAGE.

fly slicer. A cavalryman.

fly trap. A wire entanglement.

foot slogger. An infantryman.

for it. Ordered into action.

for the duration. Until the end of the war. A soldier might speak of having enlisted "for the duration."

fought the battle of Paris. To have been stationed in Paris, otherwise known as YANKEE HEAVEN. See also DIVISION THAT FOUGHT THE BATTLE OF PARIS, THE.

found. To be found deficient or wanting in anything, especially in an examination.

four-minute men. A corps of about 75,000 men on the American homefront who would go to movie theaters and other public places and, for four minutes, declaim anti-German propaganda.

fowl balls. Chicken croquettes; a Navy term.

foxhole. An excavation that would serve as an individual's shelter or **dugout.** See also under World War II.

fox pass. A false step; a social blunder. Derived from the French *faux pas* ("false step"), the term also appears as "folks pass," "fo paws," and "fawks pass."

frankies. The French; derived from the French *Français* ("French").

freeze. To lie flat on the ground in NO-MAN'S-LAND, while rockets are exploding.

Frenchyville. Paris.

frightfulness. A translation of the German word *Schrecklichkeit*. This description appeared in the *Saturday Review* of October 26, 1918: "A method of warfare characterized by brutality, horror and terrorism as conducted by the German Army in the World War of 1914–1918."

Fritz. A German; Germans as a group. The word is a common German first name. "Guess Fritz is getting more than he bargained for," says a character in Homer Randall's *Army Boys on the Firing Line* (1919).

frog. A Frenchman. This term was used for the French as early as the 1780s, but it was given a new lease on life by the American soldier during World War I. The most common theory is that this derisive term comes from "frog eater," because of the French predilection for frog's legs.

In *Words of the Fighting Forces* (1942), by Clinton A. Sanders and Joseph W. Blackwell, Jr., no less than thirteen "frog"-based words from the 1917–18 period appear: "frog cop," "frog dame," "frog dizzy shop" (a French saloon), "frog dough" (francs), "frog funny papers" (francs), "froggy" (a member of the

French armed services), "frog juice joint" (a French saloon), "frogland" (France), "frog lip pounding" (speaking French), "frogskin" (a franc note), "frog's paradise" (Paris), "frog teakettle" (a French railroad locomotive), and "frogtown" (Paris).

front and center. The command to step out of formation, usually foreshadowing trouble.

front-liner. A front-line trench

F.T.D. Feeding the dog (the occupation of a soldier killing time).

fuckin'. Paul Fussell, in *The Great War and Modern Memory* (1975), points out that this word was ubiquitous in the war: "The intensifier of all words was *fucking*, pronounced *fuckin'*, and one exhibited one's quasi-poetic talents by treating it with the greatest possible originality as a movable 'internal' modifier and placing it well inside the word to be modified. As in, 'I can't stand no more of that Mac-bloody-fuckin'-Conochie.'"

The f-word was important in another context, as Laurence Stallings points out in *The Doughboys* (1963):

> It was an axiom that a man who would not actively cooperate with one "f" verb would not fight which was the complementary "f" word. For this reason many a young man was unable to excuse himself from the action in a French whore house no matter how depressing the surroundings and no matter how obvious it was that a prostitute was loaded with disease.

full pack. A soldier carrying all of his equipment.

full pack slum. Slum with a crust baked over it.

function. To act as intended. To say that a machine or a unit was "functioning" was seen as British and American slang beginning in this war. Edward Fraser and John Gibbons, in *Soldier and Sailor Words and Phrases* (1925), give several examples, including: "The company were not up to much, but they seem to be functioning right now."

funk hole. A DUGOUT (1).

Funky Villas. Foncquevillers, France.

gadget. Any mechanical contrivance or detail; anything that one does not know the name of. An old tar is quoted in R. G. Kauffman's *Our Navy at Work* (1918):

> Well, he's had a lot of it—Philippines, Boxer Rebellion, Vera Cruz, and Haiti. You know, in the Marines, when we can't think of the generic name for anything, we call it a "gadget" or a "gilguy." Now, this man has won a Congressional Medal and has another coming. When we sighted the French coast, I was standing where he couldn't see me, just behind him; and I heard him say, while he looked over things in general:
> "I got one o' them gadgets now an' one on its way. I wonder if I'll get another over here."

galvanized iron can. A heavy shell. See G.I. CAN (2).

gas bombs. Stale eggs.

gas goggles. A gas mask.

gaspirator. A gas mask.

gassed. Said of a victim of poisoned gas, as well as a victim of the hot air of a trenchmate.

German up. A German airplane is overhead.

get down to it. To sleep.

get it. To be killed.

get the sparks. To fire machine-gun bullets at enemy barbed wire at night. When a bullet strikes wire, it generally throws off a bluish spark; thus, as explained by Arthur Empey in *Over the Top* (1917): "Machine gunners use this method at night to 'set' their gun so that its fire will command the enemy's trench."

get the wind up. To become nervous or scared; to be flustered by danger. See also PUT THE WIND UP.

G.I. can. (1) A galvanized can; "G.I." was short for "galvanized iron." (2) A German heavy shell; so-called because of the similarity to the kind of galvanized can found around a hospital.

gimper. A special and most dependable buddy; a highly competent airman. Lieutenant Eddie Rickenbacker led the group known as the GIMPER SQUADRON, and the term was discussed by him in the *Literary Digest* of August 24, 1918:

One who would stick to you through thick and thin; a member of the Gimper means a lot to us. It means more than scout, or pal, or comrade. I got the word from a mechanic I had when I was in the racing game. He was a gimper, and I knew when he finished with a motor, she would run.

In this man's life there were two kinds of people—gimpers and bums.

See also GOOPHER.

Gimper Squadron. An American escadrille headed by Lieutenant Eddie Rickenbacker. See also GIMPER.

gippo. Bacon grease; fat.

give a steady one. To growl and curse.

give her the gun. To advance the throttle of an airplane, thus feeding fuel and making the engine rev faster.

goat. A junior officer. For a different use of this term, see under the Civil War.

goaty. Awkward; ignorant.

go-away medicine. Poison gas.

gob. An enlisted man in the Navy.

Gob Word History

For starters, here is what Eugene McCartney had to say about "gob" in *Slang and Idioms of the World War* (1929):

The sailors much prefer this word to "Jackie." A popular weekly states that there is evidence that this word originated on the Chinese coast. It was employed long before the war. A newspaper clipping says that the name originated at the time of Perry's expedition to Asia, when the Orientals called the American sailors "gobshites." It seems to be generally agreed that the name originated in Asia.

As is the case with many other words whose history is forgotten, explanations are not wanting. The following is from

Logan E. Ruggles's *The Navy Explained* (1918):

Long before the Spanish-American War, out on the Asiatic Station, there was a long, lanky sailorman on the flagship by the name of Gobbles. Gobbles was a very well known character in the "mosquito fleet," as the Asiatic Squadron was termed. Gobbles was a good natured, easy-going sort of chap; he made a decided hit with the "gang" because he could drink like a sea-gull and stand up longer than any man on the station. He could swill Tansan, Tsing-tau or San Miguel and other beers of the Orient. . . . He had the goats of every Limejuice [British] sailor, marine or civilian ashore, because he could put 'em away every time in the beer battles.

They first called this gentleman "Shikepoke," and he went by this handle for some time; since his name was Gobbles, they cut the two names in half and called him "Gobshike," so Gobbles changed his name to just plain, simple "Gob," and by that name he was known until he came home to the States.

The term "Gob" later became so popular on the station that men coming home brought it back; later it was circulated in the North Atlantic Squadron, and still later throughout the service. To-day it is the sailorman's favorite, and he always refers to himself as "Gob."

Ruggles goes on to traffic in the truly odd and implausible—totally in keeping with the lore of the Navy:

In the olden days—back where ancient history started—there was a people, tribe or creed known as Gobbies. They were a ghost people and could only see at night; they lived in cliffs, high trees and deep under the ground. They were seldom seen out in daylight—in fact seldom seen at all. In later years the people were known as Gobbies, since they were of the spook variety or goblins, as they are sometimes called. And since all sailors were superstitious once upon a time, all suspicious characters were called Gobbies. And, too, sailors always abbreviate their words, and soon the term Gobbies was known as Gobs; in time, it is said that sailors began to refer to each other as "Gobs."

gob gully. A Navy supply route.

go in. To occupy enemy trenches.

G.O.K. God only knows. This term was borrowed from British physicians, who used it when dealing with large numbers of wounded and when there was not ample time for proper diagnosis.

gold brick. (1) A shirker; one who tries to avoid work or to get an easy job; a noncombatant. (2) A member of the military police. The following is from an article by George Pattullo in the *Saturday Evening Post* for September 21, 1918: "But Wally sidled up to one of the M.P.'s exhibiting his wounded arm as credentials. Ordinarily he avoided 'goldbricks' as the doughboys called the military police." (3) An unattractive girl.

goldbrick. To evade duty; to shirk. The term is defined by Mark Sullivan in *Our Times, Vol. V, Over Here* (1933): "Pretending you have sciation when what troubles you is homesickness or hangover."

goldbrick dream / goldbricker's holiday. An easy task or assignment.

goldbricker. A shirker.

goldfish. Canned salmon.

gooey. Hash.

goopher. A competent airman who is almost of top quality. This was a slang term of the GIMPER SQUADRON for an airman one level below a GIMPER. Lieutenant Eddie Rickenbacker was quoted as follows in the *Literary Digest* of August 24, 1918: "When a new chap arrives, he's an egg. All good eggs soon become vultures, and they are promoted to goopher standing."

goose step. To march stiff-kneed. German troops marched in this graceless, ridiculous fashion, as if "saluting" with their feet. The term was doubly appropriate: not only is the step imitative of the waddle of a goose, but any given marcher seems to be goosing the man in front of him. See also under World War II.

go out. To be relieved from the trenches.

go over the cognac trail. To get drunk.

go over the hill. To desert.

go over the wall. To go to prison.

"Go-to-Hell" Whittlesey. Major Charles W. Whittlesey, the commander of the so-called LOST BATTALION in the Argonne Forest. "Go to hell" was the major's answer to a German demand for surrender; in its time, it seemed the boldest of replies.

go to stir. To go to prison. The term "stir" for "jail" or "prison" is very old; it appears to derive from the Anglo-Saxon *styr* ("punishment").

got the wrinkles out. Said of a man who enlisted in the Navy to get his hunger appeased. Once sated, he scorns the **chow.**

gowed up. Drunk; a Navy term, along with the synonymous "hopped up."

go west. To die. The expression is discussed in *Notes and Queries* for December 1918: "The region of the dead is naturally in the land of the setting sun, and the dead have been 'going west' from time immemorial. When Ulysses went to pay a visit to Hades, he directed his course westward. The mythologies of many tribes retain the same tradition today."

The expression "to go west" was extended so that a soldier might speak of an airplane as having "gone west."

grandma. A fifteen-inch howitzer; so-called because it was short and stout.

gravel agitator / gravel cruncher. An infantryman.

graveyard watch. The shipboard watch from midnight till four A.M., when there was silence throughout the ship.

gray mule. Corn whiskey; so-called because of its color and its "kick." The drink was also known as "white lightning" and "white mule."

grease. Butter; also known as "pull" and "drag."

The Great War. The name used by most Americans fighting in what had first been known as the European War.

Green Hornet. The nickname of Colonel George S. Patton, in this war. Patton was the consummate fighter; it is reported that on taking command of his first Negro division, he said, "Well, men, I am happy to have you here. I don't give a damn what color you are, just so you kill those sons-of-bitches in the green suits."

groundhog. An infantryman in the trenches.

Groundhog Day. A name for Armistice Day (November 11, 1918), when the fighting stopped and everyone came out of their holes. This was a gag of the period just following the war.

ground squirrel. A man in the Aviation Corps who does not fly as part of his duties.

ground stunt. A fliers' term for an attack from a low altitude.

grouse. To grumble; to complain. This was British military slang adopted by the Americans during the war.

G.S.W. A gunshot wound.

gum the game. To interfere; to spoil things.

gun for seam squirrels. To extract lice from one's clothes.

guy. A pal; a good friend.

★ ☆ **H** ☆ ★

hairbrush. A type of bomb or hand grenade. Arthur Guy Empey discusses the term in *Over the Top* (1917): "A bomb used in the earlier stages of the war. It is shaped like a hairbrush and is thrown by the handle. Tommy used to throw them over to the Germans for their morning toilette." The term enjoyed limited American use.

half-and-half trench. A trench built up with sandbags to a height equaling the depth of the excavation, thus making the distance from the bottom of the trench to the top of the parapet twice the depth of the excavation.

half-loot. A second lieutenant.

hang on the wire. To be killed in action; to hang dead on the barbed wire of NO-MAN'S-LAND.

Hans. A German.

hardhead. A cavalryman.

hard oil. Butter.

hardtack. Hard bread; a biscuit. See also under the Civil War.

hardtail. An Army mule. This was an old southern term for a mule; it spread into the Army via farmers and mule-skinners.

haricot bean. A bullet.

Hash! hash! "Gas! gas!" The following appeared in the *Literary Digest* of February 8, 1919: "It is said that on one occasion after soldiers had tired of hash, which was being served for the n-teenth time, they hastily put on gas masks and spread the cry of 'Gas! gas!' For weeks after that the actual alarms were announced as 'Hash! hash!'"

hatrack. A horse in poor condition. This was an old farm term for any animal good for nothing more than hanging hats from.

have the cafard. To be fearful and sad.

heave eggs. To shell with artillery.

Heaven, Hell, or Hoboken by Christmas. A slogan of the DOUGHBOYS in parts of France during the summer of 1918. Hoboken was a port of embarkation.

heavy dough. An artilleryman manning heavy artillery.

hedgehog. An egg-shaped criss-crossed tangle of wire; from the nocturnal mammal of the same name, which presents its defensive spines by rolling up in a ball.

hedgehop. To fly near the ground. The following lines, by "an American in France," appeared in the *Independent* of November 6, 1918: "I went 'hedge hopping' last night. 'Hedge hopping' is the fanciful name for flying low. I think it is perhaps the most exhilarating—and dangerous—of all phases of flying, even including acrobatics. It is the splendid sensation of tremendous power and matchless speed. No other sensation is to be compared with it."

Heine. A German; from the German name Heinrich.

heine tin fish. A German submarine; a torpedo fired from a German submarine.

Hell-fighters. The 369th Infantry Regiment, from New York City.

hell's acres. The territory between the front lines. See NO-MAN'S-LAND.

hell's half hour. A strenuous half hour at bayonet practice.

Hell Terrors. Australians; a German designation.

he-man. A strong, virile man. Robert G. Skerrett writes in the *Saturday Evening Post* of October 26, 1918: "Theirs is a he man's job; and they are tackling it like red-blooded, two-fisted fighters. They are heroes all of them."

he tried to step on one. Said of a man who has a shell explode underfoot.

hickboo. A rumpus; a bombardment. According to the *Literary Digest*: "Hickboo means a good many things, but chiefly that enemy aircraft are about. If Zeppelins or Taubes are on their way, a hickboo is on. Anything, in fact, which is calculated to put the wind up the timid is a hickboo. The word is said to be a distortion of an Indian word meaning an eagle."

hickie. (1) Anything whose name one does not remember; what's-its-name; a thingamajig. (2) A pimple.

hi-ex shell. A high-explosive shell.

highball. Salute. This term does not appear to come from the name of the drink, but rather from the name of the railroad signal denoting a clear track (hence it also means "to start," "to continue moving," and "to increase speed"). The signal itself was a painted metal globe hoisted to the cross-arm of a tall pole and then brought down—analogous to a salute.

higher-up. An officer.

hike. A march; TOMMY's "route march." According to B. Matthews, in *Munsey's* (April 1919): "Perhaps 'hike' is our sole surviving linguistic legacy from our annexation of the Philippines."

his nibs. The commanding officer of an OUTFIT.

hissing Jenny. A big shell.

hitch. An enlistment. A soldier may speak of "three hitches in the Navy and two in the Army." This term had been American slang for "marriage" since about 1860; thus, an enlistment is a "marriage" to the Army.

hitch in. To enlist for the second time in the Navy.

hit the deck. To get out of one's bunk. see SNAP OUT OF IT.

hive. To discover; to catch.

Hobnail Express. The 27th Division. This division was also known as "O'Ryan's Roughnecks" and "O'Ryan's Traveling Circus." See also EMPIRE DIVISION.

hobo. A provost-sergeant.

hog table. A table for the glutton at MESS (see under the Civil War). In his article "Feeding the American Army," in *The Century* for November 1918, R. F. Wilson explains: "The 'hog table' is plainly and bluntly so labeled upon a large cardboard sign that hangs directly above it. A day or so at the 'hog table' is apt to impress any recruit with the wisdom of moderation when the roast beef is passed."

holy brick / holy stone. A stone about the size of a brick, used to scour the decks of a warship. Logan E. Ruggles writes in *The Navy Explained* (1918): "Sand is thrown upon the deck, soapy water is sprinkled around and then the holy-stone is pushed back and forth over the sand by the aid of a long stick and it cleans the deck and makes it snow white when dry. It is also called a holy-brick, or the rock of ages."

Holy Joe. (1) A chaplain. (2) Any man effecting piety.

honey wagon. A French manure cart.

Hooverize. To save. The verb was coined from the name of Herbert C. Hoover, United States Food Administrator during the war, and later President of the United States. Saving was serious business to Hoover, who sent a message to General John J. Pershing asking that he put sentries in CHOW lines to make sure that nothing was wasted. The recommendation was not heeded, and as Laurence Stallings points out in *The Doughboys* (1963): "No Doughboy ever Hooverized, though there would be days when not even cold food could reach him and he would welcome a piece of black bread from the pocket of a prisoner."

hop-over. A trench raid OVER THE TOP and into NO-MAN'S-LAND.

horizontal exercise. The "activity" of lying down or sleeping; a Navy term.

hot-stuff. To steal, "pinch," "lift," or appropriate to oneself. (2) To be excessively audacious.

hot-stuffer. A thief.

housewife. A soldier's sewing kit.

how. A toast in drinking; it means "Here's to your health" or "My regards."

how-gun. A howitzer.

H.S. Mustard gas.

hug the bathmats. To lie flat while shells fly overhead.

human cyclones. The Marines.

humdinger. Something that is excellent or the best. Private A. B. Callow, in a letter published in the *Literary Digest* of November 16, 1918, wrote: "Say, Skotchie, I forgot to mention these American nurses. They are humdingers, I want to tell you. And, Skotchie, these girls are all for you here. There isn't anything they won't do for you."

In the *Saturday Evening Post* of November 2, 1918, George Patullo wrote: "Another old French sergeant stayed with us two days. He was a humdinger. He had a gray beard and was well up in years; but there he was in the front trenches. It seemed that back in 1914 he had been in the commissary behind the line because he was considered too old.

But the boches burst through and captured him. Somehow he managed to escape."

The term is of unknown origin.

hummingbird. An artillery shell.

Hun. (1) A German. According to Arthur Guy Empey, in *Over the Top* (1918), this term was "mostly used by war correspondents."

It is reported that, in 1900, on the eve of the departure of German troops to help quell the Boxer insurrection, Kaiser Wilhelm urged them to play the part of Attila's Huns. In *Slang and Idioms of the World War* (1929), Eugene S. McCartney quotes from the *War Book of the University of Wisconsin*, which reports that the kaiser said: "No mercy will be shown! No prisoners will be taken! As the Huns under Attila made a name for themselves, which is still mighty in traditions and legends today, may the name of Germany be so fixed in China by your deeds that no Chinaman shall ever again dare to look at a German askance."

(2) A student airplane pilot. The title was a reflection of the destruction they wrought in learning their duties. According to E. M. Roberts, in *A Flying Fighter* (1918): "A student who is learning to fly is called that on account of the queer things he does. Every pilot is a Hun until he has received his wings."

hungry Liz / hungry Lizzie. An ambulance stationed at a flying field and ready for emergencies.

Hunland. Germany.

Hun pinching / Hun raiding. The practice of raiding German trenches for prisoners.

Hun sticker. A bayonet.

hunt cooties / hunt lizards. To search for lice in one's clothing.

hurry up and wait. A phrase used by the A.E.F. to describe the routine of the war.

hush-hush boat / hush-hush ship. A floating air base. Eugene S. McCartney identified them in *Slang and Idioms of the World War* (1929): "Craft to serve as floating bases for airplanes. The name originated from the secrecy with which the new type of ship was guarded. The purpose of the first boats of this type was to serve as cruisers to deal with raiders, but the guns were too powerful for the ships."

hyphenate. An immigrant to America, or an American from an immigrant family. The term is defined by Eugene S. McCartney in *Slang and Idioms of the World War* (1929): "A citizen of the United States who tries to maintain allegiance to the country from which he or his ancestors emigrated to the United States. The term was coined by Colonel Roosevelt. It was suggested by our habit of speaking of German-Americans, Italian-Americans, etc."

★ ☆ **I** ☆ ★

I.C. Inspected and condemned by an inspector.

iddy-umpties. Members of the Army Signal Corps; also known as "buzzers."

idler. The Navy man who kept the morning watch.

Illinois Division. The 33rd Division, composed of troops from the Illinois National Guard; also known as the PRAIRIE DIVISION and the YELLOW CROSS DIVISION. Its insignia was a yellow cross on a black circle.

Immelmann turn / Immelmann roll. An aerial "stunt"—essentially, a 180-degree turn made by taking half a loop followed by half a roll. It was practiced by the German ace Max Immelmann. Quentin Reynolds described it in *They Fought for the Sky* (1960): "He would pull his stick up sharply, making the nose of the Fokker rise as though he were beginning a loop; but at the top of the loop he did a half-roll and came out flying in the opposite direction, with the needed height regained. It took the British airmen completely by surprise."

Soon afterward, the British paid Immelmann the compliment of imitating the turn, which later became a standard maneuver.

I'm sorry. An insincere apology. In later wars, an equivalent phrase would be, "Sorry 'bout that."

Indian Head Division. The 2nd Division. Its insignia was a red Indian head on a white star.

in dock. Laid up with illness; in the hospital, or dock.

ink. Red wine.

in the mill. In a guardhouse.

in the pink. Healthy; fit. The term is an abridgment of "in the pink of condition."

Iron Division. The 28th Division, composed of Pennsylvania National Guard regiments; also known as the KEYSTONE DIVISION and the PENNSYLVANIA DIVISION. Its insignia was a red keystone, an allusion to Pennsylvania as the Keystone State.

Iron Jaw Division. The 32nd Division; so-called because it was employed on both flanks of the Marne salient. See also BROAD ARROW DIVISION.

iron ration. Canned food carried for use in an emergency.

Ivan. (1) Individual Russian soldier. (2) The Russian Army.

Ivy Division. The 4th Division. Its insignia was four green ivy leaves on a drab background. "The choice of ivy leaves was due to a pun," reports Eugene S. McCartney in *Slang and Idioms of the World War* (1929): "When the Roman numerals IV are regarded as capital letters and are pronounced, we get ivy."

★ ☆ **J** ☆ ★

jackass rig. Improper garb, as a pair of white pants with a blue jumper; a Navy term.

Jack Johnson. A large shell. Wrote Eugene S. McCartney in *Slang and Idioms of the World War* (1929):

This was a common designation of the German 17-inch shell, although it has been applied to missiles as small as those from the 6-inch howitzer. This nickname had a great vogue at the beginning of the war before Jack Johnson had been dethroned from the heavy-weight championship of the world. He was living in Paris at the time.

jack-of-the-dust. "A man in charge of the commissary stores and storerooms" is the definition given by Logan E. Ruggles in *The Navy Explained* (1918). "[He] keeps the keys to the issuing room and serves out the rations for the day's consumption. He is generally a ship's cook, or a man who has had some experience in the galley."

jaggie. A judge advocate general.

jake. A term that expresses satisfaction. If a girl is pretty, she is jake. If anything is right, it is jake. It has been suggested that the word is an Anglicized form of the French *chic* ("becoming"; "natty").

java. Coffee.

jawbone. (1) Credit; a loan. (2) To trust; to lend. This word was used nearly fifty years before in the territory of Washington, in the sense of "to get credit by talk."

jawbreaker. An Army biscuit.

Jayhawker. A country boy in the Navy who is habitually stargazing when he should be paying attention to duty.

Jayhawkers. The 89th Division, composed of men from Kansas, Missouri, and Colorado. The word was used of participants in the free-soil conflict in Kansas around 1848–1850. Its insignia was a black monogrammed MW ("Middle West"). It was also known as the Western Division.

Jazz Boes. American black troops in France; a patronizing but positive name.

jelly bean. A girl.

Jenny sass pass / Jenny's pa. I do not understand; from the French *je ne sais pas.*

Jerry. (1) A German. It has been said that the British were looking for a term of contempt for the Germans and somehow settled on this; the term became popular all over the world. (2) A steel shrapnel helmet.

Jerry jabber. A bayonet.

Jerry sausage. A German zeppelin.

Jerry whale. A German submarine.

Jersey Lightnings. The 78th Division, composed of men from New Jersey, Delaware, and New York. Its insignia was white forked lightning on a red semicircle. It was also known as the Lightning Division.

Jewish cavalry / Jews' division. The Quartermaster Corps; so-called because of the impression that there was a high percentage of Jewish storekeepers.

john. A greenhorn; a newcomer to the Army. Here is what Lieutenant Daniel E. Walsh wrote in a letter to his parents, published in the Baltimore *News* on October 24, 1918: "You know they call a man who has seen no service a 'John.' Well I am not a 'John' any more."

John J. General John J. ("Black Jack") Pershing.

Johnny. (1) A Turk. (2) The Turkish Army.

joyrider. A government-owned automobile when used by officials for pleasure; a person who uses such a car.

joystick. The nickname for the main control lever of an aircraft; clearly, a play on the phallic nature of the instrument. According to Edward Fraser and John Gibbons, in *Soldier and Sailor Words and Phrases* (1925): "The control lever was invented in 1907 by an M. Pelterie, who, in May 1923, was awarded over seven million francs in a law-suit against the French government for infringement of his patent during the War."

Joysticks on Parade

The term "joystick" was regarded as both funny and risqué and those who wrote about the aviators of the period never seemed to miss a chance to have someone grab a joystick. Here are three examples.

D. H. Haines wrote in *American Boy* for February 1919: "A bare minute of this (Sidmore always cut the preliminaries to a minimum), then the speed of the plane increased, it nosed up into the wind, the pilot pulled the 'joy-stick,' as the lever which operates the elevating planes is called, and the machine took the air."

Alan Bott's "Contact," in *Cavalry of the Clouds* (1918), contained these lines: "C.'s bus was then seen to heel over into a vertical dive, and plunge down, spinning rhythmically on its axis. Probably he was shot dead and fell over on to the joy-stick, and this put the machine to its last dive."

Marcel Nadaud wrote in *Atlantic Monthly* for November 1918: "Papa Charles pulled the joy-stick; the aeroplane nosed up, leaped, took a tail-dive of several hundred metres."

juice. Gasoline; any other source of power.

jump. To admonish

jumping-off point. The point from which an attack begins. "Jumping-off place" is a phrase of frequent occurrence in journals of early western travel, designating the starting point on the frontier.

jump off. To go OVER THE TOP.

jump ship. To leave a ship without proper authorization.

jump the bags. To go OVER THE TOP.

just a minute. A bistro; from the French *estaminet* (a small cafe).

★ ☆ **K** ☆ ★

kaput. Finished; over; shot. It is from the German *kaputt*.

kenoozer. Connoisseur; an Anglicization of the French word.

Keystone Division. The 28th Division, composed of Pennsylvania National Guard Regiments; so-called because Pennsylvania is the Keystone State. It was also known as the IRON DIVISION and the PENNSYLVANIA DIVISION.

K.G. 5. King George V.

kicked. Dishonorably discharged.

kick the bucket. To die. See under the Civil War.

Kings of No Man's Land. The 2nd Brigade of the 1st Division. According to A. H. Chute, in *The Real Front* (1918), the men of that division "have won for themselves the title of 'Kings of No Man's Land.' To them that dread country between the trenches is no longer known as No Man's Land. They call it 'The Dominion of Canada.'"

kip. (1) To sleep. (2) A bed.

kissing the earth. Said of an airplane standing on its nose after a crash.

kitchen police / K.P. Men detailed to help the cook in menial tasks. It is a World War I term, not World War II, as some have wrongly stated. The verb "police," meaning "to clean up an area," is first recorded in 1893; it may be a corruption of "polish."

One soldier who had been assigned to the kitchen police wrote home as follows, in a letter published in *The Outlook* (May 15, 1918): "Dear Mother:—I put in this entire day washing dishes, sweeping floors, making beds, and peeling potatoes. When I get home from this camp, I'll make some girl a mighty fine wife."

Sing a Song of K.P.

A popular song of the war days ran thus:

K-K-K-Katy, beautiful Katy,
You're the only g-g-g-girl that I adore.
When the m-moon shines over the
   cowshed,
I'll be waiting at the k-k-k-kitchen
   door.

This was the soldiers' parody of it:

K-K-K-K-P, damnable K.P.
You're the only kind of work that I
   abhor.
When the m-moon shines over the
   guardhouse,
I'll be mopping up the k-k-k-kitchen
   floor.

Songs proclaiming the indignities of K.P. were not rare during World War I, and at least one was written by a man of some ability. As related in Elbridge Colby's *Army Talk: A Familiar Dictionary of Soldier Speech* (1943):

In *Yip-Yip-Yaphank*, a musical review put on by the soldiers of the 1918 Camp Upton, Irving Berlin—himself one of them—appeared on the stage with scrub pail and mop and sang:

Poor little me,
I'm a K.P.;
I scrub the mess hall on bended knee.
Against my wishes I wash the dishes
To make this world safe for
   democracy.

kite. A weight used on the sweepwire in a minesweeping operation. The following passage appeared in the *National Geographic* of February 1920:

Sweeping mines . . . is not a particularly intricate process. It consists essentially in dragging a heavy wire between two vessels. In order to bury the wire to a sufficient depth beneath the surface to insure catching the mines, "kites" are attached to the sweepwire just astern of each vessel. These kites fly down in the water in much the same manner that an ordinary kite flies up in the air.

kiwi. A nonflying member of the Air Corps; from the name of the flightless New Zealand bird.

knitting needle. A sword.

knock civvies into shape. To train raw recruits.

knocked off. Killed.

knock koo-koo. To render unconscious; to mortally wound; to kill.

knuckle knife. A dagger blade with a studded steel guard over the grip.

K.O. The "kommanding" officer of a large unit; "C.O." designates the commander of a smaller unit.

K.P. See KITCHEN POLICE.

kraut. A German; from "sauerkraut."

kraut fish. A German submarine.

Krautland. Germany.

kraut outfit. A unit of the German armed forces.

kraut ship. A German man-of-war.

★ ☆ **L** ☆ ★

lachie. Milk (from the Spanish *leche*).

Ladies from Hell / Ladies of Hell. The Scotch "Kilties" (units whose uniform included kilts). The term is a translation of the Germans' name for these fierce fighters. The expression may have first been applied to the Canadian Highlanders at Langemarck, but afterward it designated all Kilties.

"Lafayette, we are here." Words reported to have been uttered by General John J. ("Black Jack") Pershing as he stood by the tomb of Lafayette in Paris. In fact, however, these words were spoken, not by Pershing, but by Colonel Stanton, a member of Pershing's staff. The phrase was widely repeated among the American troops pouring into Paris.

Lafayette Division. The 11th Division, organized at Camp Meade, Maryland, in August 1918. Its insignia includes the profile of the Revolutionary War hero the Marquis de Lafayette.

laid out. Injured; having fainted.

land battleship / land cruiser / land ship. A tank, when tanks were in the experimental stage.

lathouse. Latrine; presumably a blend of "latrine" and "outhouse."

latrine rumor. Startling news, almost always incorrect.

latrine sergeant. A private whose duty it was to keep the latrines in order, clean the floors, keep the fires going, etc.

leather. Meat.

leather bumper. A cavalryman.

leatherneck. A Marine, either British or American. According to sources on both sides of the Atlantic, the name—it has long been claimed—derives from the tight-looking military collar, but, perhaps, as John Ciardi asserts in *A Browser's Dictionary* (1980) because the Marine uniform had a leather lining in the collar of the dress uniform ca. 1880. A song of the U.S. Marines runs as follows:

> The Leathernecks, the Leathernecks, with dirt behind their ears!
> The Leatherneck's the man that mops up all the beers;
> The infantry, the cavalry, and the dirty engineers
> Couldn't lick the Leathernecks in a hundred thousand years.

American Leatherneck

Joe, as they is so few things you know, not meanin' you're dumb or the like, only thick, I will tell you what a Leatherneck is. Joe, a Leatherneck is the baby they send for when Mexico or some of them other South-American joints which is under the protection of Uncle Sam gets fresh and tries to go Republican. The Leathernecks is rushed special delivery on a battleship and lands at this joint and the next mornin' the papers says, "A detachment of United States marines was landed at Porto Bananas to put down a revolution. They was no trouble. The revolutionists was buried in lots of a thousand each. One marine got wounded. He stumbled over the Porto Bananas army whilst comin' back to his ship."

—H. C. Witwer, *Marines' Bulletin Holiday Number* (1918)

---

leave one cold. To annoy; to bore. Edward Fraser and John Gibbons, in *Soldier and Sailor Words and Phrases* (1925), provide the following etymology: "Presumably from the French colloquialism 'cela me laisse froid'—i.e., It's a matter of complete indifference. It doesn't interest me."

Lee Division. The 80th Division. The following account of the naming of this division is quoted from the *Army and Navy Journal*, in *The New York Times* of December 29, 1918:

> The 80th Division of the National Army, in real Winter quarters in the "Sunny South"—the mercury hovering at a point between 4 and 6 degrees below zero—received its distinctive designation. The baptism occurred at Camp Lee, just outside Petersburg, Va., in connection with a memorable tribute by soldiers to a departed soldier, the leader of the lost cause. The occasion was the birthday anniversary of General Robert E. Lee.
>
> The baptism occurred at the climax of a brief but inspiring address by Brig. Gen. Lloyd M. Brett, commanding the 80th Division and the camp. After thanking the people of Virginia for their hospitable treatment of the soldiers of the command, General Brett concluded: "When the great call comes for us to go 'over there' and we have stood the acid test of battle, then—and not until then—bestow on us the name Lee Division."
>
> Enthusiastic cheering followed General Brett's suggestion, and it was adopted unanimously, with this slight modification, the 80th Division will not have to wait until it has stood the acid test of battle; it was then and there named Lee Division, and as such it will be known in history until the end of time.

See also BLUE RIDGE DIVISION.

leg it. To run away.

Les Terribles. The 32nd Division, composed of troops from Michigan and Wisconsin. It was so-called by the French because of the bravery and initiative shown by the men of this division. Edwin L. James wrote of them in *The New York Times* for September 9, 1918: "No unit in our army presents men of better physique than these Indians, lumberjacks, and farmer lads from the Northwest." The division was also known as the BROAD ARROW DIVISION and the IRON JAW DIVISION.

Lewisite. A poison gas developed under the direction of Winford Lee Lewis at the American University, in Washington, D.C.

liaison. A link between two units. Thus, an "officer de liaison" is a staff officer charged with the duty of coordinating different units. In a letter published in the *Literary Digest* of November 16, 1918, Corporal H. E. Hilty writes: "As we were supposed to keep up a liaison with the next post where the sergeant was, I crouched by a tree to sort of get a hold of myself and decide what to do, for I couldn't keep up the liaison myself and watch the post, too."

liberty cabbage. Sauerkraut. *The New York Times* for November 30, 1918, reported as follows: "'Liberty cabbage,' made in Germany and there still known as sauerkraut, has been served at many American army messes during the week, five carloads of the edible having been left behind by the withdrawing German army."

liberty clover. German clover; a name used by some American farmers.

Liberty Division. The 77th Division, composed of troops drafted from New York. Its insignia was the Statue of Liberty on a blue field. This division was also called the MELTING-POT DIVISION, the METROPOLITAN DIVISION, and the UPTON DIVISION. The name "New York's Own" has been applied to both the 27th and 77th divisions.

liberty measles. German measles.

liberty steak. Chopped steak.

lid. A helmet.

light hands. A gentle touch in handling the JOYSTICK.

Lightning Division. The 78th Division. See JERSEY LIGHTNINGS.

limey. A British sailor or ship; also, "lima." This use of the word comes from the old "lime-juicers," for ships on which lime juice was given to ward off scurvy.

Lincoln Division. The 84th Division, composed of men from Illinois, Indiana, and Kentucky. It was so christened while stationed at Camp Zachary Taylor, Kentucky.

little Archibald. A special gun for firing parachute flares.

little Bertha. A German "105" (artillery piece).

little Jesus. A corporal.

Little Willie. The German crown prince.

loggin. A recruit. After the war, this term came to mean "boob," "sap," or "dope."

Lone Star Division. The 36th Division, composed of National Guard troops from Texas and Oklahoma. The name derives from the fact that Texas is called the Lone Star State. Its insignia was a white star on a red disk. The name replaced PANTHER DIVISION.

The following is from *The Statesman* of October 19, 1918:

> After consultation of representative officers of the National Guard of Texas and Oklahoma, it was decided that the appellation Panther Division was in no way appropriate, and that hereafter the Thirty-sixth Division shall be known as The Lone Star Division, and that its emblem shall consist of a five-pointed star with the numerical designation "36" superimposed in the center of the star.

In fact, however, the divisional insignia became a blue Indian arrowhead with a khaki "T" superimposed upon it, the "T" representing Texas and the arrowhead representing Oklahoma, formerly Indian territory.

longhorn. See MECHANICAL COW.

long Tom. A French 155-mm rifle.

looie. A second lieutenant.

look-see. A look through the raised-up periscope of a submarine.

look spare. To have nothing to do; to be at leisure.

Looneyville. Luneville, France.

loophole. A concealed aperture through which one could snipe at the enemy. It is a very old term, dating back to the sixteenth century.

loot. A first lieutenant.

lose one's can. To be killed; most commonly used to refer to men shot through the head.

Lost Battalion. The 1st Battalion, 308th Infantry (77th Division), commanded by Major Charles W. Whittlesey. Its communications were cut in late September 1918 and again in early October, while it was advancing into the Argonne Forest. Its position, however, was always known. See also "GO-TO-HELL" WHITTLESEY.

lota [pronounced: "lah-tah"]. Anything incredible.

Lufberry circle. An aerial maneuver whose invention is credited to Raoul Lufberry, a famous World War I American ace. Groups of planes, if attacked while flying in formation, shift into a circular formation with each aircraft protecting the one ahead. Also known as the "Lufberry show," the maneuver was, according to Don Lawson in *The United States in World War I* (1963), used by all air forces in fighter-plane combat up through the Korean War.

★ ☆ **M** ☆ ★

madamoizook. A Frenchwoman of easy virtue.

mad minute. The firing of fifteen rounds from a rifle in sixty seconds.

maggot. A small, fast airplane that guards reconnaissance planes; also called a "viper."

make knots. To move fast; a Navy term.

male tank. A tank armed principally with rapid-fire cannon. A female tank was designed for lighter work and was equipped with machine guns.

man trap. A booby trap. As described in *My Company* (1918), by Captain Carroll J. Swann, man traps were "ingenious devices of the huns for killing us after they had retreated."

Marinette. A woman who enlisted in the Marines to do clerical work.

marmite. A shell; from the French word for a pot.

Marne Division. The 3rd Division. Major General Joseph T. Dickman conferred this name on the division after its exploits on the Marne opposite Château-Thierry. According to *National Geographic* for December 1919:

> The three white stripes of its insignia are symbolical of the three major operations in which the division participated—the Marne, St. Mihiel, and the Meuse-Argonne. The blue symbolizes the loyalty of those who placed their lives on the altar of self-sacrifice in defense of the American ideals of liberty and democracy.

meal ticket. A wrist tag used for purposes of identification; also known as a DOG TAG.

mechanical cow. An airplane that is clumsy in the air. Such aircraft are described by V. Drake in his *Above the Battle* (1918): "Some machines of this type possessed an elevator situated out in front of the body and supported by two long outriggers. The machines with these long outriggers were called Longhorns, those without them Shorthorns."

mechanical flea. A Ford automobile, especially one used by the military.

Melting-pot Division. The 77th Division. According to Eugene S. McCartney, in *Slang and Idioms of the World War* (1929): "The Seventy-seventh Division, so named because composed of a sprinkling of all the nationalities that make up the cosmopolitan population of New York. It is said that hundreds of the men could not speak English when they were drafted. The Division acquitted itself in true American style." See also LIBERTY DIVISION and UPTON DIVISION.

merchant of death. A manufacturer or other businessman who made money from the war. This postwar term comes from the title of the book *The Merchants of Death* (1920), by H. C. Engelbrecht and F. D. Hanighan, which argues that munitions manufacturers were among the major forces behind the outbreak of the war.

mercy blow through / messy bucket. Many thanks; from the French *merci beaucoup.*

mess gear. A mess kit.

mess up. To get into or cause trouble.

Metropolitan Division. The 77th Division. See LIBERTY DIVISION, MELTING-POT DIVISION, and UPTON DIVISION.

mex. Any non-American currency; perhaps from the derogatory use of the same term to refer to anything cheap or inferior (from "Mexican").

Middle West Division. The 89th Division, composed of men from Colorado, Kansas, and Missouri. The insignia was a circle with a w in the center, which, when inverted, becomes an M.

military census. The draft.

milk squadron / milk battalion. The third squadron in cavalry; the third battalion in infantry. In his book *First Call* (1918), Arthur Guy Empey explains that "milk" is taken from the letters of the companies from which the squadrons come: "I," "K," "L," and "M."

mill. A guardhouse. See also under World War II.

mind your eye, judge. Be careful.

Minnehaha. A German trench mortar; from the German *Minenwerfer* ("mine thrower"). The British term was "minnie."

missing. Dead and unburied.

Missouri hummingbird. A Missouri mule.

miss the bus. To lose out on an opportunity.

M.O. A medical officer.

moan. To complain; to grumble.

moaner. A pessimist.

mob. A regiment; used at Gallipoli.

monkey drill. Rough-riding (in the Cavalry); also, a reference to the act of leaping on and off the back of a galloping horse.

monkey meat. Canned beef. Sometimes, the term referred to canned meat and carrots. This account by Major General Omar Bundy appeared in *Every-*

body's Magazine for March 1919: "We received the French ration, a part of which was canned beef shipped from Madagascar. It had a peculiar taste which our men did not like. They called it 'monkey meat' and it soon became known by that name throughout our Army."

monkey motions. Physical exercises.

monkey suit. A fur suit for high flying.

moocher. A politician who takes graft or who "bolts" (opposes his or her party's position). The following appeared in *The New York Times* of October 10, 1918:

> Many "charges" have been "hurled" at Miss Jeannette Rankin, at present a Representative in Congress from Montana, but the height and depth of political "slang-whangin" in the State can best be judged from the Fergus County Argus, which includes her among "political moochers."
>
> In the old English slang, to "mouch" was to steal, to prig. If one doesn't quite understand the process of importation, one sees how "moucher" passes into "grafter." Nobody has accused or could accuse Miss Rankin of having been that. As a politician, she may have been brought into temporary political alliances with thinkers of the Nonpartisan League school, found guilty of "graft" by politicians of the opposing school. So far as can be made out from Fergus County, however, she is a political "moocher" and "one of the most despicable of politicians," because she is a bolter. If a "moocher" is only a bolter, it is a title of honour and respect which Miss Rankin can accept with pride.

moo-cow farm. Mouquet Farm, the scene of especially fierce fighting in the battle of the Somme.

moosh. A guardroom.

mopper-up. One whose duty it is to kill or subdue the defenders of enemy trenches passed over by an assaulting force.

mosquito fleet. The small boats, pleasure boats, and other craft pressed into service as submarine chasers. See also under the Civil War.

mother. A howitzer not so large or heavy as a GRANDMA (in general, a twelve-inch howitzer).

mother ship. A vessel that accompanies submarines to supply their needs and act as a base.

mounseer. A Frenchman; from the French monsieur.

mousetrap. A plant in Willoughby, Ohio, built for the manufacture of LEWISITE. According to Eugene S. McCartney, in *Slang and Idioms of the World War* (1929): "It was so called by the workmen because every one who entered the eleven-acre stockade did so under an agreement not to leave until the end of the war. The purpose of this action was, of course, to guard the secret of manufacture."

movies. A searchlight. A man working a searchlight is said to be "on the pictures" or "on the movies."

M.P. Military police.

muck in. To share rations.

mud cruncher. An infantryman.

mudlark. An engineer.

muffler. A gas mask.

mule skinner. A teamster; a wagoner.

Mulligan. A stew made of the regular ration issue and whatever extras may come to hand; from hobo vernacular, probably derived from "salmagundi" (a potpourri).

Mulligan battery. A cook wagon.

mungey / mobgee. Food; from the French *manger* and Italian *mangiare* ("to eat").

munition mongering. Profiteering. See also MERCHANT OF DEATH.

mustard gas. A gas that smells like mustard, makes the eyes water, and has a devastating blistering effect when it comes in contact with the skin. It was also known as YELLOW CROSS.

mustard imitator. LEWISITE; from its use in response to mustard gas. It was much more deadly than mustard gas, as indicated by this description from *Harper's* (November 1919): "Lewisite is a gas so deadly that it has seventy-two times the killing power of the most deadly gas used in the war."

mystery ship. A vessel that can be quickly converted from a seeming tramp steamer into a warship. According to Eugene S. McCartney, in *Slang and Idioms of the World War* (1929): "Mystery ships were designed for use against the submarine. They were so named, of course, from the veil of secrecy which was thrown about them. The designation has been applied to submarine monitors also."

A news item on mystery ships in *The New York Times* of December 22, 1918, attests to their importance in the war at sea:

> London, November 30 (Associated Press)—One of the most exciting chapters of the war against U-boats is a series of accounts of notable engagements between British decoy ships and the submarines, made public by the British Admiralty. While the whole story of the part played by these decoy vessels, "mystery ships" or "Q" craft has not been revealed, it is evident that several of them were used to lure the undersea craft to destruction.

See also Q-BOAT / Q-SHIP.

★ ☆ **N** ☆ ★

Nancy. An NC type of seaplane. The New York *World* of May 17, 1919, saw this word as evidence of linguistic innovation during war: "The NC type of seaplane becomes at once the 'Nancy' of aircraft in popular parlance. And what with this coinage and 'blimps' and 'hop offs,' linguistic inventiveness goes on augmenting the vocabulary in the time-honoured way which is the despair of purists and precisians."

napoo / napoo-fini. Gone; dead; finished.

napper. One's head.

native son. A prune.

N.C.O. Noncommissioned officer. Humorously interpreted as "noncombatant officer," this initialism was applied to officers stationed in Washington, D.C.

near go, a. Almost killed.

nest. (1) A DUGOUT. (2) A machine-gun position or emplacement. (3) A sniper's place of concealment.

New England Division. The 26th Division. See YANKEE DIVISION.

New York Division. The 27th Division. See EMPIRE DIVISION.

New York's Own. A title given to both the 77th Division (the LIBERTY DIVISION) and the 27th Division (the EMPIRE DIVISION).

night ops. Night operations or maneuvers.

night roll. To drive an ambulance at night.

ninety-day wonder. A second lieutenant. See also under World War II.

no bon. No good; from the French *bon* ("good").

No-Man's-Land. The devastated territory between the hostile front-line trenches; so-called, according to the troops, because no one owns it and no one wants to. In *The Great War and Modern Memory* (1975), Paul Fussell writes: "The phrase 'No Man's Land' has haunted the imagination for sixty years, although its original associations with fixed positions and static warfare are eroding."

No-Man's-Land

The designation "no-man's-land" is interesting whatever its origin, and as with so many expressions of this war, there is more than one explanation of its history. The *Oxford English Dictionary* says: "A piece of waste or unowned land; in early use as the name of a plot of ground, lying outside the north wall of London, and used as a place of execution."

In discussing plowing, F. Seebohm, in *The English Village Community* (1890 edition), writes: "In other cases little odds and ends of unused land remained, which from time immemorial were called 'no man's land,' or 'any one's land,' or 'Jack's land,' as the case might be."

Mark Twain, in *Following the Equator* (1897), has some comments on the expression: "Australia has a slang of its own. This is a matter of course. The vast cattle and sheep industries, the strange aspects of the country, and the strange native animals, brute and human, are matters which would naturally breed a local slang. . . . The wide, sterile, unpeopled deserts have created phrases like 'No Man's Land' and the 'Never-never Country.'"

Webster's Ninth New Collegiate Dictionary says the term first appeared in print in the fourteenth century.

noncom. A noncommissioned Army officer.

nonstop. Said of an airplane trip without intermediate landings. Here is a very early use of the term in *The New York Times* (1919):

London, June 16 (Associated Press)—London celebrated today the achievement of the two British airmen who yesterday completed the first non-stop transatlantic flight, meanwhile preparing for a formal reception to the air victors, Captain John Alcock and Lieutenant Arthur W. Brown.

nose cap. A gas mask.

nose dive. To make a downward plunge in an aircraft.

nothing to write home about. Not worthwhile. This phrase appears to have been a Briticism adopted by Americans during the war. Here is how it was defined in Ward Muir's *Observations of an Orderly* (1917): "Miserable conditions in the desert or in the trenches, bad accommodation, doubtful food—anything that cannot arouse the faintest enthusiasm of any sort—these, in the lingo of the much-travelled and stoical troops, are 'nothing to write home about.'"

★ ☆ **O** ☆ ★

O.B. Observation balloon.

Ocean Villas. Auchonvillers, France.

O.D. (1) Officer of the day. (2) Olive drab. Mark Sullivan, in *Our Times*, Vol. 5, *Over Here* (1933), describes it as follows: "The color of an Army shirt before it is worn over six weeks or sent to the laundry."

O.D. pill. A pill, olive drab in color, taken as a physic.

officers' papers. Cigarette papers that are bought separately, in contrast to those that come filled with tobacco.

off the tail. Said of an airplane that is picked off from its position at the end of a formation.

O.F.'s. Offensive hand grenades (i.e., those thrown at the enemy).

oil can. A German trench mortar shell; so-called because of its canlike shape.

oil slick. A telltale mark left by a submarine on the surface of the water.

Oil Slick—A Verbal Novelty

The *Saturday Evening Post* for October 12, 1918, discussed the term:

The submarine when running close beneath the surface leaves what is known as an "oil slick." That is, the oil that is discharged in the exhausts floats on the top of the water in tell-tale streaks, and where there is an oil slick there also is likely to be a destroyer.

"Oil Slick" is American terminology. The British Admiralty did not approve of the use of the term at first, but nobody in the Admiralty could present a better descriptive phrase, so now it is officially recognized, but with due British reservation.

---

old. An adjective used by both the British and Americans to indicate what J. B. Priestley called a "half-affectionate familiarity," as in a trench song that contained these words about a missing battalion:

It's hanging on the old barbed wire.
I've seen 'em, I've seen 'em
Hanging on the old barbed wire.

Old "Fighting 69th." The 165th Infantry of New York.

old file. An old officer.

Old Hickory Division. The 30th Division. Colonel J. K. Herr, in *The New York Times* of March 2, 1918, had this to say about the unit:

> The division is constituted of National Guard troops of North Carolina, South Carolina, and Tennessee, augmented by many thousands of selective draft troops from the states of Indiana, Illinois, Iowa, Minnesota, North Dakota, North Carolina, South Carolina, and Tennessee. The Division was dubbed "Old Hickory" after the warrior and statesman Andrew Jackson, who was so closely identified with the history of the states furnishing the major portion of the personnel.

According to Eugene S. McCartney, in *Slang and Idioms of the World War* (1929), this division was frequently called the Wildcat Division, because its men came largely from the same states that supplied the 81st Division (see WILD-CAT DIVISION).

Its insignia was a blue monogrammed O surrounding an H, with three x's (i.e., Roman numeral for 30) forming the crossbar of the H.

old issue. An old soldier.

old man. The captain of a company. Arthur Guy Empey, in *Over the Top* (1917), says he is called "'the old man' because generally his age is about twenty-eight."

Old man Joss. The patron saint of all submarine men.

olive oil. *Au revoir* ("good-bye," in French).

One O'clock. A nickname for the German general Heinrich von Kluck.

one-up. A lance corporal who wears one stripe.

one-winger. An air or combat observer, who wears a one-winged badge. See also TWO-WINGER.

on official terms. Not on speaking terms, except officially.

on the carpet / on the mat. Hauled before an officer to answer questions about possible misdeeds.

on the cot. Refraining from drink; "on the water wagon."

on the pegs. Under arrest.

on the tack. See ON THE COT.

on the wire. Said of a man who cannot be found, suggesting that he might be dead and hanging on the barbed wire at the front.

oojiboo. A "gadget"; a "thingummy"; a "what-d'ye-call-it."

opener. A cathartic pill.

orderly bucker. A soldier who strives by extra neatness of appearance to be designated as an orderly for the commanding officer.

orderly room. A company office.

orphan. A soldier who fails to get an attractive mademoiselle to give him "French lessons."

O'Ryan's Roughnecks / O'Ryan's Traveling Circus. The 27th Division. See EMPIRE DIVISION and HOBNAIL EXPRESS.

ou-la-la girl. A French girl; from a French exclamation of glee.

outfit. Almost any Army unit or group of soldiers. "I have yet to see a drunken American private in Paris," wrote Elizabeth Frazer, in the *Saturday Evening Post* for November 2, 1918. "For the most part they are to be seen in groups of twos or threes, 'gangs' or 'outfits' as they call themselves, strolling about the streets."

outlaw. An unruly horse; a Cavalry term.

out of the trenches by Christmas. A rallying cry of those who wanted to end the war relatively quickly. A hater of war, Henry Ford failed with his 1915 "peace ship" effort to get the boys "out of the trenches by Christmas."

over the hump / over the lump. Beyond the halfway point in one's period of enlistment.

over there. France and other allied European nations.

over the top. An order directing the troops to jump out of the trenches and attack the German lines. Traditionally, it was accompanied by the phrase, "With the best o' luck and give 'em hell." It was the British who mostly used "over the top," while the Americans mostly used "jump off."

The term "over the top" found many applications in civilian life. Here is an early example from the *Daily News* of Greensboro, North Carolina (March 13, 1919): "He pleaded that those who went over the top in bond drives and in giving money to support the war relief work again go over the top in the cause of the Kingdom of God."

★ ☆ **P** ☆ ★

pacifist. One opposed to the use of force as a means of settling international disputes. In *Slang and Idioms of the World War* (1929), Eugene S. McCartney notes: "This is an emergency war word and does not appear in the dictionaries printed before the war."

Pacifist—How to Cope Linguistically

Arthur H. Weston, in *The Nation* of August 16, 1917, addressed himself to dealing with this new term:

Theoretically, there is no question but that we should say "pacificist" and "pacificism," just as we say "publicist" and "Catholicism." But a false sense of analogy has made itself felt in this case. People think of economic, economist; lyric, lyrist; philanthropic, philanthropist; and so they say pacific, pacifist. The analogy is false because "pacific," as mentioned above, is formed with the suffix -fic and not with the suffix -ic, which usually represents the Greek -ikós. It is common, though not invariable, in the case of these words derived from the Greek, for the -ic to be dropped before the -ist or -ism is added. So that, although we are quite justified in saying "heroism" instead of "heroicism," we ought not to say "pacifism," but "pacificism." There is no sense in cutting off the -ic of -fic and leaving the lone f remaining. Added to the false sense of

> analogy is a phonetic reason of some weight. "Pacifism" is shorter and easier to say than "pacificism," and the contraction avoids one of a rather disagreeable series of sibilants.

pals battalion. An American or British unit in which men who joined the Army together could stay together during their enlistment.

pancake. To stall or slow down a dropping airplane while keeping the machine parallel to the ground; to land flat.

panic party. A demonstration of alarm or panic on board a MYSTERY SHIP in order to trick the commander of a submarine into coming alongside. When a mystery ship was torpedoed, the panic party took to the boats, apparently abandoning the vessel, but leaving a crew on board to man the guns.

Panther Division. The 36th Division; so-called while it was in training at Camp Bowie, Texas. See also LONE STAR DIVISION.

According to *The New York Times* of December 29, 1918: "The 36th Division had as its insignia the picture of a fighting panther and below it were three Latin words that translated into English meant: 'We'll do it in spite of Hell.' Of course it was christened the 'Panther Division.'"

pants rabbits. Lice; COOTIES; CHATS.

Paradise. Paris.

pass. To die.

pass the buck. To shift responsibility to another. Here is how the term was discussed by Frederick Palmer, in *Collier's* of April 19, 1919:

> He did not "pass the buck," as they say in the army, which means that you shift the responsibility to another fellow. The phrase which is particularly applicable to the army system in peace time probably originated in the old poker-playing days of the frontier. It is possible to keep "passing the buck" in a circle for a long time if nobody finds "openers."

Pathfinder Division. The 8th Division, which was organized at Camp Fremont, California, in December 1917. Its insignia was a gold arrow pointing upward, running through a white figure eight.

pay a drill. To perform an extra drill as punishment.

P.B.I. Poor bloody infantry. According to *Notes and Queries* for December 1918, the predominantly British "P.B.I." was "applied by the weary 'foot-slogger' to himself, seeing that he gets a greater share of the kicks than, and the fewest halfpence of, any arm of the service."

peace-time trench. A trench in a quiet sector.

Pennsylvania Division. The 28th Division; also known as the IRON DIVISION and the KEYSTONE DIVISION.

Percy. A type of German naval artillery. As G. V. Williams wrote in *With Our Army in Flanders* (1915): "A certain German long-range naval gun, whose shells have the peculiarity of bursting before you hear them arrive."

persuader. (1) A short club with a nail-studded head used to induce prisoners to follow. (2) A bayonet.

In World War II, this term was used to mean virtually any weapon.

picture show. A big battle.

piece. A rifle, especially one used in drills.

pie-up. A crash; a smash.

pie wagon. A ship's prison; so-called because no pie was served to prisoners.

pig nose. A French gas mask preferred by British and American troops to those issued by their own armies.

pillbox. A small, low structure of reinforced concrete, with very thick walls and roof, employed as a minor fort. Pillboxes were developed by the Germans for use in their "elastic" defense and employed as machine-gun nests.

Writer Floyd Gibbons described them in the New York *Tribune* of September 9, 1917: "The cement dries and hardens quickly, and when finished presents a solid yard of reinforced concrete in all directions. In these shelters machine-gun crews and quotas of 40 front-line reserves are safe from any shelling except a direct hit from a 10-inch high-explosive shell."

pillow. A balloon shaped roughly like a pair of rectangular wings and used as a target by airmen.

pill rollers. The hospital corps.

pills. A surgeon.

pimple. A hill.

pineapple. (1) A type of bomb; so-called because of its shape and the criss-cross pattern of lines marking off the segments into which it bursts. (2) A type of German aerial torpedo; so-called because of its shape. (3) A light trench mortar.

pink. To strike with a bullet.

pipe down. To cease talking; to shut up.

pipsqueak / popsqueak. (1) A shell; an onomatopoeic name. Wrote R. Derby Holmes in *A Yankee in the Trenches* (1918): "The 'pop-squeak' is a shell that starts with a silly 'pip,' goes on with a sillier 'squeeeeee,' and goes off with a man's-size bang." (2) A temporary second lieutenant; from the diamond-shaped insignia called a "pip" that was used by the British to indicate rank.

pistol light. A rocket shot from a pistol.

Pistol Pete. See RICOCHET OFFICER.

Plymouth Division. The 12th Division; so-called because it was recruited mainly from the New England states.

pocked. Pitted with shell holes. Land frequently shelled bore some resemblance to the face of a person who has had smallpox.

pogey bait. Candy; any kind of sweets.

poilu. A French soldier at the front. The term means "hairy" in French and alludes to the traditional thick whiskers worn by the soldiers of the French infantry.

police. To clean up. See also KITCHEN POLICE.

politician. (1) A sailor having a "soft" job, such as compartment cleaner, storeroom keeper, JACK-OF-THE-DUST, yeoman, or signal boy. These are known as "political jobs." (2) A soldier with a job that excuses him from assemblies and musters.

pom-pom. A small antiaircraft gun, essentially a large-caliber machine gun; so-called because of the noise it makes.

pop off. To rant; to criticize; to brag.

porridge pot. A spent shell.

possum playing dead. A dud shell; used by Americans from the South.

pot hole. A shell hole.

pound one's ear. To sleep; a Navy term.

pow-wow. A conference of senior officers; from the Algonquin Indian term for a ceremony.

Prairie Division. The 33rd Division, composed of men from the Illinois National Guard. It was also known as the ILLINOIS DIVISION and the YELLOW CROSS DIVISION.

profiteer. To take advantage of wartime conditions for purposes of gain; formed on the analogy of "commandeer."

prop. A propeller.

prune picker. A Californian; a Navy term.

pull his belt. To confine a sentry for a breach of the regulations in the guard manual.

pumfrits. Fried potatoes; from the French *pommes frites.*

pump handle. A salute; from the stiff, snappy character of the salute.

punish. To shell; a translation of the German *strafen.* See also STRAFE.

punk. Bread. This word was used in New York breadlines before the war.

pup. A type of airplane. The pup was described at the time as being "of minute dimensions, playful temperament and powerful disposition."

pup tent. A small tent. Here's how it was described in *Collier's* of April 21, 1917:

> Each man in the United States Army and in the National Guard carries half a shelter tent for use in the field. Half a tent consists of a sheet of canvas about five by eight feet, a jointed tent pole, five metal tent pegs, and a length of cotton line. When a halt is reached, each pair of men set up their tent poles, stretch the line as a ridge, tie their canvas sheets together, and peg them down as a cover. The result is familiarly called a "pup" tent.

push. An attack in force; a major offensive.

push and pull / push pull. A sighting and aiming drill.

push off. To go; to leave.

push up the daisies. To have been killed and lie buried in France.

put a sock in it. Be quiet (as if one had a sock stuffed into one's mouth).

put dots on one. To bore; to tire.

put in a bag. Killed; wrapped in a shroud.

put the wind up. To make afraid. See also GET THE WIND UP.

putts. Puttees, or wrapped leggings. See also PUTTEE, under the Spanish-American War era.

P.X. Post exchange.

★ ☆ **Q** ☆ ★

Q-boat / Q-ship. A decoy vessel used to lure German submarines to destruction. Q-boats were equipped with gun mountings concealed beneath hatchway covers and masked by deckhouses that collapsed at the jerk of a lever. They were also known as MYSTERY SHIPS and "queer q's." The reason for the letter "q" is elusive; perhaps it came from "question" or "queer." The German equivalents were known as "trap ships."

Q.M. Quartermaster.

quiet sector. An area of the front where, by mutual consent of the opposing forces, there was little or no fighting. The quiet sectors were south of Verdun

and were used by the U.S. to prepare green troops for the "noisy sectors" and bring the war weary, as Robert Leckie puts it in *The Wars of America* (1965), "to rest, to gorge themselves on cheese, sausage, fresh bread, and low-priced wines, and to try to forget the nightmare of battle."

quimp. Unsoldierly; slack.

quirk. A pupil; a term used by aviators.

★ ☆ **R** ☆ ★

racker. A hard-trotting horse.

radish. A bogus communist. The term was defined in the *Literary Digest* of January 10, 1920: "A 'Radish,' Bolshevistically speaking, is . . . a man who fervently professes devotion to the Communist cause while harboring a secret longing for its overthrow. In other words, he is 'red' on the outside, but 'white' within, and that makes him a radish."

railroad trains. Certain kinds of very large shells; from their size and sound.

Rainbow Division. The 42nd Division, composed of men from twenty-six states and the District of Columbia; it was among the first divisions to land in France. Its insignia was a red, yellow, and blue rainbow.

ranked out. Compelled to vacate by a senior (e.g., "to be ranked out of quarters").

rathskeller. A DUGOUT; from the German *Ratskeller* (a basement restaurant or tavern).

rations. Bombs for an airplane.

rat tail. A mule; presumably, because its tail lacks hair.

Rattlesnakes. A nickname for the 369th Negro Regiment, of New York.

read one's shirt. To search for lice in one's shirt seams.

rear. A toilet; a latrine.

Red Baron, the. Manfred von Richthofen (1892–1918), the top German ACE, who shot down eighty allied planes before he was killed in combat. He was also called the Red Knight and the Red Devil. All these names derive from the fact that he flew a bright red Albatross biplane, not because he had red hair or spilled so much blood, as has been alleged by some.

The Red Baron Lives

The Red Baron legend became part of popular culture with the 1930 publication of *The Red Knight of Germany*, by Floyd Gibbons. Here is an example of Gibbons's purple prose: "Into the grisly story of the World War there came a refreshing gleam of the chivalry of old, when the pick of the flower of youth on both sides carried the conflict into the skies. Into the Knighthood of the Blue, Richthofen has been given a place of highest merit by those he fought with and against."

Such period movies as *Hell's Angels* and *Dawn Patrol*, as well as serials, featured thinly disguised von Richthofen characters. "Hell's Angels" was the name given to a World War II bomber and, on March 17, 1948, to the notorious motorcycle gang.

Red Diamond Division. The 5th Division. Says the *Literary Digest* of May 31, 1919: "Two derivations of this unit's nickname are given. The first is as follows: 'Diamond Dye—it never runs.' The second derivation is quoted from a staff officer and states, 'The Red Diamond represents a well-known problem in bridge-building—it is made up of two adjacent isosceles triangles, which make for the greatest strength.'"

red eye. Catsup.

Red Knight. See RED BARON.

Reds. Communist revolutionaries in Russia and Germany.

red tab. A British staff officer; so-called from the bright red tabs worn on either side of the collar to indicate rank.

red tape. Official formality; the close or excessive observance of forms and routine in the transaction of business. See also under the Civil War.

regimental monkey. A drum major.

regular feller. A shipmate who is a good sport.

repeaters. Beans; sausages. The term refers to the gas these foods produce.

rest-camp. A cemetery. The following is from the *Literary Digest* of March 29, 1919: "The German snipers were very active, now and then killing or wounding one of us. At one time a trench-mortar shell hit so close to my hole in the ground, that I was completely buried and for a moment or two I thought I was going to a rest-camp."

rest in pieces. R.I.P. (on military graves). Arthur Guy Empey, in *Over the Top* (1917), notes that the term was used especially "if the man under the cross has been sent West by a bomb or shell explosion" (in other words, if the man had been blown to bits).

re-up. To reenlist. The term is thought to be a blend of "reenlist" and "sign up."

ricco. A ricocheting bullet.

ricochet officer. An officer used for emergency jobs. The following paragraph appeared in the St. Louis *Post-Dispatch* of November 24, 1918:

> CAMP KEARNEY, CAL.—Two new bits of army slang have come into use here. The latest one is "ricochet officer." A "ricochet officer" has nothing to do with the artillery range, it was explained, neither does he attempt to restrain glancing rifle bullets on the small arms target ranges. He merely "ricochets" from one job to another within the camp, "pinch-hitting" wherever the need for officers may exceed the supply, or serving in such temporary organizations as the casual company or recruit-receiving battalion. The other term is "Pistol Pete," and it is applied to any "hard-boiled guy" who is unapproachable, belligerent, a martinet or unduly strict with his men.

rig in your booms. Put down your elbows; an expression used at mess in the Navy.

rise and shine. Turn out of your bunks and get moving.

riveter. A machine gun.

rob de night. A nightgown; from the French *robe de nuit*.

rookie / rooky. A raw recruit. In 1917 General John J. ("Black Jack") Pershing took a look at two battalions of raw recruits and proclaimed: "They are sturdy rookies. We shall make great soldiers out of them." But the pioneer in using this term may have been Rudyard Kipling, in *Many Inventions* (1893): "You can't drill, you can't walk, you can't shoot . . . you awful rookies."

rooty. Bread.

Rosalie. One's bayonet.

rubber heel. A shell that gives no warning of its approach.

rumble. To annoy; to anger.

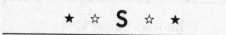

★ ☆ **S** ☆ ★

salvage. To steal.

salve. Butter.

Sam Browne. A military belt worn by officers; by extension, an officer. As Laurence Stallings points out in *The Doughboys* (1963), the troops jested about the belt because it allowed French prostitutes to identify officers, who were likely to have more cash than the soldiers without one. Stallings quotes a soldier song of the war in which "Sam Browne" is a verb and the noun "love" is a euphemism:

> They say that love is a blessing,
> A blessing I could never see,
> For the only girl I ever loved
> Has gone and made a sucker out of me.
> She can Sam Browne out of Bordeaux,
> She can Sam Browne all over Paree,
> She can love herself to death in the A.E.F.
> But she'll never find a sucker like me.

The belt is named after its originator, General Sir Samuel Joseph Browne, an English officer prominent in the early Indian campaign and the Indian mutiny, who lost an arm in the battle of Seeporah. It was the loss of the arm that caused him to devise a new sort of saber belt. Colonel T. Bentley Mott says of him, "He devised it in the 'seventies, along with a leather covered scabbard of the same color for the sword. The whole affair was inconspicuous in battle and looked smart on khaki uniforms."

The belt saw its first wartime use in the British expedition to Afghanistan in 1879. It was then used in the Boer War (1899–1902), and in 1914 the British expeditionary force brought it to France. One by one the allied armies adopted it during the war, and now practically every fighting man and woman officer in the world wears one.

Sammy. An infantryman; a DOUGHBOY. The name is evidently the result of an effort to find a cousin for TOMMY and was suggested by the nickname Uncle Sam. The appellation was utterly lacking in spontaneity, so it is not strange that American troops strongly objected to it. In *Stars and Stripes* of March 29, 1918, an editorial is headed "Down with 'Sammie.'"

A Canadian account of 1918 gives the following apocryphal origin of the name:

"The welcoming French shouted enthusiastically 'Vive les amis,' pronounced 'Veev lay zammie,' and the soldiers thought that instead of cheering their arriving friends, the crowds were giving them a nickname referring to Uncle Sam."

Sammy heaven. Paris.

sand. Sugar; a Navy term.

sand and specks. Salt and pepper.

sandbag Mary Ann. That's all right; don't worry about it. The following is from *Notes and Queries* of October 1918:

> Mary Ann started her career as Fairy Ann in the well-known phrase, Celane Fairy Ann, which is army French for Cela ne fait rien, one of the half-dozen items necessary for conversing with the remaining natives. Fairy Ann, not being sufficiently homelike for old soldiers, becomes Mary Ann; while—owing either to cherished idols at home being protected by sandbags or to the ignorance of the "18-pounders" (as the underage recruits are affectionately called) when Sammy apologizes to Tommy for pushing past him in the trenches—the cryptic phrase, "Sandbag Mary Ann," is more readily uttered and understood than the conventional "That's all right, chum."

sand rat. A soldier or officer on duty in the rifle pit at target practice. Eugene S. McCartney defines the term as follows, in *Slang and Idioms of the World War* (1929): "a man who at target practice signals a miss when you are sure you have made a 'Bull.'"

Sandstorm Division. The 34th Division, composed of troops from Iowa, Minnesota, Nebraska, and North Dakota.

Says Eugene S. McCartney in *Slang and Idioms of the World War* (1929): "Trained in Camp Cody, where sand storms sifted grit into almost every meal, they come by their name honestly." Its insignia was a red bovine skull superimposed on a dark field.

sauce. Gasoline.

sausage. (1) A German. (2) A military observation balloon shaped like a sausage.

sawbones. A regimental doctor.

S.C.D. Surgeon's Certificate of Disability (a paper given to a soldier who is unfit for duty when he is discharged from the Army).

school of the soldier. The fundamentals of Army life, drilled into recruits before being sent overseas.

scooter. A motor-driven handcar used for quickly traveling about an Army supply base.

scrap. An engagement; a fight (even a major battle).

scrap of paper. A broken promise, treaty, or pledge. At the beginning of the war the British government decided to make the violation of Belgium a casus belli. The German chancellor hastened to Sir Edward Goschen, the British ambassador at Berlin, and made an appeal to have England disregard the Belgian treaty, referring to it contemptuously as a "scrap of paper."

To this Eugene S. McCartney adds, in *Slang and Idioms of the World War* (1929): "It is interesting to note that when the German Chamber of Deputies protested to Emperor William I that the expenditure of funds without their sanction was a breach of the Constitution, the ruler dissolved the Chamber, and boldly declared that he would do his duty without regard to 'pieces of paper called constitutions.'"

Among British and American troops, the phrase came to be used ironically—a death notice might be referred to as a "scrap of paper."

scrounge. To appropriate; to misappropriate. In *Behind the Barrage*, published shortly after the war, British writer G. Goodchild discusses the term:

In the category of "odd jobs" came "scrounging." "Scrounging" is eloquent armyese; it covers pilfering, commandeering, "pinching," and many other familiar terms. You may scrounge for rations, kit, pay, or leave. Signalers are experts at it, and they usually scrounge for wire. Scrounging for wire is legitimized by the War Office, and called by the gentler name of "salving." We were informed that it was our duty to economize in the cost of the war by salving the wire that was disconnected by shell fire, or which appeared to be serving no useful purpose. We had first to "tap it" on the line with a field telephone, and if we got no response the wire was ours. . . . We made "scrounging" a daily affair, and not infrequently "scrounged" wire that was not disconnected and belonged to other batteries.

British in origin, this term was eagerly accepted by Americans and by the time of World War II was seen by many as pure G.I. See also under World War II, and **SCROUNGER**, under the Korean War.

seabag. A type of large shell.

sea dust. Salt; a Navy term.

sea gull. (1) A Navy airman. The term dates from 1914, at the Naval Air Station at Pensacola, Florida. (2) Chicken; a Navy term.

sea hornet. A destroyer.

sea lawyer. (1) A Navy man who believed himself omniscient on things naval, including shipboard rules and law. (2) A troublemaker; a malcontent.

Sears and Roebuck lieutenant / Sears and Roebuck loot. A new officer (i.e., one recently commissioned, usually a second lieutenant). The allusion is to the idea that the commission has come by mail order, as if ordered from a Sears, Roebuck catalogue.

seconds. An extra helping of food.

sector. That portion of the front lines occupied by a battalion.

sent up with the rations. Common; commonplace.

sewed in a blanket. Dead and buried.

shackles. Army stew; thick soup.

shag. French or other foreign tobacco; from its shaggy, rough cut.

shake a mean lip. To tell irresponsible stories; to indulge in "a mean line of chatter."

shavetail. An officer recently graduated from West Point; a second lieutenant. In the Quartermaster Corps young, unbroken mules were also known as "shavetails." See also under the Spanish-American War era.

shellitis. Initial horror and fear of war. The term came into play in the fall of 1917 when a letter from American ambulance driver Lawrence Copley Thaw to a girl back home was published. Thaw, a man of wealth who had been known as "the boy with the $25,000 allowance," wrote of the "shellitis" that baptized American soldiers with the shock of warfare.

shell shock. Battle fatigue.

Shell Shock

It was immediately thought that these conditions were the result of violent concussions occurring in the vicinity, and the striking but misleading term of "shell shock" came into being. The name was applied to all queer nervous and mental symptoms, and these patients suddenly acquired considerable notoriety. . . . The nervous symptoms included under the misleading and forbidden term, "shell shock," are not called war neuroses, or simply nervousness. They are known to be similar to peacetime neuroses, and they are peacetime neuroses with a war-time colouring.

—Frederick W. Parsons, *Atlantic Monthly* (March, 1919)

When famed British war poet Siegfried Sassoon died in 1967 at age eighty-one, obituaries noted that he had been honored for his bravery in combat but—after throwing his Military Cross into a river—had been sent to a sanatorium for victims of shell shock.

---

she said there'd be days like this. A phrase expressing a fatalistic attitude; a direct reference to "mama said there'd be days like this."

shimmy. A shirt or blouse; from the French *chemise.*

shirt hunt. A search for cooties; one who conducts such a search is known as a "shirt explorer." See also the entries beginning with "cootie."

shivoo. A party; from the French *chez vous* ("your house").

shock dump. A corrugated iron Army shelter.

shoestring corporal. A Marine lance corporal, who wears one stripe on his arm.

shot. An inoculation.

show. A military action. The following discussion appeared in the *Saturday Evening Post* of May 25, 1918:

> Anything in the nature of a thrust or a blow delivered against the enemy is a show. A great offensive on a wide front is a big show; a raid by night into hostile territory is a little show; a feint by infantry, undertaken with intent to deceive the other side at a given point while the real attack is being launched at a second given point, and accompanied by much vain banging of powder and much squibbing-off of rockets and flares and star-shells, is a Chinese show.

shrap. Shrapnel.

shrapnel. Grape Nuts (the cereal).

sick bay. A ship's hospital.

sicker. A sick report from a medical office.

sidekicker. A sleeping companion; a bosom chum.

Sightseeing Sixth. The 6th Division. "This division is reported to have marched more than any other in the A.E.F. and was known as the 'Sightseeing Sixth,'" reported the *National Geographic* for December 1919. "The insignia is a six-pointed star in red, and is frequently seen with the figure '6' superimposed on the star, but that was never authorized."

silent Sue / silent Lizzie. A shell that gives no warning of its approach.

silver plate. Please. From the French *s'il vous plait.*

sink. A toilet; a latrine.

sinker. A dumpling; a doughnut.

six for five. The practice of lending someone five dollars and getting back six dollars on payday.

six-sixty. A punishment of six months in the guardhouse and a fine of sixty dollars.

skee. Whiskey.

skilligalee / skilly. A stew of whatever leftovers are available.

Skilligalee Described

The best thing in a fixed camp is the stock-pot—a large covered pot or enamelled pail is reserved for this and nothing else. Into it go all the clean fag ends of game, head, tails, wings, feet, giblets, large bones, also left-overs of fish, flesh and fowl of any and all sorts. Vegetables, rice or other cereals, macaroni, stale bread, everything edible except fat and grease. The pot is always kept hot. Its flavors are forever changing, but ever welcome. It is always ready, day or night, for the hungry varlet who missed connections, or who wants a bite between meals. No cook who values his peace of mind will fail to have skilly simmering at all hours.

—*The Outpost Cook*, by Captain Joseph W. Gosling (1917)

sky pilot. An Army chaplain.

slackers' paradise boat. A submarine patrol boat; an ironical description.

slum / slumgullion. A stew composed chiefly of meat, potatoes, and onions. Cadets at West Point used to refer to hash as "slumgudgeon." See also under the Civil War.

small ticket. A dishonorable discharge from the Navy. A BIG TICKET was an honorable discharge.

Smash the Hun. A Navy slogan.

smoke a thermometer. To have one's temperature taken.

smoke screen. Smoke created for the purpose of concealment. In the report *The Enemy Submarine*, by the U.S. Naval Consulting Board (May 1, 1918), the tactic is described:

Under favorable conditions of wind and position many vessels have saved themselves from torpedo attack by the production of a smoke screen. This may be formed either by incomplete combustion of the oil used for fuel by most naval vessels, or it may be created by burning chemicals, such as phosphorus and coal tar, or mixtures in which both of these and other materials are used.

smoke wagon. A gun of the field artillery.

snake eyes. Tapioca.

snap out of it. To get out of one's bunk. The phrase is discussed in the *Saturday Evening Post* of December 21, 1918:

The captains transmitted their orders to their respective companies by a wave of their hands, while the sergeants and corporals emphasized the command to rise with sharp injunctions to "Snap out of it!", "Hit the deck!", "Rise and shine!", and other such nautical tricks of expression, all of which were traditionally sacred in this organization (the U.S. Marines), which, entrained or afloat or afield, never permitted itself to forget that it was essentially a seafaring set of men.

snipe. A fireman in the BLACK GANG. Says Logan E. Ruggles in *The Navy Explained* (1918): "In a gang of snipes below, there is generally one dude who is known as the 'king snipe.'"

An earlier, possibly related meaning of snipe is "a contemptible person."

sniper. A concealed sharpshooter whose duty it was to pick off enemy soldiers.

snow digger. A man from the New England states.

so-called salt. A dry-land sailor.

S.O.L. Strictly out of luck; soldier out of luck (in print and politely, but really "shit out of luck"). Mark Sullivan, who discusses it as "soldier out of luck" in *Our Times*, Vol. V, *Over Here* (1933), says it is an "expression used of one who is late for mess, has lost his hat-cord, or been given thirty days' confinement to the post for shooting crap."

soldier. To serve; to shirk.

soldier's one percent. One hundred percent.

soldier's supper. Nothing; that which does not exist.

solo. To fly alone.

solo-hop. A solo flight.

Somewhere in France. The only return address allowed by military censors on letters mailed from anywhere in France.

Somewhere in France

James M. Beck writes in *Defenders of Democracy* (1917): "The war has enriched our language with many new expressions, but none more beautiful than that of 'Somewhere in France.' To all noble minds, while it sounds the abysmal depths of tragic suffering, it rises to the sublimest heights of heroic self-sacrifice."

The following poem by John Hogben appeared in the *Spectator* of September 25, 1915:

"Somewhere in France"—we know not where—he lies,
Mid shuddering earth and under anguished skies!
We may not visit him, but this we say:
Though our steps err his shall not miss their way.
From the exhaustion of War's fierce embrace

He, nothing doubting, went to his own place.
To him has come, if not the crown and palm,
The kiss of Peace—a vast, sufficing calm!

---

sootbox. A German artillery shell that emits black smoke upon exploding.

soup gun. A rolling kitchen.

souvenir. (1) A shell. (2) A penny or a morsel of food. The term was used by French children when begging.

sow belly. Bacon.

Spad. A small biplane. The aircraft is described by Bertram W. Williams in *Scientific American* of October 6, 1917: "Till recently the French pinned their faith on an improved and speedier type of the well-known Nieuport, a monoplane upon which many records were made in the early days. Still faster is the 'Spad,' a tiny biplane."

Spanish flu. Influenza, in the epidemic of 1918–1919, which caused more deaths than did the war itself.

spare. At leisure; off duty.

spick. A Hispanic person. Logan E. Ruggles discusses the term in *The Navy Explained* (1918): "A Mexican or Spaniard, or any dark-skinned people are known to the navy men as spicks. It was, some years ago, almost always called spiggoty, but since the days of abbreviations, spick. The term is said to have originated during the Spanish-American War."

The term was used in the Army also, especially on the Mexican border.

spiderweb. A wire entanglement.

splash. Flying splinters from the inside of a tank wall, caused by the impact of bullets striking the outside. The *Atlantic Monthly* of December 1918 reported:

> While bullets do not penetrate the armor (of tanks), but only ruffle it up a bit at the point where they are deflected, a great deal of bullet "splash" does come in. This is more annoying than serious, and after an action one could pick out any number of these tiny splinters from one's face. So, as a means of protection against "splash," face-armor was invented. This looks much like a bandit's mask, with a steel-mesh chain hanging from it. The mask itself is of thin steel, with slits for the eyes, the whole padded for the face and adjustable to it.

splinter house. A corrugated iron shelter that splinters when hit by enemy fire.

splitass. To do stunt flying; to fly in a reckless manner.

splitass merchant. A reckless individual; an expert stunt flier.

spotter. (1) A soldier who telephones ranges to gun crews. (2) An airman engaged in locating enemy guns or submarines.

spruce. To deceive; to tell tall tales.

spudhole. A guardroom (akin to the dank place where potatoes [spuds] are stored).

square head. A German. Eugene S. McCartney, in *Slang and Idioms of the World War* (1929), writes that this was "a term which was very popular with the Americans of 1917–1918. This is a translation of the French expression tête carrée but the term appears in English as early as 1589 and was used by thieves to mean an honest man."

squeeker. A young courier pigeon. An explanation of the need for young birds appears in the collection *Stories of Americans in the World War* (1918):

> How can Uncle Sam break the pigeons he buys for service in France of their instinct to return to the United States? He cannot. Once a homer is settled it is no good to our government except for breeding purposes. The only birds useful for courier purposes are those that are brought into service before they are old enough to settle. These are eight weeks old or less, and are called "squeekers."

stand-to. A special time in the morning and in the evening. The term is discussed by H. R. Peat in *Private Peat* (1917): "The name given to the sunrise hour, and again that hour at night when every man stands to the parapet in full equipment and with fixed bayonet. After morning stand-to, bayonets are unfixed, for if the sun should glint upon the polished steel, our position would be disclosed to some sniper."

star light. A flare.

stars and stripes. Beans with bacon; so-called because of the striped appearance of the bacon served with the beans.

star shell. A rocket used to light up NO-MAN'S-LAND at night.

start arguin', bastards. An expression of mock provocation.

stone frigate. A prison ashore; from the fact that worn-out boats were once used as prisons.

Stonewall Division. The 81st Division. See WILDCAT DIVISION.

stop. To be hit by a bullet or shell fragment.

storm cellar. A DUGOUT.

stove lizard. One who likes to hang around the stove at the Y.M.C.A. or Red Cross canteen.

strafe. To punish; from the German *strafen*. The word was so greatly extended that soldiers could speak of "strafing" a fly. The word is used also as a noun (e.g., "Next strafe we 'ave, 'ell's goin' to pop for fair"). See also under World War II.

straggler barrage. A cordon of military police who follow the infantry OVER THE TOP and prevent any straggling toward the rear.

straight kick. A summary discharge by the commander of a vessel.

strategic retreat. The German high command's explanation of the retirement from the Somme in the spring of 1917. Eugene S. McCartney, in his *Slang and Idioms of the World War* (1929), adds this definition: "During the following year there was a tendency to give the expression a slang connotation, and to use it when a person yielded a point or receded from a position he had taken."

strawberries. Prunes.

striker. A soldier who works for an officer. See also DOG ROBBER, under the Civil War.

strip. To reduce in rank.

sub. A submachine gun; a submarine; a substitute.

submarine. (1) A bedpan; a urinal. (2) A duck.

submarine shark. A salmon.

Sugar Sticks. The Ordnance Corps.

Suicide Club. The Machine Gun Corps. British writer Captain Herbert W. McBride, in *The Emma Gees* (1918), writes:

> During the early part of the war, before the advent of the Lewis and other automatic rifles, the only machine guns in general use were of the heavy tripod-mounted type and it was necessary for them to advance with or even ahead of the attacking troops. As the guns and tripods were very conspicuous objects, they naturally became the especial targets for enemy riflemen and snipers and the casualties ran far above the average for other troops.

suicide ditch. A front-line trench.

suicide fleet. The small boats of the American Patrol Squadron in European waters. According to an article in the *Literary Digest* of March 22, 1919:

> In boats that were never expected to fight, the largest of them hardly more than seven hundred tons gross, many of them so delicately balanced that the weight of the single gun they had to carry was almost enough to turn them topsy-turvy, any of them sure to be instantaneously distributed over the sea if touched by a torpedo,

life is likely to be a precarious and brief matter.

Sunset Division. The 41st Division, composed of troops from Washington, Oregon, Idaho, and Wyoming. Its insignia was a setting sun of yellow on a field of red.

Sunshine Division. The 40th Division, composed of troops from Arizona, California, Colorado, and Utah. Its insignia was a shining sun of gold on a blue field.

S.W. Shell wound. As Arthur Guy Empey puts it in *Over the Top* (1917): "What the doctor marks on your chart when a shell has removed your leg."

swamp. To put on airs; to show off.

swing the lead. To boast; to exaggerate.

★ ☆ **T** ☆ ★

tadpole. A small French child.

tail-end Charlie. The last aircraft in a formation.

tailor-made. A ready-made cigarette.

take another blanket / take on. To reenlist within three months of one's discharge.

tank. An armor-plated motor vehicle operated by a crew and armed with a cannon and machine guns. Tanks were first used by the British on September 15, 1916, in the battle of the Somme.

In their early days, tanks were often referred to as "military tanks."

Tales of the Tank

Major General Sir E. D. Swinton, the inventor of the tank, explains the origin of the name in *World's Work* for September 1917:

Quite a large part of the earlier stage of manufacture would consist of the rolling of steel plates and their assemblage and erection into boxes, which to all except those who made a close examination might well be intended for vessels to hold water, petrol, or oil. The fact that the boxes would be bullet-proof would merely lend color to the idea that they might be intended to move up into the fighting zone. This theory would not necessarily be discredited even when the stage of fitting them with engines and caterpillar tracks was reached. It would not be until the time for mounting the armament that the real purpose must become plain, up to which an alias might to some extent conceal it. "Reservoir" and "Cistern" were long-winded and clumsy; "Tank" was equally accurate and shorter. And "Tank" it became. As a matter of fact, various rumors about the new machines were current among those who got wind of them. One was that they were intended to carry water for the troops across the deserts of Egypt and Mesopotamia. A second hinted at snow-ploughs for use on the Russian front. It is perhaps unnecessary to say that no special trouble was taken to contradict these yarns. It was also bruited about that experiments had been made in some wild-cat scheme which had failed absolutely.

Additional information is provided by Brevet Colonel J. F. C. Fuller in *Tanks in the Great War* (1920):

Up to December 1915, the machines now known as "tanks" were, in the experimental stage, called "landships" or "land cruisers," and also "caterpillar machine-gun destroyers."

On December 24 ... it occurred to Colonel Swinton that the use of the above names would give away a secret which it was important to preserve. After consultation with Lieutenant-Colonel W. Dally-Jones, assistant secretary of the "Committee on Imperial Defence," the following names were suggested by Colonel Swinton—"cistern," "reservoir," and "tank," all of which were applicable to the structure of the machines in the earlier stages of manufacture. Because it was less clumsy and monosyllabic the name "tank" was decided on.

Swinton invented the tank, but its propelling principle was that of the "caterpillar" farm tractor, invented about 1900 by Benjamin Holt of Stockton, California.

taxi. To drive an airplane along the ground without rising into the air or in order to acquire sufficient speed to ascend. Here is the explanation given to readers of the February 1919 issue of *American Boy*:

The plane bumped across the rough ground, acting very much like an automobile, nosing this way and that as Sidmore sought and finally found the direction of the wind. This maneuvering along the ground was known, in the slang of the camp, as "taxi-ing," being designed as a final test of the motor and other parts before leaving the earth.

T-bone steak. Tenderloin steak; from the fact that the cut contains a T-shaped bone.

teakettle / teapot. A French locomotive.

tell it to the Marines. A phrase that expresses doubt. Arthur Guy Empey discusses it in *First Call* (1918): "An old army phrase used when a man is trying to get away with a fishy statement. The marine is half soldier and half sailor. He generally receives his preliminary training on land; after that, on a ship. Upon arriving on board the sailors tell him many impossible tales and he is supposed to believe them."

In spite of the origin and meaning of this expression, it was employed in recruiting posters in slightly altered form: "Tell that to the Marines." See also under the Civil War.

terps. An interpreter; especially important in dealings with the French.

third lieutenant. See DOVETAIL.

three beans. Very good; very well; from the French *tres bien*.

three-point landing. An airplane landing in which both wheels and the tail hit the ground at the same time.

three-thirty. A punishment of three months in the guardhouse and a fine of thirty dollars.

thumbs up. A phrase or gesture meaning everything is fine. It is a popular idea that the Romans held their thumbs up when a defeated gladiator was to be spared, but classical scholars are by no means unanimous on this point. In *Over the Top* (1917), by Arthur Guy Empey, it is noted that the phrase or gesture is "Very seldom used during an intense bombardment."

tick. To complain; to find fault.

tickler. A hand grenade.

tick off. To administer a reproof.

ticky. Tending to find fault or to complain.

tie bags. To get married; from the fact that Navy chums used to tie their seabags together on the same jack stay, or rod to which sails are affixed. In the old Navy, to "tie bags" with a man meant to hang out with him.

tin derby / tin dip / tin hat. A steel helmet. The first American wearers of steel helmets in battle were a group of Marines, on August 13, 1917.

tin fleet. Pleasure boats refitted and armed as submarine hunters.

Tin Lizzie. A Model-T Ford, especially the Ford ambulance in combat areas. Laurence Stallings writes in *The Doughboys* (1963): "I was thinking of the blood that dripped upon my face from the boy above me in the Tin Lizzie."

tinned cow. Condensed milk.

tin willie. (1) Canned corn beef. (2) A Ford ambulance.

Tommy. See **Tommy Atkins.**

Tommy Atkins. A British soldier. The term was used by the soldiers themselves, the English people, and American soldiers.

Tommy

"Tommy" was familiar to readers of Rudyard Kipling long before the war. Kipling's *Barrack-Room Ballads* is, in fact, dedicated "To T.A.," and one stanza of the poem "Tommy" runs as follows:

> While it's Tommy this an' Tommy that, an' "Tommy, fall be'ind,"
> But it's "Please to walk in front, sir," when there's trouble in the wind,
> There's trouble in the wind, my boys, there's trouble in the wind,
> O it's "Please to walk in front, sir," when there's trouble in the wind.

The Philadelphia *Public Ledger* of August 24, 1919, explains the origin of the name:

It happened in this way. The war office issued a little note-book to the men requesting each one to fill out the little blanks in the front as to name, age, date of enlistment, etc. So that they would not make any mistakes a copy of the front page was filled out properly in each book under the name of Tommy Atkins. It did not take long for the name to stick to all the soldier boys, and it is today as significant of the English fighting man as John Bull is of England itself.

---

toot and scramble. All together; from the French *tout ensemble.*

tootfinny. All finished; everything done. It is from the French *tout finis.*

toothpick. A bayonet; in imitation of the French *curedent* ("toothpick"), which was French slang for a bayonet. In the same spirit, Americans on the frontier in the midnineteenth century would call a large fighting knife an "Arkansas toothpick."

toots sweet. Hurry up; look sharp. It is from the French *tout de suite.*

top cutter / top kicker / top sergeant / top soldier. A first sergeant.

torp. A torpedo.

torpedo plane. An airplane designed to launch self-propelled torpedoes. The torpedo plane was invented by Rear Admiral Bradley A. Fiske, in 1912.

toy shop. The factory in France where decoy papier-mâché soldiers and various camouflaged objects were made.

trace beans. Very good; very well. It is from the French *tres bien.*

treat 'em rough. Handle the machinery roughly. This was the motto of the Tank Corps during the war.

trench. A type of military excavation. The term is defined in *Over the Top* (1917), by Arthur Guy Empey: "A ditch full of water, rats and soldiers."

Paul Fussell wrote about a number of "trench" constructions in *The Great War and Modern Memory* (1975): "Of the *trench* words like *trenchmouth, trenchfoot, trenchknife,* and *trenchcoat,* only *trench fever* has not survived. *Trenchcoat* (originally *Burberry*) has recently spawned the adjective *trenchy* to describe a trend in women's clothing: 'This year it's the trenchy look.'" Fussell adds: "In the *Sunday Times Magazine* for August 8, 1972, a caption celebrating the vogue of the trenchy announces that 'Fashion Goes Over the Top.'"

trench broom. A machine gun. An explanation of this term appears in John Ellis's *The Social History of the Machine Gun* (1975): "In the summer of 1918 the first working model of the Thompson submachine gun had appeared. The gun had been designed by Colonel J. T. Thompson specifically as a weapon for trench warfare, and he dubbed it the 'trench broom' to be used in close quarter combat when troops were trying to clear an enemy trench."

trench derby. A helmet.

trench dreams. Fear, especially the fear that one will show cowardice.

trench fever. A malady of the front whose symptoms included fever, aches, pains, and homesickness.

trench foot. A disease of the feet contracted in the trenches from exposure to extreme cold and wet. P. Giggs wrote of the condition in *The New York Times* for April 6, 1919:

> In winter, when the water was ice cold, it may be imagined what our men endured. They were always wet. They slept in wet clothes, sat in wet dugouts, stood in wet boots, and the cold slime of mud in Flanders encased them, and put its clammy touch about their very souls. In the first two winters of the war, they were stricken with a disease called "Trench Foot." Its symptoms were exactly like those of frostbite, a sense of burning until all sense was deadened and the feet blackened and rotted. Battalions lost 40 per cent of their men for a time from this cause, and in the old Ypres salient I have seen men of the 49th (Yorkshire) Division crawling back from the trenches, or carried pick-a-back by their comrades, unable to walk a yard, and with both feet tied up in cotton wool at the field ambulance.

The term had analogues in later wars, including the JUNGLE ROT of World War II and the PADDY FOOT of the Vietnam War.

trench horrors. Fear and cowardice, or fear of same.

trenchitis. A combination of FEDUPNESS and homesickness, as defined in *Over the Top* (1918), by Arthur Guy Empey.

trench moppers. Troops hunting for Germans concealed in German trenches.

trench mouth. A disease that causes ulceration and bleeding of the gums. It is caused by A.P.C. (adenoidal-pharyngeal-conjunctival) viruses. Here is a description that appeared in the British newspaper *The Mail*, on May 1, 1918:

> We have trench mouth just as we have trench feet. Otherwise known as ulcero-membranous stomatitis, or Vincent's disease, it has for some considerable time now, engaged the attention of both the medical and the dental services. The result of a bacillus that causes ulceration and bleeding of the gums, it occurs on the German as well as on our side of the war zone. A satisfactory method of treatment has been discovered, the painting of the gums with salvarsan or an arsenical solution, and a cure is generally effected within two or three weeks' time. The Germans credited their war bread as one of the contributory causes, a cause that up to the present is absent from the British war zone.

Trench Mouth

After the war, "trench mouth" was applied to civilians so affected, although it is not as commonly heard now as it once was. The malady was linked to kissing and even thought to be a sexually transmitted disease. In the San Francisco *Examiner* of October 21, 1969, a mother wrote this appeal to a medical advice columnist:

> My husband and I are terribly upset because our daughter has developed a severe case of trench mouth.
>
> The attitude of her classmates in the senior year of high school makes her feel as if she has a venereal disease.
>
> I hope you can tell your readers that this is not so.

When war breaks out the term is still relevant. A Washington *Post* dispatch of February 21, 1991, from the Persian Gulf on the health of the soldiers fighting there contains this line: "The Army calls it 'trench mouth' and it happens when soldiers at war neglect to brush their teeth for days."

trench talk. Military slang.

trench warfare. Warfare conducted from relatively permanent positions in trenches. It was the dominant form of warfare for the final four years of the war. In American football, intense interior line play has been called "trench warfare," and those that play there are said to be "in the trenches."

tres bon / tres bong. Very good; from the French *tres bien*.

trick. A turn at sentry duty. The word was borrowed by the Army from seamen's language, in which it meant a turn at any task or duty.

triple. A German Fokker triplane.

troops. Foot soldiers.

tube. A kind of DUGOUT. It was described by J. S. Smith in *Over There and Back* (1918): "If you took half a subway car, stuck it in the ground, and covered the top with two or three feet of earth, you would have a 'tube' dugout. Inside are seats as in the subway, and through the center runs a rudely constructed table."

tune up. To make a final inspection and adjustment of the parts of an airplane before flying.

turn off the juice. To shut off an engine. "Juice" means "gasoline."

two and a butt. An enlistment period of under three years. "Butt" means a portion of a year.

two-twenty. A punishment of two months in the guardhouse and a fine of twenty dollars.

two-winger. A pilot, who wears a two-winged badge. See also ONE-WINGER.

typewriter. (1) A machine gun. (2) A manual lawn mower.

★ ☆ **U** ☆ ★

u-jah. See CUM-SAH.

up against the wall. The position of a man about to be shot by a firing squad; by extension, anyone in a desperate position.

upstairs. In flight.

Upton Division. The 77th Division; so-called because it trained at Camp Upton, on Long Island. See also LIBERTY DIVISION and MELTING-POT DIVISION.

used up. Killed.

★ ☆ **V** ☆ ★

venereal list. A list of men with venereal diseases. They were not allowed to go on leave until they were removed from the list by a medical officer.

Very light. A kind of flare fired from a pistol; named after the inventor.

victory. The downing of an enemy plane in combat. During World War II, this term was replaced by "a kill." (This fascinating semantic change was pointed out in the obituary of Charles Dolan, the last member of the Lafayette Escadrille, in *The New York Times* of January 2, 1988.)

victual office. The stomach; from the long-established term (sometimes pronounced as "vittles") for food.

vinegar blink. White wine; from the French *vin blanc.*

viper. See MAGGOT.

Von Hutier tactics. The system whereby a spent division would not fall back as customary, but as explained in Homer Randall's 1919 novel, *Army Boys on the Firing Line,* "simply opened up and let a fresh division pass through and take up the burden."

von Woodenburg. A nickname of the German general Paul von Hindenburg. "We would inquire after the health of old 'Von Woodenburg,' old 'One O'clock,' the 'Clown Prince,' or 'One Bumstoff,'" wrote H. T. Peat, in *Private Peat* (1917).

These parodies referred to von Hindenburg, Heinrich von Kluck, the Crown Prince, and Johann von Bernstorff, respectively.

vulture. See GOOPHER.

★ ☆ **W** ☆ ★

WAAC. A member of the British Women's Auxiliary Army Corps. The U.S. would not have a women's Army corps until the next war, but Americans were fascinated by the concept, as indicated by this account by Hamilton Holt in the December 14, 1918, *Independent:*

> Here we saw hundreds of "Waacs" and "Penguins" working. England is the only nation that has allowed women in her army, unless it be Russia and her Battalion of Death. The Waacs (Woman's Auxiliary Army Corps) consists of many thousands of British women who have enlisted in the army, wear a regular khaki uniform, and live under strict military discipline. At least twenty thousand of them serve close behind the front lines in France as waitresses, housekeepers, clerks, chauffeurs, stenographers, etc., while many more are stationed in post all over England.

waders. Rubber hip boots. They were of especial importance in the ever-waterlogged trenches.

wagon soldier. A light artilleryman; a field artilleryman.

waltzing Matilda. An Australian soldier; from the Australian anthem, "Waltzing Matilda."

wampus. An insect inhabitant of oatmeal and other dry foods. By the time of World War II, the following claim could be made by Francis Raymond Meyer, in *Fighting Talk* (1942): "Scrupulous cleanliness and sanitation now makes the wampus about as rare as the dodo bird."

wangle. To obtain by whatever means necessary. It was one of the war words commented upon in the *Spectator* (September 21, 1918): "Now, contrary to what might have been expected, the war has not depreciated the lingual currency. It has indeed circulated camouflage and strafe but provided they are not naturalized and remain merely denizens, they may be serviceable, while 'carry on' actually supplies a word that was badly missed. Nor do we object to wangle."

The word also turned up in an article by Samuel G. Blythe in the *Saturday Evening Post* of October 19, 1918: "And wet—always, always wet, unless the weather is clear and the sea is calm—but good sea boats. They [the submarine chasers] wangle through somehow. They weather it out."

war baby. (1) A child, legitimate or illegitimate, fathered by a soldier. (2) On Wall Street, a factory producing goods for the war that showed sudden and spectacular profits.

war of attrition. A characterization of the trench war on the western front, in which a tremendous price in casualties was paid for tiny advances in territory—territory that was often given back a few days later.

washed out. Killed.

washout. (1) A failure; something of no account. This expression began in the British navy and then crept ashore to land in the trenches, where it was used by both the British and the Americans. The term appeared in the *Atlantic Monthly* of January 1919: "At the end of the week you will be given an examination. Those who do well will remain with the tanks; the washouts will go back to the infantry."

As a verb, "wash out" means "to fail."

(2) A day on which aircraft are not sent up.

wave. A line of men advancing side by side OVER THE TOP. The waves were often numbered—first wave, second wave, etc.

W.D. War Department.

weary Willie. A German shell that approaches with a "nerve-racking whine."

weed ration. An issue of tobacco and cigarettes.

Western Division. The 89th Division. See JAYHAWKERS.

westerner. One who maintained that the only way the war could be won was with a decisive victory at the western front. See also EASTERNER.

wet canteen. A military saloon. In this sense, "wet" means that the sale of alcoholic beverages is permitted, whereas "dry" means it is prohibited.

wet nurse. One who tests a gun "under the special direction of the inventor or promoter" (according to Eugene S. McCartney, in *Slang and Idioms of the World War* [1929]).

we we town. Paris; from the French *oui, oui* ("yes, yes").

whacked. Exhausted; played out.

what-for. Punishment. *The New York Times* of March 2, 1919, reported: "To give an enemy 'What-for' was to play the very mischief with him."

whee. A big shell; an onomatopoeic name.

whispering Jimmy. A howitzer shell.

whispering Willie. A large German shell that traveled at a velocity so high that one hardly heard it in its flight.

white hope. A German high-explosive shell.

white ink. White wine.

white lightning. Corn whiskey; so-called because of its color and its "kick." The drink was also known as "gray mule" and "white mule."

white man. A good and brave man. The term was used by both British and American troops and was almost certainly racist in origin. British writer T. Tiplady discusses it in *The Soul of the Soldier* (1918):

> In the army it is a term of supreme praise to call a man white. When you say a comrade is a white man, there is no more to be said. It is worth more than the Victoria Cross with its red ribbon, for it includes gallantry, and adds to it goodness. A man must be brave to be called white, and he must be generous, noble and good. To reach whiteness is a great achievement. To be dubbed white is, in the army, like being dubbed knight at King Arthur's Court, or canonized saint in the Church. He stands out among a soldier's comrades distinct as white handkerchiefs among khaki ones.

white mule. Corn whiskey; so-called because of its color and its "kick." The drink was also known as "gray mule" and "white lightning."

whizz-bang. A high-velocity antipersonnel schrapnel; an onomatopoeic name. R. Derby Holmes describes the device in *A Yankee in the Trenches* (1918): "The 'whizzbang' starts with a rough whirr like a flushing cock partridge, and goes off on contact with a tremendous bang."

whutt. A bullet; an onomatopoeic description. In *Between the Lines* (1915), B. Cable writes: "When a bullet whistles or sings past, it is a comfortable distance clear; when it goes hiss or swish, it is too close for safety; and when it says whutt very sharply and viciously, it is merely a matter of being a few inches out either way."

wigwag. To signal with flags.

Wildcat Division. The 81st Division, composed of men from Florida, North Carolina, South Carolina, and Puerto Rico; also known as the Stonewall Division. According to Eugene S. McCartney, in *Slang and Idioms of the World War* (1919): "The name has also been frequently applied to the Thirtieth (Old Hickory) Division, because the men in it came largely from the same states. The name is due to the fact that a small stream which flows through Camp Jackson, S.C., where the unit was organized, is called Wildcat Creek." Its insignia was a cat on a disk, with the color of the cat varying according to the brigade.

wildcat trains. Trains that the Belgians sent into the German lines outside Antwerp at the beginning of the war.

Wild West Division. The 91st Division, composed of troops from Alaska, Colorado, Idaho, Montana, Nevada, Oregon, Utah, Washington, and Wyoming. Its insignia was a green fir tree.

wild woodbine. A cigarette "composed of glue, cheap paper, and a poor quality of hay" (according to R. Derby Holmes, in *A Yankee in the Trenches* [1918]). "Woodbine" is a generic name for several honeysuckles and creepers.

will-o'-the-wisp. A shell.

win. To steal; to lift; to SCROUNGE; to obtain by other than fair means. "I won it," was a common expression in the trenches.

windjammer. A trumpeter; a bandsman.

windy. A coward.

Wipers. Ypres, France.

wire, the. Barbed wire.

wobbler. An infantryman.

wolf. A daredevil pilot who does stunts near the ground.

Wolverine Division. The 14th Division; so-named because wolverines were once very common in Michigan, where the division was organized. The head of a wolverine appears on the insignia.

woodbine. (1) An English soldier. (2) See WILD WOODBINE.

wood butcher. A company carpenter.

wooden shoe factory. A derisive name for a French village dance.

woolly bear. A shell that on exploding gives out dense black smoke and rolls about in such a manner as to suggest the animal for which it is named.

work one's ticket. To feign illness or insanity.

WRENS. Woman's Royal Naval Service. The WRENS were attached to the British navy and, like the **WAACs,** attracted much American attention.

★ ☆ Y ☆ ★

Yankee Division. The 26th Division, composed of New England troops; also called the New England Division. Its insignia was a dark blue YD monogrammed on a khaki diamond.

Yankee heaven. Paris.

Yank Tommy. An American soldier in the British army.

yard bird. A guardhouse prisoner.

yellow cross. MUSTARD GAS; probably from the yellow crosses that appeared on the shells and containers in which it was stored.

Yellow Cross Division. The 33rd Division, composed of troops from the Illinois National Guard. The name is derived from its insignia, a yellow cross on a black circle. According to Eugene S. McCartney, in *Slang and Idioms of the World War* (1929): "The colors of this division were due to the fact that only yellow and black paints were available when it became necessary to mark the equipment in Texas before leaving for France."

It was also known as the ILLINOIS DIVISION and the PRAIRIE DIVISION.

yellow leg. A cavalryman; from the traditional yellow trouser stripe.

yellow ticket. A dishonorable discharge; from the color of the paper on which it was printed.

you'll find it on the payroll. A phrase said when a soldier loses a piece of equipment, referring to the fact that the cost of the item will eventually be deducted from the man's paycheck.

you must come across. Y.M.C.A.

young Charlie. A haversack.

youngster. A young officer; a first or second lieutenant.

your number. Fate (e.g., a bullet that has your number on it). It alludes to the small metal disk with a personal serial number, worn by all American soldiers and sailors.

★ ☆ Z ☆ ★

zepp. A zeppelin.

zeppelins in a cloud. Sausage and mashed potatoes.

zero / zero hour. The time fixed for an attack. The time before or after was spoken of as a certain number minus or plus zero or zero hour.

zero day. The day fixed for an attack.

zigzag. Drunk.

zing. Pep; vim.

zoom. To make an aircraft climb at an extreme angle for a short distance and then resume a level course before the machine stalls. This description appeared in Century for January 1919: "My trouble now was to 'zoom' over the fringe of trees and fences. There was a heartbreaking moment when I thought that I was going to be 'hung up' on a tall treetop, but the gallant old girl rose to the occasion, and the leaves seemed just to graze my wheels. I breathed a stupendous sigh of relief."

See also under World War II.

Zouave. A cook. For a vastly different meaning, see under the Civil War.

zowie. So forth and so on.

Sources

★

MILITARY SLANG

Empey, Arthur Guy, *First Call.* G.P. Putnam's Sons, New York, 1918. (A very important collection of "American Army Terms" by one of the most well-read American participants in the War.)
———, *Over the Top.* G.P. Putnam's Sons, New York, 1917. (This is essentially a compilation of British trenches slang—which the author says, ". . . Tommy Atkins uses a thousand times a day as he is serving in France"—but is a most valuable reference.)
Fraser, Edward, and John Gibbons, *Soldier and Sailor Words and Phrases: including slang of the trenches and the air force; British and American war-words and service terms and expressions in everyday use; nicknames, sobriquets, and titles of regiments, with their origins; the battle-honours of the Great War awarded to the British Army.* E.P. Dutton & Co., New York; 1925.
Funk and Wagnalls War Words, Funk and Wagnalls, New York, 1915.
Fussell, Paul, *The Great War and Modern Memory,* Oxford University Press, New York, 1975. (The chapter "Oh What a Literary War" has much on the use of language and euphemism in describing the war.)
Hargrave, Basil, *Origins and Meanings of Popular Phrases and Names, including those which came into use during the World War.* J. B. Lippincott Co., Phila., 1925.
Holmes, R. Derby, *A Yankee in the Trenches,* Little Brown, and Co., Boston, 1918.
Lawson, Don, *The United States in World War I,* Scholastic, New York, 1963.

LITERARY DIGEST: These articles graphically followed the slang of the War: "Active-Service Slang," 50:907, "How War Enriches Language," 50:1081–1082, "French Soldier-Slang," 52:643, "Slang of the Airmen," 54:1957 and the most important "Recruits' Primer of Trench Idiom," October 27, 1917.

MacDonald, Lyn, *The Roses of No Man's Land*, Atheneum, New York, 1989.

McCartney, Eugene S., *Additions to a Volume on the Slang and Its Idioms of the World War*, Michigan Academy of Arts and Sciences, 1929. (For purposes of brevity I have called this *Slang and Idioms of the World War* in the body of the text. This is the most important reference on American slang of the War and was used more than any other single reference in preparing this chapter. The word "additions" in the title refers to the addition of American slang to the Fraser and Gibbons volume which is overwhelmingly British in emphasis. This reference is extremely hard to locate and the author has used copies in the Library of Congress and the Boston Public Library.)

McKnight, George H., *English Words and Their Background*, D. Appleton and Company, New York, 1923.

Randall, Homer, *Army Boys on the Firing Line*, The World Syndicate Publishing Co., New York, 1919.

Reynolds, Quentin. *They Fought for the Sky*, Holt, Reinhart and Winston, New York, 1960.

Ruggles, Logan E., *The Navy Explained*, Appleton, New York, 1918.

Smith, C. Alphonso, *New Words Self-Defined*, Doubleday, Page and Co., Garden City, New York, 1919. An extremely important reference which provided many of the newspaper and magazine quotations used in this chapter.

Springs, Elliott White, *Nocturne Militaire*, New York, Grosset and Dunlaps, 1927.

Stallings, Laurence, *The Doughboys*, Harper and Row, New York, 1963.

Sullivan, Mark, *Our Times: The United States, 1900–1925*, Vol. V, *Over Here, 1914–1918*, Scribner's, New York, 1933.

Swann, Captain Carroll J., *My Company*, Boston, Houghton Mifflin, 1918.

Weseen, Maurice H., *Dictionary of American Slang*, Thomas Y. Crowell, New York, 1934.

Winter, J. M., *The Experience of World War I*, Oxford University Press, New York, 1989.

3

THE MANY WORDS OF WORLD WAR II

★

G.I.'s, Jeeps, Kilroy, and V-Signs from Two Theaters of War

★

Three quotations from three different sources serve as a good introduction to the slang of World War II, a period of unprecedented linguistic experimentation and innovation.

"Tell that apple knocker to stop bull-dogging the belly-robber's bomb heaver or he'll soon be a China clipper, the big zombie!"

That, ladies and gentlemen, is soldierese. It means:

"Tell that upstate hick to quit dancing with the mess sergeant's beautiful girl or he'll soon be a dishwasher, the big clown!"

The navy and the marines would have a slightly different way of saying this. But the fact is that all service men whether in khaki, blue, or field green, are speaking a fresh and vigorous tongue these days, one all their own.

What does this new language imply? Some might say: "Not much." But perhaps they don't know their history. The new language means a lot. It indicates that all men are united by the words they speak. So the welding value of a fighter's jargon is nothing to sneeze at.

—*Fighting Talk*, by Francis Raymond Meyer (1942)

Our fighting men are makers of slang because they are adventurous individuals and they are not restricted by decorum and their taste is unlimited. Their hunting ground for new terms is in their native tongue as well as foreign. They adopt traditional devices of similitude, making attributes do work for the whole. They use hidden resemblances, they know no limitations and have no boundaries. They have substituted far-fetched figures for a hundred literary descriptions, using abbreviations most freely, compositions, formations of words to resemble the sound and picturesque synonyms. Their transfer of proper names into common usage has been so much "duck-soup" (that which is done with ease), giving remote figurative significances to the coining in question. They have enriched the national vocabulary with many new verbs and verb phrases.

It must not be forgotten that our fighting men have come from all walks of life, that all sections and divisions of a free social order are represented and each man has brought the peculiar and colorful language of his section of the country with him. Ours is a fighting force of a hundred races and as many creeds speaking a language called American.

—*Words of the Fighting Forces*, by Clinton A. Sanders
and Joseph W. Blackwell, Jr. (1942)

World War II may be remembered for a number of reasons, and probably the least of these is that it provided a king-size fund of new slang for the diversion of lexicographers.

—"Dogfaces and Dog Soldiers," by Jonathan E. Lighter (1974)

Every once in a while an apprentice lexicographer gets lucky and bumps into a bona fide Rosetta Stone, as I did with the prime source used in this chapter: *Words of the Fighting Forces (A Lexicon of Military Terms; Phrases & Terms of Argot, Cant, Jargon & Slang Used by the Armed Forces of the United States of America)*. This work, which exists only in manuscript form, was researched, compiled, and arranged by Clinton A. Sanders and Joseph W. Blackwell, Jr., and completed in September 1942. It was prepared under the auspices of the Language Section of the Military Intelligence Service, located in the Whitehall Building on Battery Place in New York.

The original 495-page, four-volume typescript was found in the Pentagon library. It does not appear in other card catalogues, in bibliographies, or in books on World War II. It is quite likely that the copy in the Pentagon is the only copy.

To say that this is a major discovery is not to overstate the case. It is a first-rate compilation created during the war, apparently for the use of a small group of officers. It "is dedicated to the fighting men of our forces on land, sea and in the air."

It then moves to a disclaimer: "This compilation is offered to the United States War Department without fee or reward, obligation or legal responsibility as a contribution to the war effort."

The introduction offers an overview of the work:

> *Words of the Fighting Forces* is a dictionary of military lingo, specialized language, argot, cant, jargon and slang used by American fighting men, including a supplement of military terms. We hope that this shall not be classed as "just another slang dictionary," but a volume characteristic in general design, profitableness to some valuable end, a scholarly preparation and up-to-date information and accuracy. In this volume it will be found that both the English spellings in common usage in the United States and conventional English spellings are recognized.
>
> Specialists have been located who have generously donated large blocks of terms.
>
> Terms which are found to overlap in one branch of the service running into another have been classified as general usage and are not listed with a classification code. Terms which have distinctive meaning and belong to a particular branch of the service have been listed with a classification code.
>
> There are terms appearing herein that will no doubt "shock" the clergy, appeaser, isolationist and puritan. We offer no apology nor have we deleted a term or terms because of what we feared such a group would do or say. These terms are part of a picturesque and living language of men who live close to earth and closer to death, words of men who fight the battles of free men for our America and her Allies on remote and distant battlefields, who man our ships in dangerous seas, and fight up there on high.

For convenience, and because of the importance of this source to this chapter, references to *Words of the Fighting Forces* will be by title only.

On to the slang, with the note that this is the first war to see the large-scale introduction of initialisms and acronyms. While it can be argued that such terminology is not slang in the traditional sense of the word, it is hard to imagine a slang portrait of this war that did not include G.I., WAC, and the sound of A.A. fire.

★ ☆ A ☆ ★

A.A. Antiaircraft; one of the war's most persistent initialisms. It was commonly used in the expression "A.A. fire."

A.B. (1) An able-bodied seaman. (2) An "area bird" (a cadet walking a punishment tour in the area of the barracks).

A.B.C.D. America, Britain, China, and the Dutch East Indies; used in referring to the combined forces of these powers in the western Pacific.

able. The letter A, in the official communications code. The complete alphabet was Able, Baker, Charlie, Dog, Easy, Fox, George, How, Item, Jig, King, Love, Mike, Nan, Oboe, Peter, Queen, Roger, Sugar, Tare, Uncle, Victor, William, X-ray, Yoke, and Zebra. (In the Navy, A, I, N, O, and P were represented by Affirm, Interrogatory, Negat, Option, and Prep.) See ACK-ACK for the British alphabet.

above the salt. Any rank above that of ordinary seaman.

ack-ack. Antiaircraft fire. This bit of British slang was picked up by the Americans. The British Library of Information gave this explanation for the term: Radio communications required an alphabet code for words that had to be spelled out. In the British code, "ack" stood for A; thus, "ack-ack" ("A.A.") stood for antiaircraft fire.

The complete alphabet in the British communications code was Ack, Beer, Charlie, Don, Edward, Freddy, George, Harry, Ink, John, King, London, Monkey, Nuts, Orange, Pip, Queen, Robert, Sugar, Tock, Uncle, Victor, William, X-ray, Yorker, and Zebra. The British used their alphabet for the first three years of the war, then switched to the American alphabet for the duration and beyond. See **able** for the American alphabet.

acorn cracker. A rustic.

acre-foot. A rustic; a person with large feet. In irrigation, an acre-foot is the amount of water covering one acre to a depth of one foot (43,560 cubic feet).

Adam with an anchor / Adam with a dead battery / Adam with a dead pan / Adam with a flickering flame / Adam with a frozen puss / Adam with a sour puss. A married man; a cold, unresponsive man; a gloomy, dull man.

A-day. The code name for the day set for the landing on Leyte, in the Philippines.

A.D.C. Alaska Defense Command; known to many of the soldiers who served in it as "all damn confusion."

admiral of the Swiss navy. A self-important person.

admiral's watch. A good sleep.

after Tokyo. A slogan adopted by sailors in the Pacific Fleet, signifying their belief that Tokyo should be the Navy's first objective (according to *Newsweek* of April 13, 1942).

A.G. An adjutant general.

agony buggy / agony bus / agony chariot / agony crate / agony hack / agony wagon. An ambulance.

air can. A bomb when dropped from an aircraft.

air canary. See **air Jane.**

airedale. An airplane handler on an aircraft carrier; from the name of a breed of dogs.

air goose. An amphibian airplane; mostly a Marine Corps term.

airgraph mail. Letters written on specially prepared blanks and photographically reduced in size by microfilming. The films were flown to Washington, enlarged by the War Department, and then forwarded to the addressees. The use of airgraph mail was not mandatory, but it saved shipping hundreds of tons of regular mail overseas. Airgraph mail was also known as "V-mail."

air hawk. A combat pilot.

air hog. One who flies at every opportunity.

air Jane. A female aviator; a pilot assigned to fly aircraft to combat areas (also called a "ferry patrol" pilot), as opposed to a combat pilot (invariably a man). Another name for an air Jane was "air canary."

air Lizzie. An airplane manufactured by the Ford Motor Company; an allusion to the "tin Lizzy" (Model-T Ford motorcar).

air merchant. A talkative person.

air rock. A disturbance of the air.

airstrip. A hurriedly prepared landing strip, usually for fighter planes (according to *Newsweek* of December 7, 1942).

airtorial. An editorial on aviation.

albatross. Chicken—roasted, broiled, or stewed.

Al K. Hall. Alcohol.

all-American chump. A stupid person.

all guts. A fat person; a person of great courage.

all hands. Everybody; all the members of a squad, company, etc. The term derives from the traditional Navy call, "All hands on deck."

all hot and bothered. Angered; emotional; lustful; passionate.

alligator. A kind of amphibious armed vehicle, of American manufacture, designed for landing cargo and personnel; a landing barge. The command used to land these barges was, "Beach the 'gators."

alligator bait. Fried liver.

all in the wind. Wavering (i.e., as uncertain as the weather).

all-out. With full vigor, determination, or enthusiasm. According to *American*

Speech of February 1941, it came to be used in such phrases as "the struggle still may be far short of the 'all out' air warfare to come"; "the twelfth raid since Germany began her 'all-out' assaults on London"; and so on. "Total," as a synonym of "all-out," is usually applied to activities on a larger scale (e.g., "all-out battle" but "total war").

all-outer. An advocate of an all-out policy (as of aid to Great Britain or of national defense).

all the aces. First-rate; excellent. The term derives from the game of poker, which was ubiquitous among American forces.

all the whole cheese. A self-important person.

all wool and a yard wide. First-rate; excellent.

almond-eye. An oriental.

alphabet job. An easy assignment or task; a government civilian job. The term alludes to the many New Deal and wartime agencies known by acronyms or initialisms rather than by their full names.

American Club. The American fighting forces (not to be confused with an American League baseball team).

AMGOT / AMG. An allied military government of occupied territory. According to A. Marjorie Taylor, in *The Language of World War II* (1948), the first AMGOT was set up by British and American armies in Sicily in July 1943.

The term was shortened to AMG on August 25, 1943, after it was discovered that *amgot* was an unprintable word in Turkish (according to *The New York Times* of August 26, 1943).

ammo. Ammunition.

ammunition wife. A mistress.

amphibious operations. Military operations involving the combined efforts of land and sea forces.

anchor. A spouse.

Andy Gump. A person with a small chin and a prominent nose; from the cartoon character of the same name.

angel. A thousand feet in aircraft altitude. The term is radar code; thus, the phrase "bandit at four angels" would refer to an enemy aircraft (see BANDIT) at four thousand feet.

angel factory. (1) A theological seminary. (2) An aviation plant employing females.

angels of Bataan. The Army nurses who served in the Bataan campaign. Until the liberation of Manila, they endured three years of fearful misery as prisoners of the Japanese.

angel's scream / angel's whisper. A bugle call.

ank. (1) An anchor. (2) To anchor.

ankle chokers. Narrow-bottomed Army-issue trousers.

Ann. The *Anopheles* mosquito (according to *Newsweek* of October 23, 1944). The insect carries malaria, and the Army conducted a drastic campaign against it.

answer the last call / answer the last muster / answer the last roll / answer the last roll call. To be killed; to die.

answer to a she-gal's dream. A male member of the armed forces.

anti-gas heater. A gas mask; an Army term.

antipersonnel mine. A bomb that sprayed a wide area with shrapnel. The weapon, introduced by the Germans in the fall of 1939, was seen as horrific, and the term itself served as anti-German propaganda. The December 1942 issue of *Reader's Digest* introduced many Americans to the term as a description of a Nazi instrument whose chief feature was an arrangement whereby the mine, on being tripped, was boosted out of the ground to about the height of a man's waist before exploding, in order to inflict maximum harm.

Anzac. Australian and New Zealand Army Corps; a nickname given to members of this corps. See also under World War I.

Anzio amble. A fast shuffle from one shelter to the next. The term undoubtedly originated on the Anzio beachhead where, according to *American Speech* of April 1945, Americans discovered "Anzio anxiety" (jitters), "Anzio foot" (when the scream of a shell suddenly makes you change course), and "Anzio walk" (jumping and twitching to dodge shells).

A.P.C. Armor-piercing cap (an armor-piercing artillery or tank cannon shell).

ape with a frozen pan / ape with a sour puss. A gloomy, dull man. See also the terms beginning with "Adam."

apron. A girl or a woman.

apron chaser / apron crazy / apron dizzy / apron jumper / apron screwy. One fond of women; a seducer.

apron with a flickering flame. A cold or unresponsive woman.

apron with a nip. A virgin; a virtuous, respectable woman. The significance of the term "nip" in this context has been lost, but it could have something to do with old criminal cant in which "nip" alluded to the ability to open a locked door.

apron with round heels. A woman of loose morals.

A-ration. A balanced ration for troops in the field, issued by regular mess units.

Arctic whiteout. A condition in far northern flying in which land features are camouflaged by snow and ice; earth and sky blend, and the horizon and all landmarks disappear.

arm dropper. An artilleryman who gives the signal to fire the gun, by dropping his raised arm.

armed to the teeth. Well equipped with firearms; alert; fully prepared; awake to danger.

armored heifer. Condensed milk; from the fact that it comes in a metal can.

Army Bible. Army regulations.

Army brat. A child of an Army officer.

Army chicken. Franks and beans.

Army dick. A military policeman.

Army lid. A radio operator. According to *Newsweek* of March 10, 1941, Army lids were so-called because they "talk through their hats." (In the general slang of the era, one's hat was a "lid.")

Army-stitch Day. Armistice Day.

Army strawberries. Prunes.

Army worm. An informer; one who betrays a trust.

A.R.'s. Army regulations.

arsenal wear. Government-issue lingerie for women in the armed forces; not the kind that could be bought in a department store.

asbestos Joe / asbestos papa. A Navy seaman whose duty is to wear an insulated asbestos suit so he can make rescues in case of fire aboard an aircraft carrier. Sometimes he was simply known as "the man in asbestos."

as close as five minutes to eleven / as close as twenty minutes to eight. In love.

ash can. (1) A shell. (2) A bomb. (3) A depth charge used in antisubmarine warfare. All of these meanings derive from the shape and heft of the large garbage cans used to haul ashes.

ash-can patrol. Minelayer units; from the shape of the mines.

asparagus bed. (1) An antitank obstacle; from its resemblance to the tangle of an asparagus patch. (2) An obstacle to airborne landings. See also ROMMEL'S ASPARAGUS.

asparagus stick. A submarine's periscope.

asthma. A company wit; so-called because he's full of wheezes (jokes).

A.T. Antitank.

atabrine. A synthetic antimalarial drug used in lieu of quinine. The wide use of the drug was the occasion of much World War II humor, as in this excerpt from *Atabrine Times* (1946), the self-published memoir of a soldier known only as Kilroy:

> Atabrine; the army's cure for gastritis, corn-beefitis, goldbrickitis, neuritis, neuralgia, insomnia, athlete's foot, pregnancy, and incidentally, malaria. It doesn't really cure athlete's foot though.
>
> In New Guinea everything was dedicated to Atabrine. It was Atabrine Night Club, Atabrine Diamond, Atabrine Boxing Ring, Atabrine Mess Hall, Atabrine Juke Joint, and many other tributes to its worthy suppressive and therapeutic powers. In front of our tent hung this sign:
>
> ATABRINE ASYLUM
> 10 cents cover charge to keep out riff-raff and other insects

at low water. Short of funds.

atomic age. The period that began on August 6, 1945, with the bombing of Hiroshima.

Aunt Jemima. A high explosive mixed with flour and smuggled to Chinese saboteurs behind the Japanese lines; from the name of a popular brand of pancake mix.

awkward squad. Men who require extra instruction at drill.

A.W.O.L. Absent Without Official Leave; commonly pronounced "a-wall." See also under the Civil War and under World War I.

Axis rat / Axis snake / Axis water-moccasin. A German submarine.

axle grease. Butter.

★ ☆ **B** ☆ ★

B.A. Busted aristocrat (a cadet officer reduced to the ranks). The term originated at West Point.

baby. Mustard; from its resemblance to that which comes out of the hind end of an infant.

baby carriage. A machine-gun cart.

baby elephant. A large, gray corrugated-iron shelter used by the Army.

B-ache / bellyache. To complain.

backbiter. A tattletale.

backbone. Moral courage; one's chief support; a mainstay.

back in your hole. Return to your room or barracks.

back patter / back scratcher / back slapper. An obsequious person; a sycophant.

badgy. Underage (referring to an enlistee).

Baedeker invasion. The invasion of Sicily; from the fact that troops were issued booklets about the island. The famous Baedeker series of travel guides had been popular for decades.

Baedeker raids. Certain German air raids on Great Britain. The phrase appeared in the English press on April 29 or 30, 1942, after German officials stated that the Luftwaffe, in attacking such cities as Bath and Norwich, was deliberately aiming to destroy buildings of high historic interest (i.e., those listed in the Baedeker guidebooks). According to *American Notes and Queries* of December 1942, the official German bulletin described these raids as reprisals for allied raids on the German cities of Cologne and Lübeck.

baffle paint. Camouflage.

bagoose. Good. Used by troops in the South Pacific, the term is explained in *Atabrine Times* (1946), by the pseudonymous Kilroy: "If the word 'bagoose' were eliminated from the Malayan dialect, it would be completely lost. The literal translation means good, but it has more uses than our O.K. Anything not bagoose was 'tita bagoose.' Soon we were bagoosing everything and they were saying O.K. Joe."

bags of mystery. Sausages.

bail out. To parachute out of an airplane; by extension, to get out of a situation (e.g., to bail out on a blind date).

bail-out ration. The smallest and most compact of all emergency rations (composed of a bar of D-RATION chocolate, dextrose tablets, concentrated bouillon, and chewing gum). It weighed only 8¼ ounces and would fit into the shirt pocket of an airman or a paratrooper.

baka / baka bomb. A Japanese KAMI-KAZE (suicide) airplane; a pilot of a kamikaze airplane; a bomb carried by a kamikaze airplane. The term is from the Japanese *baka* ("stupid"; "crazy"; "foolish"). Other nicknames were "booby wagon," "loony Joe," and "highpockets" (according to *Newsweek* of May 7, 1945).

bakehead. (1) A stupid person. (2) A member of a ship's engineering crew (whose brains were "baked" in the sweltering conditions below decks).

baksheesh. An air mission on which no enemy opposition is encountered.

Balbo. A flight formation involving hundreds of aircraft; from the name of the Italian general Italo Balbo, who in 1933 led a huge flight of airplanes from Italy to the United States and back. A Balbo is often seen at the end of a movie about the war.

baldheaded. Cleared for action (said of a ship's decks). See also GO IN BALD-HEADED.

ball of fire. An energetic person.

balloon barrage. Balloons anchored near land objectives or attached to ships in convoy, to snag attacking aircraft. Such obstacles were also called "old floppies" and "flying elephants."

balloonist. A merchant who charges excessive prices for his goods.

balloon juice. Helium.

balls of fire. See FOO-FIGHTERS.

Baltimore steak. Calf's liver.

bam. A "broad-assed Marine" (i.e., a woman Marine).

Bamboo Fleet. The Navy fleet assigned to the waters near the Philippines prior to December 7, 1941.

bamboo juice. Wine; mostly used in the South Pacific.

bandit. An enemy aircraft. See also **angel.**

bang it out. To fight; to quarrel.

bang-up. (1) Excellent; first-rate. (2) To do violence. (3) To inject drugs.

banjo. (1) A short-handled shovel. (2) A bedpan.

bantam. A JEEP.

banzai. An attack cry of the Japanese; interpreted as a desperate or suicidal cry during the war. Robert Hendrickson writes in *Encyclopedia of Word and Phrase Origins* (1987):

> Before World War II, when the Japanese Navy and those of the Western powers were on good terms, banzai parties, or shore parties, were held where seamen from Japan and other nations mingled. The expression derives from the general Japanese felicitation, banzai, which has been variously interpreted as meaning "May you live forever" or "May you live 1,000 years." During World War II, the once pleasant banzai was shouted by Japanese soldiers making bayonet charges.

baptized by fire. To have been under enemy fire for the first time; to have received one's first wounds.

B.A.R. Browning Automatic Rifle. The weapon was invented by John M. Browning (1854–1926), of Ogden, Utah. According to Robert Hendrickson, in *Encyclopedia of Word and Phrase Origins* (1987):

> The BAR, an air-cooled weapon capable of firing 200–350 rounds per minute, was generally assigned one to a squad. It is said that none of the prolific Browning's designs ever failed. These included the light and heavy Browning machine guns, the caliber .45 pistol, the caliber .50 machine gun, the 37mm. aircraft gun, and a number of shotguns and repeating rifles. Browning took out his first patent in 1879, on a breech-loading, single-shot rifle that the Winchester Arms Company purchased. After his entry into the military field, the U.S. Army relied almost exclusively on Browning's automatic weapons.

bark. (1) To graze the skin. (2) To complain about an assignment or duty. (3) To cough.

barker. (1) A heavy artillery gun. (2) One who complains. (3) A cougher.

barking of the dogs of war / barking of the sea dogs / barking of the war dogs. Gunfire; a bombardment.

barracks bag. A bag used to hold one's clothing and other possessions.

barracks bags. Morning-after bags under one's eyes.

barracks lawyer. An enlisted man well-versed in Army regulations and able to use them to advantage.

barracks 13. A guardhouse. According to *Slanguage Dictionary of American Slang* (1942), it was where "they lock up bad little boys."

barrack wacky. See **shell shock,** under World War I.

barrel. A cylinder of an airplane engine.

basin crop. A close haircut. The term almost certainly derives from the notion of putting a bowl or basin over one's head and cutting off all the hair that shows.

bathtub. (1) A motorcycle sidecar. (2) A ball turret.

battery acid. Coffee.

bat the breeze. To talk.

battle bowler. A steel helmet; from the bowler, a domed hat favored by Englishmen.

battle breakfast. Steak and eggs; a Navy term. *Fighting Talk* (1942), by Francis Raymond Meyer, contains this passage: "This heavy menu is actually served before a ship's company goes into battle. After eating a battle breakfast, all hands man battle stations with range finders and gun pointers warming up with orders from the fire control station."

battle the watch. To do one's best in difficult circumstances.

battlewagon. A battleship.

battling bastards of Bataan. Veterans of the battle of Bataan, in the Philippines (1942).

battling sons of the air. Airmen.

bayonet course. Hospital treatment for venereal diseases. "Bayonet" refers to the male member.

bazooka. An antitank gun. This new weapon was immediately seen as a godsend in disabling German tanks. It used the rocket method of propulsion and was operated by two men: one man loaded and aimed it, and the other, who fired it, carried it on his shoulder. Army officials declared it capable of destroying any enemy tank, according to an article in *Popular Mechanics* for August 1943.

The name came from its similarity in appearance to the freak musical instrument known as the bazooka, which had been invented by comedian Bob Burns (the "Arkansas Traveler") and used by him on the radio in the late 1930s. According to Stuart Berg Flexner, in *I Hear America Talking* (1976), the name was bestowed on the weapon in 1943 by Major Zeb Hastings. Burns later compared his instrument to the weapon and noted "both have a more or less devastating effect."

b-bag. A column in the soldiers' newspaper *Stars and Stripes* where letters from soldiers were printed. It was a good place in which to air grievances and "bitch" about the war and Army life.

B.C. Battery commander (in the field artillery).

beachcomb. To search for female companionship.

beach comber. A sailor on shore leave. This use derives from the earlier meaning of one who lives idly on the seashore.

beached. Without funds; mostly a Navy term. It alludes to a ship run aground and rendered useless.

beachhead. (1) A beach where invading forces land. (2) A fortified position on a beach.

beachmaster. (1) An officer in charge of logistics during an invasion. (2) A sailor very fond of women.

beach pounder. A member of the Coast Guard (i.e., one who patrols, or "pounds," the shore).

beacon. A sailor's home.

beam. (1) A constant unidirectional radio signal transmitted from an airfield to guide pilots. (2) Any correct course; sanity. See also OFF THE BEAM and ON THE BEAM.

bean. (1) One's head. (2) One dollar, in coin or paper. (3) To strike on the head.

bean gun. A rolling kitchen.

bean jockey. A table waiter, on KITCHEN POLICE duty (see under World War I).

bean king. An Army mess officer.

beans. A mess sergeant; a commissary.

bean shooter. An officer in charge of the commissary.

bean spiller. An informer; a telltale.

Beantown special. Boston baked beans.

bear cat. A hard-fighting soldier.

bearded lady. A searchlight with diffuse rays.

beast. A cadet in preliminary training at West Point.

beat all creation. To be excellent.

beat a retreat. To withdraw.

beat one's gums. To talk a lot.

beat someone's ears in. To do violence; to assault.

beat the breeze. (1) To talk; to boast. (2) To travel with great speed.

beat the can off of / beat the devil out of / beat the hell out of / beat the sap out of / beat the tar out of / beat to a frazzle / beat to a jelly / beat to a mummy. To do violence.

beat the mill. To type. A "mill" was a typewriter.

beat-up. Damaged; worn out; of unimpressive appearance; completely exhausted.

beat up on. To do violence.

beaut. (1) A beautiful woman. (2) Something first-rate; something excellent.

become a gold star in mother's window. To be killed in action. This allowed one's mother to become a "Gold Star Mother" and place a symbolic gold star in her window.

bedpan commando. A medical corpsman.

beef. (1) A tedious or annoying thing or person. (2) To complain loudly.

beef boat. A cattle boat; a supply ship.

beep. A jeep.

before the wind. (1) Out of debt. (2) Moving in the direction of the wind; moving by the impulse of the wind.

behavior report. A reply to a love letter.

belcher. An informer; a telltale.

bell tent. A conical Army tent.

belly cousin. A man who has slept with a woman you slept with. The term is of British origin.

belly landing. An aircraft landing without the benefit of wheels (i.e., to land on the belly of the aircraft).

belly tank. An auxiliary gasoline tank under the belly or wing of a plane. When empty, it could be released if necessary to lighten the load.

below the salt. Of inferior rank; a Navy term.

bend a bend / bend a corner / bend 'er. To round a curve or corner at great speed.

bend the throttle. To fly an airplane or drive a vehicle at very high speed.

benzine board. A board of Army officers having authority to demote other officers. "Benzine" is an old generic term for a number of highly combustible fuels and solvents; thus, the benzine board would light a fire under the demoted officers.

benzine wagon. An automobile; a truck.

better fraction. One's wife; a play on the reference to one's wife as one's "better half."

B-girl. Bar girl (a woman who encourages soldiers and sailors to drink; she was often paid a commission by the bar). In *I Hear America Talking* (1976), Stuart Berg Flexner notes that this term was first recorded in print in 1937 and got a lot of work during the war.

big America. The United States.

big bean. A person of importance.

Big Ben. The aircraft carrier *Franklin* (named for Benjamin Franklin).

big blue team. A group of regular pilots.

big bow-wow. (1) A regimental sergeant major. (2) An important person.

big boy with a fever. (1) A passionate man. (2) A man with a venereal disease.

big bozo. A corpulent man.

big brawl / big fracas / big mix-up / big row / big rumpus / big show. War.

big bus. A large airplane.

big chump / big cluck / big clunk. A stupid person.

big dame hunter. A philanderer; one fond of women; a play on "big game hunter."

Big E, the. The aircraft carrier *Enterprise*. According to *Newsweek* of October 22, 1945, sailors of the *Essex* began using the nickname for their newer, larger carrier and calling the *Enterprise* "the Little E"; *Enterprise* men (proud of their ship's achievements, definitely not in the "little" class) beat them up.

big friend. A bomber.

big girl with the torch. The Statue of Liberty.

big guy. An important man; a corpulent man.

big Jeep. A large bomber.

big John. A recruit; one who is in basic training.

bigot. Highly secret information (e.g., invasion plans); a code word.

big set-to / big show. A major engagement.

big ship. A large airplane; a bomber.

Big Three. The United States, Great Britain, and the Soviet Union.

big ticket. An honorable discharge.

big wheel. Anyone with a little authority.

bilge rat. A member of a ship's engineering crew in the Navy. "Bilge" is a traditional naval term for dirty water, specifically that found at the bottom of the ship where the engineering crew works.

bimbo dough. Money for a date.

bimbo dust. Face powder.

bimbo nuts. Fond of girls.

bingo. A close antiaircraft shot.

birdboat. An aircraft carrier.

bird in the monkey suit. An aviator.

bird of paradise. A discharge button (because it depicts an eagle at rest). See also RUPTURED DUCK.

birdseed. A silly or stupid person.

bird's-eye view. A view from the air.

biscuit blast. Damage caused to teeth when biting down on the rock-hard "dog biscuit" in the Army's K-ration.

biscuit gun. An imaginary weapon, said to be used to shoot food to novice pilots who are having a hard time making a landing. The term was commonly used in flying schools.

bite the dust. To be defeated; to be killed in action; to be wounded; to be shamed; to be mortified.

blab off. To talk out of turn.

blackbird. A black; a black aviator.

Black Cat. The Catalina Flying Boat (a Navy aircraft); so-called because of its black paint and nocturnal habits.

black hawk. The black Army necktie (as opposed to the khaki necktie).

black market. (1) The business of illegal transactions (including the sale of stolen goods). This term first cropped up in European dispatches in 1939, referring to the practice of hoarding goods and selling them at inflated prices. In *I Hear America Talking* (1976), Stuart Berg Flexner notes that the term had seen limited use during World War I, when it entered the English language as a literal translation of the German *Schwarzmarkt*.

(2) An illegal market in merchandise declared "frozen" (i.e., available only at a fixed price in the regulated market). It was in this context that the term became a household word in the United States; black markets were seen as a very real menace to law-abiding Americans.

blackout. (1) An extinction of lights as protection against enemy aircraft. The blackout in London was lifted in April 1945, after 2,061 nights of dangerous and distressing darkness. In the United States, practice blackouts were held at intervals so that people would be prepared in case the real thing became necessary. (2) Unconsciousness, especially from the centrifugal force created in an aircraft. (3) Long underwear.

black strap. Thick black coffee (i.e., coffee that seems as viscous as black-strap molasses).

Black Umbrella. The "all Negro" 99th Pursuit Squadron of the Army Air Corps; so-called because of their protective role.

blanket drill. An afternoon nap.

blankets. Hotcakes.

blanket soldier. A military policeman; so-called because his other names are unfit for publication.

blanket wife. A prostitute.

blank file. A stupid soldier.

blast. To shoot; to kill.

blaze away at. To shoot at.

blind flying. (1) Flying by instruments only. (2) Going on a blind date.

blind pig. (1) A place where liquor is illegally sold. (2) A miniature tank packed with twenty-five pounds of TNT, developed by the Crosby Research Foundation in Pasadena, California. The idea was to turn such machines loose on a battlefield. (They were featured in the *PM Daily Picture Magazine* for July 21, 1942.)

blip. An "echo" on a radar screen; from the sound made when the image flashes.

blister foot. An infantryman.

blister mechanic. A hospital corpsman.

blitz. (1) The German bombing of Britain, from August 1940 until the end of May 1941; from the German *Blitzkrieg* ("lightning war"). (2) An air patrol. (3) A German. (4) To attack a task in the manner of a blitzkrieg (e.g., to blitz the barracks in a quick cleanup). (5) To hurry.

Blitz—From the Horror of War to Football

A number of words have made a quick transfer from war to civilian life, and "blitz" was one, as indicated by a story in the San Francisco *Examiner* of July 22, 1941:

FOOTBALL CLAIMS CREDIT FOR BLITZ

NEW ORLEANS, July 21 (AP)—America's football coaches, says one of them, would know how to stop a blitzkrieg—because they invented it!

> "Those fellows in Europe are just doing what we've been doing for years," declared Tulane's coach "Red" Dawson, sitting before an electric fan in his office.
>
> He diagrammed tactics used in the Russo-German war, and compared them with plays he was outlining for his own fall campaign.
>
> "Football used to be a 'war of position,'" he said, "but changed to a 'war of movement' before you ever heard of a blitzkrieg. . . . Your downfield blockers operate just as the advance units of panzer divisions."

blitz baby. A child born in Britain during the German BLITZ.

blitz bachelor. A British man who sent his wife and children to the country to avoid the bombing of London during the BLITZ. Because of the number of American males stationed outside of London, this term had a certain relevance.

blitz buggy. A reconnaissance car, especially a midget truck manufactured by the Ford Motor Company for the Army.

Blitz Day. Hawaiian name for December 7, 1941 (the date of the Japanese attack on Pearl Harbor), according to *Time* of December 19, 1949.

blitzed out. Forced to leave because of damage caused to premises during the BLITZ.

blitz flu. Influenza that floors its victim and then suddenly disappears.

blitz it. To polish or spruce up with vigor and speed. According to sources of the time, the expression is from the trade name of a brass-polishing cloth, rather than directly from the German BLITZ.

blitzkrieg. An attack by powerful forces at lightning speed. This German term appeared in *The Nation* of September 10, 1938, with the definition "lightning stroke." The word captured the popular imagination and appeared in innumerable short-lived forms (e.g., "airblitz," "blitzlizzies," and "blitzrhythm").

blitz wagon. A staff car.

blitzy. Showing the marks of a BLITZ.

blob stick / blob stock. A simulated bayonet used in training.

blockbuster. An aerial bomb large enough to knock down a whole block of houses. The term originated in Britain, where "block" had a different meaning. Writing in *American Speech* for December 1944, Robert Trout of CBS explained: "Many Americans who are accustomed to this word do not realize that the 'block' is not an American city block, but a large modern building. As the British say, 'A block of flats,' or 'A block of offices.'"

Blockbuster

Like BLITZ, "blockbuster" made a quick entrance into civilian life, as demonstrated by the following examples.

If Congress does not put some pay-as-you-go income tax payment plan into operation before next March 15th, there is likely to be a nationwide explosion which will punch at the foundations of our entire federal income tax structure.

> The present income tax collection system has become a time bomb of block-buster proportions, and it is set to go off next March 15th.
> —"Danger: Time Bomb, An Editorial," in *Collier's* (January 2, 1943)
>
> "The Brazilian blockbuster—Aurora Miranda."
> —Orson Welles, on his radio show (May 10, 1944)

blockbusting. Scathing; annihilating.

blond and sweet. Coffee with cream and sugar.

blood. Catsup.

blood, sweat, and tears. All one's effort or resources. In a speech in the House of Commons on May 13, 1940, after receiving a commission from the king to form a new administration, Winston Churchill said: "I would say to the House, as I said to those who have joined this government: 'I have nothing to offer but blood, toil, tears, and sweat.'"

blood bank. A place where blood and plasma is stored for use in transfusions. In January 1941 the American Red Cross announced plans for a giant blood bank that would furnish thousands of liters of plasma to the British Red Cross for the treatment of war victims.

bloodbath. A massacre; from the German *blutbad*.

blood wagon. An ambulance.

Bloody Nose Ridge. A place of carnage. In *Marines at War* (1961), Russell Davis writes: "Old Marines talk of Bloody Nose Ridge as though it were one, but I remember it as a series of crags, ripped bare of all standing vegetation, peeled down to the rotted coral, rolling in smoke, crackling with heat and stinking of wounds and death."

bloomers. Gun covers; a Navy term.

blotter machine. A machine gun.

blotto. Dead. Before the war, this meant "dead drunk."

blouse. To tuck the bottoms of one's pants into rubber bands—generally, condoms knotted at the ends—above the first buckle of one's combat boots. This made the trousers puff out at the bottom (an effect called "blousing").

blow job. A jet-propelled aircraft. The term figured in several long-recalled headlines, such as the postwar "First Blow Job in Japan" (in the English-language daily *Japan Times*, published in Tokyo).

blow one's top. To lose one's temper.

blue job. The Navy; from the traditional color of the Navy uniform. See also BROWN JOB.

blue letter mail. Letters that soldiers did not want their immediate superiors to censor. Such letters were handled by the Base Censorship Detachment of Military Intelligence, and soldiers could send two of these a month (according to *Newsweek* of March 27, 1944).

boar's nest. An untidy bunk and bunk area.

bobtail. (1) A dishonorable discharge. The allusion is to the former practice of cutting out the portion of a discharge certificate that referred to "service honorable and faithful." (2) A truck tractor without a trailer in tow.

bobtail hotel. An Army disciplinary barracks.

body snatcher. A stretcher bearer.

bogey. An unidentified enemy aircraft, in radar code.

bog pocket. A tightwad.

boilermakers. An Army band. Elbridge Colby defines the term in *Army Talk: A Familiar Dictionary of Soldier Speech* (1943): "The service's affectionate descriptive term for the average army band. Whether the music is good or bad, they are 'boilermakers' just the same."

bolo. An inept marksman. See BOLO SQUAD, under the Spanish-American War era, and BOLO, under the Vietnam War.

bolognas. Automobile or truck tires; from their plump, sausagelike quality.

bombardier. One who releases bombs at a target, especially from aircraft. The word "bomb" had once been synonymous with "shell."

bombardier's dream. To sink an enemy battleship, submarine, or aircraft carrier.

bomb bay. That portion of the fuselage in an airplane where the bombs are lodged.

bomber's moon. A moon full enough to give light for bombing operations.

bombs on. Bombs are aboard; said of an airplane.

bomb-up. To load an aircraft with bombs.

bomphlet. A propaganda leaflet dropped by air in enemy territory. The word was coined by A. P. Herbert, a British author. The term "bomphleteer" was applied to airmen engaged in dropping such leaflets in the early days of the war.

bone. To study.

bone bootlick. To flatter; to curry favor.

boob. (1) A stupid person. (2) A Navy recruit.

boob squad. A squad of newly recruited soldiers.

booby trap. Any concealed device used by the Germans or Japanese to kill allied soldiers. Booby traps took many forms, one being mines placed under the bodies of dead or wounded soldiers, which would explode when the bodies were moved. Here is how they were described in a 1944 CBS radio dispatch: "And then there are the booby-traps. Maybe you see a bottle of wine lying beside a bombed building, but you don't touch it. And maybe there is a tempting apple tree beside the road . . . but you leave that tree alone too because it might blow up in your face if you pulled a branch down."

booby-trap. To fit with booby traps.

boodle. Cake, candy, ice cream, etc. A "boodle fight" is a party at which boodle is served. The term seems to derive from "kit and caboodle." See also under the Spanish-American War era.

boodle bag. A kit or Army haversack into which one stuffs boodle.

boom dust. Dynamite; black powder (an explosive).

boom wagon. A truck transporting high explosives.

boondockers. Combat boots or field shoes used in the BOONDOCKS (see under the Spanish-American War era).

boot. A Marine or Navy recruit. See also under the Spanish-American War era and under World War I.

boot camp. The place and process of basic training in the Navy and the Marine Corps.

boot hill. Hill 89 (the last stronghold of the defeated Japanese army on Okinawa); so-called by Colonel M. M. Finn, commander of the 32nd Regiment of the 7th Division, because so many booted Japanese feet could be seen sticking up from the soil (as told in *American Notes and Queries* of June 1945).

bootle. A WAVES recruit.

bootleg. Coffee of an inferior grade; akin to "bootleg" whiskey.

bootlick. To flatter; to curry favor.

bore an ape / bore a nip / bore a nippo. To shoot a Japanese. The derogatory terms "nip" and "nippo" are derived from the Japanese name for Japan, Nippon.

bore a ratzy. To shoot a German. "Ratzy" was a blend of "rat" and "Nazi."

boreconstrictor. A bore; an unpopular person.

bore war. The period of comparative inaction on the western front from the outbreak of war in September 1939 until the German offensive in May 1940; a pun on "Boer War."

borrowed brass. False courage inspired by drugs or drink.

bosom chums. Lice.

bottle baby. A woman with dyed blond hair; from the fact that hair dye comes in a bottle.

bottled sunshine. Beer.

bottleneck. An impasse in production or in the movement of men or matériel. There was some British fascination with the term, as evidenced by this question and answer from a 1944 issue of *Punch*: "What exactly are bottle-necks? Are they really numerous? The term bottle-neck is a useful Americanism. It means a temporary stoppage of production caused by a shortage, a surplus or a sufficiency of supplies. It is such a useful American-ism that journalists can always find a suitable excuse for its use."

bottlenecker. One who obstructs na-tional defense.

boudoir. A squad tent; from the French *boudoir* (a woman's dressing room or bedroom; itself derived from the French *bouder* ["to pout"]).

bought guts. False courage inspired by drugs or drink.

boy in blue. A sailor.

boy in brown. A soldier.

Boyington's Bastards. The Black Sheep squadron, under Lieutenant Colo-nel Gregory Boyington, a Marine flying ace.

boy upstairs. A pilot, gunner, or bom-bardier, when in flight.

brace. An extreme position of atten-tion. The term probably originated at West Point. See also BRUSS.

brain gang. The staff of general head-quarters.

brain trust. A group of highly qualified military advisors.

branch. A large functional subdivision of the Army—Infantry, Supply, Transpor-tation, Air Corps, etc.

brass, the. Officers, as a class or caste. Higher-ranking officers were usually called "the big brass." The term derives from the fact that officers' insignias are usually made of brass.

brassed off. See BROWNED OFF.

brass hat. A higher-ranking officer (spe-cifically, one with gold braid on his cap visor).

brass lip echo. A bugle call.

brass looie / brass loot. A second lieutenant.

brass pounder. A radiotelegraph op-erator, who works a brass telegraph key.

B-ration. A balanced ration for troops in the field, issued by regular mess units. The Army described it as follows: "This ration will correspond as nearly as prac-ticable to the components of Type A field ration, with the exception that nonper-ishable processed and canned products will replace items of a perishable na-ture."

breadbasket. An aerial bomb that combines explosives and incendiaries.

bread sergeant. A private assigned to work as a dining-room orderly, one of his main duties being to slice and serve bread.

break out a flag. To request a loan from a friend in the Navy. A "flag" is a bill, and "break out" is a traditional na-val way of saying "take out of storage."

breaks of the game. Luck, good or bad.

bred to arms. Brought up and educated for the life of a soldier.

bridge ape. A member of the Army Engineer Corps. Among other things, they build bridges and dams.

bridgehead. An offensive or defensive position established at a bridge or at a point where one fords a river.

brief. To instruct with regard to upcoming operations.

briefing room. A room in which pilots are BRIEFED (e.g., they receive their instructions for air raids over enemy territory).

bright-light fellow. One who requests repeated leaves (i.e., one who seeks the bright lights and good times of the city).

broad on fire / broad with a fever. A passionate woman.

broad with a heat wave. A passionate woman; a woman with a venereal disease.

broad with a load of lettuce. A woman of wealth.

broad with a soft conk. A stupid or silly woman; "conk" was common 1930s slang for "head."

broad with canned goods. A virgin.

broad with round heels. A woman of loose morals.

broom ship. A Navy ship that won an efficiency award. Such ships frequently hoisted a broom to the masthead to signify the award.

brown. To curry favor; to BOOTLICK.

browned off. Fed up. According to A. Marjorie Taylor, in *The Language of World War II* (1948), other such phrases included "brassed off" (very fed up) and "cheesed off" (utterly disgusted). "Browned off" originated in the British army in India (c. 1932). "Cheesed off" was probably suggested by "browned off," the link being the brown rind of cheese. "Brassed off" was originally a naval term, derived from the excessive polishing of a ship's brasswork. In the R.A.F., "cheesed off" became the favorite of the three phases. All of these terms were readily adopted by American forces, beginning with those pilots who had frequent contact with their R.A.F. counterparts.

brown job. The Army. This term was extended by the British, who referred to soldiers as "brown jobs." See also BLUE JOB.

brownnose. A soldier or cadet who curries favors; an "ass kisser."

brownout. A partial BLACKOUT.

brushing the bushes. Flying close to the ground.

brush-off club. Men in the armed forces who have been dumped by their girlfriends.

Brush-off Club

EX-DARLING CLUB

The Brush-off Club, which was founded at a U.S. bomber base in India and is fast becoming a global affair, is composed of soldiers whose gals have thrown them over since they got into the army. Local chapters are being organized wherever our troops are stationed. Requirements for membership are: (1) She has married somebody else. (2) She is engaged or "practically engaged" to somebody else. (3) She mentions dates with other guys and doesn't start out "Dearest Darling" any more. (4) The soldier's folks have reported seeing her out with other joes.

There is also a "Pending or Prospective Membership" for the "Just Sweating Member." He doesn't know where the hell he stands but the mail doesn't bring in sugar reports any longer. All members are eligible for the Good Hunting Committee, which convenes as often as two or three men can get leave anywhere females are in evidence. A Corresponding Secretary keeps track of new telephone numbers to exchange among members.

One new member joined the club with particularly high qualifications—a six-page letter from his fiancee back in Texas. In the last paragraph she mentioned casually, "I was married a week ago but my husband won't mind you writing to me once in a while. He's a sailor and very broadminded."

—*Reader's Digest* (September 1943; adapted from *Yank, The Army Weekly*)

bruss. An exaggerated BRACE.

B-2. Unidentified aircraft. According to the New York *Herald Tribune* of September 11, 1944, "B-2" came from the phrase "be too bad if they are not friendly."

bubble dancing. Dishwashing; from the fact that the activity covers one with suds, like a bubble dancer.

buck. To work hard to qualify (e.g., for a higher rank, an assignment, or a transfer); to cram for an examination.

buck for orderly. To give special attention to one's uniform and equipment before going on guard, with a view to competing for the position of orderly for the commanding officer.

buck for Section VIII. To purposely make mistakes or get into trouble; to pretend to be crazy. Such behavior could get a soldier a Section VIII discharge, granted to those unable to perform military duties.

buck passer. One who evades work and responsibility.

buck private. The lowest rank in the Army.

buck sergeant. An ordinary sergeant (as opposed to a staff sergeant, a technical sergeant, etc.).

buck slip. A slip of paper on which certain information is requested from another department or office. The information is usually returned on the same slip. The term almost certainly came from the phrase "pass the buck."

buffalo. A huge, armored amphibious vehicle for carrying soldiers and weapons.

bug. (1) Any solid matter in soup. (2) An Army supply truck. (3) A defect in a machine. (4) A telegraph speed-key. (5) A stupid or silly person. (6) A germ or an illness (as in, "I just came down with a bug").

The "bug" in the machine is discussed by Elbridge Colby in *Army Talk: A Familiar Dictionary of Soldier Speech* (1943):

> Our modern mechanical army is using this word a lot. (No! It has nothing to do with "cooties.") It was brought into the service by the motor hounds, the men of the motor transport schools and the tank school. It is a pure borrowing from civil life. A "bug" is something in the nature of a defect of design or of adjustment in a machine.

bug juice. (1) Gasoline. (2) Whiskey of very poor quality.

bug sender. A telegraph operator using a semiautomatic key-instrument, or BUG (4).

build a stew. To cook a stew.

build a wooden horse. To make an imperfect landing.

built-in head wind. A low cruising speed (said of an airplane); The implication is that the airplane's designer intentionally lowered the cruising speed.

bullhorn. A powerful amplifier on an aircraft carrier, through which orders are given.

bull in the can. Canned corned beef.

bullpen. A military prison yard.

bully beef. Canned meat.

An Ode to Bully Beef

BULLY BEEF

You can eat it with your eyes closed
And a clothespin on your nose.
You can eat it in the mess hall,
Or out where the kunai grows.
You can serve it up in dishes,
Camouflaged beyond belief.
But no matter what you call it,
It will still be Bully Beef.

You can boil it, fry it, stew it,
Serve it cold or piping hot.
You can mix it up with gravy,
Or leave it there to rot.
But no matter how you mix it,
You will always come to grief.
For no matter what you call it,
It will still be Bully Beef.

—*Atabrine Times*, by "Kilroy" (1946)

---

bumble bomb. See BUZZ BOMB.

bumped. To lose one's accommodations or seat to one of a higher rank.

bunk fatigue. Napping on one's bed. The term is a compound—a bunk is a bed, and "fatigue" is an Army term for labor.

bunkie. One who shares a bunk, tent, or other shelter. It was civilian slang adopted by the Army.

Burma Road. The 700-mile road from Burma to China, used as a military supply route. Figuratively, it came to mean any supply route of similar importance.

burn and turn. The game of blackjack.

burned broad / burned hooker / burned hustler / burned quail. A woman with a venereal disease.

burp gun. Practically any type of German automatic or semiautomatic small arms. The term came from the sound made by the weapons.

bus. An aircraft.

bus a town. To fly low near a town.

bushwhack. To ambush; to cheat; to steal; to lie.

bust. To reduce in rank. Usually, being busted meant being reduced to the rank of private.

buster. To fly at normal speed; radar code. "To gate" meant to fly at the greatest speed possible. Such terms were often created more for their ability to be heard over the radio than to make logical sense.

butch. A medical officer; from "butcher."

butcher. (1) A company barber. (2) A doctor.

butcher's bill. A bulletin, or list, of those killed in action.

butcher shop. A hospital.

butt. A remainder. It could refer to the remainder of an enlistment period as well as that of a cigarette or cigar.

butt-end Charlie. A tail gunner in a bomber; also called "tail-end Charlie."

button chopper. A laundry worker; a laundry.

buttoned up. (1) A phrase meaning "orders carried out." In British slang, it meant "thoroughly prepared." (2) Home from a mission and locked up for the night (said of an aircraft). (3) A tank closed to the outside. (4) A ship whose portholes, bulkheads, and companionways are closed to contain damage.

butts on you. A request for a partly smoked cigarette.

buy another star (for the flag). To be fined.

buzz. To fly low and fast over an area.

buzzard. A member of the Army Air Corps.

buzzard meat. Chicken; turkey.

buzz a town. To fly low and fast over a town; by extension, to "do" a town (i.e., to go there and carouse).

buzz bomb. A jet-propelled, one-ton "flying bomb," or "robot bomb," used by the Germans to bomb England and Belgium in 1944. Other synonyms for "buzz bomb" included "bumblebomb," "buzzer," "doodlebug," "dynamite meteor," "Goebbels's gizmo," "whizbang," and "whizzer." Buzz bombs were a major topic in U.S. newspapers and on the radio.

buzzer. A member of the Signal Corps.

by the board. (1) Correct; an Army term. (2) Close to the deck; a Navy term.

by the numbers. In a routine manner; as rehearsed. A. Marjorie Taylor explained the term in *The Language of World War II* (1948): "In training, certain fundamental operations, such as putting on a gas mask, were taught by the numbers—at the count of one, the carrier was unfastened, two the mask was removed, and so forth."

★ ☆ C ☆ ★

cabbage. Money.

cackleberry. An egg; from the fact that chickens cackle.

cadet widow. A young woman popular with several classes of cadets.

cadre. A group of officers and enlisted men who administer and train a new unit.

California strawberries. Prunes.

cam. Camouflage.

camoufleur. One who applies or uses camouflage.

camp strawberries. Beans.

canary. A gas mask; also called a "dicky-bird" and a "nose-bag." The link between the mask and the bird is that canaries are used to warn miners of the presence of gas (the birds die when gas first enters the work area).

C. and S. Clean and sober.

candy wagon. A light truck.

canned morale. A movie.

canned news. A newsreel.

cannibalization. Using parts from one machine to repair another. The term was defined officially as: "Removal, on authority, of parts from major items for the repair of other major items."

Canol. The Canadian oil development project. The word was formed from the abbreviated linking of "Canada" and "oil." The project was initiated early in 1942, when the decision to build the Alcan (a blend of "Alaska" and "Canada") Highway made it feasible.

can opener. (1) A bayonet. (2) A cook. (3) An aircraft equipped to destroy (i.e., open) tanks and other armored vehicles.

Can Opener

Many of the slang terms of the war were moved around the English-speaking world in news accounts. This excerpt from a wire service story in the San Francisco News of April 22, 1943, helped establish one of the meanings of "can opener":

SECRETS OF NEW RAF "CAN-OPENER" PLANES
REVEALED

LONDON, April 22—The secret of the RAF's tank busting planes which have earned the name "Can-Openers" because of their work in North Africa, was officially revealed today.

The "Can-Openers" are Hurricanes designed especially for use against armored vehicles. They carry two 40 mm. guns, one in each wing. The guns are capable of automatic or single shot fire with a shell weighing 2½ pounds.

The gun itself, especially designed for aircraft use, weighs only 320 pounds.

The plane also carries two Browning machine-guns.

cans. Radio headphones; from their resemblance to tin cans.

canteen. (1) A flask carried in the field. (2) A military post exchange, snack bar, or other place where the troops went for refreshment (e.g., the Stage Door Canteen, on Lafayette Square, across from the White House).

canteen check. A credit coupon used at post exchanges.

canteen medal. A stain on one's clothing from food or drink.

canteen soldier. One who wears non-regulation clothing or insignia.

CAP. Civil Air Patrol. It was established under the Office of Civilian Defense on December 9, 1941, with Major General John F. Curry of the Army Air Corps as national commander.

captain's butt. A cigarette less than half smoked; an Army term. See also COR-PORAL'S BUTT.

captain's mouthorgan. A company clerk.

captain's wash. A display of signal pennants.

care boy. A tank driver.

carpet / carpet bombing / carpet raid. A bombing attack that attempts to clear the way for advancing ground troops by laying out exploding bombs like carpet being unrolled.

carpet knight. A soldier who remains at home during a war and does not go into combat.

carrier pigeon. An officer's messenger.

carry a bone in the teeth. To cut through the water making waves of foam about the bow.

carry a heavy load. To be fatigued; to be melancholy.

Casey Jones mission. An air attack against enemy railroad installations. The Casey Jones in question is the train engineer of song and legend.

cash in one's checks / cash one's chips. To die.

cast-iron bathtub. A battleship.

cast the last anchor. To die; to be killed.

cat beer. Milk.

caterpillar club. Those aviators who have had to BAIL OUT in an emergency.

cathead kid. A sailor guarding a mine cable over the cathead, or projecting portion of a ship.

cat house. A garage for a tractor or similar vehicle; from the Caterpillar tractor.

cat jabber. A bayonet.

C.B. Confined to barracks.

ceiling. An upper limit; from the aeronautical use of the term. It was used in reference to the price limits placed on goods by the government, in an attempt to prevent inflation.

Celestial Chicken. A member of the "Flying Tigers" (the American Volunteer Flying Group, attached to the Chinese army).

C.G. (1) Commanding general. (2) Captain of the guard. (3) Coast Guard.

chamber pot. A steel helmet. The helmet is likened to the portable toilet pot of bygone days. Chamber pots (often called "thunder mugs") were used to avoid cold trips to the outhouse in the days before indoor plumbing.

chase guardhouse visitors. To guard prisoners while they are working.

chase the cow. Pass the milk.

chatterbox. A machine gun.

chatter of the guns. Gunfire; a bombardment.

chauffeur. A pilot.

cheap liberty. A look at the shore from aboard ship.

check out. To be killed; to die.

check ride. A flight on which an instructor evaluates a pilot's ability; an Army Air Corps term.

cherry picker. A heavy crane used by the Seabees in the Pacific for construction work; so-called because it looked like it would work perfectly for harvesting cherries from high in a tree.

chew off. To dress down; to reprimand.

Chicago atomizer. An automatic rifle.

Chicago banjo / Chicago blotter / Chicago chatterbox / Chicago chopper / Chicago coffee-grinder / Chicago grind-organ / Chicago mowing-machine / Chicago riveter / Chicago Tommy / Chicago typewriter / Chicago violin. A machine gun.

Chicago piano. A multiple antiaircraft gun.

chicken. (1) Mean, petty, or annoying, especially as regards regulations. (2) Unnecessary discipline or regimentation. (3) A person who adheres too closely to Army rules and regulations or abuses his authority, especially in minor or petty matters. (4) The silver eagle that a colonel wears on each shoulder. A colonel's eagles were first called "chickens" in World War I, as noted in a popular song of the day: "I'd rather be a private with a chicken on my knee than a colonel with a chicken on my shoulder."

chicken berry. An egg.

chicken colonel. A full colonel, whose rank is designated by a silver eagle (a CHICKEN) on each shoulder; also known as a "bird colonel."

china clipper. A dishwasher. The "china" in question here is dishware.

chicken shit. The G.I.'s name for service regulations and the seemingly endless make-work chores. In his *Browser's Dictionary* (1980) John Ciardi links the term to chores because the one "unending labor on any chicken farm used to be the shoveling up of droppings, which were forever immediately renewed in place."

Chindits. Wingate's Raiders. It has been written that General Orde Wingate "called his men 'Chindits' after the Chinthey—the mythological beast, half lion, half griffin, statues of which stand guard over Burmese pagodas to ward off evil spirits."

Chinese landing / Chinese ace. An airplane landing with one wing low; from the fact that, to westerners, "one wing low" sounds Chinese.

Chinese three-point landing. An airplane crash.

chinkberries. Rice. "Chink" is a derogatory term for "Chinese."

chisling. A quota chiseler (i.e., a firm that fails to conform to production quotas set up by the War Production Board).

chow bumps. Two bugle blasts, giving preliminary notice of mess.

chow hound. Someone always at the head of a mess line.

chowmobile. A CANTEEN (2) pulled by a tractor and serving hot meals.

chow-table muscles. Fat.

chuck spoiler. A cook. "Chuck" is an old Americanism for "food," as in "chuckwagon."

chute. A parachute.

chutist. A parachutist.

C. in C. Commander in chief.

Cinclant. Commander in chief of the Atlantic Fleet.

Cincpac. Commander in chief of the Pacific Fleet.

CINCUS. Commander in chief of the U.S. Fleet. This acronym was used by the Navy until 1942, when, because of its resemblance to "sink us," it was changed by Admiral Ernest J. ("Rey") King to COMINCH.

cinder shifter. An infantryman marching on a drill field packed with cinders.

circus water. Iced drinks served with meals.

cit. A civilian; from "citizen."

cit duds / cit rags / cits. Civilian clothing.

cits army. The National Guard.

city cow. Canned milk.

civvies. Civilians; civilian clothing.

C.J. The civilian jeep, or CJ-2A (the first nonmilitary version of the Army vehicle).

C.L. A light cruiser; from the military designation, "cruiser, light."

Clara. The all-clear signal after an air raid.

class A liberty. Freedom. The term derives from the classification of military passes. The class A pass serves as a reward for efficiency and good conduct; it permits absence at all times when not on duty. The class B pass permitted absence only between taps and reveille.

cloak and dagger. Said of a person or activity that is secret, exciting, dangerous, and highly important. It stemmed from the popular notion that a spy always carried a dagger beneath his cloak.

clocks. Cockpit instruments.

cloud kissing. Touching the clouds in an airplane.

cloud wagon. An airplane.

clutter. Images on a radar screen caused by noise, permanent echoes, or jamming.

C.N.O. Chief of naval operations.

C.O. (1) Commanding officer. (2) Conscientious objector.

cockpit fog. A state of confusion.

coffee cooler. One who seeks and secures a duty more congenial than his regular duties; one who is always looking for an easy job; a loafer. The term describes a person whose major "activity" is to stand around waiting for his coffee to get cool enough to drink.

coffee grinder. (1) A machine gun; from the noise it makes. (2) A portable radio set for sending out S.O.S. signals; so-called because the machine resembles an old-fashioned coffee mill. These machines were part of the equipment on lifeboats of vessels in war zones.

coffin corridor. An area of Normandy, France. It is described by A. Marjorie Taylor in *The Language of World War II* (1948):

> As the Allied troops were driving on across France toward Paris in August 1944, there was still a narrow route in Normandy along which the German Seventh Army expected to be able to withdraw to a safer position at the Seine. When the gap was closed by Allied advances 100,000 to 200,000 German troops were forced to turn for a battle to the death.

C. of S. Chief of staff.

C.O. highball. Castor oil.

cold. Absolute; without error.

cold feet. Fear.

cold steel. Bayonets (in hand-to-hand fighting).

collision mats. Pancakes; waffles.

combat boots. Standard Army boots. After 1942, they replaced the World War I–style boots and leggings. Combat boots have a "cuff" of leather, with two buckles above the laced-up "high-top."

combat fatigue. See SHELL SHOCK, under World War I.

comb it. To make a detailed inspection of an Army tank.

come in through the cabin window. To obtain a commission; a Navy term.

COMINCH. Commander in chief of the U.S. Fleet. See CINCUS.

commander of the Swiss fleet / commander of the Swiss navy. See ADMIRAL OF THE SWISS NAVY.

commando. A member of a special British assault force, trained in raiding and in hand-to-hand combat. The first commando raid took place on March 7, 1941; the commandos destroyed a plant in occupied Norway making glycerine for the Germans.

The term dates back to the Boer War, when it was adapted from the Afrikaans *kommando* (a unit of troops under one command). It was first heard by Americans during World War II and used by them to describe military actions involving shock and surprise (e.g., "commando tactics" and "commando attack").

commissary bullets. Beans.

commo. Communication.

common soldier. A private; an enlisted man.

company punishment. Punishment fixed by the company commander.

company stooge. A company clerk.

completely cheesed. Bored to an extreme.

compo. Compensation.

conchie. Conscientious objector.

condition black. A situation of extreme danger. A number of such "colorful" conditions existed, as indicated by this extract from *Words of the Fighting Forces:* "Degrees of danger in this war are described in shouted warnings of CON-DISH-SHUN YELLOW, RED, BLACK, etc. 'Condition Red' means enemy planes are approaching. 'Condition Black' is the most imperative of all; it means enemy landing parties are approaching."

conk out. (1) To stop working suddenly (said of an aircraft engine during flight). (2) To become unconscious. "Conk" was established slang for the head and, sometimes, the nose.

convoy. One or more troop ships or supply ships escorted by warships.

cooking with gas. Having become wise to something.

cooking with stardust. In love.

cook someone's goose. To ruin someone.

cool as a cucumber. Alert and aware; self-possessed; calm.

cool card / cool customer / cool fish / cool hand. One who is COOL AS A CUCUMBER.

cootie. A body louse. See also the COOTIE entries under World War I.

cootie frisk. A search for lice in one's clothes.

cootie trap. A bed; a bunk.

cork down / cork off. To go to bed; to sleep.

corner turner. A deserter.

corporal's butt. A cigarette more than half smoked. See also CAPTAIN'S BUTT.

cosmolines. The Artillery Corps; so-called because cosmoline was the grease in which small arms were packed and stored.

costume jewelry. An officer's insignia; a WAC term.

coughing Clara. A heavy artillery gun.

count off. To determine the different positions in ranks.

Country Club. Randolph Field, Texas, the air training center for the Army Air Corps; so-called because pilots were given better accommodations than other servicemen.

couple of jugs. Several beers.

cousin. A close friend.

covered wagon. An aircraft carrier.

cow in a tin barn. Canned milk; canned corned beef; canned beef.

cow juice. Milk.

coxswain of the plow. An inexperienced Navy recruit. A coxswain traditionally steers a boat, so this term alludes

to one whose only steering has been of a farm implement.

C.P. Command post.

crab. (1) A person who complains a lot. (2) A girl from Annapolis, Maryland (see CRABTOWN, under the Civil War). (3) To complain. (4) To head an airplane's nose into a crosswind to keep the plane from drifting off course.

crab fleet. The warship squadron on which midshipmen make their annual practice cruise.

crack. (1) To speak. (2) To become nervous or afraid. (3) To wreck an airplane.

cracked egg. A silly or stupid person.

crack regiment. A first-class regiment; an Army term.

crapper. A latrine.

crash. An omelet.

crash boat. A Marine rescue boat, for rescuing aircraft personnel and planes making forced landings at sea.

crash dive. To dive hastily in a submarine.

crash land. To make a forced airplane landing, with a crash.

crash wagon. An ambulance.

crate. An automobile; an old airplane.

C-ration. A balanced ration for troops in the field. It was developed just before the United States entered the war, with advance billing as the "balanced meal in a can." The Army Subsistence Research Laboratory first offered it for trial in 1940, as a ration in six cans, two for each meal of the day. Three of the cans were meat units, while the other three contained concentrated biscuits, ingredients for a drink (soluble coffee and sugar), and five pieces of hard candy. In all, the six cans added up to 3,500 well-balanced calories of varied foods. An accessory packet included cigarettes, matches, chewing gum, and toilet tissue. As the war progressed, the C-ration became the basic ration used when mess units were not accessible. The ration was bulky and, after a few days of continuous use, hard to get down. Many troops were, however, sustained on it for weeks.

A small C-ration was called a BAIL-OUT RATION. A version of the original C-ration was still in use in the Vietnam War, when it was called a C-RAT.

creamed foreskins. Creamed chipped beef.

creepers. (1) Lice. (2) The feet. (3) Soft-soled shoes.

creeping crud. See JUNGLE ROT.

crewman. A member of an airplane crew other than the pilot.

crossbar hotel. A guardhouse.

crown on the conk. To strike on the head.

crow tracks. Chevrons; from their appearance as inverted v's.

cruiser. A prostitute, especially a street-walker.

crumb gob. A dirty sailor; from the older slang term "crumb" ("dirty" or "lousy").

crumb hunt. A kitchen inspection; an Army term.

crumb up. To get a haircut, shoeshine, freshly pressed shirt, etc., in preparation for an inspection.

crump hole. A shell hole.

cry always. Bromobenzylcyanide (a type of teargas).

cunt cap. A soft overseas cap; from the shape of the hat, which resembles that of the female pudenda.

cunt hair. A unit of measurement, smaller than a millimeter, used in directing cannon fire (as in, "a cunt hair to the left").

cupid's itch. Any venereal disease.

cup of Java / cup of J. Cup of coffee.

curfloozie. A woman wandering the streets. The term is discussed in *Newsweek* of March 20, 1955:

> After curfew order was put into effect in February 1945, the midnight closings of restaurants, places of entertainment, etc., threw onto the streets (especially in the large cities) thousands of GI's (and women) with nowhere to go. This gave rise to a serious social problem which many felt far outweighed any advantage the curfew order may have had. It was in this connection that the *Daily News* coined the word "curfloozie."

cut-and-run operation. A military operation consisting of a sudden attack followed by an immediate withdrawal, before a counterattack can be mounted.

cut her water off and read her meter. To stop a truck with a mechanical problem and find the trouble; to make a driving error in traffic.

cut one's cable. To die; a Navy term.

cut the gun. To turn off the motor of an aircraft.

★ ☆ **D** ☆ ★

D.A. A delayed-action bomb.

Dad. The oldest member of a group.

daily details. A daily work schedule issued by the company sergeant.

dame with an anchor. A married woman.

dan. Dynamite; also known as DINO. Perhaps the volatile nature of the substance dictates that nicknames for it be short.

darby kelly. The belly. This bit of Cockney rhyming slang was picked up by the American Army.

dawn patrol. (1) An early morning patrol. (2) Those reaching camp or post just before reveille.

Day of Infamy. The day of the Japanese attack on Pearl Harbor (December 7, 1941). The first draft of Franklin Delano Roosevelt's historic Pearl Harbor speech, which he wrote himself, began: "Yesterday, December 7, 1941, a date which will live in world history, the United States was simultaneously and deliberately attacked by naval and air forces of the Empire of Japan." According to Robert Hendrickson, in *Encyclopedia of Word and Phrase Origins* (1987): "In the second draft FDR substituted the infinitely better 'infamy' for 'world history' and 'suddenly' for 'simultaneously,' making a sentence that will live in world history." Most people immediately began using "day" as part of the phrase, rather than "date," the word Roosevelt actually used.

day room. A recreation room.

D.B. Disciplinary barracks (i.e., a prison).

D.C. Speaker. A mythical character, created on June 15, 1943, by Kent Cooper of the Associated Press. "D.C. Speaker" was quoted as the source of news, when the true identity of the source could not be disclosed.

D.D. Dishonorable discharge.

D-day. The day of the Normandy invasion (June 6, 1944). According to Robert Hendrickson, in *Encyclopedia of Word and Phrase Origins* (1987):

Many explanations have been given for the meaning of D-day, June 6, 1944, the day the Allies invaded Normandy from England during World War II. The Army has said that it is "simply an alliteration, as in H-hour." Others say the first D in the word also stands for "day," the term a code designation. The French maintain the D means "disembarkation," still others say "debarkation," and the more poetic insist D-day is short for "day of decision." When someone wrote to General Eisenhower in 1964 asking for an explanation, his executive assistant Brigadier General Robert Schultz answered: "General Eisenhower asked me to respond to your letter. Be advised that any amphibious operation has a 'departed date'; therefore, the shortened term 'D-day' is used."

dead battery. An irritable or gloomy person; a pessimist.

dead can. A shell that fails to explode.

deadlined. Laid up for repairs (said of a vehicle).

dead nuts on. Fond of; in love with.

dead soldier / dead dog. An empty beer bottle or liquor bottle.

Dear John. A letter from one's wife or sweetheart informing one that the relationship is over. A contemporary radio program included the reading of letters addressed to "Dear John," and the phrase became a permanent part of both military and civilian slang. In the film *Dr. Strangelove*, the two nuclear warheads were named "Hi There" and "Dear John."

death gratuity. Money sent to the family of one killed in action. It was officially defined by the War Department as:

> Payment to beneficiaries of military personnel who die from wounds or disease not the result of their own misconduct, while on active duty. Gratuity amounts to six months' pay (excluding allowances) at the rate received by such person at the time of his death, officially reported or administratively determined.

Because this definition made the gratuity sound like a tip for good service, it was much lampooned by the troops.

deck ape. A sailor whose duties keep him on the deck.

deck monkey. A member of the deck crew of an Army minelayer. Many mine-laying operations were conducted by the Army rather than the Navy.

decode. To explain.

deep dunkers. A little-known and exclusive official submarine servicemen's organization. According to *Newsweek* for October 2, 1944, it was established in the spring of 1943 with the objective of recognizing officers and men who had not qualified for medals (usually awarded only to skippers). Membership was restricted to crewmembers of submarines that, on war patrol, had either sunk an enemy ship of more than one thousand tons, damaged a major warship (e.g., an aircraft carrier or a battleship), or performed a mission (usually secret) of comparable importance.

deep-sea chicken / deep-sea turkey. Canned salmon.

"defense" biscuits. See K-RATION.

delousy. Anything unpleasant; in contrast with "delightful."

deplane. (1) To disembark from an aircraft. (2) To be granted a furlough in the Army Air Corps.

depth bomb. A bomb designed to explode underwater. In *The Language of World War II* (1948), A. Marjorie Taylor gives this description, based on a 1940 newspaper account:

> Three hundred pounds or more of high

explosives in a thin shell with an adjustable hydrostatic mechanism to touch it off at any desired depth under the sea. Pitched or rolled from fighting ships, particularly destroyers, it was the nemesis of submarines. Direct hits were unnecessary. Water-transmitted shock of nearby explosion was sufficient to buckle plates of submarines or damage steering or elevating apparatus.

devil beater. A chaplain.

devil-dogs of the sea. The Marines.

devil-dogs on the march. Marines on the march, especially in battle.

devil's piano. A machine gun.

devil's voice. A bugle call.

die in a blaze of glory. To die fighting bravely; to die while killing the enemy.

dihedral oil. An imaginary substance. Recruits are sent to procure some, as a joke or in being hazed.

Dilbert. A sailor who is a foul-up or a screwball. Dilbert was a cartoon character created by Robert C. Osborn, along with another character, a wacky mechanic named Spoiler. Dilbert and Spoiler became known to naval combat fliers the world over as horrible examples of what *not* to be.

dimout. A dimming of lights, or partial BLACKOUT, especially along the coast where bright lights would offer a background against which passing ships would be silhouetted, making them easy prey for U-boats.

ding how. Swell; okay; all right. The phrase was first used by the Flying Tigers. It derives from a Chinese phrase meaning "very good."

dinky. A short, coupled truck.

dino. Dynamite.

Dirty Gertie of Bizerte. A sluttish woman.

dirty mixture. Gasoline.

dis. Discipline.

ditch. To bail out of a disabled airplane over water; to crash-land a plane in the water.

dit da. Radiotelegraph operations; from the sound of the keys.

dit da artist. A radiotelegraph operator.

dit happy. A little crazy from copying too much radio code.

dive bomb. To dive an airplane at a steep angle so as to bomb with greater accuracy than from level flight. During the war, dive bombers were specially constructed to stand the strain of high-speed dives. Stuka dive bombers were considered "terror weapons" at the start of the war.

diviz. An Army division.

dizzy painting. Camouflage.

do a hitch. To serve an enlistment.

do a porpoise. To dive a submarine at a sharp angle.

dock. (1) To forfeit pay by sentence of a court-martial. (2) A hospital.

dodo. A cadet before he starts solo flying; from the dodo bird, which could not fly.

dog / dogface / doggie. An infantryman; probably from the fact that infantrymen lead a dog's life, compared with soldiers in other branches of the Army. The military brass railed against these names, but the dogfaces themselves seem to have reveled in them. The expression occurs in many songs—for example, "I'm Just a Dog Face Soldier" (words and music by Bert Gold and Ken Hart). Set to a jazzy marching tune, the lyrics announced:

> I wouldn't give a bean
> To be a fancy-pants marine,
> I'd rather be a dog face soldier like I am.
> I wouldn't change my B.V.D.'s
> For all the navy's dungarees,
> 'Cause I'm the walking pride of Uncle Sam.

In "Dogfaces and Dog Soldiers" (1974), Jonathan E. Lighter writes: "Th[is] tune quickly became a favorite march of U.S. army bands, and was even featured in the 1955 film biography of Lieut. Audie Murphy, America's most decorated soldier of World War II."

dog and bystander. Silhouette targets, one standing and one prone, set up side by side.

dog fashion. Askew; not in line. The term is used to describe a truck trailer that does not track, so that the unit looks like two canines mating.

dogfight. A fight between two or more airplanes.

dog food. Corned beef hash.

dogleg. A chevron.

dog show. Foot inspection. The term "dogs" is slang for "feet."

dogs of war. (1) Artillery. (2) Bombers. (3) Warships. (4) Marines.

dog tags. Identification tags worn by soldiers on a chain around the neck. A dog tag became symbolic of a dead soldier, because one tag was sent home after he was killed and the other remained with the body for purposes of identification. For this reason, a line widely attributed to General George S. Patton was especially relevant: "I have sent home one truckload of dog tags, and by God I'll send home another."

doll's-eyes factory. An unimportant factory (e.g., one manufacturing parts for toys).

donagher sergeant. A soldier assigned to cleaning the latrine. "Donagher" (or "donnicker") was underworld slang for "toilet."

doodle. (1) To draw or scribble idly and absentmindedly. (2) A drawing so produced.

doodlebug. A light tank.

doodle gadget. A contrivance; a thingamajig.

do one's bit. To serve in the military in time of war; to engage in war work.

doorkey children. Children left to

fend for themselves (with a doorkey hanging on a string around their necks). Most of them were children of war workers or those with parents in the armed forces. The phrase appeared frequently in discussions of the rising tide of juvenile delinquency.

dope head. (1) One fond of Coca-Cola. "Dope" was slang for Coca-Cola because the soft drink was once said to contain a drug. (2) One given to spreading false information and rumors.

dope off. To act in a stupid manner.

do-re-mi. Money; from "dough" as slang for money.

double-bottomed. Insincere; implying one thing and meaning another.

double-silver-bar john. An Army captain, whose insignia is two parallel bars.

dough beater / dough roller. A baker; a cook.

doughboy. An infantryman. See under World War I.

doughfoot. An infantryman. According to The New York Times of December 10, 1944, the term alludes to the disagreeable, even miserable, conditions endured by the infantryman because of mud. Also, the infantryman's big four-buckle galoshes, worn over his regular G.I. shoes, make his feet look like oversized rolls of chocolate dough after a few hours in the fall and winter mud of the front lines. Some say the term originated in Italy; others, in North Carolina, Georgia,

or Louisiana; and still others, in France or Germany.

doughnut dugout. A one-room recreation and refreshment center set up in Britain by the Red Cross for G.I.'s overseas.

dough puncher. A baker.

downhill. The second half of an Army enlistment.

do you dig me? Do you understand?

D.P. Displaced person; a term applied to persons driven from their homes by war and cared for in refugee camps. There were many such camps in Europe after the war, and in the late 1940s, many emigrated to America.

draft bait. (1) A SELECTEE (one waiting to be drafted into the armed forces). (2) A prospective bride (in the sense that she is about to be "drafted" into matrimony).

drafted malted-milk shaker. A jeep.

draftee / draftie. One conscripted for military service under the Selective Service Act of 1940.

drag an anchor. To have a blind date with an ugly or dull woman.

dragon's teeth. Concrete or steel anti-tank obstacles resembling teeth pointing upward.

D-ration. A highly concentrated emergency ration for troops in the field. It consisted of three four-ounce chocolate bars. The special chocolate bar was mixed with oat flour to raise the melting point. It was not to be eaten except under orders, or in an extreme emergency.

draw crabs. To attract fire from the enemy by exposing oneself.

draw the long bow. To exaggerate.

dream sack. A sleeping bag.

drive it in the hangar. Let's stop it!

drome. An aerodrome.

drone. A pilotless, radio-controlled aircraft.

drugstore nerve. False courage inspired by drugs or drink.

dry dock. A ship's hospital; a ship's jail.

dry run. Something done for practice only (e.g., a simulated bombing, in which no bombs were dropped); by extension, a rehearsal for any kind of event, from a parade to an appointment with a superior officer.

D.T. Double-time.

dual. A flight with an instructor; a date accompanied by a chaperone.

duck. An Army amphibious truck; from its official designation, D.U.K.W. The vehicle was described by Winston Churchill in a speech in the House of Commons in 1944:

The marvelous "Duck," the American invention spelt D.U.K.W., is a heavy lorry which goes at between 40 and 50 miles per hour along the road, and can plunge into the water and swim out for miles to sea in quite choppy weather, returning with a load of several tons, coming ashore and going off to wherever it is specially needed.

duckbills. Metal flanges welded to tank treads to give them a wider grip so they would not flounder in the mud.

duck day. The day on which a G.I. received his discharge papers; from RUPTURED DUCK.

duck soup. An easy task.

dude up. To dress in one's best uniform.

duke. A self-important person.

dum-dum / dummy. A gun made of scrap material, intended to fool the enemy as regards the strength and position of one's forces. Aerial photography usually exposed such tactics; however, the Chinese had some success in fooling Japanese airmen with dummy wooden airplanes.

dunker. A submarine.

Dunkirk. A disastrous retreat; from the retreat from Dunkirk of British forces in June 1940 (one of the epic events of the war).

dustbin. The enemy rear gunner's lower position in an airplane.

dust disturber. An infantryman.

D.X. man. A radio operator who uses his radio to contact people in other countries.

★ ☆ **E** ☆ ★

eager beaver. An underclassman of the Army Air Corps during the first thirty days of training; by extension, a soldier so anxious to impress superiors that he would volunteer for any job offered or in other ways display unusual diligence.

eagle. (1) A student pilot. (2) A bomb.

eagle day. Payday; also known as "the day the eagle shits." The term was a reference to the American eagle that appears on some coins. Among the phrases used to announce payday were "the eagle flies," "the eagle screams," and "the eagle shits."

eagles' nest. An airfield.

eaglet. A young aviator.

earn wings. To be commissioned as a second lieutenant in the Army Air Corps; from the insignia, a pair of wings.

earthquake bomb. A six-ton bomb that penetrates deeply into the earth before exploding, with earthshaking effect.

ear wardens. Small nipple-shaped devices made of neoprene. They were inserted into the ear to prevent injury resulting from noise shock. The term is a play on "air wardens."

echo. A reflection on a radar screen.

E.D. Extra duty.

egg. (1) A man (as in "good egg"). (2) An aerial bomb. (3) An error; a Navy term.

egg in the deep. A depth bomb, after being released.

egg in your beer. Too much of a good thing.

eight ball. A soldier who got into trouble so much that he was a liability to his unit; from the old notion that it is bad luck to be behind the eight ball in pocket billiards.

Eisenhower jacket. A short, fitted, belted jacket of the type made popular by General Dwight D. Eisenhower during the war.

electric cow. A machine used for mixing powdered milk and water.

electric stooge. See MECHANICAL RAT.

electronic raspberry. The effect of jamming radar by dispersing quantities of aluminum foil from airplanes.

Elsie. A fine imposed by an Army court-martial.

Emily Posters. Naval cadets; so-called because they were given a condensed edition of an etiquette book by Emily Post.

Enola Gay. The airplane (a B-29 Superfortress) that dropped an atomic bomb on Hiroshima, Japan.

erk. An airman; an airplane mechanic; a beginner. This bit of British slang was adopted by many Americans. According to the April 1944 issue of *Nineteenth Century*: "In World War I and for some years afterwards, an erk meant an air mechanic. The word was probably a shortened pronunciation of air and ch from mechanic. In World War II, it came to mean a beginner in any field."

Erpel Heart. A mythical medal. As recounted in *Newsweek* for March 26, 1945, the 9th Armored Division seized the Remagen bridge over the Rhine in March of that year, and thousands of tons of supplies crossed it before it collapsed. Many drivers of supply trucks crossed it so often that they were awarded the order of the "Erpel Heart"—a pun on "Purple Heart" and on "Erpel," the name of a little town on the Rhine's east bank. The "medal" was awarded to drivers who made five trips in a single day.

ersatz. Substitute; synthetic. It was not until World War II that the term became widely used on the fighting and home fronts to signify materials of inferior quality, such as ersatz coffee or ersatz beer. A. Marjorie Taylor notes in *The Language of World War II* (1948) that it was later applied to people, as in "The heroine called him an ersatz gentleman." See also under World War I.

E.T.A. Estimated time of arrival.

E.T.O. European theater of operations.

E.T.O. happy. Bored.

expendable. Anything considered only as a means to an end. In the words of A. Marjorie Taylor, in *The Language of World War II* (1948): "In World War II, the term came into general use. It meant troops or equipment of any kind that for military purposes might be considered by the authorities worth consuming entirely to achieve an end."

They Were Expendable (1942), by W. H. White, did much to fix the term in the mind of the public:

> Well, it's like this. Suppose you're a sergeant machine-gunner, and your army is retreating and the enemy advancing. The captain takes you to a machine gun covering the road. "You're to stay here and hold this position," he tells you. "For how long?" you ask. "Never mind," he answers, "just hold it." Then you know you're expendable. In a war anything can be expendable—money or gasoline or equipment or most usually men. They are expending you and that machine gun to get time.

eyeball. To look over the immediate area.

eyes of a ship. Scout duty airplanes.

eyes of the Army. The Army Air Corps.

Eyeties. Italians.

eyewash. (1) To pretty up barracks and grounds for inspection. (2) Something done for effect only. In *Words of the Fighting Forces*, the term is seen in a much more negative context: "A deplorable interest in a spick-and-span appearance rather than an efficient performance of a soldier, regiment, army automobile, etc." (3) A garnish on food (e.g., raisin sauce on plain white cake).

★ ☆ F ☆ ★

face muffler. A gas mask.

face the enemy. To meet one's wife after being out drinking.

factory buster. A bomb larger than a BLOCKBUSTER.

fall out. To quarrel; to dissolve a friendship.

fan. A propeller.

farmyard nugget. An egg.

fatal pill. A bullet.

fat friend. A balloon.

fatigue dress / fatigues. A loose uniform worn when working; work clothes.

F.B.I.'s. Forgotten boys (or bastards) of Iceland. Army soldiers in Iceland gave themselves this nickname.

F.D. coat. Full-dress coat.

feather merchant. A civilian; a lazy person. Here is an excerpt from the jacket copy of Max Shulman's 1944 classic of wartime humor, *The Feather Merchants*: "Dan Miller is just a happy soldier going home on furlough. But he is ambushed by an advance patrol of feather merchants as he gets off the train in Minneapolis."

Feather Merchant—Word History

Here are three theories about the origin of the term:

(1) Hillbilly dwarfs in the Barney Google comic strip were considered (prewar) "feather merchants" because they "pick up large feathers and fly off, waving them like wings" (according to *American Notes and Queries* of April 1945).

(2) The phrase originated with the Navy. According to a letter by William B. Mellor, Jr., in *Newsweek* of April 23, 1945, it "comes from the crossed-feather device worn on the shoulder boards of ships' clerks, who are commissioned officers, and as a part of petty officers' rating badges to signify that they are yeomen. Hence a yeoman is a 'feather merchant.' The implication, of course, was that the yeoman took things easy on a swivel chair while the fighting men manned the guns. The term is now loosely applied to anyone with a 'soft berth.'"

(3) In *The Feather Merchants*, Max Shulman notes that theories abound but only one seems worthy of even provisional credence—that of Professor Herk Betzimmer, the famous "one horse philologist" of Wilkes-Barre, Pennsylvania. To wit:

Circa 4500 B.C. two neighboring tribes, the Puntangi and the Snafu, went to war over the possession of a gap-toothed idol named Ed to whom they attributed widespread curative powers. At that time Ed was well concealed by the Snafu. Gluk-Os, chief of the Snafu, was taken prisoner and brought before Miklos the Scaly, prince of the Puntangi. Upon refusing to divulge the location of Ed, Gluk-Os was bound and subjected to a favorite torture of the day—tickling the soles of the feet with feathers. For weeks two shifts of Miklos's warriors tickled Gluk-Os's feet day and night, but he spoke not a word. All the feathers in Miklos's court were worn to the nub. Miklos ordered more feathers brought to him at any cost so that the torture could continue. Civilians by the thousands plucked their fowl and wives' hats and sold the feathers to the army. Hence "feather merchants."

Shulman then adds: "Gluk-Os, incidently, never did tell where Ed was hidden. The tickling bothered him not in the least, for, had the Snafu known, he was wearing history's first pair of shoes."

feed one's face. To eat.

feeds like a hotel. Said of a ship with a sumptuous bill of fare.

fellow traveler. A person working secretly for a foreign government; a treacherous person. The term originated in the 1930s as the name for a follower of communist doctrines who did not belong to the party.

femarines. The women's reserve of the Marine Corps; also called "jungle Juliets" and "leather-nectarines." The Marines insisted that the proper term was "Marines."

ferry pilot. An aviator engaged in flying aircraft from the factory to the field.

fiat money. Money made legal by degree, or fiat, usually by a dictator.

FIDO. Fog investigation and dispersal operation. FIDO systems kept fifteen British airfields active even during the winter fogs, with the help of landing-strip pipes loaded with gasoline; when the pipes were ignited (by men running alongside the pipes), the flames burned off the fog.

field officer's weather. Perfect flying conditions.

field piece. A field artillery piece.

fifinella. A female gremlin character designed by Walt Disney as an emblem for the WASPs (Women's Airforce Service Pilots, under the direction of Jacqueline Cochran), who reveled in the motto, "Fifinellas don't cry."

fifth column. Individuals and groups engaged in sabotage, espionage, or other subversive activities. See also SIXTH COLUMN.

Fifth Column—Word History

Some say that the expression "fifth column" originated with General Francisco Franco, head of the victorious rebel forces in the Spanish Civil War; others say the originator was General Emilio Mola, another rebel commander. Late in 1936, in the early stages of the war, Franco (or Mola) observed that he had four rebel columns to send against loyalist-held Madrid, and a fifth column of rebel sympathizers waiting inside the city to attack the defenders from the rear, when the time was ripe. The expression was adapted by the allies to refer to traitors or enemy sympathizers.

52-20 club. World War II veterans who, rather than take low-salaried jobs, accepted the twenty-dollar-a-week unemployment compensation that the government would pay for fifty-two weeks.

fighting-hole feet. A disease contracted from life in foxholes. See also TRENCH FOOT, under World War I.

fighting tools. Eating utensils (namely, a knife, fork, and spoon).

figurehead. A company clerk (because he often served as a stand-in for the commander).

file 13. A wastebasket.

Filthy Thirteen, The. An Engineers Corps demolition unit, composed of Yaqui and Cherokee Indians; also called "the Braves." They adopted the name "The Filthy Thirteen" in training. A communiqué from the 9th Air Force troop carrier base in England, quoted by A. Marjorie Taylor in *The Language of World War II* (1948), reported that this group of American Indians, in full war paint, were among the first paratrooper units to go into action in France on June 6, 1944 (D-day).

find out the score. To get the correct information.

fireworks. An artillery bombardment; a disturbance; the end of life.

first hitch. A first enlistment.

first line. Troops or ships directly confronting the enemy.

fish eyes. Tapioca; from its appearance.

fish hooks. Fingers.

fishtail. To swing the tail of an airplane from side to side to reduce speed when coming in for a landing.

five-in-one rations. Prepackaged food that would feed five men for one day or one man for five days.

flak. Antiaircraft fire; from the German *Fliegerabwehrkanone* (a gun used to drive off aircraft). Other possible sources for the term are discussed in *Words of the Fighting Forces*:

> A burst of fire from an anti-aircraft gun or guns. This is a term used by the military, however, it comes first from the theater. That alert weekly, "Variety," birthplace of numerous Americanisms, tried to coin the word "flack" as a synonym for publicity agent. The word is said to be derived from Gene Flack, a movie publicity agent; one who sends up interference or messages in the hope that some of what he is offering will be heeded. Something "Variety" may have overlooked, however, is that a Yiddish word similar in sound means "one who goes around talking about the other fellow's business."

flak happy. (1) The condition of one suffering from combat fatigue; an Army Air Corps term. (2) "Slap happy" (slightly muddled mentally).

flak jacket. A padded vest worn by airmen as a protection against FLAK. See also FLAK SUIT.

flak shack. A rest home where men who have had too much battle strain—who have taken too much FLAK—go to relax and regain their composure.

flak suit. A protective coverall worn by military aviators.

flanker. A tall person.

flap. (1) A scare or an alarm; by extension, any kind of row, inquiry, or excitement. The term is defined in the novel *Ten Fighter Boys:* "To be in a flap—to be all of a dooda—to get all excited about nothing. Normally associated with doing things in a hurry." (2) An ear. (3) A mechanical device on the wing of an aircraft used to increase lift or drag.

flash. A brief, usually telegraphic news dispatch.

flasher. A member of the Signal Corps.

flash gun. A machine gun used in training. It is linked to a spotlight to identify "hits."

flathatter. A careless pilot; a Navy term.

flat out. At top speed; in an "all out" manner.

flat spin. To act confused.

flattop. An aircraft carrier; from the flat flight deck. The following etymology, perhaps mythical, appeared in an article on the war's new vocabulary in the April 1944 issue of *Word Study:* "This name was first applied by a jubilant bomber pilot who yelled into his microphone, 'Scratch one flat top' after he sank a Jap carrier. He was pledged not to reveal important information and he thought the Japs wouldn't be able to decipher that."

flea circus / flea pasture / flea trap. A bed; a bunk.

flier. (1) An aviator. (2) An airplane or other flying machine. (3) Anyone or anything that moves with great speed.

flivver. (1) A Ford automobile (a cheap motorcar used by the military). (2) A Navy destroyer of the 750-ton class.

floater. (1) A mine that has broken adrift. (2) A woman who follows the fleet.

floating coffin. An unsafe ship.

floating elephant. A military balloon.

floating palace. A large and comfortable ship.

flowerpot. A movable, powered turret on an airplane.

fly-away. An airplane that is flown to an overseas command instead of being shipped; an airplane flown from the factory to a storage depot in the United States.

fly blind. To fly by instruments only. See also BLIND FLYING.

flyboat. A hydromonoplane.

flyboy. A glamorous pilot. In *I Hear America Speaking* (1976), Stuart Berg Flexner noted that the term was "usually used ironically."

fly by the seat of one's pants. To fly by instinct rather than by instruments.

flying boat. A seaplane with a hull fit for floating and designed for long flights.

flying boxcar. A bomber.

flying Chinese. See **Chinese landing.**

flying coffin. A dilapidated airplane.

flying column. A strong, fast military detachment made up of well-armed, highly mobile troops and operating independently.

flying corps. An air force subdivision of an army.

flying dustpan. A device for dropping bombs so they explode in a concentric pattern rather than linearly.

flying eyes of the Army. Reconnaissance or observation airplanes. They were used to obtain immediate, accurate information about the enemy. The value of aerial reconnaissance greatly increased with the improvement of aerial photography. Panchromatic and infrared film enabled pictures to be taken through haze, fog, and even light clouds.

Flying Fortress. The Boeing B-17 heavy bomber, capable of carrying tons of bombs and a large crew. The Joint Aircraft Committee, in considering names for airplanes, favored names of one word, so Flying Fortress was officially changed to Fortress. However, Flying Fortress is what the plane continued to be called by just about everyone except the Joint Aircraft Committee.

flying pig. An aerial torpedo.

flying Scotchman. An expert pilot who is very thoughtful about the other members of the flying crew.

flying shotgun. Shrapnel; from its scattershot patterns.

flying streamers. The streams of smoke from an airplane swirling downward to its doom.

flying wreck. A nervous, careless person; an Army Air Corps term.

fly light. To go without a meal.

fly the iron beam. To fly along a railroad line.

fly the wet. To fly along a river.

fog factory. A locality where fogs are plentiful.

Foo / Mr. Foo. An imaginary observer of military actions, known to American and British troops alike. He was described in a naval magazine in 1946: "Mr. Foo is a mysterious Second World War product, gifted with bitter omniscience and sarcasm."

foo-fighters. Mysterious balls of fire, widely alleged to have been sent into the air by the Germans. They were described in a series of articles in the Rochester, New York, *Democrat & Chronicle* of January 2 and January 3, 1945, as reported by A. Marjorie Taylor in *The Language of World War II* (1948):

> The balls traveled along at the same rate as the night flying planes on raids over Germany. They were apparently an electrical phenomenon related to lightning. They followed not only the speed of the plane, but changed speed and direction as the plane changed its speed and direction. Apparently designed by the Nazis as a psychological weapon, since the balls did not attack the planes.

foofoo. Perfume; a WAC term.

foot locker. A small trunk. It is described in Louise D. Parry's *The War Dictionary* (1942) as "a small olive-drab-colored trunk of a standard size issued to each soldier in the army for storing his clothing and personal equipment and so called because it usually stands at the foot of his bed."

foot slogger. An infantryman; a poor dancer.

for a hell of a long time. Death; for a long time; for an indefinite period of time.

forget it, sign off. Drop the matter; pay no attention; stop talking.

forty-eight. Two days' liberty.

four-by-four. A JEEP; from its four wheels and four-wheel drive.

four freedoms war. World War II.

400W. Maple syrup; from the name of a thick oil.

four-o. All right; from the highest Navy efficiency rating (4.0).

four-starrer. A general; an admiral.

four-striper. A Navy captain; from the four stripes indicating rank.

fourth arm. The Army Air Corps (because it came after the Army, Navy, and Marine Corps).

fowl balls. Chicken croquettes.

foxes. The veterans of the battle of Bataan, in the Philippines (1942); so-called because of their fighting from FOXHOLES.

foxhole. A one-man slit trench.

Word History—Foxhole

The term "foxhole" originated in World War I, but came into its own during World War II.

Elbridge Colby writes in *Army Talk: A Familiar Dictionary of Soldier Speech* (1943):

Officially this was long called a "skirmisher's trench," but beginning on the campaign in France and continuing to this day, the soldier speaks of it as a "foxhole"—which covers all varieties of hasty field entrenchment whether for a man kneeling, sitting, standing, or prone. This very unofficial character of the name simplifies language, making one term easily cover all forms without being too particular about which form. Now, for protection against aerial bombs he digs narrower and deeper and calls it a "slit trench."

---

foxhole circuit. A U.S.O. tour of overseas military bases and camps.

Foxhole University. The United States Armed Forces Institute. The term was coined by Stephen G. Thompson in *This Week Magazine* (of the New York *Herald Tribune*) of November 19, 1944.

frat. See FRATERNIZE.

frat bait. Such items as candy, chewing gum, and cigarettes, used by American and British soldiers to attract German women during the occupation. The practice hastened the relaxation of the non-fraternization rules for allied troops.

fraternize. (1) To associate with enemy nationals. (2) To have close relations, usually sexual, with a female enemy national (according to an article in *American Speech* for December 1946). By extension, the word came to be used also with respect to the women of allied countries and even American women.

free board and your own washing. An enlistment in the Navy.

freeze. To hold things where they are; to keep prices constant. Early in the war, prices in the United States were "frozen" at a certain limit. In a separate move, foreign assets were "frozen" in American banks and could not be withdrawn.

freighter. (1) A slow airplane. (2) A ship that carries goods, not passengers.

fresh fish. A Navy recruit.

fresh-fish squad. A squad of new recruits.

fried egg. (1) The insignia of West Point, worn as the headpiece on the full-dress hat. (2) The Japanese flag; from the image of the rising sun.

frigate. A large woman; from a class of ship.

frigo. Frozen meat.

fritzkrieg. A German attack; a play on FRITZ (see under World War I) and BLITZKRIEG.

fritzville. Berlin.

frog sticker. A bayonet; an infantry sword.

from Maine to California. All over; from one end to the other; everywhere.

front and center. Step forward!

fruit salad. Colorful chest decorations. "Fruit salad" was the name given by servicemen to theater of operations ribbons, service ribbons, and battle stars worn on the left side of the uniform jacket.

fubar. Fouled up (or fucked up) beyond all recognition.

Fujiyama flivver. A Japanese tank.

full feather. Full naval uniform.

full fig. Full naval uniform.

full house. The condition of having several diseases at the same time.

full pack. A soldier's complete equipment.

full-pack slum. A meat pie; from SLUM/SLUMGULLION (see under the Civil War and under World War I).

funeral glide. The flight of an airplane gone out of control.

fuselage. One's body; a woman's body. In its nonslang meaning, the term refers to the body of an airplane.

★ ☆ G ☆ ★

galley sight. An incorrect determination of the ship's position. Orlo Misfeldt discussed the term in his article "Argot of the Sea," in *American Speech* of December 1940: "This term is applied to false reports as to ship's position, the inference being that the unreliable information probably came from the cook [who works in the ship's kitchen, or galley], who would know less of where the ship was than anyone aboard. 'Shaft-alley sights' has the same meaning."

galley yarn. (1) A tall tale; a rumor; false information; a swindle; a falsehood. (2) Empty talk.

galvanized gelding. A tank.

galvanized Guernsey. Canned milk; from the Guernsey breed of dairy cow.

gangplank. (1) An ugly woman. (2) Bail from jail.

gangplank greased for him. Said of a sailor dishonorably discharged.

gangster nations. Germany, Italy, and Japan. The description was made popular by President Franklin D. Roosevelt.

Garand. The M-1 rifle. This standard semiautomatic weapon was so-named after its inventor, John Garand, a Pratt and Whitney engineer who complained, "Not only did I not receive a penny in royalties, but nobody pronounced the name correctly." ("Garand" is pronounced with the accent on the first syllable.)

garbage catcher. A metal tray with eight depressions in which food is served.

garrison floats. Army dress shoes.

garrison sport. A soldier who loafs about the post exchange.

gas hog. One who used too much gasoline during the gasoline shortage, abusing the gasoline-rationing privileges.

gas house. A beer garden; a saloon.

gas-house gang. Chemical warfare instructors (because the training they gave was to take troops through a "gas house" to expose them to war gases).

gasket. A pancake.

gasoline cowboy. A member of the armored force (usually, a tank driver).

gaspirator. A gask mask.

gator. See ALLIGATOR.

gear. Radio equipment.

gear adrift. Disorderly clothing.

gedunk. Snack food, especially ice cream. In a 1982 article on cooking in a nuclear submarine, Washington *Post* writer Phyllis Richman reported that young sailors insisted that this term for junk food came from the sound of vending machines dispensing food. But as Richman pointed out, the term almost certainly first applied to the rich ice cream sundaes, sodas, and other confections served at prewar soda fountains.

gedunk stand. A snack bar that serves ice cream. The term was soon picked up by visitors to Navy ships and installations. Lee G. Miller, a reporter for the San Francisco *News*, reported from a cruiser in May 1945 on a trip below decks: "When we finally emerged from our tour we were bathed in sweat and so limp it was all we could do to stagger to the gedunk stand for life-saving ice cream."

Ice cream was terribly important to Navy morale, and cooks and supply officers did all they could to provide it. A young Navy man who had learned to make ice cream in the South Pacific and then to flavor it with the exotic fruits and flavorings of the area went home to parlay his flavoring ability into an empire. He was the late Burt Baskin, cofounder of Baskin-Robbins.

geese. Bombers in flight formation.

gen. Inside information; anything genuine. Thus, "bad gen" is false information.

general court. A general court-martial.

General Grant. A type of Army tank. It was first used in combat in the Libyan campaign.

generalissima. The woman commander of the Women's Army Corps (the WACs); a play on "generalissimo." Chiang Kai-shek of China and Francisco Franco of Spain were called "generalissimo."

General Lee. A type of Army tank. It was first used in combat in the Libyan campaign.

general's car. A wheelbarrow.

germ. A person with gonorrhea.

germ in the hut. A person in a hospital being treated for a venereal disease.

Geronimo! The battle cry of the paratroopers in North Africa. It was first used in combat during the airborne invasion of November 1942.

Geronimo!

In *The Language of World War II* (1948), A. Marjorie Taylor offers this explanation of the origin of "Geronimo!": "Parachute troops have to be tough—'tough as the wily old Indian warrior Geronimo, that the Army fought in the Southwest in the 1880's and from whom the paratroopers got their battle cry.'"

According to Stuart Berg Flexner, in *I Hear America Talking* (1976):

The yell was coined and popularized by the many American Indians, especially Yakis and Cherokee, in our paratroop units. Geronimo (1829–1909), of course, was the Apache renegade, the prototype of the savage Indian killer to the U.S. Army, which had called him "the Human Tiger" (he was captured in 1886 and by 1904 was on exhibit at the St. Louis World's Fair). After the war Geronimo! became a popular exclamation of surprise or delight.

In *Why Do We Say Such Things?* (1947), Bruce Chapman offers a revisionist and perhaps more plausible explanation:

Several members of the first unit of parachute troops formed at Fort Benning, Georgia went to see the motion picture "Geronimo." Afterwards, in derisive reference to the mock heroics of their practice jumps, they started calling each other by this name. From this grew the paratrooper's practice of shouting "Geronimo" as he leaps from the plane.

Gertrude. An office clerk.

get. To kill.

get a grass sandwich. To copulate (i.e., to roll about in the grass while making love).

get a Jap headache. To be wounded in action.

get a Jap sardine. To sink or destroy a Japanese submarine.

get a Jerry battlewagon. To sink or destroy a German man-of-war.

get a Jerry fish. To sink or destroy a German submarine.

get a Jerry sky wagon. To shoot down a German aircraft.

get-alongs. Legs.

get a pasting. To be badly bombed.

get cracking. To get started; to get into the air. The Army Air Corps borrowed this slang phrase from the R.A.F.

get eager. To strive to be the best.

get off the ground. To accomplish something.

get one's head out of the cockpit. To pay attention.

get on someone's tail. To attack from the rear in air combat.

get the barbwire garters. To receive no decorations, special honors, or mentions. See also BARBWIRE GARTERS, under World War I.

ghost. An unusual radar echo for which no definite source can be found.

ghost man. An aircraft carrier's signal officer on night duty. Dressed in a fluorescent-striped suit and using fluorescent paddles, he directs night fighters to safe landings on the carrier's deck (as reported in *Newsweek* of July 30, 1945).

ghost walks, the. Said on the day salaries are paid. The theater brought this term into use about 1853; it derives from a line in Shakespeare's *Hamlet* where Horatio asks the ghost if it walks because, in life, it buried ill-gotten gains.

ghost walks on the deck, the. Said on payday in the Navy.

G.H.Q. General headquarters (the main office of the commander in chief in the field).

G.I. (1) Government issue. In this usage, the term refers to any article carried by the quartermaster. By extension, it came to be synonymous with "Army."

(2) An enlisted soldier; any member of the armed forces. This meaning of "G.I." did not really take hold until the last half of the war. In an April 1943 article in *Word Study*, "Army Slang," Private Richard A. Herzberg says the use of "G.I." to mean a soldier himself is "a comparatively rare usage." However, by the latter days of the war the situation had changed. General Dwight D. Eisenhower, referring to the death of war correspondent Ernie Pyle, said: "Every G.I.

in Europe—and that means all of us—has lost one of his best and most understanding friends."

G.I.

We now know something of the way the G.I. regarded the two worlds to which he belonged, but how did he see himself? The answer probably lies in the term he chose to describe himself: G.I. The origin of this abbreviation is much debated, but it was undoubtedly used in the Old Army for "government issue." One story is that the Regulars used it as a derogatory label for early draftees, since they were content to wear what the Army gave them—i.e., government issue—rather than buy commercially made items of uniform that would have given them a smarter appearance. If obscurity surrounded the derivation of "G.I.," its various meanings were also a source of much confusion for the uninitiated. Thus, a man who had *the G.I.s* was afflicted with the Army's version of diarrhea. Used in another way, as in "too G.I.," the term meant a person or organization that rigidly adhered to regulations.

—*G.I.: The American Soldier in World War II*, by Lee Kennett (1987)

G.I. ashcan. A heavy artillery shell.

G.I. Bill. Legislation setting up financial benefits for veterans of World War II. The benefits were outlined in *Time* for June 26, 1944: (1) speedy settlement of all disability claims; (2) the aid of a veterans' placement bureau in finding a job, and unemployment insurance for a maximum of one year; (3) government guarantee of fifty percent of any loan for as much as $4,000 to be applied toward the purchase or repair of a home, farm, or business property; (4) a free year or more of college, depending on length of service, if the veteran was under twenty-five when he entered the service. The bill was signed into law by President Franklin D. Roosevelt in June 1944.

G.I. brat. A child of a member of the armed forces.

Gibson girl. A hand-cranked radio transmitter included in aircraft life rafts; so-called from its wasp-waisted shape, reminiscent of the beautiful, idealized women drawn by Charles D. Gibson.

G.I. can. (1) An ashcan or a garbage can. This term was in use in the Army long before World War II; in this instance, "G.I." stands for "galvanized iron." (2) An artillery shell. (3) A cooking vessel.

G.I. cocktail. A dose of salts used as a laxative.

gigadier brendal. A brigadier general.

G.I. haircut. Hair cut to a length of one inch.

G.I. hop. A government-sponsored dance for enlisted men to which "G.I. girls" were brought by official chaperones.

G.I. Jane. A member of the WACS; also called "G.I. Jill" and "G.I. Josephine."

G.I. Joe. A soldier. Dave Breger, the popular cartoonist, claimed to be the originator of the term in a February 26, 1945, letter to *Time* magazine. "G.I. Joe Trooper" was the name of his cartoon hero, whose exploits and misadventures he used in a series of cartoons for *Yank*, the Army weekly. The first of the Breger strips appeared in the issue of June 17, 1942.

G.I. moe. An Army mule.

gimper / goofer. A skilled airman. See both terms under World War I.

gink. A stupid person.

ginkus. A contrivance; a thingamajig.

G.I. party. The traditional Friday-night major cleanup of barracks to prepare for Saturday-morning inspection.

G.I. round table. An educational program, sponsored by the War Department, planned for all the camps and theaters of war.

G.I. shits. Diarrhea; almost certainly from the medical term "gastrointestinal."

G.I. sky pilot. A chaplain.

gism. Gravy.

G.I. struggle. A dance at an Army post.

G.I. turkey. Corned beef.

G. Ivan. A Russian soldier; a play on G.I.

give a bellyful of hot lead. To shoot; to riddle with bullets.

give a bum steer. To give false information.

give a dirty eye / give a dirty blim / give a dirty lamp / give a dirty orb / give a dog eye. To give a hostile look.

give a good working over. To do violence; an Army term.

give an inch of cold iron. To stab; a Marine Corps term.

give cold steel. To stab; to attack with a bayonet.

give half a chance. To supply an opportunity.

give it the air. (1) To apply power to an airplane. (2) To apply the air brakes on a truck.

give it the deep six, brother. Forget it; from older naval slang for burial at sea, which was known as "the deep six," probably from the custom of burying people six feet underground.

give it the gun. To step on the gas.

give lead medicine to a Nip. To shoot or kill a Japanese. See also NIP.

give someone a dose of his own medicine. To take revenge; to retaliate.

give the gun. (1) To apply power; to increase speed. (2) To shoot; to kill.

give the weeps. To attack with tear-gas bombs.

G.I. war. An Army military maneuver.

gizmo / gismo. Anything or anyone with an unknown or forgotten name.

glamor boy. A draftee; a recruit. Soldiers of the regular Army used the term to refer to National Guard soldiers as well as inductees.

glass house. A power-operated glass and metal turret in an airplane.

glide bomb. To bomb from an airplane by descending at an angle of less than sixty-five degrees from the horizontal when releasing bombs. See also DIVE BOMB.

glider. (1) An expert dancer. (2) An engineless airplane.

gloom pan / gloom puss / gloomy pan / glump / glum pan / glum pot / glum puss on a holiday. An irritable or gloomy person; a pessimist.

glory wagon. A FLYING FORTRESS.

G-Man. A garbageman.

gnome. A member of the 2nd Battalion; also called a "runt."

go-ashores. A sailor's best uniform.

go-away cart. A hearse; an ambulance.

go-away cog. Fast driving.

go-away kiss. A bullet.

gobbledygook. Talk or writing that is long, pompous, vague, or tangled, usually with Latinized words. The word was created by Maury Maverick when he became the wartime chairman of President Franklin D. Roosevelt's Smaller War Plans Corporation. Taking aim at the bloated language of government, he drafted a famous memo containing the line: "Anyone using the words 'activation' or 'implementation' will be shot." Maverick coined the term with the turkeys of his native Texas in mind. The birds would end their gobbling with a loud "gook" sound.

go down blazing. (1) To be killed or wounded while fighting the enemy. (2) To fall in flames (said of an airplane or of the people in it).

go downstairs. To parachute from an aircraft.

God's country. The United States.

go for a Spanish walk. To desert from the Navy.

go in baldheaded. To be prepared for any eventuality.

go into a scramble. To take off in an aircraft.

go into a tailspin. To get mad.

go into dry dock. To be hospitalized (as a ship is taken out of the water for repairs).

gold bird/gold buzzard. An eagle insignia.

goldfish / goldfish in a tin coat. Canned salmon.

Gold Fish Club. An organization whose membership was limited to airmen who had crashed into the ocean. It was founded by Lieutenant Colonel Baden-Powell Weil.

good show. Well done (a term of praise). This R.A.F. slang was eagerly adopted by American airmen. "Cracking good show" was the highest possible praise, while "bad show" conveyed criticism or functioned as a comment on any regrettable happening.

good-time Charley. A person given to carousing; a generous person.

good-time Charley act. (1) Dissipated behavior. (2) Generous behavior.

goof burner. A person who uses marijuana.

goof off. To loaf; to avoid work; to make a mistake. A person could goof off in any number of ways.

goofs off. A person who makes mistakes.

gook. A derogatory term for a Melanesian or Polynesian native in the Pacific theater. See also under the Spanish-American War and under the Korean War.

goon. (1) A soldier who falls into the lowest category in Army classification. This term dates back to the fourteenth century (in the writings of Geoffrey Chaucer, it means "thug"). In the "Popeye" comic strip during the 1930s, a stupid character was called the Goon. (2) Any person of subnormal intelligence.

goop bomb. A 500-pound incendiary bomb made of clusters of six-pound bombs packed with jellied oil and magnesium, each of which spread flame over a radius of thirty yards; so-called because the "fiery jellied oil contents" of the bomb suggested a sticky mass, which in laboratory slang is known as "goop." Goop bombs were dropped on Japan in March 1945.

goose it. To feed gas to an engine in irregular spurts; from "goose" in the sense of a poke in the anus.

goose step. The German straight-legged marching step, which came to symbolize the Germans as rigid, conformist, and grotesque. See also under World War I.

Bruce Chapman, in *Why Do We Say Such Things?* (1947), gives this history of the term:

> The name "goose step" was originally applied to a British setting-up exercise in which a new recruit was made to stand on one leg and swing the other backward and forward without bending the knee, just as a goose stands on one leg and swings the other. Because of a similarity of appearance—in particular, the straightened knee—the term was applied to the German military march step in which the foot is raised sufficiently to give it a twenty-inch stride.

go over. To parachute from an aircraft; to attack.

go over the blue wall. To be committed to a hospital for the insane.

go over the hill. To go absent without leave; to desert.

go over the side. (1) To parachute from an aircraft. (2) To leap from the side of a ship.

goozlum. Gravy; syrup. This old logger's term was adopted for Army use.

go to Davy. To be buried at sea. See also DAVY JONES and DAVY JONES'S LOCKER, under the Civil War.

go-to-hell hat. A soft overseas cap.

go to the mat for. To uphold; to support; to be willing to fight for. "Mat" here refers to a wrestling mat.

go to the movies. To go into air combat.

go to work on. To assault; to attack.

go up. To take off in an airplane.

go upstairs. To climb to a high altitude in an airplane.

government bouquet. A government issue of laundry soap.

government mouth-organ. (1) A military counsel. (2) A member of the judge advocate general's department.

grandma. A heavy howitzer.

grand slam. The enemy plane has been shot down (radar code).

grapeshot. Pudding.

grapevine. Rumor; unconfirmed gossip. See also under the Civil War.

grass. Salad.

grass cutter. (1) A fragmentation bomb that explodes on contact, spraying metal fragments over a wide area. The same instinct to give a horrific weapon a bucolic name can be seen in the naming of the powerful "daisy cutter" used in the Vietnam War. (2) The A-20A attack plane (because it flies so low).

grasshopper. A reconnaissance airplane.

gravel crusher. An infantryman.

graveyard stew. (1) Milk toast. (2) A weak stew consisting mostly of bones (like slumgullion without body—see SLUM / SLUMGULLION, under the Civil War).

A Stanza to Graveyard Stew

Francis Raymond Meyer's *Fighting Talk* (1942) quotes this song about graveyard stew, sung to the tune of "God Bless America":

God bless our graveyard stew
No other stew will do
Like graveyard stew
Be careful what you take
Over upon your plate
Or you will get a bellyache
On graveyard stew

---

graybacks. (1) Lice. (2) German soldiers; from the color of their uniform.

gray ghost. A flight school commander's airplane; so-called because it is the last plane one rides in before being WASHED OUT.

grease ape. A mechanic.

grease hound. A mechanic.

grease monkey. A mechanic's assistant.

greasepot. A cook.

great one, the. (1) God. (2) A general. (3) A person of importance.

great unknown, the. (1) Death. (2) Hash; meat loaf; meat pie.

green hornet. A difficult military problem that must be solved quickly.

greenhouse. A shell of light, durable, transparent plastic that covers a bombardier's or gunner's cockpit.

greenie. A recruit.

green light hotel. A "prophylactic station" (i.e., a place where one gets condoms before getting a green light to proceed to town).

gremlin. One of the mythical "little people" who make things go wrong, particularly on airplanes. In *Time* of September 14, 1942, many Americans first heard of them with this account: "The R.A.F. first learned about the little creatures in 1923 and called them gremlins—probably from the obsolete Old English transitive verb greme, meaning to vex. Yet it was not until World War II that the R.A.F. really got to know the gremlins."

Another account, by John Moore, from the *Observer* of November 8, 1942, says that they were called gremlins because "they were the goblins which came out of Fremlin beer bottles."

Newsweek of September 7, 1943, quotes the following dispatch from Merrill Mueller, chief of the magazine's London bureau:

> The great-grandaddy of all "bloody Gremlins" was born in 1923 in a beer bottle belonging to a Fleet Air Arm pilot whose catapult reconnaissance plane was cursed with perpetual engine trouble. This pilot was overloaded with beer the night before a practice maneuver, when the engine failed and he crashed into the waves. Rescued he said the engine failed because little people from a beer bottle had haunted him all night and had got into the plane's engine and controls during the flight. . . . "the bloody Gremlins did it."

This article also says that American gremlins are called "Yehudis" because they are always "fiddling about" (this was a play on the name of violinist Yehudi Menuhin).

Expert "gremlinologists" recorded the characteristics of four new species in *American Notes and Queries* for November 1942: genus *Jockey*, which guided seagulls or pigeons into an airplane's windscreen; genus *Incisor*, whose young teethed on an airplane's control wires; genus *Optic*, which cast a kind of glow over the bombsight just as it was being lined on a target; and genus *Cavity*, which riddled airfields with troublesome little holes.

gremlin grange. A rest home for airmen suffering from battle fatigue. The phrase originated with the R.A.F.—anyone who saw a GREMLIN was ready for the gremlin grange.

grind organ. A machine gun.

grind to hamburger. To do violence.

grizzle guts. (1) A quarrelsome or ill-tempered person. (2) A drill sergeant.

ground. To prohibit an aircraft or an airman to fly.

groundage. Prohibition from flying.

ground gripper. A person who does not fly.

groundhog. A nonflying member of the air service.

ground rat. An infantryman.

gruesome twosomes. Government-issue shoes; a WAC term.

grumlin. A "saboteur of the spirit" on the home front. The name was coined by Sam Rayburn, speaker of the House of Representatives. "The Grumlin," Rayburn declared, "does the same job of sabotage on the home front that the Gremlin does to the airplanes of our pilots fighting the Axis."

grunt. An electrician's helper; an Army Signal Corps term. See also under the Vietnam War.

grunt and growler. A fault finder; a complainer.

g-suit. A suit adopted by the Army Air Corps for fighter pilots, to keep them from losing consciousness in steep dives. It was also called an "anti-g suit"; "g" stands for "gravity."

G-2. (1) Military intelligence. (2) Inquisitiveness. (3) To figure something out; to prophesy.

guardhouse lawyer. (1) A soldier who has some knowledge of regulations and military law and gives advice freely to men who are in trouble. (2) A talkative soldier.

gu-gu. A Filipino. See also GOO-GOO under the Spanish-American War.

gump on the brown. Fried chicken. "Gump" was an old hobo term for chicken.

gun. The throttle of an airplane engine.

gung ho. The nickname for Lieutenant Colonel (later Brigadier General) Evans Fordyce Carlson, and the battle cry of the unit he organized and led, the 2nd Marine Raider Battalion. Gung Ho was also the name given to the Raider camp on Espíritu Santo, in the New Hebrides. See also under the Korean War.

Gung Ho—A Word History

"Carlson of the Raiders," an article by Don Burke in *Life* of September 20, 1943, quotes Carlson on the origin of the Raiders' use of "gung ho":

As we went along, I told the boys everything we were doing and invited criticism and suggestions. And we got them. I was trying to build up the same sort of working spirit I had seen in China where all the soldiers dedicated themselves to one idea and worked together to put that idea over. I told the boys about it again and again. I told them of the motto of the Chinese Cooperatives, Gung Ho. It means Work Together—Work in Harmony. It was hard at first to make them understand since we are essentially a selfish people. But gradually, the longer we were together and the more I had a chance to talk with them, they began to feel it. My motto

caught on and they began to call themselves the Gung Ho Battalion. When I
designed a field jacket to replace the
bulky and orthodox pack they even
called it the Gung Ho jacket. And they
named every new thing Gung Ho. It became the watchword.

gun the potatoes. To replenish the potato dish at mess.

gun-up. To attack; to go into action.

gunwale. A large woman; from the
suggestion of "gun whale" in the gunwale of a ship, which is the upper edge
of its side.

gut-packings. Food; rations.

guy with a round haircut. A recruit;
an unsophisticated person. The expression derives from the bowl-style haircut
given to recruits.

gyrene. A Marine. The term was used
very generally throughout the Pacific
theater of operations and was said at the
time to have been applied to the Marines
by the Chinese. It has also been suggested that the term may be a blend of
"G.I." and "Marine." Another possibility
is that it derived from an old British sea
term. In *Sea Slang of the Twentieth Century,* Wilfred Granville asserts that **ger-
ines** was a 19th century Royal Navy term
for the Royal Marines.

The term has remained in use since
World War II despite efforts by the De-
partment of Defense to eliminate it. *The
New York Times Magazine* for June 5,
1955, in an article entitled "Pentagon
Parlance," reported: "Few terms in the
Pentagon's current lexicon have pro-

voked official disapproval, and even
those that have don't disappear because
of it. Despite a Navy directive to cut it
out, Navy pilots remain 'Airedales' and
Marines are still 'Gyrenes.'"

gyrenes on the march. Marines going
into action.

gyrenes on the wing. Marine Corps
airmen.

gyrene's picnic. An attack by Marines
against the Japanese.

★ ☆ **H** ☆ ★

half-lieut. A second lieutenant (i.e., not
a full lieutenant).

half-track. A vehicle with wheels in
front and a track assembly in the rear;
often miscalled by civilians an "armored car."

halt and freeze. To come to attention.

ham. (1) A recruit; a novice; an awkward person. (2) An amateur radio operator.

hamfist. An airman who wishes to become a pilot but has no instinct for flying. Such men often remained in the Air
Corps in other capacities.

ham shack. An amateur radio station;
a building from which an amateur radio
station does its broadcasting.

hand a gong. To hand out a medal to
a flier.

handcuff volunteer. One who is ordered on a work detail.

hand grenade. A hamburger.

handmade. A handmade cigarette.

hand out the washing. To hang up a display of signal flags.

hand to hand. (1) Married; in close union. (2) Close fighting.

hangar. A drinking establishment.

hangar flying. Conversation about flying and kindred subjects.

hangar lice. Airplane mechanics.

hangar pilot. One who does his best "flying" in conversation.

hangar shyster. An airplane mechanic who talks a lot about airplanes in the manner of a conniving lawyer.

hangar warrior. An airplane mechanic who boasts about what he would do if he were a pilot.

hang fire. To hesitate; to hold in a state of suspension. The term derives from being said of a gun when the charge does not rapidly ignite.

hang out the laundry. To drop paratroopers from airplanes.

-happy. Crazy about; exhilarated by (a combining form). According to an article by Dwight L. Bolinger, in *American Speech* of February 1944, "slap-happy" was apparently the first such term. Others included "Hitler-happy," "bar-happy," "stripe-happy," "bomb-happy," and "trigger-happy."

harborlight. A companion; one who takes care of a friend who has been drinking.

harbormaster. One's wife or mistress.

hard-case. A quarrelsome or ill-tempered person.

hard-roll. A packaged cigarette (in contrast to a HANDMADE).

hard soup. Liquor.

hardtail. An Army mule.

hardware. Firearms.

hash burner. A cook.

hash mark. A straight stripe on a soldier's uniform that denotes a period of service, usually a minimum of three years per stripe. Hash marks are not to be confused with chevrons, which are v-shaped and indicate rank.

haul. The distance flown by an aircraft on a military mission.

have one's number on it. Said of a bullet or piece of shrapnel that hits one.

haywire. Broken; out of order. The term derives from the notion that broken farm implements are often repaired with hay baling wire.

head. (1) A head man. (2) A latrine.

head for the barn. To return in an airplane to an aircraft carrier.

head resistance. The resistance offered by a head wind.

headset. A radio receiver worn on one's head.

heartburn. (1) A sweetheart, wife, or mistress. (2) To be in love.

heaven kissing. (1) Dreaming. (2) Touching the clouds in an airplane.

heavies. Heavy artillery.

heavy heeled. Well armed.

heavy weapons. A company or other unit armed with machine guns.

hedgehopper. A pilot who flies so low he has to hop over obstacles on the ground.

Heinie. A German; anything German. The term derives from the name Heinrich, the German equivalent of Henry.

hell afloat. A ship commanded by a stern captain.

hell buggy. A tank.

hell cat. A bugler.

hell chariot. A tank.

hell to pay. The need to make up for one's mistakes.

hen. A bombardier; so-called because he is responsible for the "laying of the eggs" (dropping bombs).

hep. Intelligent; wise to what is happening. The term is a variant of "hip."

herdbound. A soldier or work animal unfit for military duty.

Hershey bar. A gold insignia worn on a soldier's lower left sleeve, denoting six months' overseas duty; named for the fact that the nation's most popular chocolate bar had the same name as Lewis B. Hershey, director of Selective Service.

high and dry on a tub. Aboard a ship when aground; beached.

highball. To run with the throttle wide open, as a train.

higher than a Georgia pine. Very excited.

higher-up. A person holding senior rank or office.

high flier. A person inclined to go to extremes in anything; an aviator.

high hat. An expert aviator.

highpockets. A tall, lanky person.

Hit and Muss. Hitler and Mussolini.

hit-and-run battleship. A battleship used for making sudden attacks on merchant shipping and then escaping. President Franklin D. Roosevelt used the term in a radio broadcast of May 27, 1941: "In this second world war, however, the problem is greater because the attack on the freedom of the seas is now fourfold: first, the improved submarine; second, the much greater use of the heavily armed raiding cruiser, or hit-and-run battleship . . ."

hitch. An enlistment. See under World War I.

hitch mark. An Army service stripe, denoting a certain number of years of service.

Hitler hearse. An Army tank. The term seems to have been coined by Walter Winchell in his "On Broadway" syndicated newspaper column for July 31, 1942.

Hitlerist. One who believes in Hitlerian dogma.

Hitlerize. To make into a HITLERIST.

Hitlerland. Germany; the countries conquered by Germany.

hit the beach. To go on shore leave.

hit the deck / hit it. (1) To land an airplane. (2) To get out of one's bunk in the morning. Medics on a surprise early-morning SHORT-ARM INSPECTION would shout, "Hit the deck for pecker check."

hit the hay. To go to bed.

hit the silk / hit the silkworm. To parachute from an airplane (parachutes of the time were made of silk).

hive. To discover; to catch.

hivey. Quick to learn.

Hobby lobby. The office of Colonel Oveta Culp Hobby, commander of the WACs.

hog caller. A portable loudspeaker.

holiday. A space left unswept in a minesweeping operation.

Hollywood private. An acting corporal (one waiting for a corporalcy).

Holy Joe. A clergyman.

Holy Joe's mate. A Navy chaplain.

home west of the divide. One's "location" after death.

homing device. A furlough.

honey barge. A garbage scow.

honey wagon. A rolling toilet; a wagon or truck used in collecting refuse at an Army post.

hook. (1) A hypodermic needle. Calling it a hook was undoubtedly a way of terrifying recruits. (2) A chevron; from its V-shape.

Horehouse Heato. Emperor Hirohito.

horizontal drill. Sleep; resting in bed.

horse a ship. To point the nose of an airplane toward the earth.

horse croaker / horse doctor. A veterinary surgeon.

hot landing. An airplane landing made with the plane not in a fully stalled attitude, usually with excess speed.

hot pilot / hotshot. An expert aviator; a person of extraordinary ability.

hot plane. An aircraft requiring careful handling because of its high takeoff or landing speed.

hot spot. (1) A dangerous position while under fire. (2) Hell.

hot stuff. (1) Large-caliber shells. (2) An exclamation of approval.

how. A toast; probably short for "Here's how!"

howler. (1) A faultfinder; a complainer. (2) An air-raid siren.

H.P. Hot pilot (an expert pilot).

hubba hubba. An exclamation of approbation, thrill, or enthusiasm by a man for a woman. According to an article in *American Speech* of February 1947, the term was very widely used during the war—on the radio, in the movies, in several popular songs, and in general conversation. The *English Dialect Dictionary* (1898) notes this possible etymology: "Hubba—a cry given to warn fishermen of the approach of pilchards." This meaning accords very well with the way "hubba hubba" was used during the war.

huff duff. High-frequency direction-finding device (an instrument for detecting and plotting the direction of radio signals from distant sources). During the war, the device was used to determine the location of covert transmitters.

hulaland. Hawaii.

human cyclones. Marines.

hump. The spur of the Himalayas that separates Assam and Yunnan and cuts through western China. See also OVER THE HUMP.

hungry hill. The married noncommissioned officers' quarters.

hush boat. A mystery boat.

hustling hooker. A prostitute.

Hyde Park Ranger. A British streetwalker.

hydroship. A hydroplane.

hypo happy. Enamored of photography. "Hypo" is sodium thiosulfate, used as a fixing agent in developing.

★ ☆ **I** ☆ ★

I.C. Inspected and condemned (as unfit for further military use). These letters are placed on any article so acted upon.

icebird. A soldier or Coast Guardsman assigned to duty in the far north.

ice up. (1) To have ice form on the wings of an airplane. (2) To snub or neglect.

ice wagon. A large Catalina Flying Boat.

I.D. (1) Intelligence Department. (2) A soldier given to spreading rumors.

I'll see you in hell first. I will not do so.

I'm with you. Yes; I agree (i.e., an affirmative response).

in a spin. In an unsettled state of mind.

in a tight spot. In difficulty; in trouble.

incendiary. A bomb that, upon exploding, spreads a fire that cannot be extinguished with water but has to be smothered with chemicals, sand, or some other substance. Originally, the term referred to a person who willfully set fire to a building or other property.

in everybody's mess and nobody's watch. Said of a pest or busybody (i.e., one who is there for meals, but not work).

ink. Black coffee.

in low water. Short of funds.

in stir. In confinement as a punishment.

international date line. A date with a woman in a foreign port.

in the drink. Downed at sea.

in the gravy. In comfortable circumstances; assigned to an easy task.

in the library. Flying by instruments.

in the tub. (1) Aboard Ship. (2) About to be WASHED OUT; a play on "washtub."

invasion foot. A condition characterized by a tingling, burning sensation in the lower extremities followed within forty-eight hours by numbness and swelling (a form of frostbite); also called "immersion foot." This malady and the terms for it had an unwelcome revival during the Korean War.

in velvet. Well supplied with money; assigned to an easy task.

Irish grapes. White potatoes.

Irish horse. Tough corned beef.

Irish promotion. A demotion in rank.

iron Betsy. A rifle.

ironcladder. A severely chaste woman.

iron crab. A steel pillbox that could be moved from place to place.

iron derby / iron hat. A steel helmet.

iron fireman / iron Mike. An automatic pilot for an airplane. The device made an early appearance in Zack Mosley's "Smilin' Jack" comic strip for May 10, 1942.

iron horse / iron mule. A tank.

iron pineapple. A grenade with a pineapple-like surface.

island hop. To make military advances by seizing an island and using it as a base to seize the next island. The term was used in the Pacific theater.

is-was. A calculating device resembling a circular slide rule (used to get bearings in a submarine).

★ ☆ **J** ☆ ★

J. Coffee, short for java.

jaafu. Joint Anglo-American foul-up (or fuck-up).

jacfu. Joint American-Chinese foul-up (or fuck-up).

jack. A corporal.

jack of the dust. A petty officer in charge of coffee, cream, and sugar.

Jackson. A soldier (a form of address).

J.A.G. Judge advocate general.

jalopy. An old, reconditioned aircraft or automobile.

jam. To interfere with radio reception by transmitting on the same frequency.

jam card. A report of bad conduct.

jamming. Intentional introduction of spurious radiation into radio and radar frequencies to make the message unintelligible.

jamoc / jamoke. Coffee; from the blending of "Java" and "mocha," two types of coffee yielding a strong black drink.

jamoke-hound. A coffee addict.

jamoke-tub. A vessel used for brewing coffee.

jane. A woman.

jane-crazy. Overly fond of women.

janfu. Joint Army-Navy foul-up (or fuck-up).

Jap. (1) A Japanese. (2) Anything Japanese.

Japanazi. A Japanese or a German. This term was a wartime coinage of columnist and radio commentator Walter Winchell.

Japanese powder. Cocaine.

Jape. A Japanese. The slur was given to the Japanese by the Marines in the Marianas Islands. The word, a combination of "Jap" and "ape," was reported by Ernie Pyle in his dispatches.

Japland. Japan.

Jap sugar. Cocaine.

Jap whale. A Japanese submarine.

jarhead. (1) An Army mule. (2) A Marine.

Java. Coffee (whether actual Java coffee or not).

Java and sidearms. Coffee with cream and sugar.

jawbone. (1) Credit. (2) To charge, as an account.

jawbreakers. Army biscuits.

jayhawker. A lawless soldier; a guerrilla fighter.

jazz it. To dive close to the ground in an airplane.

jeep. (1) A small, low, khaki-colored car in general use in the Army. (2) A rookie; a recruit.

Jeep—Word History

A powerful, sturdy, and versatile vehicle, the jeep became known everywhere American soldiers went. The name gained immediate approval and now seems to be universally accepted. It is applied to any number of jeep-style vehicles, including some made in countries that were America's enemy during the war.

As A. Marjorie Taylor reports in *The Language of World War II* (1948): "The car itself was not invented by any one person, but evolved gradually, a need for such a type of car being felt in World War I. The earliest experimental models (made by Willys-Overland, American Bantam, and Ford) were nicknamed Beep, Bug, Blitz, Buggy, Chigger, Midget, Puddle Jumper, Peep, etc."

Several sources, including *American Speech* of February 1943, give this account of its nicknaming. In February 1941, the first Willys model was being put through tests in Washington, D.C., with Katharine Hillyer, a staff writer for the Washington *Daily News*, as a passenger. Someone asked the driver the "name of that thing, mister," and was told, "It's a Jeep." A picture of the car, with "jeep" in the caption, appeared in the Washington *Daily News* on February 19, 1941.

The term "jeep" had appeared in E. C. Segar's "Popeye" comic strip as early as March 16, 1936, which may have been the source for the name of the car, according to this letter of June 23, 1944, written by William Howlett, of Carl Byoir and Associates:

Your recent letter to Willys-Overland Motors regarding the genesis of the word Jeep has been referred to this office for answering since we handled public relations matters for the company.

We feel that the word originated with Segar, King Features cartoonist, who until his recent death wrote the Popeye strip. You will recall that in this feature there was a character called the "Jeep" which lived on orchids and could go anywhere and do anything.

It is our contention that the boys in the service picked this name up from Segar and applied it to the Willys vehicle which has many of the "go anywhere, do anything" characteristics of the Popeye character.

However, the following two items focus on an alternative explanation.

The first is from an article by Marsh Maslin in the San Francisco *Call-Bulletin* of November 22, 1941: "Do you know why those swift little army cars are called 'jeeps'? It's Model G-P produced by that automobile manufacturer—and G-P easily becomes 'jeep.'"

The second is from *Why We Say* (1953), by Robert L. Morgan: "The pronunciation of initials sometimes gives the English language a brand-new word. This is what happened when a new kind of United States Army vehicle was officially named 'General Purpose Car.' It was first referred to by its initials, G.P., and you can easily see how this became the very popular 'jeep.'"

---

jeepable. Impassable except by jeep (said of a rough road).

jeep nurse. A jeep driver.

jeepny. A jitney bus built on a jeep body and an important mode of transportation in the Philippines after the war.

jeeptown. Detroit, Michigan (because Army jeeps were manufactured there).

jeepville. (1) Detroit, Michigan (because Army jeeps were manufactured there). (2) The barracks or quarters of incoming recruits (presumably because one first encountered jeeps there).

jeepy. Screwy.

jeeter. A lieutenant.

jerk. An unpopular, clumsy, or odd person; probably from "jerkwater town."

jerk-pot. A spendthrift.

jerrican / Jerry-can. A five-gallon container designed by the Germans (see JERRY) and used mostly to hold gasoline. A great many of the flat-sided cans could be stacked in trucks and then thrown out along the roads used by military forces, so ready supplies of gasoline would be available, enabling the forces to move rapidly in the field. German field marshal Erwin Rommel used this tactic to great advantage during the Libyan campaign (as reported in the Manchester *Guardian* of November 25, 1944). Allied forces used a copy of the jerrican (hastily produced in England) during the march from El Alamein and, later, during the liberation of France.

Jerry. A German; anything German. Originally, the term was British slang for a German fighter pilot or his plane.

jetty. (1) A small woman. (2) A small pier.

jig. A frame for holding airplane parts together while the airplane is being assembled.

jitterbug. A jeep; a reconnaissance car.

jitters. A nervous sensation.

job. A woman (e.g., a "neat job," a "fast job," etc.).

Joe. (1) Coffee. (2) G.I. JOE.

Joe and sidearms. Coffee, cream, and sugar.

"Joe Blow" biography. A short biographical article featuring a fighting man, written for publication in a hometown newspaper.

Joe pot. A coffeepot.

John / Johnny Raw. A recruit.

join the bird. To become an airman.

join the cat club. To parachute from an airplane in an emergency or in combat.

joker. A wise guy; an arrogant soldier.

JOOM. A junior observer of meteorology. During the war, JOOMs were trained to replace weather bureau men who had gone to war.

joy hop. A flight for pleasure only.

joyride. A short flight for pleasure only; a student aviator's initial flight.

J.P. Jet propulsion.

jughead. (1) A mule. (2) A stupid person.

juice. Electricity.

juice jerker. An electrician.

juicy. First-rate; excellent.

jumping jeep. An autogiro with "jump takeoff."

jumping-off point. (1) A place of assembly for an attack. (2) A place disliked.

jump on someone's tail. (1) To do violence. (2) To attack from the rear in air combat.

jump out the window. To parachute from a glassed-in gun turret.

jump pay. Extra pay given to paratroopers.

jungleer. An infantryman specially trained and equipped for jungle warfare. In *The War Dictionary* (1942), by Louise D. Parry, a jungleer is described as "specially garbed in lightweight camouflaged coveralls and hat . . . [and] . . . equipped with a short carbine (instead of a rifle) as well as a razor-edged machete. . . ."

jungle juice. Illegal moonshine liquor made from the dried fruits contained in J- or K-rations. A review of G.I. liquors of the Pacific theater published in the January 1946 issue of *Esquire* reported on jungle juice and other libations, including: "night fighter"—fermented sap of the nipa palm; "plonk"—Australian table wine; "tuba"—fermented sap from the heart of the coconut palm; and "kava"—from the roots of the kava tree.

Jungle Juice—A Short Memoir

Not to be outdone, the division sent down a directive giving the men Good Conduct Medals. When the notices were posted, I was overjoyed. Wouldn't my folks be proud of me! A Good Conduct Medal and promoted to Pfc all in one day. The colonel, however, took care of that situation. After lunch, a special notice appeared on the bulletin board rescinding the medal of a guy named Kilroy. The colonel said it was for the illicit manufacture of alcoholic beverages. "Tain't true" no one in his right mind would call Jungle Juice manufactured. By accident, some corn fell into a gasoline drum, fermented, and I was fortunate enough to find it. (Said beverage is known farther north as the "Aleutian Solution.")

—*Atabrine Times*, by "Kilroy" (1946)

---

jungle Juliet. A female member of the Marine Corps.

jungle rot. Any kind of skin disease. Other, equivalent terms included "creeping crud" and "New Guinea crud."

junior birdman. A recipient of the Air Medal.

junior prom. A dangerous mission in the Army Air Corps.

juniper. A raw recruit.

★ ☆ K ☆ ★

kaiten. A Japanese human-steered torpedo.

kamikaze. A term used to describe Japanese "suicide" aircraft and pilots. The term is also applied to a defense strategy of suicidal resistance. In Japanese, the literal meaning is "divine wind."

kangaroo John. An Australian soldier.

kay o. The commanding officer of an Army unit (usually, the commander of a regiment).

keelhauling. A reprimand from a superior officer; from KEELHAUL (see under the Civil War).

keep 'em flying. A popular slogan urging civilians to contribute to the war effort (thereby keeping air squadrons flying).

keep the field. To continue active operations.

keep the tail clear. To maneuver an airplane so as not to allow an enemy airplane to attack from the rear.

Kennel Ration. Hash or meat loaf; from the name of a popular dog food.

khaki-whacky. A woman overly fond of men in uniform.

kick. (1) A dishonorable discharge. (2) The recoil of a rifle.

kick downstairs. To demote in rank.

kick his teeth down his throat. To do violence.

kick in the can. (1) To kick in the posterior. (2) To confine in the guardhouse.

kid. A bomber copilot.

Kilroy was here. A motto that was written on fences, buildings, sidewalks, and restroom walls all over the world. It also became a popular civilian expression.

Kilroy: He Was There, but Who Was He?

Folklore about Kilroy grew up among the boys of the Air Transport Command, who, wherever they flew, found that Kilroy had been there before them, though no one ever saw him. "Kilroy was here," "Kilroy ate here," "Kilroy slept here," and other items of information about Kilroy appeared at airfields all over the world. In *I Hear America Talking* (1976), Stuart Berg Flexner points out: "This most popular piece of graffiti of all time meant 'a U.S. serviceman was here' and 'a stranger was here.'" Imitators such as "Corduroy" and "Clem" also appeared, but they failed to attain the vogue of Kilroy.

The expression even held on for a while after the war. After the first H-bomb test, scientists went in to check the guinea-pig battleships used in the test and found "Kilroy was here" freshly painted on one of the hulls.

Who was he? An ad for the Association of the U.S. Army gave this answer:

Some say he was a foreman in a Seattle munitions plant during World War II. Equipment shipped overseas carried his name on the side, showing that it had been inspected and approved. Others insist that he was an unknown infantry soldier who got tired of hearing the Air Force brag that they were always first on the spot. So he began to leave his message wherever his unit saw action. . . . But everyone knows that in a sense Kilroy is no one. No single person, that is. He's every soldier.

According to *Newsweek* of December 3, 1945, the real Kilroy was Sergeant Francis J. Kilroy, Jr. One day in 1943—after the phrase was in circulation—a notice appeared on the bulletin board at Boca Raton Field, Florida: "Kilroy will be here next week." It had been written by Sergeant James Maloney as his friend Sergeant Kilroy lay ill with influenza. That started a campaign that made Kilroy the most famous man in the Army Air Corps. Transferred to another station, Maloney kept writing notices about Kilroy.

However, in 1962 the Associated Press put an obituary on the wire for a James J. Kilroy of Boston, who had died at the age of sixty. The AP declared that of all the claims to having originated the expression, this Kilroy's was "generally credited as the soundest." The obituary went on to say that Kilroy had gone to work as an inspector at the Fore River Shipyard, in Quincy, Massachusetts, two days before Pearl Harbor and had immediately begun writing "Kilroy was here" on the equipment that his gang had checked. As the equipment was shipped around the world, the slogan caught on. The AP added that when the war was over the American Transit Association held a contest to see who the original Kilroy was, and this Kilroy, still working at the shipyard, presented his evidence and won. His prize: a twenty-two-ton trolley car.

The James Kilroy claim is further bolstered by an article in *Time* for December 2, 1946, in which the same James J. Kilroy, then of Halifax, Massachusetts, is quoted as saying that he first wrote "Kilroy was here" on the hull of the *Lexington* in a shipyard. He won a contest for

the best explanation of how the Kilroy thing started. He said he had been a war worker at the Bethlehem Steel Company's Quincy shipyard. His job was to inspect the tanks, double bottoms, and other aspects of warships under construction. In order to let his superiors know that he was doing what had been assigned to him, he followed the practice of scrawling "Kilroy was here" in yellow crayon on the items he inspected.

Some investigators have found so many conflicting claims that they have thrown up their hands. Stuart Berg Flexner wrote in *I Hear America Talking:*

There have been dozens of stories about who the original Kilroy was or what "Kilroy" meant to its originators—so many stories that no one knows for sure who or what the original Kilroy was. Many graffiti writers made a drawing to accompany the phrase "Kilroy was here," showing a wide-eyed, bald-headed face peering over a fence which hid everything below his nose, except for his fingers, which were shown gripping the top of the fence—Kilroy was the mischievous outsider, staring at, and probably laughing at, the world.

kite. A slow plane with a big wingspan.

kite full of flak. An airplane hit heavily by antiaircraft fire.

kiwi / kewie. A GROUNDHOG; a timid pilot. The kiwi is a flightless bird.

klink. (1) A guardhouse; a ship's prison. See also CLINK, under World War I.

knee pad. A pancake.

knight of the silkworm. One who has jumped from an airplane in a silk parachute.

K-9 Corps. Dogs used in war. The Army's K-9 Corps, organized during the war, was originally called D4D ("Dogs for Defense").

knockabout. A small dorylike boat.

knock civvies into shape. To train or drill recruits.

knock down / K.D. To take apart a piece of equipment, partially or entirely.

knocker. (1) A small fulminate cap. (2) A faultfinder; a complainer.

knock for a goal / knock hell out of / knock hell, west, and crooked / knock into a cocked hat / knock someone's block off / knock someone's ears down / knock the sap out of / knock the spots off of. To do violence.

knock-knock. An acoustic mine.

knuckle buster. A crescent wrench.

konshine. A conscientious objector.

K.P. See KITCHEN POLICE, under World War I.

K-ration. A balanced ration for troops in the field. The K-ration was put out by the Army Subsistence Research Laboratory, starting out as the "Parachute Ration," or "Pararation." Some called it the "blitz ration" while it was under development. Its wide use by many different combat groups necessitated a more general name, and it was called "Ration K," after the leader of the team that created it, Dr. Ancel Keys. In the late 1950s and early 1960s Keys was in the news as the author of *Eat Well and Stay Well*, the first book on the dangers of animal fat in the American diet.

The K-ration came in three sealed boxes—breakfast, lunch, and dinner units. It contained over 3,000 calories and all the required vitamins. The inventory of foods in the ration changed several times during the war, but this is what was most often in the three packages: in the breakfast unit—two types of biscuits, one meat and egg unit, a fruit bar, one soluble coffee unit, three sugar tablets, a stick of gum, four cigarettes, and one can key; in the dinner unit—two types of biscuits, one cheese unit, one confection unit, one lemon powder unit, three sugar tablets, a stick of gum, four cigarettes, one clip of matches, and one can key; in the supper unit—two types of biscuits, one meat product, one two-ounce D-ration candy bar, one bouillon powder unit, a stick of gum, and four cigarettes. The biscuits included were known as "defense" biscuits; they were made of molasses, whole wheat flour, and soybean flour and flavored with spices.

Two items in particular were widely disliked: malt-dextrose tablets and ersatz lemon powder, which in theory could be used to make a lemon-flavored drink, but the drink was so bad that it tended to be used for hair rinse or stove cleaner.

kraut. A German; from "sauerkraut" (popularly supposed to be the staple food of the Germans).

kraut-head of the krauts. Adolf Hitler.

★ ☆ L ☆ ★

ladies' fever. Syphilis.

lame and lazy list. The sick and injured list.

lam man. A deserter (i.e., one who is on the lam).

land crab / land swab. A landlubber.

landing gear. One's legs.

land of the rising sun. Japan; from the image of the sun on its flag. After December 7, 1941, Japan was often called the "land of the setting sun."

land shark. One who preys on seamen ashore.

latrine humor. The kind of humor shared among men using the latrine, or group toilet. To illustrate, here are two stanzas from "When I Begin to Clean the Latrine" (sung to the tune of "Begin the Beguine"), a song of the men serving in the South Pacific:

> When I begin to clean the latrine,
> I take up a mop in my hand so tender,
> I scrub all the seats till they shine in splendor,
> And polish the bowls till they have a sheen.
>
> . . .
>
> Just a short year ago I was green,
> And I didn't know that the word latrine ever existed,
> But I found out soon enough when I enlisted,
> Now I know but too well what it means.

latrineogram / latrine rumor / latrine telegram. An unfounded report.

laundry. A board that passes on the promotion of a flying cadet; from the fact that this board decides who will or will not WASH OUT.

lay an egg. To drop a bomb.

lay a smokescreen. To lie; to cheat; to flatter.

lead Grape-nuts. Shrapnel.

lead pill. A bullet.

lead swinger. A shirker.

leapfrog march. A march in which troops alternately marched for five miles and then rode on trucks for fifty miles or for an hour.

leaping lena / leaping lizzie. A tank; an old jeep or other automobile.

leatherhides. Lice.

leave calling cards. To bomb a locale and then return.

leave hound. A soldier who doesn't return from his leave until the last minute.

let daylight into. To shoot or stab.

let fly at. To assault; to attack.

Lex. The aircraft carrier *Lexington*, sunk in combat in the Coral Sea.

liberate. To SCROUNGE; to steal; to loot.

liberty. A shore leave.

liberty card. A card giving permission to go on shore leave.

liberty ships. Ships of about 10,000 gross tons built in great numbers during the war years.

library. A latrine.

lieutenant's landing. A perfect airplane landing.

life raft. A savings account; a home; a wife.

lift. To discharge; to get rid of.

limejuice gob. A British sailor; from **limey** (see under World War I).

limey-navy carrier. A British aircraft carrier.

limp line. A line of men reporting to sick call.

lip burner. A cigarette stub.

Little America. Grosvenor Square (London) and the surrounding area (the site of apartment houses and public buildings occupied by U.S. troops).

little poison. A 37-mm gun.

little red wagon. A rolling toilet.

live wire. An energetic person; a passionate young woman.

looey / looie. (1) An Army second lieutenant. (2) A Navy lieutenant.

loose lips sink ships. A slogan urging care in talking about war-related matters, lest one be overheard by enemy spies. Other such slogans are recalled by Rob-

ert Hendrickson in *Encyclopedia of Word and Phrase Origins* (1987): "The slip of a lip may sink a ship," "Slipped lips sink ships," and "Idle gossip sinks ships." Still another was, "Don't talk chum. Chew Topps gum."

looseners. Prunes.

loto. A lieutenant.

Louie the Louse. A seaplane.

lovebird. An airplane.

low-hole Charlie. The wing man in a formation of airplanes.

low-neck gown. A sailor's jumper or blouse.

low on amps and voltage. Lacking ambition and ideas.

loxygen. Liquid oxygen.

lozenge. A pistol bullet.

L.P. Leg puller (i.e., a joker).

lullaby in lead. An attack with machine guns.

★ ☆ **M** ☆ ★

mac. A sailor.

machine gat / machine rod. A machine gun. "Gat" and "rod" were gangland words for a gun.

machine oil. Syrup.

made. Promoted to noncommissioned officer.

madhouse. A control tower.

Mae West. A life jacket worn by R.A.F. airmen. It was an inflatable rubber belt, and it saved the lives of many aviators who had been forced to bail out over water. Americans adopted the term and loved its cheeky (or should it be bosomy?) allusion to the quintessential American sexpot. This information on the term appeared in *American Speech* of December 1944:

> Miss West sent a letter to the RAF, on hearing that her name had been attached to a life-saving jacket. The last two paragraphs read: "If I do get in the dictionary—where you say you want to put me—how will they describe me? As a warm clinging life-saving garment worn by aviators? Or an aviator's jacket that supplies the woman's touch while the boys are flying around nights? I've been in *Who's Who* and I know what's what, but it'll be the first time I ever made the dictionary."

Maggie. A magnetic mine.

Maggie's drawers. A red flag that indicated a clean miss on the rifle range.

MAGIC. Military Advisory Group in China. This American group assisted the Chinese government in military matters.

magic carpet. The warships used to bring servicemen back to the United States after the war.

magpie. A shot that strikes the inner circle of a target, signaled by a flag also known as a "magpie."

maiden run. (1) A first date with a woman. (2) A ship's first sea voyage.

maiden trip. A ship's first sea voyage.

main dish. A wife, sweetheart, or mistress.

make a forced landing. To slip and fall down.

make a Pittsburgh sky. To spread smoke to cover the movements of naval vessels. Pittsburgh, Pennsylvania, was a manufacturing town full of smokestacks.

make do. To manage to do something despite less than ideal circumstances.

Make it snappy! Make it lively! Be quick!

make knots. To travel at high speed; from the fact that the Navy measures velocity in knots.

makings. Cigarette papers and tobacco.

mama. A girlfriend.

mama's pets. The military police; a play on M.P.

man, the. The commanding officer; the officer in charge; the executive officer of the guardhouse or brig; the officer of inspection; the officer of the day.

man-bound. Detained in port because of a lack of crewmen.

Manhattan Project. The atomic bomb research project. Three huge plants were built: at Oak Ridge, Tennessee; at Pasco, Washington; and at Los Alamos, New Mexico.

man in brown. An officer; a soldier.

Marauder. The Martin B-26 medium bomber.

Marfak. Butter; from the name of a brand of machine oil.

marge. Margarine.

Marines. Women in the Marine Corps. At the time, women in the military were usually given cute names, so this passage from A. Marjorie Taylor's *The Language of World War II* (1948) is notable: "The Marine Corps announced firmly that its new women's reserve would be called—not WAMS, not MARINETTES—but simply MARINES. The group was established February 13, 1943."

marsh grass. Spinach.

mash in. To push in the clutch pedal.

maskee. Okay.

master of the pills. A hospital steward or orderly.

MAT. Military Air Transport.

max. A complete success; the maximum.

Maytag Charlie. A type of Japanese scout airplane. The plane's engine made a distinctive sound, much like that of a washing machine. (Maytag was, and still is, a well-known brand of washing machine.)

McCoy. A trustworthy person or thing; from "the real McCoy."

M-Dogs. A group of Army dogs. A note in the August 1944 issue of *American Notes and Queries* defined this term as follows: "Army-trained dogs capable of detecting anti-personnel mines and booby traps laid by the enemy; called 'the elite of the K-9 Corps.' Involving an ability to spot metallic and non-metallic objects, the temperament of the dog was more important than the breed."

meat can. A tight compartment in a bomber (where men are packed in like tinned beef).

meat hound. One who is overly fond of food.

meatlegger. A person who sells meat in defiance of rationing restrictions; analogous to "bootlegger."

meat wagon. An ambulance.

mechanical rat. A two-way loudspeaker system connecting the soldiers' barracks with the noncommissioned officer's room; also called an "electric stooge."

mechanized dandruff. Fleas; lice.

medico. A medical person.

men behind the men behind the guns. The Quartermaster Corps.

Merrill's Marauders. An Army unit under Brigadier General Frank D. Merrill, who called for volunteers for a "dangerous and hazardous mission," then welded them into a fighting group patterned after Wingate's Raiders. They went into action in Assam in 1944.

metal mustang. A JEEP.

meteorskrieg. An exceptionally powerful BLITZKRIEG. The term was coined by American general Stephen O. Fuqua to describe the speed and power of the German drive in France and Belgium in the spring of 1940.

Mexican strawberries. Beans.

M.I.A. Missing in action.

Mickey Mouse. (1) The lever that releases the bombs in an airplane. (2) A training film, especially one dealing with venereal disease.

Mickey Mouse money. Japanese paper occupation currency in the Philippines.

Mickey Mouse rules. Petty rules, red tape, and regulations. In his marvelous book on nautical terminology, *Salty Words* (1984), Robert Hendrickson writes: "One theory holds that World War II U.S. Navy Military Indoctrination Centers, or M.I.C.s, where undisciplined sailors were restrained, gave their initials to this expression for petty rules."

middle of the scow in a jam. The central portion of a ship during an emergency.

midget. Tiny; miniature. The term was used especially in describing naval vessels (for instance, "midget submarine").

mighty atom. A JEEP. This Army tip of the hat to atomic power dates from 1942.

military architecture. A handsome soldier.

military wedding. An enforced wedding.

milk battalion. The 3rd Battalion.

milk route. A short, easy flight.

milk run. (1) A routine mission flown daily. (2) A mission completed without loss of either aircraft or personnel.

milk squadron. The 3rd Squadron.

mill. (1) A guardhouse or other place of confinement. (2) A motor, especially an aircraft engine.

millimeter Pete. Japanese artillery.

mine planter. A ship for sowing mines at sea.

minuteman. A person engaged in selling war bonds and stamps. The image of a Revolutionary War minuteman was used to promote their sale.

miny. Abounding with naval mines.

misery pipe. A bugle.

missing link. A second lieutenant (seen as prehuman).

mission. A bomber raid.

Missouri nightingale. An Army mule.

miss wing. A female pilot.

Mitscher shampoo. Any of a number of large-scale and successful air attacks under the command of Vice Admiral Marc Andrew Mitscher.

mitt flapper / mitt flopper. A soldier who does favors for his superiors; a yes-man; one who raises his hand (mitt) to volunteer.

M.O. Medical officer.

moan and wail. A jail; an Army adaptation of Cockney rhyming slang.

mobile pillbox. A tank.

mockup. (1) A panel on which working models of aircraft parts are flat mounted. They were used as teaching aids by the Army Air Corps. (2). A design model of an aircraft.

MOINC. Medical officer in command. See OINC.

mole hole. A darkroom.

mole-rat. A sapper.

Molotov bread basket. A big container filled with small bombs. The baskets would be dropped by a bomber, and the bombs would be released on the way to the ground. It was named after Vyacheslav Molotov, a Soviet diplomat and minister for foreign affairs, as is the next entry.

Molotov cocktail. A glass bottle of gasoline tied to a flaming rag and thrown. The improvised incendiary weapon was first used against tanks but found many other applications. Properly done, the burning gas heats the tank and drives the crew out of the tank to be shot or captured.

Mona. An air-raid signal; from its moaning sound.

Mona and Clara. Air-raid and all-clear signals. "Clara" is echoic of "clear."

M-1 thumb. An injured thumb. Many recruits would get a mangled, black-and-blue thumb while learning to deal with the bolt of the M-1 rifle.

monkey. (1) A fellow; a company clerk. (2) A Japanese.

monkey island. (1) The exposed top side of a ship's wheelhouse. (2) Japan.

monkey meat. (1) Canned beef. (2) A dead Japanese.

monkey suit. (1) An aviator's coverall. (2) A formal military uniform.

month and a month. A sentence of one month in the guardhouse and a fine of one month's pay.

mooch. To borrow (with no intention of repaying).

moo juice. Milk.

moonlight requisition. Illegal requisition, unauthorized trade, or downright thievery of supplies. Here is a passage by Quentin Reynolds, from an article in *Collier's* of October 23, 1943:

> Officers watched them carefully. They had to, lest the men from one outfit grab supplies assigned to another outfit. Our Army is great for that. They will steal a battleship if they can get away with it. At night, every jeep driver cannibalizes his car, removes the magneto. Otherwise, his jeep would be gone. Our boys don't call it stealing. They call it "moonlight requisitioning."

moo oil. (1) Butter. (2) Insincere talk.

moosh. A guardhouse.

mop up. (1) To clear a position of debris and wounded. (2) To clear ground of remaining enemy combatants after an attack. (3) To win a large sum of money at gambling.

morning headache. A bugle call.

Morse music. The noise created by operating a telegraph instrument.

mosquito. (1) A British fighter-bomber plane. It was a plywood airplane that British enthusiasts called the world's fastest aircraft. (2) A torpedo boat.

mosquito craft. Torpedo boats; small men-of-war.

mosquito navy. A fleet of small warships; a fleet of small torpedo boats; a group of PT boats.

mother-in-law of the Navy. Pensacola, Florida (home of a gigantic naval air station).

Mother McCrea. A sob story; from the traditional Irish song of the same name.

Mother's Day. Payday.

motorized dandruff / motorized freckles. Insects and other bugs.

motor pool. A collection of motor vehicles; a garage.

Mount Plasma. Mount Suribachi, on Iwo Jima. *Newsweek* described it in its issue of March 5, 1945: "The Japanese had set more than 115 guns in the volcano. The Mount was taken February 23, 1945. The campaign on Iwo was one of the toughest in Marine history."

mousetrap. A submarine (because of its confining atmosphere).

move in on. To attack; to court another soldier's sweetheart; to take possession of by trickery.

mowing machine. A machine gun.

M.P. Military police.

Mr. Dowilly. An air cadet.

Mr. Foo. See FOO.

muck. Muscle.

mud. (1) Coffee. (2) Chocolate pudding. (3) Unclear telegraphic signals.

mud crusher. An infantryman.

mud eater. An infantryman.

mud on a shingle. Creamed beef on toast; mostly used as a sanitized version of SHIT ON A SHINGLE.

mugwump. Opossum meat. It was eaten by the Japanese and by the natives on Bougainville.

Mulligan battery. A rolling kitchen (where one could get Mulligan stew).

mustang. (1) Any Navy officer who entered the service through the merchant marine instead of graduating from the Naval Academy. (2) After the war, an officer in any service who had risen from the ranks.

mustang of metal. A reconnaissance car; a **jeep.**

mustard. A smart pilot.

muster a bean for a shag. To borrow a dollar to be used in purchasing tickets to a dance.

mystery. Hash.

mystery ship on the blue. A ship in convoy during time of war (because its position is kept secret).

★ ☆ **N** ☆ ★

naviation. Naval aviation.

navvator. A naval aviator.

Nazidom. The political and philosophical system of the Nazis; Germany.

Naziest. Anything relating to the Nazi Party.

Nazify. To introduce the political and philosophical doctrine of the Nazis into the national life of another country.

Nazi tin fish. A German submarine.

N.C.O. Noncommissioned officer.

N.C.O.I.C.O.Q. Noncommissioned officer in charge of quarters.

needful, the. Money.

Neptune aspirin. A depth bomb.

nervous boot with a heel. A recruit (boot) who tries to impress others with his knowledge of naval affairs.

netted. Tuned on the same frequency (said of a radio sender and receiver).

never lose outfit. The U.S. armed forces; so-called because the U.S. had never lost a war.

New Guinea crud. See JUNGLE ROT.

new wheeze / new wrinkle. A new device or tactic.

N.G. (1) National Guard. (2) No good.

Niagara onion / Niagara pineapple. A tear-gas bomb.

nickels. Leaflets dropped over enemy territory.

night bomber. A pilot who sleeps in the daytime and visits nightclubs at night.

nighthawk. (1) A guard on night patrol. (2) A PT boat.

night maneuver. A date; a WAC term.

ninety-day wonder. An officer who received a commission after a three-month course at an officers' candidate school. The term was popular among graduates of West Point and Annapolis, who spent four years earning their commissions.

Nip. Japan; short for "Nippon." Racist by today's standards, this term was used routinely in broadcasts, news dispatches, and conversation during the war, as was the term "Jap."

Nippo box kite. A Japanese combat aircraft.

N.L.D. Not in line of duty.

N.O.B. Naval operating base.

noncom. A noncommissioned officer.

North Dakota rice. Hot cereal.

nose dive. (1) Intoxication. (2) A temperamental tailspin.

number 14 roller skate. A JEEP. The vehicle was described by an Army wit as: "A number 14 roller-skate, equipped with motor, mud-guards, windshield and a place to seat 'two heels' instead of one."

number-one man. A machine gunner.

number ones. One's best uniform.

"Nuts!" Brigadier General Anthony C. McAuliffe's response to a German demand for surrender during the siege of Bastogne. The reply was given on December 22, 1944, before the siege was broken. McAuliffe was commander of the 101st Airborne Division and was known as "Old Crock" to his troops. Robert Hendrickson wrote in *Encyclopedia of Word and Phrase Origins* (1987): "There are those who believe that McAuliffe, a tough airborne officer, after all, said something much stronger—Shit! to be exact—but no proof has been offered. In any case, he meant 'Go to hell!' and Nuts! has become immortal."

N.W.-N.W. No work—no woo. The slogan was adopted by women war workers at the Albina shipyards in Portland, Oregon. It was explained in the January 1944 issue of *Reader's Digest*: "They agreed not to date men who were absent from work."

nylon. A synthetic fiber. Robert Hendrickson wrote about this product in *Encyclopedia of Word and Phrase Origins* (1987): "Though it was first mass produced during World War II and hurt our enemy Japan's silk industry, nylon is not an acronym of 'Now You Lousy Nips,' as the old story goes. Formerly a trademark, nylon is an arbitrary name with no meaning, though the symbols NY in its chemical formula may have suggested the word."

★ ☆ O ☆ ★

O.A.O. One-and-only (as in "one-and-only girl").

O.C. Officer in charge.

ocean bullets. Beans.

ocean greyhound. A destroyer.

o'clock. A term used, largely by fliers, to indicate direction. Thus, "twelve o'clock" means straight ahead; "three o'clock," directly to the right; and so on. This crude but very effective system is still in use. In actual use, it is often heard as "o'—fuckin'—clock."

O.D. (1) Officer of the day. (2) Olive drab (shirt, pants, or uniform).

off duty. Free from responsibility.

office. The cockpit of an airplane.

officers' line. A row of houses occupied by officers and their families.

off the beam. Incorrect; from navigation by radio beam.

of the old school. (1) Said of officers who served in World War I. (2) That which is old-fashioned or traditional.

O.G. Officer of the guard.

"Oh, So Social." Nickname given to the O.S.S. (Office of Strategic Services) by those who saw it as a harbor for high-born Ivy Leaguers.

oil slick. (1) Clever; talkative. (2) A streak left by a submarine's exhaust on the surface of the water.

oil tanker. (1) A large woman. (2) A prostitute with a venereal disease.

OINC. Officer in command. The acronym was meant to be built-on—e.g., MOINC (medical officer in command) and SOINC (supply officer in command).

Okies. Okinawans. The term was used stateside for people from Oklahoma.

old fogy pay. Extra pay for additional service after four years in the armed forces.

Old Glory. The American flag.

old guard. Mess-hall syrup.

old issue / old file / old settled. An old soldier.

old Joe. Syphilis.

old lady of the Pacific Fleet. The aircraft carrier Enterprise.

old man. A company or regimental commander (sometimes, any commander).

Old Man, The. Major General George S. Patton.

old shell. An old sailor.

one-star wonder. A second lieutenant.

one-wheel landing. (1) Intoxicated. (2) An airplane landing on one wheel.

only apple in the orchard / only oyster in the stew / only pebble on the beach. A self-important person.

on the beach. Without funds.

on the beam. Correct; alert.

on the blink. Defective; not working.

on the carpet. Called before the commanding officer for disciplinary action.

on the deck. At minimum altitude in an airplane.

oof. Money.

openers. Cathartic pills.

open out. To increase the distance between airplanes in formation flying.

orchid hunt. A furlough.

orderly room. Company headquarters.

'orsetralian. An Australian (mimicking the Cockney pronunciation).

oscar. A submarine.

oscar hocks. Socks (in rhyming slang).

ossifer. An officer.

otter. A device used for cutting mine anchor cables. The mines then rise to the surface, where they can be swept up. The device is equipped with powerful, sawlike jaws and is towed at a distance by a minesweeper. It is also called a "paravane."

out for blood. Determined to take revenge or to retaliate.

out of uniform. Not wearing the proper uniform.

outside. Civilian life.

out-touch. To treat another more roughly than one is treated.

overboard. (1) Out of a ship and in the water. (2) Without funds. (3) Jilted by one's sweetheart.

overcoat. A parachute.

Overlord. Code name for operational plans to attack the Axis fortress in Europe—the Normandy invasion. This name replaced the earlier code name Roundup.

overshoot. To overestimate.

over the bump. Retired after thirty years of active duty.

over the hump. The air route over the Himalayas from India to China. At the war's end, supplies were being flown over this route at a rate of two tons a minute.

owl. A military guard or picket.

ozzieland. Australia; a play on "Aussieland."

★ ☆ P ☆ ★

pacifico. A peaceful person; a pacifist.

padre. A chaplain; from the Spanish word for "father" or "priest."

paint a wet anchor. To do unnecessary work.

pal. (1) A chum; a partner. (2) To chum; to make friends.

pancake. To level off a plane near the ground before landing.

pancake and light. Land, refuel, and rearm (in radar code).

pan rattler. A cook; a talkative person.

pants leg. A wind indicator; because of its shape.

panzer division. A German armored division; a German tank division. In German, *panzer* means "armored."

paramarine. A Marine parachutist.

parapooch. A dog dropped by parachute for military purposes.

parasaboteur. A parachutist equipped to perform acts of sabotage.

paraskier. A soldier trained as a parachutist and a ski trooper.

paratrooper. An Army parachute soldier. In a letter dated May 16, 1942, to the editors of *Collier's* David W. Maurer states: "I seem to have a memory of this term (paratrooper) being used by the British or perhaps United States correspondents before 1941, in the first news stories that came out regarding the use of parachute troops."

paring knife. A bayonet.

part teeth. To shoot with extreme accuracy.

pathfinders. Specially picked air crews who locate a target and drop incendiaries, lighting the way for the main attacking force.

Paul Pry. A giant searchlight.

payday for Sam. The day when debts are discharged; the day when payment is to be made.

pay hop. A flight made so that one can qualify for flight pay.

p-a-y number. A mocking cry. It is defined in *Fighting Talk* (1942), by Francis Raymond Meyer: "What the lads cry when a mess attendant or a sailor on mess duty breaks a dish or cup. (The expression derives from the practice of charging broken dishes against the sailor's pay if breakage is caused by carelessness.)"

PCAU (pronounced "pee-cow"). Philippine Civil Affairs Unit. After Manila was freed from Japanese dominance, it was the Army's PCAU that kept the city alive, serving hundreds of thousands of meals and making sure drinking water was available.

P.C.S. Previous condition of servitude.

peanut. The Bruster Buffalo fighter plane (because of its short, stubby shape).

pearl diver. A dishwasher.

Pearl Harbor. A treacherous, devastating attack (after the Japanese attack of December 7, 1941).

peashooter. A pursuit pilot; a pursuit airplane.

pecker checker. A medical person who checks for evidence of venereal disease.

pecker parade. See SHORT-ARM INSPECTION.

peel off. (1) To curve away from another aircraft. The movement is supposed to resemble the act of peeling off the skin of a banana. (2) To dive out from the bottom of an echelon formation.

peep. A small car; used when the word JEEP is applied to larger vehicles.

peewee Matilda. A small tank.

pencil pusher. A navigator on an airplane.

pencil pusher / pencil shover. A clerk.

pending a C.M. Awaiting a court-martial.

penguin. A nonflying member of the Army Air Corps; from the flightless bird.

Pentagon pip. An imaginary illness. It is described in the July 1945 issue of *American Notes and Queries:* "An affliction common among Army officers and enlisted men stationed in Washington; brought on by an Army order proposing overseas duty for men whose war work has kept them heretofore in the United States."

pep tire. A doughnut; so-called by American Red Cross workers in England and other places where they served G.I.'s.

Peter-boat on the prowl. A PT boat on patrol.

petty officer. A Navy enlisted man with a rank corresponding to that of a noncommissioned officer in the Army.

Philip. A Filipino male.

photo Joe. A pilot of a single-seat photoreconnaissance airplane.

P.I. (1) Philippine Islands. (2) Post inspection.

pick-and-shovel boy. An engineer.

pick 'em up and lay 'em down. To run.

pickle barrel. A bombardier training target.

pickle lugger. A torpedo-carrying naval aircraft.

pickup. (1) A light truck for transporting goods. (2) A casual acquaintance that one takes home.

pick up one's brass. To get out of the road.

Pidgin. A simplified mixture of English with any of a number of indigenous tongues of the South Pacific. It was used in communicating with the native populations.

Basic Pidgin

Survival manuals issued during the war contained glossaries of pidgin English for use in the South Pacific. One does not survive after being shot down over the Bismarck Archipelago by asking, "Is the water good to drink?" but must know enough to ask, "Good fella water?" A manual published by the Army Air Corps during the war, entitled *Jungle, Desert and Arctic Emergencies*, contained this advice and basic glossary:

Learning to speak Pidgin consists in memorizing a small vocabulary of native words and becoming accustomed to the peculiar way of putting together the native and English words. Two or three weeks of practice . . . will normally suffice to gain a working knowledge of Pidgin. The glossary on the following pages is short but should give you a basis of communicating with natives, if they don't understand English.

English	Pidgin
Aircraft	Balus ("a" as in "far")
Landing ground	Place balus
Shore, coast, or beach	Nambis (or nabeach)
Food	Kai kai (rhymes with "sky")
Water	Water
Sea	Sola water
Path or track	Road
House, hut, or shelter	'ouse

English	Pidgin
Stream, creek, or river	Water
Village	Place kanaka
Village headman	Luluai (rhymes with "sky")
White man	Master (or government man)
Japan or Japanese	Jap-pan (or Yap-pan)
To hide, secret	Kali fai (rhymes with "sky")
To injure, wound	Killim
To kill	Killim e die
Paper money	Kunda money
Lantern	Lamp walkabout
Flashlight	Shoot lamp
To leave; to forget; past, ago	Lose
Native woman, female	Mary
What?	What name?
To work; to make	Work-im
Bring me food	Bring em kai kai
Bring me water	Bring em water
I want sleep	Me like sleep
Where is the (or a) path?	Where stop road?
Guide me to the coast	One fellow boy brings em me long nambis
Guide me to a village	Bring em me long place kanaka
Tell the chief to come	Luluai e come
Are Japanese in the district?	E got Jap-pan e stop?
How long ago did the Japanese leave here?	Long what name time Jap-pan e los em harpir?
Where is a path to avoid the Japanese?	Where stop road being sackin Jap-pan?
How many days ago?	How muss day e lose?
A long distance (20 miles or more)	Long way

English	Pidgin
A moderate distance (usually 3 or 4 miles)	Long way lik lik
You will be well rewarded later	Bye'm bye all e givim you good fellow pay
Do you understand me thoroughly?	You savvy finish?
Is the water good to drink?	Good fella water?
Where does the track go?	Road e go where?
Did you see the plane crash?	You lookim balus e fall down?
Where is the plane?	Balue e stop where?
Take me to the plane	Bring im me along balus

"Long" (from "along" and "belong") is a general preposition meaning "to," "at," "by," "with," and "for." Few of the natives are reliable in the use of numerals above "twelve."

pig. A torpedo plane.

pigboat. A submarine. The term was resented by those who served on them.

piggyback. A large plane that carries a smaller one.

pig snout. A gas mask.

pig's vest with buttons. Fat salt pork.

pill peddler / pill pusher / pill roller / pill shooter. A doctor; a member of the medical corps.

pilots' ready room. A room on land or aboard an aircraft carrier where pilots and other members of the air service await calls to take to the air.

pineapple. A hand grenade (because of its pineapplelike surface).

ping. A radar echo.

pinpoint. To locate the position of an aircraft or a target with great accuracy; to bomb with precision.

pinup. A picture of a woman for a soldier to pin up on the wall of his quarters. According to an editorial in *Newsweek* of July 16, 1945, pinups were not new with this war: "The demand for decorative damsels existed among the troops of Spanish-American war times and it increased considerably when the Yanks started 'over there' in 1917. But the GI's of today have boomed pin-ups into big business, with one firm alone having sold more than 60,000,000 pictures since Pearl Harbor."

In *The Language of World War II* (1948), A. Marjorie Taylor writes about the term:

But even though the idea is an old one, the term pin-up (or pinup, as it is sometimes written) seems to have first come into general usage in this war. Pin-up girls were mentioned on the back cover of *Yank* (the Army weekly) March 12, 1943, and later issues published pictures of photogenic Hollywood stars and models for GI use as pin-ups. At the outset of the war Walter Thornton, recalling the enthusiasm of soldiers in World War I for pinning up photographs, offered General Powell (of Fort Dix) some 5000 photographs from his files. General Powell's letter of acceptance was the beginning of the Thornton Pin-ups, which soon became a familiar sight in all parts of the world. The Thornton pictures typified the wholesome girl-back-home type, rather than the glamorous show-girl type. According to a survey made by editors and photographers of *Life* magazine in 1941, Dorothy Lamour outnumbered all others as the soldiers' favorite pin-up girl. This mention of "pin-up" is the earliest noted in print in *Life*, July 7, 1941.

pipeline time. The elapsed time between a requisition's leaving a depot and the arrival of the requested supplies; also called "turnaround time."

piperoo. That which is excellent.

pipped. Wounded.

pipsqueak. Airborne radio transmitter with pip and squeak sounds used to identify friendly from enemy aircraft. Compare to WWI meaning of this term.

piss cutter. A soft overseas cap.

pits, the. The worst; a bad place or situation.

The Original Pits of "The Pits"

Elbridge Colby defines "the pits" in *Army Talk: A Familiar Dictionary of Soldier Speech* (1943):

The protected place behind the parapet or embankment at the target end of a rifle range, where men manipulate and mark the targets during practice shooting. Usually there are no pits there at all, merely an open place between the embankment and the hillside backstop for the bullets passing over. The phrase, however, is old and comes from days when there actually were pits. It has remained in the living speech of the soldier folk long after its accuracy has passed. The army man says: "at the butts," "in the pits," "take this detail down to the pit," and "you are on pit detail."

---

plain butch. An officer in the medical corps. The "butch" here stands for "butcher."

plane pusher. (1) A pilot. (2) One who wheels an airplane out onto the deck of an aircraft carrier.

platters of meat. Feet.

play soldier. To shirk duty.

plow into. To begin; to attack.

plow the deep. To sleep.

plucking board. (1) A board in charge of the retirement of officers. (2) A board that removes the worst examples.

pocket lettuce. Paper money.

P.O.E. Port of embarkation.

pogey. A hospital; from the hobo term for a poorhouse.

pogie bait. Candy.

pogled. Dazed; confused. It was defined in the November 1943 issue of *American Notes and Queries*: "Word used by British and American soldiers to describe the condition of Germans taken prisoner in the Salerno region, meaning 'slap-happy in its most acute and superlative degree.'"

pogue. Sissy in the Marines. Jeremiah O'Leary wrote on the term in the *Washington Times*, February 18, 1993:

"I first heard the word in May 1942, when I was going through "boot camp" at Parris Island, S.C., and whole platoons of us recruits were denounced as "pogues" by drill instructors in the sense that we were a bunch of sissies, unfit to wear the globe-and-anchor."

pointie-talkie. A phrasebook. According to *Word Study* of May 1946, it was: "A linguistic manual issued during the war, mainly for the use of airmen grounded in strange territory. If they met natives, they could point to certain phrases in the book in the native's language and thus give out information or ask questions. It worked satisfactorily when the natives could read!"

P.O.L. Petroleum, oil, and lubricants.

police. (1) To clean up. (2) The soldiers detailed to cleaning up.

polish the outfit. To make clean or neat.

POM. "Preparation for Overseas Movement," a War Department publication that was a guide to the prompt and systematic preparation and movement of units to overseas destinations.

pom-pom. An automatic machine cannon that fires one-pound shells from a looped belt; from the drumming sound of its fast fire. The first weapon to be called the pom-pom was the Swedish Bofors 40-mm gun.

poodle palace. A commanding officer's fancy headquarters.

pool. The officers and enlisted men available for assignment; also called "replacement pool." More generally, a pool is any reserve of military personnel, civilian personnel, or equipment (e.g., a motor pool).

poontang / poon. Sexual intercourse.

poop sheet. A drill schedule; any written announcement. "Poop" refers to information, not excrement.

pop it out. To expand one's chest to the limit.

popsicle. A motorcycle.

porthole. One's anus; from the name for an opening in the side of a ship.

pot / pot hat. A steel helmet.

potato masher. A type of German grenade; from its shape.

pound brass. To transmit telegraph signals using a brass hand key.

pour on the soup. To give gas to an aircraft engine by opening the throttle.

pour the heat. To shell; to bombard.

P.O.W. Prisoner of war.

powder birds of war. Army Air Corps cadets.

powder monkey. A girlfriend of an artilleryman.

powder puff. A woman flier.

power stall. A power-on approach to a landing in which the airplane is allowed to settle slowly at an air speed just above the stalling point.

p-rade. A dress parade.

prairie dog snarl. Mine cables twisted together.

praise the Lord and pass the ammunition. A popular motto during the war. A. Marjorie Taylor reports on it in *The Language of World War II* (1948): "First attributed to Chaplain William Maguire (and so quoted in *Life*, November 2, 1942), but he is reported as claiming that he didn't remember saying it and 'positively didn't man a gun' at Pearl Harbor. Real author of the phrase seems to have been Naval Lieutenant Howell Forgy, Presbyterian chaplain." The phrase is also the title of a popular song, with words and music by Frank Loesser, which came out in September 1942.

prang. (1) To bomb a place, especially to bomb it heavily (originally R.A.F. slang). The term may be a blend of "paste" and "bang." (2) To smash up. (3) A crash.

pretty perch. A well-executed airplane landing.

prick a chart. To trace a ship's course on a chart with pins or tacks.

priority. Importance. For example, war plants engaged in vital production were given top priority (or first chance) to get scarce materials.

P.R.O. Public relations officer.

proof house. A place where gun barrels are tested.

prop. A propeller.

prop wash. (1) Gossip; from the nonslang meaning of a wind stream from a propeller. (2) An expression of disbelief.

P.S. man. One with previous military experience; one with a previous term of enlistment.

P.T. A patrol torpedo boat.

P-38. A soldier over the age of thirty-eight; a play on the name of the P-38 aircraft.

puddle jumper. (1) An observation plane designed for short flights, sometimes with bazookas on its wings. (2) A JEEP; a PEEP.

pull rank. To use one's superior rank unfairly.

pull-through. An oiled rag on a cord used in cleaning the bore of a rifle.

pulpit. The cockpit of an airplane.

pumpkin rinds. Military shoulder straps.

pump ship. To urinate.

pungyo. A comrade or buddy; from a Chinese term.

punk and plaster. Bread and butter.

Purple Heart. A medal, created in 1932 and containing the words "For Military Merit." Early in the war it became the medal given to soldiers who were wounded and was awarded posthumously to those killed. According to Elbridge Colby in *Army Talk: A Familiar*

Dictionary of Soldier Speech (1943), it was inspired by an order issued by General George Washington at Newburgh, New York, on August 7, 1782, prescribing that the figure of a heart in purple cloth be worn over the left breast by soldiers who performed "any singularly meritorious action . . . not only instances of unusual gallantry but also for extraordinary fidelity and essential service in any way."

purple heart corner. The position of the outside plane in the lowest flying element of a bomber formation; also known as the "coffin corner." The term is explained by Norman Longmate in the book *The G.I.'s: The Americans in Britain, 1942–1945* (1976), when he points out that the position was "the favorite target for enemy fighters, and hence the likeliest place to earn a Purple Heart for being wounded in action."

pushbutton pilot. A pilot who was trained in an airplane relatively easy to fly.

pusher. An airplane having the propeller behind the main wings.

push someone's nose so far through his face he'll smell coming and going. To do violence.

push up the daisies. To be dead and buried.

puss blanket. A gas mask (i.e., a blanket for the face [puss]).

put that in your mess kit. Think it over!

put the bug on. (1) To turn on a light; to flash a flashlight. (2) To make a self-inflicted sore on one's body in order to shirk duty.

P.X. Post exchange.

★ ☆ **Q** ☆ ★

Q company. (1) An AWKWARD SQUAD. (2) A recruit receiving center.

quad. (1) A drill ground, or quadrangle. (2) A four-wheel-drive truck.

quail on toast. Creamed beef on toast.

Quaker. A dummy cannon used to deceive the enemy; a dummy gun used for drilling recruits; allusions to the pacifism of Quakers. See also QUAKER GUN, under the Civil War.

Quakers were traditionally placed in the portholes of ships or in the gun holes of forts. Correspondent Philip Chaplin of Canada reported: "In 1941, at least two Canadian corvettes went overseas with quakers mounted on their bandstands because the production of 4″ guns had not gotten underway in Canada."

George Washington used dummy cannon (painted logs) on Dorchester Heights, frightening the Redcoats into evacuating Boston, on March 17, 1776.

Quaker ballet. A blessing or prayer.

quartermaster gait. A step longer than the regulation thirty-inch pace.

queen of the flattops. The aircraft carrier *Lexington*, sunk by the Japanese in the Coral Sea.

quick thinker. A pursuit pilot.

quill. To report for a delinquency.

quinine Jimmy. A medical officer; from the name of the substance used to treat malaria.

quirk. A student pilot.

quisle. To act as a traitor; from QUISLING.

quisling. A traitor.

Quisling: The Man and the Word

This version of the story behind the word "quisling" is from *Words of the Fighting Forces*, written while the man still had power in Norway:

The original Quisling is Major Vidkun Quisling of Norway, who made his name a synonym for "traitor" by conspiring with the Germans to assist them in the seizure of Norway and, when they invaded his country, announcing himself as Premier. He is now "sole political leader" of Norway, while the German Governor General is Josef Terboven. According to the London *Times*, "Major Quisling has added a new word to the English language. . . . To writers, the word Quisling is a gift from the Gods. If they had been ordered to invent a new word for traitor . . . they could have hardly hit upon a more brilliant combination of letters. Actually, it contrives to suggest something at once slippery and tortuous. Visually, it has the supreme merit of beginning with a 'Q,' which . . . has long seemed to the British mind to be a crooked, uncertain and slightly disreputable letter, suggestive of the questionable, the querulous, the quavering of quaking quagmires and quivering quicksands, of quibbles and quarrels, of queasiness, quackery, qualms and quilp. . . . Major Quisling is to be congratulated. He has performed the rarish feat of turning a proper name into a common one." Now the name is even declined as a verb: "I quisle, you quisle, he quisles, etc." Before the outbreak of the war, Quisling was the head of the Nasjonal Samling, a political party he founded in 1933 to advocate the suppression of "revolutionary" parties and the "freeing" of labor from union domination. The party had never succeeded in electing a single member to the Norwegian Parliament.

quonset hut. A shelter used for many different purposes. This report on the term is from an article in *The New Yorker* of March 16, 1946:

Developed by the Navy at Quonset Point, Rhode Island, and used as barracks, garages, schools, machine shops, apartments and many other things. In shape they resemble a long cylinder, cut in half lengthwise, with the flat side on the ground. The Navy began investigation of prefabricated housing in 1941 and by June of that year, huts were being sent to England under lend-lease. By the end of 1942, having made more than 34,000 huts, the Navy handed the job to the Stran-Steel Division of the Great Lakes Steel Corporation. The huts come in different sizes—20' × 48' and 40' × 100' being the most usual. Several can be joined together. The greatest single collection of "40"s was a warehouse on Guam. It covered 54,000 square feet and was nicknamed the Multiple Mae West.

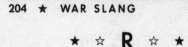

★ ☆ R ☆ ★

radar. Radio detection and ranging. According to *Time* of August 20, 1945, quoting the Navy, the man who coined the word "radar" was Commander (later Captain) S. M. Tucker. In *The Language of World War II* (1948), A. Marjorie Taylor reported: "The word Radar was kept under close military secrecy for some time but news of it was released to the public by the United States War and Navy Departments in the spring of 1943."

ragpicker. A member of the Field Salvage Corps.

railroad tracks. A captain's insignia of parallel silver bars.

rainmaker. (1) A heavy artillery gun. (2) A meteorologist.

rainmakers. The drum and bugle corps.

raise the wind. To brag.

rake. To fire along the length of a target.

ramble handle. The throttle of an airplane.

Ranger. A commando; from Rogers' Rangers, of the Revolutionary War.

ranger gang. Personnel of the aircraft carrier *Ranger*.

ranked out. To be superseded or compelled by a superior (e.g., forced to vacate quarters).

rap it back. To pull in one's chin.

rate a leather medal. To be mean or contemptible, hence deserving a boot in the rear.

rations spoiler. A cook.

rat race. (1) A type of aerial maneuver. It is defined in *Dive Bomber* (1939), by Robert A. Winston: "Tail-chasing. Open order squadron maneuvers, usually through air made turbulent by the slip streams of planes ahead." (2) A mounted review.

rattle-and-tat. A machine gun.

ratzy. A German; a blend of "rat" and "Nazi."

raunchy. According to *The Slanguage Dictionary of Modern American Slang*, "a name applied to anything that is in bad shape or dirty." In the Army Air Corps it simply meant "sloppy."

raw recruit. A newly enlisted soldier.

real stuff, the/real thing, the. Anything genuine; anything excellent.

rear line. The troops in the rear of an army.

rear of snoose. A pinch of snuff.

red ball express / red ball highway. An Army unit created to carry high-priority freight to the front. First organized in World War I after the breakthrough at St. Lo, the truck convoys made their reputation by keeping pace with General Patton's advance. The term "red ball" derives from an old American railroading system of marking priority cars with a large red dot.

red ink. Red wine; catsup.

red lead / red paint. Catsup.

redneck. A drunkard; a rustic.

redski. A Russian; a Red (i.e., a communist).

red triangle. The emblem of the Young Men's Christian Association (Y.M.C.A.), which, along with the Red Cross, was an important factor in the life of the serviceman.

reefer cargo. Perishable foods. The word "reefer" refers to refrigeration equipment.

refloat a fish. To float a submarine unable to surface under its own power.

reg'lar. Regular; first-rate; excellent; a regular soldier.

regular Army / regulars, the. The standing Army.

repple depple. A replacement depot.

retread. A veteran of World War I fighting in World War II.

re-up. To reenlist.

revival tent. A tent like those used in revival meetings. According to *The Slanguage Dictionary of Modern American Slang* (1942), they were: "Tents providing bath facilities, new clothing, etc., located near the front lines for the use of men temporarily relieved from battle duty for this rehabilitation."

rhino tank. Four pieces of angle iron sharpened at one end and welded to a steel plate at the other, and attached to the front of a tank, making it resemble a rhinoceros. Invented by Sergeant Curtis G. Culin, of Cranford, New Jersey, rhino tanks were used in the Normandy campaign to break through hedgerows.

R.H.I.P. Rank has its privileges.

rhubarb pilot. A pilot who flies low (i.e., he returns to base with pieces of rhubarb stuck to his airplane).

ribbon happy. Dazzled by one's own decorations (said of an airman).

ricco. A ricochet bullet.

rice belly / rice cracker. A Japanese.

ride the beam. To keep eyes front.

ride the sick book / ride the sick list. To feign illness to get out of work.

rigger. One who packs, or rigs, parachutes.

rigging. One's clothes and other personal belongings.

rig in one's booms. To pull in one's elbows.

ringtail. A Japanese.

rinkeydink. A Navy pilot still in the training stage of his career.

ripcord. A cord attached to a parachute pack, which is pulled after jumping, freeing the parachute so it opens up.

ripcord club. An aviators' and paratroopers' club.

ripper. A bayonet; one using a bayonet.

riveter. A machine gun; one who operates a machine gun.

roadblock. A barrier, sometimes fortified, to prevent movement of enemy traffic; any obstruction.

roblitz. Severe bombardment by robot bombs; a combination of "robot" and "blitz."

robomb. Robot bomb.

robot bomb. See BUZZ BOMB.

rock-happy. Bored, especially on the rocky islands and atolls of the Pacific.

roger. A pilot's radio message to his operational base meaning that a message has been received satisfactorily.

roller skate. A tank.

roller-skate baby. A soldier who has lost both legs above the knees.

rolls-rough. A JEEP; a tank; an old automobile. The term is a play on "Rolls-Royce."

roll up one's flaps. To stop talking.

Rommel's asparagus. Stakes placed in the ground by the Germans to thwart airborne landings. The technique was pioneered by Field Marshal Erwin Rommel in France.

RON. (1) Remain overnight; an Army Air Corps term. (2) Squadron (as a suffix); a Navy term. For example, "comdesron" stands for "commander, destroyer squadron."

ronchie. Slipshod; careless.

rootin', tootin' son of a gun. An energetic person.

rosebud. (1) A hand grenade. (2) A debutante.

round the clock. Continuously, night and day (said of aerial bombing attacks).

royal order of whale bangers. An "exclusive" club open only to airmen who have mistakenly dropped depth charges on whales, supposing them to be enemy submarines.

RSOP. Reconnoitering, surveying, and occupying a position (pronounced "arsop").

rubber band. An undersized tire.

rubber boot. An airplane deicer.

rubberneck roost. A stag line of soldiers at a dance.

Rudolf. A dummy used to test parachutes. Rudolfs were named after Rudolf Hess, according to *Newsweek* of December 1, 1941.

rugged. Wonderful; terrific; awful; difficult. According to A. Marjorie Taylor in

The Language of World War II (1948), the term was "in very general use among members of the armed services; the particular meaning has to be gathered from the context."

run / run in / bomb run / bombing run / bomb-aiming run. A steady approach of aircraft to a target immediately before bombs are released.

runaround. A mock errand given to recruits and new men.

Parade Rest: Runarounds

This glossary of runarounds appeared in *Fighting Talk* (1942), by Francis Raymond Meyer.

No dictionary of service slang would be complete without listing the runarounds. They are gags which the poor recruit must suffer before he is accepted as a seasoned comrade-in-arms. The runaround, too, provides a traditional channel for the serviceman's humor. The following have long been laugh-producers in the Army and are now being revived, sometimes with embroideries:

adjutant's post. Recruits often walk miles to borrow one. Actually it's the place on the parade ground where the adjutant stands during a review.

cannon report. Definitely required for Army bookkeeping.

invisible paint for camouflage. Rookies hunt for gallon buckets of it.

key to parade grounds. Self-explanatory.

key to rifle range. Self-explanatory.

leggins stretcher. Self-explanatory.

muster button. Imaginary item that a recruit must show before the Army paymaster will give him his check.

post exchange (called PX). General store. Not a secondhand lumberyard for swapping fence posts.

raincoat chevrons. Rookies hunt these fantasy items on rainy days to keep experienced troopers amused.

rubber flag. "Sounds very logical for use on a rainy day. Rookie searches. He gets wet but smart."

skirmish line. Rookies try to locate six feet of it.

sky hooks. Hooks holding targets to a cloud for antiaircraft guns.

tent stretcher. Self-explanatory.

Here are some of the most popular Navy runarounds:

a dimmy gadget for a wazzel. Old-timers send rookies for it, and it means anything and nothing in particular.

"Drugstore on the starboard (or port) bow, sir." That's how rookies are instructed by their weisenheimer elders to report port and starboard lights. (Drugstores used to have red and green vials in their windows.)

freshwater wrench. Self-explanatory.

"Get Charlie Noble." "You can't miss Charlie," the jokester assures the rookie. "He smokes all day." Later, much later, the rookie learns that "Charlie Noble" is the ship's stack or funnel.

"Go look for a mail buoy." This assignment comes after the rookie's more seasoned shipmate tells him a plausible story about buoys placed in the sea by the Government as mail boxes for the sailors and that launches empty the buoys at regular intervals and refill them with letters brought from the shore.

hammock stretcher. There's no such object. Every man does it for himself.

key to the keelson. The keelson is a beam running lengthwise above the keel of the ship.

key to the starboard watch. Self-explanatory.

pie tickets. Rookies need them if they want to eat, so they are told.

smoke preventer. Self-explanatory.

Tuscorora. A mythical ship which is something like the hobo's "Big Rock Candy Mountain." It has thirteen decks, a straw bottom and rubber stacks. It is talked about to test the credulity of recruits.

ruptured duck. A button that honorably discharged World War II veterans wore in their lapels; also called "screaming eagle." It bore the image of an eagle, inspired by a bas-relief in Trajan's Forum in Rome.

Russ. Russian; a Russian; the Russian language.

Russki. A Russian.

★ ☆ S ☆ ★

sack. (1) A bed. To "hit the sack" means to go to bed. (2) Civilian clothes.

sack of bull. A package, or sack, of Bull Durham tobacco.

sack time. Time spent sleeping or just lying on one's cot.

Sacred Cow. A nickname given to the plane especially designed by Douglas Aircraft for the use of President Franklin D. Roosevelt.

sad sack. (1) A G.I. who means well but never does anything right; from the cartoon character Sad Sack, made immortal by *Yank* cartoonist Sergeant George Baker, who gave the pathetic private his 1942 debut. Private Sad Sack symbolizes all the bewildered ex-civilians who blunder their way through the mazes of Army life. (2) Any inept, bewildered person.

sailorette. An enlisted woman assigned to Navy duty to relieve men for seagoing service. The law creating this branch of the service was passed by Congress on April 17, 1942.

salt and batter. Assault and battery.

saltwater cowboy. A Marine.

Sam's big house. A guardhouse; the disciplinary barracks. This and the next four terms allude to Uncle Sam.

Sam's circus. The U.S. armed forces; a war in which the U.S. is involved.

Sam's cop. A military policeman.

Sam's punk. A naval mail orderly.

Sam's sugar. Money.

samurai. A Japanese militarist; from the ancient term for a warrior class.

sand and specks. Salt and pepper.

sandpaper the anchor. To do unnecessary work.

sand rat. A soldier on duty in the rifle range pit.

Santa Claus in the pits. Good marksmanship on the target range.

sarge. Sergeant.

satchel. (1) A fat man. (2) A pocket of fat on a person's body.

saturate. To bomb very heavily.

saturation bombing. The bombing of a complete area (as contrasted with precision bombing, aimed at a specific objective).

sauerkraut face. A German.

scag. A cigarette.

scattergun. A shotgun; a machine gun.

scorched earth. The destruction of anything of possible value to the enemy, usually performed on the eve of retreat.

scrag. A cigarette.

scrambled eggs. Gold braid on the caps of naval officers; the officers themselves.

scratch one flattop. An enemy aircraft carrier has been sunk.

screamer. An aerial torpedo.

screwball. An odd or irrational person.

script. A set of special orders.

scrounge. To appropriate; to misappropriate. According to *Reader's Digest* of May 1940, this was: "A slang term which dated back to World War I, but became more prevalent in World War II, especially during the blackouts in London." See also under World War I, and **scrounger,** under the Korean War.

scuttlebutt. Gossip. See under the Civil War.

scuttlebutt chatter. Empty talk.

sea ape. An old sailor; an ugly man or woman.

Seabees. (1) Construction battalions (in the Navy). (2) Members of the construction battalions.

According to *Words of the Fighting Forces:* "When the first construction battalion was organized last spring (1942), the nickname Sea Bees was adopted because it sounds like the initials 'C.B.'s' and indicates at the same time that the men are connected with naval work and that they are busy workers."

Collier's of September 19, 1942, had this to say: "Work of the Seabees was formerly done by civilians, but experience at Guam, Wake and Cavite led to the Navy decision to put their construction men in uniform. Supposed to land at the same time or just after the Marines. Their work was to make a landing field, hospital, fortifications, docks, barracks—in short to build secret naval bases."

sea cop. A Marine; a Navy master-at-arms.

sea cow. Canned milk.

sea dust. Salt.

seagoing bellhop. A Marine.

seagoing oilcan. An oil tanker.

sea jeep. An Army amphibious armored vehicle.

sealed in a blanket. (1) Dead and buried on the field of battle. (2) Dead and buried at sea (i.e., literally sent off sewn in a blanket).

sea ooze. Worthless talk.

sea pad. A Marine assigned to police duty aboard a man-of-war.

sea puss. A face wrinkled from the winds of the sea.

sea robin. (1) A talkative person; one given to spreading false reports. (2) A prostitute in a port.

sea scooter. A PT boat.

sea skimmer. An antisubmarine boat equipped with pontoons. Power was supplied by an airplane propeller and engine. This gadget could skim the waves at fifty miles per hour and couldn't be heard with sonic detectors by enemy submarines.

sea sled. A motorboat of sledlike form, capable of great speed, having a square bow and stern, and characterized especially by an inverted V-shaped hull.

sea squatter. An aviator forced down at sea, successful in inflating a rubber raft, and rescued alive.

seaweed. (1) Spinach. (2) Whiskers; a beard.

SECNAV. Secretary of the Navy.

second Louise. A WAC second lieutenant.

seconds. Second helpings at mess.

seconds on that snipe. A request for a partly smoked cigarette.

Section VIII / Section 8. (1) An other than honorable discharge, as a result of an inability to adapt oneself to Army life. It was formerly called "one-forty-eight-and-a-half," but was changed to "Section 8" when a revision of Army regulations changed the numerical designation of the part that dealt with such matters. (2) A misfit; a candidate for such a discharge.

seep. A seagoing JEEP. It was especially developed for the use of the Marines.

see service. To come into contact with the enemy.

see the chaplain. A suggestion that one should resign oneself to an unpleasant situation. This standard advice to one with a grievance about which nothing could be done probably derived from the fact that the chaplain was the one person always ready to listen with sympathy.

see the world. To enlist in the Navy.

selectee. A man inducted into the Army through the Selective Service Act of 1940.

self-commencer. An engine hand crank.

send a fish. To discharge a torpedo.

separatee. A soldier awaiting discharge at a separation center.

serum. Whiskey; a play on "blood serum."

set her down. To land an airplane.

seven hours in the ditch. Transit through the Panama Canal. It takes about seven hours to make this fifty-mile journey by water. The canal is also known as the "big ditch."

seventy-two. Three days' liberty.

sewer trout. Whitefish.

S-4. A supply officer.

shack rat. A soldier who has friends in the city and usually goes to visit them when he is on leave.

shack up. To live with a woman to whom you are not married.

shack up with a blister. To live on the beach with a mistress or prostitute when on leave from sea duty.

shanghaied. Transferred without one's request and/or contrary to one's wishes.

Shangri-La. This term, the setting of James Hilton's very popular book *Lost Horizon* (1933), came to mean an imaginary or secret military base. President Roosevelt announced in 1942 that the American planes that had bombed Tokyo had taken off from a secret base in Shangri-La (later revealed to be the aircraft carrier *Hornet*).

shavetail general. A brand-new brigadier general.

shavetail in the box. One having completed his training and awaiting commission.

shingle. The wing covering of an airplane.

shingles. Toast.

ship over. To reenlist.

shit on a shingle. Chipped or creamed beef on toast. See s.o.s.

shivering Liz. Jell-O.

shoot. Go ahead and talk.

shoot down in flames. (1) To give someone a reprimand. (2) To jilt someone.

shooting gallery. The front line.

shoot the breeze. To converse; also BAT THE BREEZE.

shoot the gas to her. To open the throttle of an airplane.

shoot the scuttlebutt. To gossip. See **scuttlebutt,** under the Civil War.

short arm. A penis.

short-arm inspection. An inspection for venereal disease.

short-arm practice. Copulation.

short circuit between the earphones. A mental lapse.

short snorter. A member of a crew that has made a transoceanic flight.

short timer. A soldier nearing the end of his enlistment period.

shot. An inoculation.

shotgun. A machine gun.

shoulder patch. A division insignia.

shove off. To leave; to get moving, from the action of getting a ship away from a dock. It shows up in an oft-told anecdote in which an Army man asks a sailor to say something in SWABBIE and the sailor responds, "Shove off, @#$%¢&*+?>M<."

shrapnel. Grape-Nuts (the cereal).

shrubbery. Sauerkraut.

shutters. Sleeping pills.

S.I. Saturday inspection.

sick-bay veteran. A chronically ill sailor.

sidearms. Cream and sugar in coffee.

side dish. A mistress.

side-slip. (1) To dodge an issue; to shirk duty. (2) To lose altitude in an airplane by drifting to the side and down in one motion.

sideswiper. A speed key on a radio transmitter that moves from side to side when operating.

sights. A bombardier; from "bombsight."

silent service. The submarine service. See under the Cold War.

sin buster. A chaplain.

single-seater. A single-seat airplane.

sitzkrieg. An inactive period during a war; from the German for "sitting war." It was a derogatory term for the inactivity on the European western front during the winter of 1939–1940.

six-and-twenty tootsie. A woman who leads one into temptation. The term is defined in *Words of the Fighting Forces:* "A girl who makes a flying cadet so heedless of time that he returns late from week-end leave thereby incurring six demerits and twenty punishment tours."

six-by-six. A standard heavy truck used to haul personnel and materials.

six months and a bob / six months and a kick. A punishment of six months' confinement and a dishonorable discharge.

six-sixty. A punishment of six months' confinement and a sixty-dollar fine.

sixth column. People who have a negative influence on the home front. The term was popularized by President Franklin D. Roosevelt, applying it to those Americans who, according to Louise D. Parry's 1942 *War Dictionary*, "practice complacency, rumor mogering, race hatred, unwarranted criticism of the war effort, labor baiting and hoarding; persons who wittingly or unwittingly provide the vehicle for distribution of propaganda created by fifth columnists." See also FIFTH COLUMN.

skibby. A Japanese. According to *Words of the Fighting Forces*: "This term is used on the Pacific Coast. It originally meant a Japanese prostitute, however, is now applied to all persons of the race."

skid grease. Butter.

skip-bombing. Low-level bombing with delayed-action bombs that ricochet into the target.

skipper. (1) The commanding officer of a unit. (2) The commanding officer of a naval station, base, ship, or squadron, who is usually addressed by the personnel under his command as "Captain," no matter what his rank.

skip the rope. To make a power-off airplane landing over an obstruction, which can be aborted if undershot.

skirt patrol. G.I.'s on the lookout for women.

skivvies. Underwear.

sky baby. An aviator.

sky buggy. An airplane.

sky pilot / sky scout. A chaplain.

sky saddle. A parachute.

sky winder. (1) A member of the Army Air Corps. (2) A tall tale.

sky wire. A radio antenna.

slap it on. To fine someone for a minor offense.

sleds. Shoes issued by the government.

sleeping Jesus. A lazy, slow person.

slick-up. (1) To dress in one's best uniform. (2) A cleanup.

slig. An acronym of "sucker, lowbrow, idiot, and goodwill buster" used as a verb. Invented early in the war, the term was cited by an Algiers correspondent early in February 1944, who defined it as an "act of discourtesy or stupid criticism" that, among the armed forces, becomes an "added shell for the guns of Axis propaganda."

sling one's hook. To desert.

slip. Recorded tape (in the Army Signal Corps).

slip one's cable. To die.

slip the chute. To tug on a parachute's cords so as to make it change direction.

slip the clutch. To criticize; to engage, as one would a clutch.

slipway. A slope in a dock or shipyard from which ships can be launched.

slop house. A mess hall.

slow roll. A slow rotation of an airplane on its longitudinal axis through an arc of 360 degrees.

slum / slumgullion. A vegetable and meat stew. See under the Civil War. See also GRAVEYARD STEW.

slum in heavy marching orders. A meat pie with a heavy crust.

slum wagon. A large bomber.

SMOE. An electronic **gremlin.** *Newsweek* of December 21, 1945, cites an unidentified Navy man's explanation of the term's origin: "Our explanation of Smoe's origin is as follows: the electrical term OHMS which appears on drawings of radio circuits, when held up backward to the light reads SMHO. This little gentleman who knew what was going on behind the circuit changed his name to SMOE."

smoke jumpers. Parachutists who fight forest fires. They were recruited largely among conscientious objectors, according to the New York *Herald Tribune* of March 1, 1944.

smokestacker. A person who tells unbelievable tales.

smoke sticks. Airplane machine guns.

smoke wagon. A field artillery gun.

smoke watch. A nonexistent errand offered as an excuse by one of the engine crew so that he may go on deck.

smug boat. A vessel carrying contraband on the Chinese coast. Smug boats were later used to run the Japanese blockade. The word "smug" here means "trim" or "smart," rather than "self-satisfied."

snafu. Situation normal, all fouled up (or fucked up). The word is defined in a 1944 slang dictionary as "temporary turmoil resulting from an abrupt change in orders."

snake's ankle / snake's eyebrows / snake's hips / snake's pajamas / snake's pants / snake's toenails / snake's whiskers / snake's yoohoo. Something excellent. The term is in the tradition of "the cat's pajamas."

snap maneuver. An airplane maneuver in which the airplane is whipped quickly into the desired position by suddenly moving the controls.

snore rack. A sleeping bag.

snowdrops. White-helmeted American military police; a bit of London slang.

snow under. To exaggerate.

snow whites. Army nurses who wore white duty uniforms.

snuff box. A depth charge; from the notion that it could kill (snuff out) a submarine.

S.O. (1) Scout observation. (2) Special orders.

Soapsuds Row. The married noncommissioned officers' quarters. See under the Spanish-American War era.

sofar. Sound fixing and ranging; a system developed by the Navy, according to *Newsweek* of May 27, 1946, for locating survivors far at sea.

soger / sojer. A soldier.

SOINC. Supply officer in command. See OINC.

S.O.L. Shit out of luck; often sanitized as "sure out of luck" or "soldier out of luck."

soldier bull / soldier cop. A military policeman.

soldier of the seven seas. A Marine.

soldier's one percent. An agreement by which a soldier borrows a dollar and pays back two dollars on payday.

solid bundle of blitz. A large formation of enemy aircraft.

solo. To fly an airplane alone.

some groceries. Good food.

sonar. Sound navigation and ranging; a system used in detecting enemy submarines and, on submarines, in detecting enemy ships.

S-1. A staff officer who handles personnel records and paperwork.

son of a jeep. A JEEP.

son of Mars. A soldier.

soogie moogie. Any cleaning solution.

S.O.P. (1) Standard operating procedure; any prescribed, preferable, or habitual method. (2) Senior officer present.

soppin's. Gravy.

S.O.S. (1) Shit on a shingle (i.e., chipped or creamed beef on toast). (2) Services of supply.

S.O.S. for 100

The following recipe is from *The Army Cook* (1942):

Beef, dried, chipped or sliced on toast (for 100)

7 pounds chipped or sliced dried beef
2 pounds fat, butter preferred
1 pound flour, browned in fat
4 cans milk, evaporated
2 bunches parsley, chopped fine
1/2 ounce pepper
4 gallons beef stock
130 slices bread (about 12 pounds)

Melt the fat in the pan and add the flour. Cook a few minutes to brown the flour. Add the milk and beef stock, stirring constantly to prevent lumping. Add the dried beef and cook 5 minutes. Add the parsley and pepper. Serve hot on toast.

---

soul aviator. A preacher or a priest.

sound off. (1) To gripe; to speak one's mind. (2) To identify oneself by name and rank during a military drill.

soup. (1) Clouds, rain, and, most of all, fog. (2) Dynamite.

soup jockey. A cook.

soup kitchen. A large bomber.

soup up. (1) To adjust an airplane engine's fuel mixture to increase power and performance. (2) To eat.

sow belly. Salt pork.

S.P. Shore Patrol (the Navy's military police).

S.P.A. South Pacific area.

spam can. A handie-talkie (a smaller version of the walkie-talkie); from the name of a common canned lunch meat, which in turn got its name from a blend of "spiced" and "ham."

spam fleet. Landing craft and other utilitarian, slow-moving craft.

spare tire. A "reserve" sweetheart.

sparks. A radio operator on a ship.

Spars. The Women's Reserve of the United States Coast Guard Reserve. A bill creating this special unit was signed on November 22, 1942. The name was taken from the motto of the Coast Guard, "Semper Paratus" ("always prepared").

speed artist. An expert telegraph operator.

speed buggy / speed chariot / speed crate / speed hack. A pursuit airplane.

spiders. Steel rails buried by the Germans on the beaches of Normandy (and other possible landing sites). They were meant to hamper allied landings by ship.

spider webs. Parachutes shot into the air trailing long wires with which to entangle enemy aircraft.

spill it. To confess.

spill red ink. To draw blood.

spin in. (1) To fail to recover from a spin before one's airplane crashes. (2) To take a nap.

spin one's wheels. To waste time or energy in useless activity.

spirit broker. A priest, preacher, or chaplain.

Spit. A Spitfire British pursuit airplane, which along with the Hurricane formed what was termed "the backbone of the R.A.F. Fighting Command."

spit kit. (1) An ashtray. (2) A small boat, such as a harbor tug or patrol boat.

split fly. To do stunts over an airfield.

Spokane. Pork and beans.

spoon up. To clean up.

spoony. (1) Neat in appearance. (2) Dreamy.

spread the applesauce / spread the baloney / spread the bull / spread the bunk / spread the crap. To trick or deceive, as by a falsehood or flattery.

spud duty. Kitchen police assignment (i.e., peeling potatoes, or spuds).

spud hole. A guardhouse.

spuds with the bark on. Unpeeled potatoes.

sputterbus. An old airplane.

squared away. (1) Having one's uniform and equipment in order; ready. (2) Having no debts or obligations.

squawk box. An intercom speaker.

squawk sheet. A pilot's detailed written report on defects discovered when flying an airplane.

S.S. Submarines.

stack. (1) An order of pancakes. (2) A string of radio messages.

stall. The condition of an airplane whose air speed is too low to generate the lift needed to sustain it in the air.

stamps. One assigned to duty as a mail orderly.

stand-up. A pinup of a woman who had stood her man up. According to *Newsweek* of April 2, 1945, stand-ups were: "Pictures of girls who failed to wait for the men to come home, and married someone else."

St. Anthony highball. An enema.

stateside. Of, in, or toward the U.S. According to an item in *Yank* for December 1, 1944, quoted by A. Marjorie Taylor in *The Language of World War II* (1948): "American soldiers abroad used this adjective to refer to things back in America. For example, 'There was a genuine Stateside flavor to the celebration.' The word stateside antedates World War II, having been long used in Hawaii and the Philippines, but it was picked up and popularized by service personnel overseas."

static agitator. A student radio operator.

static bender. A radio operator.

stationmaster. A commander of an airfield.

station-wagon patriot. A certain kind of woman volunteer in the war effort. The term is defined in Louise D. Parry's *The War Dictionary* (1942):

> A term of derision for those wealthy or moderately well-off women who volunteer to help America's war effort in order to satisfy their personal ambitions (to see their photos in the papers, to boss other women, etc.) rather than out of true patriotism. The name is derived from the station-wagon automobiles in which these society ladies like to drive up to whatever place they "serve" as volunteers.

steam shovel. A potato peeler.

steam tug. A large woman; from the image of a tugboat.

step high, wide, and handsome. To dissipate oneself; to go the pace.

stern. The rear end.

sternchaser. (1) A man overly fond of women. (2) A gun so mounted on a ship as to fire to the rear.

stew builder. A cook.

S-3. A staff officer who plans action and training.

stick. A number of bombs arranged for release from a bomber so as to fall in a spaced series across a target.

stickler. A strict officer.

stiff pond. The Dead Sea (in the sense that a dead person is a "stiff").

stiff sheet. A cadaver cover.

stiff snatcher. A stretcher bearer.

Stilwell stride. A marching pace. According to *Time* of June 1, 1942: "105 steps per minute. Pace at which General Joseph W. Stilwell led the group of soldiers and civilians from Burma to India."

stinger. (1) A torpedo. (2) The tongue.

stinkeroo. Poor in quality; low grade.

stir. A guardhouse or prison.

stooge. A copilot.

stop one. To be shot (wounded or killed).

storm. (1) The condition one is in when excited and not knowing what one is doing. (2) A wife.

storm tossed. Agitated by passion.

stove pipe. A mortar.

stow it / stow the gab. To be quiet.

strafe. To shoot with a machine gun from an airplane. This German term came into use during World War I, initially in the phrase *Gott strafe England* ("God punish England"). Said *The New York Times* in 1946: "Strafe is now used to describe the operation in which troops are machine-gunned from low-flying planes." See also under World War I.

straight kick. A dishonorable discharge.

stratosphere Joe. A tall man.

street monkey. A member of a band.

strike-me-dead. A small beer.

striker. An officer's orderly.

stripe. A chevron.

stripe-happy. A soldier too eager for promotion.

strip of hell. A strip of land between opposing armies.

strip the stripes. To demote to the ranks.

struggle. A dance held at an Army post.

struggle buggy. A jeep.

stuff. (1) A woman; women. (2) Clouds; weather.

stump jumper. A Marine from a rural home.

stunt. To perform aerial acrobatics.

St. Vitus davenport / St. Vitus wagon. A tank.

S-2. An intelligence officer.

sub. A submarine.

sub chaser. A small, fast craft equipped with depth charges for destroying submarines.

submarine. (1) A bedpan. (2) doughnut (a sinker).

submarine ears. The ability to wake up when there is any change in the sounds around you while sleeping. The term alludes to the use of SONAR on submarines.

submarine turkey. A fish.

sub's stinger. A torpedo.

subversive. Tending to undermine a government. According to A. Marjorie Taylor, in *The Language of World War II* (1948): "The adjective subversive, 'having a tendency to upset or overthrow,' came into general usage in World War II with the meaning, activities inimical to the war effort."

sugar report. A letter from one's sweetheart.

suicide boat. A PT boat (because of the dangers they faced).

suicide soldier. A machine gunner.

suicide squad. Those who operate a machine gun under fire.

Super Fortress. The Boeing B-29 bomber.

superman drawers / superman pants. Long woolen underdrawers reminiscent of the comic-book hero's tights.

superman suit. Long, one-piece government-issue underwear.

susfu. Situation unchanged, still fouled up (or fucked up).

swab. (1) An oversized mop used for the cleaning of a ship's decks. (2) To rub or clean with a swab; to mop. (3) A sailor; a long form was "swab jockey."

swabbie from a birdboat. A sailor from an aircraft carrier.

swallow the anchor. To give up; to quit; to desert.

swamp seed. Rice.

swanks. A soldier's best uniform (i.e., his swankiest outfit).

swear like a trooper. To swear violently.

sweat / sweat out. To wait anxiously. An item in *The New York Times* of June 4, 1944, puts this term into historical perspective:

A term meaning to wait helplessly, nervously, anxiously for something over which you have absolutely no control; that is, waiting for the return of war planes carrying your pals, or waiting for promotion, or waiting for an overdue letter from home. All branches of the services used the phrase "sweating it out" but the Air Forces claim that they started it.

sweat a crack-up. To anticipate a crash in an airplane (while avoiding the taboo word "crash").

swimmando. A type of COMMANDO. The term is defined in *Words of the Fighting Forces*: "A new American version of England's daring Commandos are the 'swimmando corps'—now adopted by the 28th Pennsylvania Infantry Division. These men are being trained to swim rivers, raid enemy shore installations, and establish bridgeheads for full-scale attacks."

swing shift. A work shift in industrial plants from three P.M. to midnight. Swing shifts were especially important to the war effort.

swing the lead. To tell a story; to bullshit; to GOOF OFF.

swish. A thermal-jet engine. The term alludes to the sound it makes.

★ ☆ T ☆ ★

tag. An officer of the tactical department in the Army.

tail-end Charlie. (1) The rear gunner in a bomber. (2) The rear aircraft in a formation.

tailspin. (1) A condition of confusion. (2) The spiraling fall of an airplane after losing speed.

tail stinger. The rear gunner in a bomber.

take a brace. To take a hazing from cadet upperclassmen; to take a drink of liquor. A brace is an exaggerated position of attention.

take a dekko. To go on deck for a look at the outside world.

take a dose of hot lead. To be shot.

take another blanket. To reenlist.

take off. (1) To leave the ground in an aircraft. (2) To jump from an aircraft in flight. (3) To go away; to get out of sight.

take the field. To open hostilities; to begin a campaign.

tall-water sailor. A sailor who has crossed the ocean several times.

tallyho. (1) The enemy has been sighted and recognized as hostile (in radio code). This signal is still in use among combat fliers. (2) A squadron leader's signal to break formation for a dogfight; an R.A.F. term borrowed from fox hunting.

tangle in the soup. To get lost in the fog.

tank-dozer. A type of combat vehicle. It was described in *The New York Times* of August 4, 1944: "A new Allied break-through weapon consisting of a medium-sized tank to which was fitted a three-and-one-half-ton blade; combined lunging power of an M-4 Sherman tank with the slashing force of a bulldozer; capable of disposing of trees eighteen inches in diameter."

tanker. A member of a tank crew.

tankette. A small tank.

tarantula soup. Whiskey.

tarfu. Things are really fouled up (or fucked up).

target paste. Gravy.

taxi up. To approach; to be in motion.

tear bomb. A gas bomb that makes the eyes smart and water, producing temporary blindness.

tear 'em out. To clash gears.

tear off a stripe. To rebuke or reprimand someone.

tell off. To **count off**; to select for special duty; to reprimand.

tempest-beaten tub. A ship beat up by storms.

ten-in-one ration. A balanced ration for ten men for one day. It is packed in five menus designed to provide each man with the equivalent of the C-RATION. Each packed menu also includes cigarettes (10), halazone tablets (50), matches (20 sticks), individual can openers (2), toilet soap (1 cake), toilet paper (125 sheets), and paper towels (20 sheets).

ten-ton tessie. A 22,000-pound bomb used in bombing German cities in February and March 1945.

terps. An interpreter.

terrier with shamrocks. Corned beef and cabbage.

T.G.'s. Torpedo planes.

that's all she wrote. That's all—a customary cry of the company mail clerk at the end of mail call.

thirty-horse putt-putt. A small commercial airplane.

thousand-mile shirt. An olive-drab Army shirt (i.e., a shirt that one might have to wear for many days and many miles).

Thousand-Mile Stare / Thousand-Yard Stare. See TWO-THOUSAND-YARD STARE.

three-baller of the deck. A money-lender.

three in the mill. A punishment of three months' confinement in the guardhouse.

three L's. Lead, latitude, and lookout; a Navy term.

three-point landing. Ham and two eggs.

three-starrer. A vice-admiral.

three-striper. (1) A Navy commander. (2) An Army sergeant.

throne gang. The officers around headquarters.

thumbs up. Everything is okay. This is usually a gesture, but it can also be spoken.

thunderbird. (1) A flier (pilot, bombardier, etc.) in the Army Air Corps. (2) A combat aircraft.

thunderbolt. A PT boat.

tickers. The Signal Corps.

tickety-boo. Fine; okay. This bit of British slang was picked up by many Americans.

tiger. Shut up; zip your lip. A. Marjorie Taylor, in *The Language of World War II* (1948), says she first heard the term in a Lowell Thomas newscast of August 11, 1943.

tiger meat. Beef.

tin can. (1) A Navy destroyer of the 750-ton class. (2) A depth charge. (3) A submarine.

tin fish. A torpedo.

tin-fish trailer. A surface mark made by the periscope of a moving submarine.

tin pickle. (1) A torpedo. (2) A submarine.

tire patches. Pancakes.

T.N.T. Today, not tomorrow.

toe parade. An inspection of feet.

togglier. A bombardier.

Tojo cigar. A midget (two-man) submarine. One of these submarines, renamed for the Japanese admiral Tojo, was washed ashore during the raid on Pearl Harbor, on December 7, 1941.

Tokyo tanks. An airplane's auxiliary gas tanks (i.e., those that would get one to Tokyo).

Tommy / Tommy gun / Tommy gat / Tommy rod / Tommy roscoe. A submachine gun.

too little and too late. A popular expression of regret that the U.S. did not send enough weapons and supplies to Europe to stop Hitler earlier.

toothpick village. Wooden barracks.

top / top kick / top knocker. A TOP SERGEANT; a first sergeant.

top cover / top flight. Fighter planes flying above bombers to give them protection.

top cutter / topper / top soak. A first sergeant.

top sergeant / top sarg. The highest-ranking sergeant in a unit, whose duty is to handle the soldiers for the commander of the unit.

topside. (1) Above; on deck. (2) The bridge of a ship.

Topside from the Top—A Word History

In *Army Talk: A Familiar Dictionary of Soldier Speech* (1943), Elbridge Colby declares that "topside" is pure PIDGIN English, "taken from a mode of language common to Chinamen and Filipinos, and meaning upstairs or a higher level." Colby continues:

For instance, on the island of Corregidor, the garrison groups on the sloping hill are, according to their locations, called "Top-Side," "Middle-Side," and "Bottom-Side." The word has been brought from the Far East with folk returning from foreign service tours, and is occasionally heard at garrisons at home. It is also frequently used to speak of persons in authority, or at a higher headquarters, as "Those Top-Side."

topside sailor. A sailor whose duties keep him on deck.

top soldier. A first-class soldier; a first sergeant.

torpedo body. A woman with a good figure.

torps. The men responsible for the torpedo tubes.

toss oars. To hold oars with their blades upright, as a salute.

tough row of buttons to shine. A hard job or assignment.

tour. A penalty march.

town major. A liaison officer between townsfolk and soldiers.

tracer. A bullet or shell that gives off a trail of smoke or fire, allowing the shooter to check his aim.

trade, the. The submarine service.

trailing edge. The rear edge of a propeller blade.

traphanded. Deceitful; sinful.

trigger talk. Shooting.

trooper. A soldier in a cavalry division, which has troops instead of companies and squadrons instead of battalions.

troubleshooter. (1) One who locates and fixes problems. (2) A member of the Army inspector general's department.

T.S. cards. Tough shit cards. They are described by Kenneth L. Dixon in an account of life at the Anzio beachhead: "Beachhead chaplains are carrying a special 'tough stuff' ticket these days which they issue to guys with complaints about which nothing can be done. One ticket says 'this slip entitles the bearer to 15 minutes of crying time on a chaplain's shoulder for each question punched below.'"

tub. A scout car.

tubes. (1) Torpedoes. (2) Those who handle torpedoes. Both meanings allude to the tubes from which torpedoes are fired.

tuifu. The ultimate in foul-ups (or fuck-ups).

Turkhead McGirk. A sailor adept at tying knots.

turn turtle. To capsize a boat (i.e., to render it as helpless as a turtle on its back).

twist a dizzy. To roll a cigarette.

two-step. A chicken.

two-striper. (1) An Army corporal. (2) A Navy lieutenant.

two submarines and a mug of murk, no cow. Two doughnuts and a cup of coffee without cream.

Two-Thousand-Yard Stare. Name given to the look of the man with a combat-harrowed psyche. The term was the title of a 1944 Tom Lea painting depicting the face of a battle-weary G.I. about whom Lea wrote: "Two-thirds of his company have been killed, but he is still standing. So he will return to attack this mourning. How much can a human being endure." Sometimes called the Thousand-Mile Stare and the Thousand-Yard Stare.

typewriter. A .30-caliber machine gun, an automatic rifle, or any other clattering gun.

★ ☆ **U** ☆ ★

ugly duckling. A LIBERTY SHIP; an ugly ship.

umbrella. (1) A type of maneuver or attack by airplanes protecting ground forces in action. (2) A protective screen of fighter aircraft. (3) A parachute.

Uncle Samdom. The United States.

Uncle Sam's boys. The men of the armed forces.

Uncle Sam's party. Payday in the armed forces.

Uncle Sam's rag. The American flag.

Uncle Sugar. The United States. Says A. Marjorie Taylor in *The Language of World War II* (1948): "Expression used widely in the Pacific (and probably elsewhere) when referring to the United States. Derived from code words used in radio to transcribe the letters US."

undergear. Underwear.

underground. An outlawed political or military movement or organization operating in secret. During the war this term described a number of very active and sometimes very efficient groups of citizens in conquered nations working for the overthrow of the occupying Axis power.

undershoot. To land an airplane short of the mark.

under steam. Angered.

underwater battlewagon. A fully armed submarine.

undress. (1) The dress of soldiers out of uniform. (2) Ordinary military dress (as opposed to full dress).

unload a fish. To discharge a torpedo.

unreel a line. To trick or deceive, as by a falsehood or flattery.

unrigged. (1) Naked. (2) Out of commission, damaged, or in dry dock (said of a ship).

up / up-check. A successful squadron flight check; from THUMBS UP.

upstairs. (1) The sky. (2) In flight.

U.S.A.A.C. United States Army Air Corps.

U.S.O. United Service Organizations. The U.S.O. was created from six preexisting nongovernmental service organizations to provide recreation and special services for the troops.

★ ☆ **V** ☆ ★

vackie. An evacuee.

VACS. Volunteer Army Canteen Service. A VAC is a person engaged or employed in that service.

Valley Forge. A temporary tent city during cold weather.

varsity crewman. A Navy officer; a backhanded reference to the many college boys who were given commissions during the war and whose only previous naval experience might have been in crew racing.

V-discs. Twelve-inch double-faced plastic records of popular and classical music recorded by outstanding artists.

They were shipped to the troops monthly by the Special Services Division.

V-E Day and V-J Day. Victory-in-Europe Day and Victory-in-Japan Day. These designations were suggested by James F. Byrnes, director of war mobilization. V-E Day was announced this way in the London *Daily Sketch* for May 8, 1945:

THIS IS VE-DAY

Prime Minister to Announce the End in Europe This Afternoon

Official statement:
An official announcement will be broadcast by the Prime Minister at three o'clock this afternoon.
In view of this fact, to-day will be treated as Victory in Europe Day and will be regarded as a holiday.

V-J Day was celebrated on August 14, 1945.

vessel man. A pot washer.

vet. A veteran.

V-for-Victory. An allied slogan and hand signal. Its importance is explained by Stuart Berg Flexner in *I Hear America Talking* (1976): "'Victory' was the key word of World War II. 'Victory' meant the end of the war, the liberation of Europe, the end of totalitarianism. It was represented by the letter V on posters, in slogans, and in the V-for-Victory hand sign, made by raising the index and middle fingers into a V."

Winston Churchill made the V-for-Victory hand sign famous by using it frequently. The smiling, cigar-chomping Churchill flashing the V was a common newspaper and newsreel image.

V—The Birth of a Symbol

In *The Language of World War II* (1948), A. Marjorie Taylor gives this account of the origin of the V symbol:

January 14, 1941, Victor de Laveleye, a member of the Belgian Parliament exiled in London, in a broadcast to his homeland, proposed the use of the letter V as a symbol of passive resistance in Nazi-occupied lands. He had heard that Belgian children were chalking the initials RAF (for Royal Air Force) on walls and sidewalks, but he thought one letter which could be chalked quickly would be safer. He chose the letter "V." . . . The V stood not only for "Victory" and for the French Victoire but also for Vrieheid and Vrijheid, the words for freedom in Flemish and Dutch respectively. The scheme rapidly evolved into the most ambitious British propaganda campaign of the war. On July 4, 1941, the British Broadcasting Corporation carried speeches in all European languages. These were sprinkled with the Morse code for V, three dots and a dash. The opening bar of Beethoven's C minor symphony, three short notes and a long note, known as the fate theme, was chosen as the leitmotif of the movement. July 20 was proclaimed by the British as "V day." V clubs were formed. Radio listeners were also told to open their Bibles to Daniel V, which contains the words written on the wall: "Mene mene tekel upharsin," or, "God hath numbered thy kingdom and finished."

V-girl. See VICTORY GIRL.

vice. (1) A vice admiral. (2) Love.

vichyate. To subject France to the Vichy regime.

victory garden / V-garden. Vegetable gardens in the U.S. planted to help in the war effort. A. Marjorie Taylor gives this account in *The Language of World War II* (1948):

A week after the bombing of Pearl Harbor, December 7, 1941, gardeners stopped talking of Defense gardens, and began calling them Victory gardens. As food prices went up and food became scarcer, and point rationing was instituted, more and more persons planted vegetables in their Victory gardens, vegetables both for eating and for canning.

victory girl / V-girl. A girl under sixteen years of age who, without chaperone, became a pickup for servicemen, especially in big cities. In New York City, they were taken into custody to protect, as it was put at the time, "the morals of juveniles and the health of our armed forces." Writing in *Life* for December 20, 1943, Roger Butterfield reported on synonyms for V-girl: "*Khaki wackies, cuddle bunnies, round-heels, patriotutes, chippies, good-time Janes, Victory girls* are terms applied to delinquent girls; *shipyard orphans* and *door key kids* are names for neglected children."

V-Girls—Who Were They?

This is how Eleanor Lake addressed the question of V-girls in the May 1943 issue of *Common Sense:*

They aren't professional bad girls, these "victory girls" and "cuddle bunnies" who raise the truancy rate in high school, go uniform hunting in every railroad station, wander arm-in-arm down Main Street late at night looking for pick-ups. They are just ordinary kids who have been swept along by a torrent of wartime excitement and free spending. When they run afoul of the law, and are asked why they are delinquent, their answers are amazingly naive. The most common reason given is: "Because there's nothing else to do in this town." Next comes that age-old excuse: "Because it's my patriotic duty to comfort these poor boys who may go overseas and get killed."

★ ☆ **W** ☆ ★

victory suit / V-suit. A suit for civilian wear designed to save materials through the elimination of such things as cuffs and patch pockets.

V.I.P. / Viper. Very important person. A Viper was considered much superior to a "Piper" (pretty important person). This nickname was given particularly to important persons traveling on planes in war areas.

visiting fireman. A visiting officer, to whom courtesies must be paid.

V-mail. Victory mail. See AIRGRAPH MAIL.

volplane. To descend in an airplane without motor power or with the power shut off.

vomit iron rations / vomit lead / vomit leaden death. To shell; to bombard.

V.T. fuse. Variable time fuse; a secret weapon that the Army code-named "Pozit" and the Navy called "Buck Rogers." The V.T. fuse was a self-powered radio transmitter and receiver small enough to fit into the nose of an antiaircraft shell and tough enough to stand the terrific shock of firing.

WAC. Women's Army Corps; a member of the WACs.

wads. A naval gunner.

WAFS. Women's Auxiliary Ferrying Squadron. Here is how they were described in *Words of the Fighting Forces:*

Members of this organization must be not less than 21 years of age nor more than 35, high school education, commercial license with 200 H.P. rating, at least 500 hours logged and certified flying time, American citizenship, and cross-country experience. The unit will have an initial strength of about 50, 40 active pilots and 10 assigned to administrative duties. They will have civil service status, without an examination, and the pay will be $3,000 a year. Headquarters will be at Wilmington, Delaware.

wagon. An aircraft.

wagon soldier. A field artilleryman.

wagon train. A caravan of Army supply vehicles.

Wags. The K-9 CORPS; from its tail-wagging members.

Waldorf. A mess hall; an allusion to the swank Waldorf-Astoria Hotel, in New York City.

walkabout bottle. Oxygen in a bottle for emergency use.

walkie-talkie. A small, portable two-way field radio. According to *American Speech* for February 1941:

The first portable two-way set was developed in 1933 in the laboratories of the Signal Corps. Walkie-Talkie was the nickname given by soldiers to the first sets made by Galvin Manufacturing Corporation, but as popularity of the device grew, "walkie-talkie" slipped into official Army jargon and is now applied to all similar sets.

walking Johnny. A Marine; from the nickname for the Marine on a recruiting poster.

walkout club. Airmen forced to walk to safety after bailing out. A. Marjorie Taylor, in *The Language of World War II* (1948), gives this report based on an *Information Please* broadcast of May 26, 1945:

So many crews of American transport and battle planes, most of them flying along the air transport route into China, had been rescued from the North Burma jungles, that they formed the Walkout Club. Membership was limited to all those on active service with American forces who spent time in the jungle after parachuting to the ground when their planes were forced down.

walrus. One who cannot swim.

waltzing Matilda. A tank.

war baby. (1) A child of a soldier born during a war or just after a war is over. (2) A stockholding whose value increases because of a war.

war bride. A woman who marries an overseas U.S. serviceman.

warfish. A submarine; a torpedo.

war of nerves. A contest in which rumors, propaganda, and other elements of psychological warfare are employed to unnerve an enemy. It was believed that the French were quick to surrender after only a little fighting in the summer of 1940 because of the "war of nerves."

war paint. Official or full dress.

warphan. A war orphan. According to *American Speech* of October 1939: "The term was used in World War I and revived in China around 1938. Though it was used in World War II, 'vackie' (from evacuee) became the more generally used term."

war shoes. Heavy shoes; combat boots.

war time. Wartime daylight savings time. It was officially termed "war time" by President Franklin D. Roosevelt in 1942.

washed out. (1) Exhausted; in poor health. (2) Dismissed before completing flight training. (3) Killed in action; killed while in flight.

washing machine. A training squadron commander's airplane, in which cadets are given qualification tests; a plane in which an unsuccessful cadet is WASHED OUT.

washing-machine Charlie. A Japanese bomber whose engines sounded like a washing machine.

wash out. To be eliminated from flight training.

wash out on the range. To fail to hit a target on the firing range.

watch the hook. A warning used to terrorize recruits about to receive injections. See also HOOK.

water buffalo. An amphibious tank.

watercan. A depth charge; a submarine.

water rat. A veteran sailor.

water wasp. A PT boat (because of its ability to sting).

WAVES. Women Appointed for Volunteer Emergency Service; a branch of the Naval Reserve.

weasel. A caterpillar-tread truck.

weather-krock. A meteorologist.

weevil. Rice; from its appearance before being cooked.

Werewolves. A German underground group pledged to destroy both allied invaders and German "traitors."

when the ducks are walking. Weather too poor for flying.

where the hair's short. At a disadvantage.

whimsy. The Y.M.C.A. (as if said quickly).

whippet. A light, fast tank; from the breed of dog.

whip stall. A STALL from a vertical climb, which makes the airplane's nose whip violently forward.

whirlwind. A fast, two-engine, single-seater airplane, with four cannons and a high tail.

whiskers. Uncle Sam; a man employed by the government. The allusion is to Uncle Sam's white beard.

whiskey warrior. Any fighting man given to alcoholic excess.

whistle dick. An unliked or undervalued person.

white discharge. Any form of discharge other than dishonorable.

whites. A white Navy uniform.

whorehouse on wheels. A house trailer used by prostitutes, in which they entertain their customers.

wilco. Will comply. This radio code was used throughout the services and taken up by civilians. "Roger—wilco" means "Okay—I'll do it." See also ROGER.

wild hangar flying. Rumors, false information, or wild theories.

willie in the can. Canned corned beef.

Wimpy special. (1) A hamburger. In U.S. Army canteens in Australia hamburgers were named after Popeye's hamburger-loving friend J. Wellington Wimpy. (2) The British Wellington bomber; no doubt from the character's middle name.

windjammer. An Army bugler.

wind sock. A wind indicator that resembles a gigantic sock.

wing and wing. A close flying formation.

winged whale. A large Catalina Flying Boat.

wing heavy. Intoxicated.

winglet. A flying cadet.

wingover. A flying maneuver in which a rapid change of direction of 180 degrees is effected.

wings. An insignia worn by airmen.

wipe out. To ruin; to kill.

wireman. One who works on telephone or telegraph wires; an operator.

wolf pack. A group of three or more German submarines raiding allied convoys in the Atlantic.

woofin. A person who tells tall tales.

woof woof. A battalion sergeant major.

work one's ticket. To shirk duty.

World War I. The war of 1914–1918, previously known as the Great War. The name came into popularity in September 1939, a week after WORLD WAR II first appeared in *Time*. Lt. Col. C. A. Court Repington published a book entitled *The First World War 1914–1918* in 1920. Repington had first used "First World War" in his diary in a September 10, 1918 entry.

World War II. The official name for the war of 1939–1945. The name was first used in *Time* magazine, in its issue of September 11, 1939, but not officially accepted in the U.S. until 1945 by President Harry S Truman.

World War II—By Any Other Name

Although "World War II" was quickly accepted as the name for the conflict, there were many other suggestions, including some by Franklin D. Roosevelt, who never liked the name. Here is a sampling of the other suggestions:

The European War.

The Fatherland War.

Hitler's War. This was one of a number of names suggested by various news organizations during the 1939 lull. Others included: *The Little War That Wasn't There, The Word War, The Weird War, The Nutsy War,* and *The Nervy Nazi War.*

The Patriotic War.

The People's War. This was suggested by Australian prime minister John Curtin.

The Teutonic War.

The Teutonic Plague.

The Tyrant's War.

The War for Survival. This was the name preferred by President Franklin D. Roosevelt, who strongly suggested it during an April 1942 press conference. He had selected it from the thousands of suggested names sent to him at the White House.

The War of Deliverance.

The War of Democracy.

The War of Freedom.

The War of Individual Liberty.

The War of Liberation.

The War of Liberty.

The War of the Ages.

The War of the People.

wound chevron. A small Army uniform stripe worn on the lower part of the right sleeve to show that the G.I. wearing it had been wounded.

wreck. An airplane, especially one that has seen action.

writ. A written examination.

★ ☆ Y ☆ ★

yardbird. A buck private; a new soldier.

year and a bob / year and a kick. A punishment of one year's confinement and a dishonorable discharge.

yearling. A recruit; a SELECTEE.

Yehudi. See GREMLIN.

yellow ticket. A dishonorable discharge; from the color of the paper on which it was printed.

yeoette / yeomanette / yeowoman. A female clerk employed by the Department of the Navy.

Y gun. A depth-charge or bomb thrower.

yimca. The Y.M.C.A.

you're gigged. You have been reported for violating a rule or regulation. (A gig is a demerit.)

★ ☆ Z ☆ ★

zebra. (1) A NONCOM with multiple stripes, or chevrons. (2) A cadet officer in the Army Air Corps.

zepp. A zeppelin (i.e., a dirigible airship of rigid type); named after Ferdinand von Zeppelin.

Zero. A Japanese navy fighter plane. It was highly maneuverable and had a top speed of 340 miles per hour.

zero a bun. To set one's gun sights.

zero-zero. (1) Range is point-blank. (2) Visibility zero, ceiling zero.

zombie. A soldier falling in the lowest category in the Army classification test.

zoom. A brief, rapid climb after flying low at full speed. One zooms at an angle steeper than one would achieve in normal flight.

Sources and Acknowledgments

★

Every once in a while an apprentice lexicographer gets real, real lucky and bumps into a bona fide Rosetta stone. I did with the prime source used in this chapter, which is a manuscript entitled *Words of the Fighting Forces*. Actually, its full title is *Words of the Fighting Forces (A Lexicon of Military Terms; Phrases & Terms of Argot, Cant, Jargon & Slang Used by the Armed Forces of the United States of America.)* It was researched, compiled, and arranged by Clinton A. Sanders and Joseph W. Blackwell, Jr., and completed in September 1942, presumably to be of use while the war was ongoing. It was prepared under the auspices of the Language Section of the Military Intelligence Service, G-2, War Department General Staff, located in the Whitehall Building on Battery Place in New York.

The work appears in four typewritten volumes and the *original* 495-page typescript was located in the Pentagon Library. It does not appear in other card catalogs, bibliographies, and books on World War II and shows no signs of ever having been published. It is quite likely that the copy in the Pentagon is the only copy in existence.

To say that this is a major discovery is not to overstate the case. It is a first-rate compilation created during the War, apparently for the use of a small group of officers. As it has never been exposed to public view—either directly or by adaptation—it is worth giving some details on it, beginning with this dedication:

"*Words of the Fighting Forces* is dedicated to the fighting men of our forces on land, sea, and in the air.

And moving to this disclaimer:

"This compilation is offered to the United States War Department without fee or reward, obligation or legal responsibilities, as a contribution to the war effort."

An introduction explains the book, its intent, and the people who helped get it put together—including a most interesting sponsor. It is quoted here in its entirety.

Introduction

Words of the Fighting Forces is a dictionary of military lingo, specialized language, argot, cant, jargon, and slang used by American fighting men, including a supplement of military terms. We hope that this shall not be classed as "just another slang dictionary," but a volume characteristic in general design, profitableness to some valuable end, a scholarly preparation and up-to-date information and accuracy. In this volume it will be found that both the English spellings in common usage in the United States and conventional English spellings are recognized.

Specialists have been located who have generously donated large blocks of terms.

Terms which are found to overlap in one branch of the service running into another have been classified as general usage and are not listed with a classification code. Terms which have distinctive meaning and belong to a particular branch of the service have been listed with a classification code.

There are terms appearing herein that will no doubt "shock" the clergy, appeaser, isolationist, and puritan. We offer no apology nor have we deleted a term or terms because of what we feared such a group would do or say. These terms are part of a picturesque and living language of men who live close to earth and closer to death, words of men who fight the battles of free men for our

America and her Allies on remote and distant battlefields, who man our ships in dangerous seas, and fight up there on high.

We, the editors, have spent many enjoyable years in the compilation of this work. Our contacts with hundreds interested in this type of language and study have brought us friendships that we trust shall not die with the years. We're indebted to a hundred persons, many of them learned in the linguistic science and military arts, the majority "lay brothers" as we. We are, in particular, indebted to our sponsor, H. L. Mencken; to Dr. David W. Maurer, who has always been generous and wise in his advice; to Dr. Earl G. Swem, who has furnished the editors with books and historical data; to Walter Winchell, who so kindly gave us permission to quote from his large files and editorials; to Jim Tully, who suggested the compilation of this and other works. The aforesaid friends are not responsible, of course, for anything that appears herein.

All additions and corrections will be appreciated, and correspondence regarding same should be addressed to Lt. Col. Arthur Vollmer, Director, Military Intelligence Language-Section, 420 Whitehall Bldg., New York, New York.

C.A.S.
J.W.B. Jr.

Richmond, Virginia.
September 1942.

Numerous other sources were used. A. Marjorie Taylor's *The Language of World War II* (New York: H. W. Wilson, 2d ed. 1948) was a most important source for this chapter and still ranks as the most important published work on the language (slang as well as official terminology) of World War II from an American perspective.

Other sources consulted for this chapter include: *Army Talk* by Elbridge Colby, Princeton University Press, 1942; *The American Language* (and supplements) by H. L. Mencken, Alfred Knopf; *A Dictionary of Forces Slang*, 1948, edited by Eric Partridge, Books for Libraries Press, 1970; *Dictionary of American Slang* by Harold Wentworth and Stuart Berg Flexner, Thomas Y. Crowell, 1960; *The G.I.'s: The Americans in Britain 1942–1945* by Norman Longmate, Hutchinson, London; and *Words: The New Dictionary*, by Charles P. Chadsey, William Morris, and Harold Wentworth, Grosset and Dunlap, 1946.

Word Studies, a periodical publication of G. & C. Merriam Company of Springfield, Mass., which was published through the war years, provided many important short articles on the slang of World War II, including these:

Herzbert, Pvt. Richard A., "Army Slang," April 1943.

Kallich, Martin, "World War II Slang," May 1943.

"War Vocabulary Study Unit," a glossary compiled from news reports by the Ninth-Year English Class of Scarborough High School, Scarborough, New York, April 1944.

Several short unsigned items: "W.A.C. Words" (October 1944); "Postwar War Words" (February 1947).

Charles D. Poe unearthed many, many sources, citations, and connections; Bob Skole (who rode liberated Imperial Guard horses with the Eighth Cavalry Regiment in occupied Japan) helped with many suggestions and references; and the Tamony Collection provided many important citations. I also used a number of ephemeral sources including ads (Camel cigarettes ran a series of ads based on service slang), postcards, and base newspapers.

4

THE CODE OF THE KOREAN CONFLICT

★

A Few Words from World War 2½

★

It was the first modern crisis of the superpowers, and it was as brutal and bloody as any other war, despite the fact that the President and the press called it a "police action" and the troops saw it as a frozen hell.

To a large degree the slang of Korea was the slang of World War II, which can be explained by the fact that many of the Americans fighting this war were over the age of twenty-one and had served—though not necessarily fought—at the end of World War II. In 1952 Bill Mauldin sent a series of dispatches from Korea in which readers were told of Navy pilots returning to their carrier "to see the sun bouncing off so many bald heads." He added, "A pretty big chunk of this war is being fought by guys who carry pockets full of pictures of their wives and kids while they bounce on the deck in an airplane shot full of holes."

But there were also linguistic differences—new slang created by new technology (this was the first war in which jet fighters and helicopters were used), a new (communist) enemy, and a new (Korean) culture. American soldiers were fighting alongside South Koreans who were being fed into their units. The South Koreans were known individually and collectively as **KATUSA** (Korean Augmentation to the U.S. Army), and each man was paired with an American "buddy." The linguistic result was described by Neil Sheehan in

A Bright Shining Lie (1988): "The Army in Korea had developed a pidgin of English, Korean, and Japanese."

In addition, new slang terms developed around the participation of many nations in the U.N. forces (in support of South Korea) and of the Chinese communists (in support of North Korea).

Meanwhile the official language of the military bureaucracy was becoming ever more bureaucratic. Everything seemed to have an official initialism or acronym. It was argued that a lot of time was saved by the Navy's saying or writing "D.R." instead of "dental recruit" or by the Army officially deeming someone a "P.E." rather than having to spend a lot of time saying that he was a "pistol expert." By 1952, officers in the medical reserve were either MORCs (Medical Officer Reserve Corps) or DORCs (Dental Officer Reserve Corps). The war also gave us MASH (mobile army surgical hospital) units.

Stiff-sounding prefixes and suffixes were in vogue, so military terms like "detrain" and "detruck" almost immediately begat terms like "detraining point" and "detrucking point." The trend was noted in an October 1951 article in *Reader's Digest*: "The Pentagon vocabulary closely resembles plain English, but must be learned. 'Implement' means do, 'formalize' means write it down."

★ ☆ **A** ☆ ★

Abdul. Any Turkish soldier in the U.N. forces.

accordion war. A war of give and take, involving lines that one could not cross. Here is an example from Joseph C. Goulden's *Korea: The Untold Story of the War* (1982): "So MacArthur began sniping at Ridgway and his 'accordion war.'"

aggie. A native Korean youngster. "Originally," writes Ralph Reppert in his feature on Korean War slang in the June 24, 1951, Baltimore *Sun*, "it was applied only to the little Korean girls who came around to beg food from the mess sergeants, but its use soon expanded to cover all native children."

aggressor republic. The supposed totalitarian force that the U.S. had been practicing against in exercises since the end of World War II. North Korea fit the bill.

air strike. A bombing attack. Writes Martin Russ in *The Last Parallel* (1957): "Propeller-driven planes of the First Marine Air Wing fly sorties over enemy positions every day. These missions are called 'air strikes.' Hill Detroit received an air strike last week."

Angry Nine. The AN/GR-9 radio. It took up the entire backseat section of a jeep. Keeping its batteries charged was rough on the motor of the jeep, but it could transmit and receive over very long distances.

Ashcan City. ASCOM (Army Service Command) City, a processing center for Army personnel, located at Inchon, South Korea.

auger in. To crash an airplane. The term was especially apropos of jet planes, which drill into the earth when they crash. As in other wars, pilots superstitiously avoided using the word "crash."

★ ☆ **B** ☆ ★

badlands. Korea. The allusion is to the savagely eroded, grassless, waterless areas of the western U.S. The terrain is described in *A Dictionary of Soldier Talk* (1984), by John R. Elting, Dan Cragg, and Ernest Deal: "At that time reputed to be the only place on earth where one could stand neck-deep in mud in a mid-winter downpour and have dust blowing into one's eyes. It was rough, folks. What's more, our air mattress sprang a leak."

bali bali. Same as HUBBA HUBBA (see under World War II).

bamboo curtain. Communist China's "iron curtain." The term was coined by Time in 1949.

B&B. Booze and broads; a play on the official R&R.

Bean Patch. A Marine bivouac area near Masan. It had literally been a bean-growing area.

bean rag. The Navy's meal pennant (a signal showing that the crew is at mess).

bed-check Charlie. A night-bombing enemy aircraft. As Robert Leckie points out in *The Wars of America*, vol. II (1968), these night raiders in prop planes did little damage, but they did affect the morale of the ground troops. The name may have been patterned on WASHING-MACHINE CHARLIE (see under World War II).

Big Eight. The most important American military prison in Japan, located near Yokohama. It was first used during the occupation of Japan after World War II.

big pickle. The atomic bomb.

big R. Rotation home; the rotation system itself. Rotation was terribly important in Korea: front-line soldiers were able to go home in nine months, rather than the eighteen of World War II.

bird. A guided missile; an aircraft.

blast furnace. A jet aircraft. This is one of a number of terms for jet aircraft that derive from the power with which their engines expel jets of burning fuel. Other names included "blow job," "blow-torch," "can," "firecan," "flame-thrower," "flute," "jet," "jet job," "pipe," "speed burner," "squirt," and "squirt job."

bloodmobile. A blood bank in a truck.

blow job / blowtorch. A jet aircraft.

boondockers. Combat boots or field shoes.

bounce. An attack on an enemy airplane.

boysun. A Korean boy.

brain bucket. A pilot's crash helmet.

brain-washee. One who has been brainwashed.

brainwashing. Systematic indoctrination used to change a person's way of thinking; specifically, the intensive interrogation and indoctrination procedures used by the North Koreans and Chinese to persuade allied prisoners to change their allegiances. Here is a headline from the April 29, 1953, San Francisco *Examiner*: "'Brain-Washed' POWs Will Receive Mental Treatment." See also MENTICIDE.

Brainwashing

The term "brainwashing" first appeared in print on September 24, 1950, in the Miami *Daily News*, in an article by Edward Hunter. Hunter's book *Brain-Washing in Red China* (1951) covered the communists' use of propaganda and indoctrination.

After the war, the term gradually came to refer to any change of opinion; for instance, a friend who changed political parties might have been said to have been brainwashed by the Republicans.

However, the more sinister sense of the term, as a form of psychological warfare, made a return at the beginning of the U.S. involvement in Vietnam. An article in the San Francisco

---

Chronicle of December 6, 1965, began with these two paragraphs:

The spectre of Americans being insidiously and irresistibly brainwashed by cunning Communists is back amongst us.

Two American soldiers released by the Viet Cong last week made anti-war statements and promised to work for an American pullout from Vietnam. "I'd say they've been brainwashed," snapped Marine Corps Commandant Wallace Greene.

B.T.O. Big-time operator.

Buck Private. A light (200-pound) experimental Air Force helicopter.

buddy system. The arrangement under which South Korean soldiers were incorporated into U.S. units. Robert Leckie writes in *The Wars of America*, vol. II (1968): "The Koreans were paired off with Americans who were supposed to give them on-the-job training in the soldier's craft.... Because of obvious differences in language, temperament and customs, it was never much of a success." See also KATUSA.

buffalo gun. A .57-caliber antitank gun. This large weapon was named for the heavy rifles used in the Old West to kill buffalo.

bug out. (1) To leave in a hurry; to retreat; to play the coward. Ralph Reppert, writing in the Baltimore Sun in 1951, noted: "'Bug out' came into use briefly during World War II, but not until the Korean war did it gain wide usage." *Life* reported that the term was used "many thousands of times a day."

(2) An act of desertion. Here is how the term is used in *The United States in the Korean War* (1964), by Don Lawson: "In these 'bug-outs' the men sometimes threw away their weapons without firing a shot."

(3) An exit; a way out. Martin Russ writes in *The Last Parallel* (1957): "If the feces really hits the fan, there are three points through which a man can run for the hills—rear exits in the trenches called 'bug outs.'"

(4) To fly an aircraft away quickly from an endangered area.

"Bugout Boogie" / "Bugout Blues." Alternative titles for "Moving On," a popular song by country singer Hank Snow, which became an anthem of the war. According to *A Dictionary of Soldier Talk* (1984), by John R. Elting, Dan Cragg, and Ernest Deal, the title was credited "to the US 2d Infantry Division, commemorating its rout at Kunuri in November 1950. Officially proscribed, but still sung, it has the catchy refrain 'We're buggin' out, We're movin' on!'"

Joseph C. Goulden wrote in *Korea: The Untold Story of the War* (1982) that the appearance of a 24th Regiment patch on a soldier's sleeve would bring jeers and sometimes the lyrics of "Bugout Boogie," because "the 24th Regiment never overcame its reputation as a 'bugout' unit."

The title "Bugout Blues" (almost certainly another name for the same song) appears in this excerpt from Robert Leckie's *The Wars of America*, vol. II (1968): "'Bugging out,' a phrase describing unseemly and precipitate flight, was already a battlefield cliche, and one regiment had already adopted 'Bugout Blues' as its theme song."

bugout gas. Gasoline reserved for the possibility of a hasty retreat.

bunny hole. A place within a fighting hole or foxhole where one could huddle during a mortar attack. It amounts to a cave dug at the bottom of a trench.

burp gun. A type of Chinese machine gun; from its sound.

buttoned up. Said of a tank that is sealed off from the outside with its hatches locked down.

butt stroke. A blow with the butt end of a rifle stock in hand-to-hand combat.

buy the farm. To die; to be killed. In *Soldier Talk* (1982), Frank A. Hailey, a veteran of World War II, Korea, and Vietnam, says that this term was coined by Americans during the Korean War, with the same meaning as "buy it," which was borrowed from the British during World War II and used during the Vietnam War.

Other evidence supports Hailey. In an article in *Life* of September 26, 1955, Bill Mauldin reports on the slang at the Air Force Academy: "to 'buy a farm' is to crash."

Peter Tamony notes that "buy the farm" is an extension of "buy it" (dating back to the R.A.F. and World War II), but that the addition of the word "farm" was purely American. He theorizes that American training bases were in rural areas and that farmers were known to sue the government for huge sums of money after a crash on their land.

★ ☆ C ☆ ★

carrier pigeon. A Korean who carried messages when radio silence was being maintained.

chair corps. Servicemen in noncombat jobs. The following item appeared in the San Francisco *Examiner* on July 29, 1951:

CHAIR CORPS' STUDY PLANNED

Washington, July 28—A new move to reduce the armed services' "chair corps" and thus increase the number of fighting men was announced today by a Senate preparedness subcommittee.

Chairman Lyndon Johnson, Democrat of Texas, said his "watchdog defense group" is sending investigators to twenty "advanced training centers" of the Army, Air Force, Navy and Marines to check on use of personnel.

Military term—The "chair corps" term is used for military personnel assigned to duty as instructors, clerks, automobile drivers, telephone operators, or similar jobs.

Earlier this year on-the-spot visits to sixteen basic training centers by the preparedness subcommittee disclosed thousands of uniformed men, qualified for combat, assigned to these jobs.

chicken / chickenshit. Petty.

Chicom. Chinese communist. The term was used especially to refer to the "volunteers" fighting against the U.N. forces in Korea. It was used as much in headquarters as by the troops and had little civilian use before April 27, 1955, when President Dwight D. Eisenhower used it in a press conference. The next day *The New York Times* carried a small explanatory item headlined: "President's Chicoms is Chinese Communists." Some who didn't know of its broad use in Korea thought it was an Ike coinage.

Chinat. Chinese nationalist. The term referred to the noncommunist Chinese living on the island of Formosa (present-day Taiwan).

chogie [pronounced "show-ghee"]. (1) To bring; to carry (specifically, on one's back on an A-frame carrier). (2) Go! Move! According to Frank A. Hailey, in *Soldier Talk* (1982), it was: "A favorite saying among soldiers who served in Korea before, during, and after the Korean War." (3) A landmark, especially a hill. (4) A Korean laborer.

chop-chop. To eat. In World War II and in Korea "chop-chop" meant "hurry up," but it took on this additional meaning in Korea. In *Dictionary of American Slang* (1960), Harold Wentworth and Stuart Berg Flexner suggest that this meaning may derive from a reduplication of the verb "chop" (to cut or slice).

chopper. A helicopter.

circuit-riding chaplain. A chaplain who went from ship to ship via helicopter.

clamp down. To sprinkle and swab down a deck.

clank / clank up. To become nervous or agitated.

clobber. (1) To attack a ground target from the air. (2) To defeat decisively.

clue in. To give information (as in, "I'll clue you in on this one").

clutch platoon. A replacement platoon; akin to the clutch hitter in baseball who is brought in to pinch-hit.

cold-weather team. A group assembled in Korea to teach others how to survive in subzero conditions.

combat fatigue. See SHELL SHOCK, under World War I. See also CRACK UP and SHOOK.

compound. A walled enclosure containing living quarters, offices, and/or storehouses. According to A Dictionary of Soldier Talk (1984), by John R. Elting, Dan Cragg, and Ernest Deal: "In Korea and Vietnam such installations were often garrisoned and fortified. From Malay kampong, 'a cluster of buildings.' The term was occasionally used by old China hands before World War II, but did not come into general use until the Vietnam War."

copter. A helicopter.

cowboy-and-Indian tactics. Close combat; hand-to-hand fighting. Perhaps the popularity of movie and television westerns, which hit with full force in the 1950s, led to this war having a number of terms with roots in the Old West. Korea itself was nicknamed the BAD-LANDS.

crack up. SHELL SHOCK. A September 5, 1950, dispatch by Jerry Thorp contained this interchange:

> The tall blond corporal sat down beside me and said he'd like to talk awhile.

> "I'm out of there for a few days, thank God," he said. "They call it combat fatigue. Combat fatigue, hell, I cracked up."

See also SHOOK.

Crybaby Division. The 40th California National Guard Division. In About Face (1989), by David H. Hackworth, the division is referred to as a "sorry, undisciplined, ineffective fighting force."

cuta chogie. To fall out (i.e., break ranks).

cutta cutta. To go away.

★ ☆ **D** ☆ ★

Daniel Boone cap. Cold-weather headgear.

debbie chon. An overweight G.I.; from the Korean term for fat soldiers.

deep kimchi / deep kimshi. "Deep shit" (i.e., serious trouble; as in, "I'm in deep kimchi now"). Kimchi is a traditional Korean cabbage dish (see also KIMCHI). The phrase survives to the present day and is found in many novels about the military, as in this excerpt from The Warbirds (1989), by Richard Herman, Jr.: "We'll be in deep kimshi with Sundown if we lose another bird." Herman adds in a 1992 letter, "Being in 'Deep Kimshi' is indeed 'Bad Juju' (Black Magic)."

The expression is discussed in A Dictionary of Soldier Talk (1984), by John R. Elting, Dan Cragg, and Ernest Deal: "Widely used in Korea by Americans stationed there, Korea service veterans, and the general Army population, which has picked up the expression by diffusion. The expression is reinforced by the almost universal American dislike for kimchi."

demoth. To take out of mothballs (i.e., to bring World War II vehicles, ships, and equipment back into service).

die for a tie. An expression used by soldiers who agreed with General Douglas MacArthur that they were fighting for a stalemate ("tie" in the sense of a tie game in sports). In Joseph C. Goulden's *Korea: The Untold Story of the War* (1982), this phrase is used to allude to a MacArthur speech that became known as his "die for a tie speech."

dink. A dinghy or other small boat. See also under the Vietnam War, in which the term was used derisively.

D.M.Z. Demilitarized zone. In this war, the D.M.Z. was a cleared area on either side of the 38th parallel, the line separating North Korea and South Korea. See also under the Vietnam War.

don't panic. Play it cool.

dough. A DOUGHBOY (see under World War I). This short form for "soldier" appeared in constructions like "squad of doughs" and "company of doughs."

D.O.W. Died of wounds.

★ ☆ **E** ☆ ★

E&E. Evasion and escape. This was the name given to the tactics used by downed pilots in getting back to friendly territory.

egg beater. A helicopter.

eyeball to eyeball. To be in close contact with the enemy. In *On Language* (1980) William Safire poses this etymology:

> Where did it come from? According to General Harold Johnson, Army Chief of Staff in the mid-60's, the phrase originated in the military and is a contribution of black English. The 24th Infantry Regiment, before integration in the armed services, was all black; in November 1950 it bore the brunt of a counterattack in Korea. When General MacArthur's headquarters sent an inquiry to the 24th regiment—"Do you have contact with the enemy?"—the reply, widely reported at the time, was "We is eyeball to eyeball."

★ ☆ **F** ☆ ★

fenced-in war. The air war in Korea (because there were lines that could not be crossed—e.g., the Yalu River). Although the ground war could also be seen as fenced in, this term was rarely used to describe it.

figmo. Fuck it, got my orders. There was no polite translation of this term, so those reporting on the slang of Korea were constrained to write absurdities, like this one from the San Francisco *Examiner* of June 2, 1957: "'Figmo' unquestionably had a good reason for being coined, but no one now in Korea seems to remember what it was."

figmo chart. A piece of paper or cardboard on which a man kept a record of the number of days he had left until rotation. Some troopers used a "figmo stick," which was a stick marked with the number of days remaining until rotation. A soldier would slice off a piece with the passing of each day.

firecan. A jet aircraft.

first shirt. A first sergeant.

5-in-1 ration. A balanced ration for troops in the field. It was introduced in World War II and reintroduced in Korea and sometimes supplied to men who had no ability to heat it up—the 5-in-1 ration was popular when served hot, but unacceptable when cold.

flame thrower. A jet aircraft.

flap. A description of the war. Many people did not see the conflict as an all-out war, but found it hard to use the official term, "police action." Curtis LeMay used the word "flap" in *Mission with LeMay* (1965): "I suggested informally, when the Korean flap started in 1950, that we go up north immediately with incendiaries and delete four or five of the largest towns: Wonsan, Pyongyang and so on."

At about the time of the French stand at Dien Bien Phu (1954), some Americans referred to that conflict as "the Indochina flap."

flute. A jet aircraft (because the sound comes out of a pipe).

fogey / fogy. An increase in pay for length of service (because one had to be on the way to becoming an old fogy before qualifying).

forgotten war. The Korean conflict. The term is still used to underscore the fact that 54,246 Americans died in a war that the nation seemed not to focus on, even while it was being fought.

friendlies. South Korean troops.

Frozen Chosin. (1) The Chosin reservoir area during the allied retreat in the disastrous winter of 1950–51. The word "frozen" was not lightly employed, as is evidenced by this excerpt from Joseph C. Goulden's *Korea: The Untold Story of the War* (1982):

> When the fighters bivouacked in snow-covered ground during combat, their feet, socks and hands were frozen together in one ice ball; they could not unscrew the caps on the hand grenades; the fuses would not ignite; the hands were not supple; the mortar tubes shrank on account of the cold; seventy percent of the shells failed to detonate; skin from the hands was stuck on the shells and mortar tubes.

(2) Korea in general. Chosin (or Chosun) is the ancient name for Korea. The term means "land of the morning calm."

★ ☆ **G** ☆ ★

gadget. The atomic bomb. The term was used by military planners from the end of World War II through the Korean War period.

galley yarn. A rumor (i.e., a story that originates—metaphorically or actually—in a ship's kitchen, or galley).

gargoyle. An unkempt pilot.

geographical bachelor. A man who, figuratively speaking, became unmarried once he left the States. The term was also applied to men at stateside military bases if they were a long way from home. Geographical bachelors, as one writer put it, were the ones who took off their wedding bands for the duration.

germ warfare. Biological warfare. North Korea insisted the U.N. forces were guilty of this war crime.

G.I. An American soldier. This term was still used in Korea despite an attempt by the Defense Department to suppress it. A June 1951 Defense Department bulletin sent to all Army public relations officers worldwide barred them from using the term: "In recognition of the dignity of the fighting man and the traditions of his service to America, Army public relations officers should make no further use of the slang expression 'G.I.'" The bulletin went on to state that the proper name for a soldier was "soldier."

girdle. A suit worn by aviators to counter g-forces.

gohong. Food. Ralph Reppert wrote about the term in the Baltimore Sun in 1951: "Gohong is one Korean word for rice. American soldiers used the word correctly for a while, then began applying it to all food. Now it's synonymous with all chow."

golfball. A TRACER bullet (see under World War II).

go mental. To be SHOOK.

goof off. (1) To blunder; to kill time. (2) A chronic blunderer.

gook. A Korean. Ralph Reppert wrote about the term in the Baltimore Sun in 1951: "Probably the most widely used slang term of this war. . . . Now it is the popular term for any native, soldier or civilian; allied or belligerent. The word is even heard in the States, used by garrison soldiers to indicate residents of the nearest town."

The term has a long history. It was used during the Spanish-American War era to refer to Filipinos; during World War II, it meant a nonfighting native of the islands of the South Pacific; and in the Vietnam War, it referred to a native Southeast Asian (mainly, of course, the Vietnamese). In all these uses, it was a racist slur.

goony. A Chinese communist soldier. The word probably derives from "goon" (a hoodlum or thug).

goonyland. Communist China. As Martin Russ explains in The Last Parallel (1957), the term had a special meaning for the Marines: "It's a small point, but the word "goonyland' has a kind of special meaning to us. Like Toyland of a department store, it suggests something innocent and—as much as I hate the word—cute."

green-apple quick-step. Dysentery; an allusion to the fact that green apples can cause severe stomachaches and diarrhea, making one step quickly to the latrine.

gung ho. Overzealous; driven. During World War II, the term had only positive connotations, but not in Korea, as can be seen in this excerpt from "A Marine Tells His Father What Korea Is Really

Like," by John W. Harper, which appeared in *Life* of December 3, 1951: "We expect to be able to rest, reorganize and prepare ourselves for the assault the next morning—but no. Someone got gung-ho and decided to jump us off as soon as possible assuming an understrength company could make a mile and a half advance in one hour of daylight!"

Here is another example, from a letter by Bill Martin in the San Francisco *Call-Bulletin* of December 11, 1950: "We've been catching hell for the last three days. You have no idea of the hell it has been for us. . . . Doesn't look like we are ever going to be relieved from up here. Did anyone say anything about Gung Ho? I'll trade places. So long, fellows."

See also under World War II.

★ ☆ **H** ☆ ★

had it. Defeated (as in, "We've had it. We're finished."). "Had it" was first heard in Europe at the end of WWII, but came into its own in Korea.

hava-no. I haven't got it.

hava-yes. I've got it.

Hawaiian Mafia. The 27th Infantry Regiment (because a large number of Hawaiians were in the unit). See also WOLF-HOUNDS.

Heartbreak Ridge. An objective that fell to U.N. troops after thirty-seven days of fierce combat.

heavy. A big machine gun.

hei-hei [pronounced "high-high"]. A black G.I. (as referred to by Chinese communist and North Korean troops).

helitrooper. A soldier who parachutes into battle from a helicopter.

hero gear. Battle souvenirs.

Hey, Kim. An expression used to address South Korean soldiers. Ralph Reppert wrote about it in the Baltimore *Sun* of June 24, 1951: "South Korean soldiers resent the term [gook]. They prefer to be called Roks (Republic of Korea). They also like to be addressed, 'Hey, Kim,' in the same tone that one G.I. hails another with 'Hey, Mac' or 'Hey, Joe.'" Kim is a common Korean name.

hit the deck. To wake up and get out of bed.

hit the sack. To go to bed.

hog pilot. A pilot who flies the F-84G Republic Thunderjet (or Hog).

home by Christmas. A phrase used by those who foresaw a quick resolution of the war. The phrase and the frustration it represented became emblematic of the conflict. It first came into play early in the war. On November 24, 1950, General Douglas MacArthur launched an offensive against North Korea and made this statement to one of his commanders: "Tell the boys for me that when they reach the Yalu, they are going home. I want to make good my statement that they are going to eat their Christmas dinner at home." A day later U.S. troops were fighting Chinese troops.

homer. A weapon with a homing (target-seeking) device.

honcho. A leader; a man in charge. This term derives from the Japanese *han* ("squad") + *cho* ("leader"). Stuart Berg Flexner, in *I Hear America Talking* (1976), reports that the term means literally "squad leader" (a corporal or sergeant). A common definition given during the war was "number-one man," suggesting the Japanese lineage. The term soon became part of general American slang.

honey bucket detail. The men assigned to emptying buckets of latrine sewage.

hooch / hoochie. (1) A bunker; other front-line living quarters. (2) The dwelling of a prostitute; any place where an American serviceman set up housekeeping with a Korean woman. (3) Any building.

The word "hooch" derives from the Japanese *uchi* ("house"). There is no connection with the slang term "hooch" for liquor, which derives from the Chinook *hoochenoo* (a homemade liquor). The term was used during the Vietnam War, too.

horde. Chinese communist or North Korean troops.

Horde Knocks

The overuse of the term "horde" during the war was something of a joke. Nelson DeMille writes of it in *By the Rivers of Babylon* (1978): "That had been an American infantryman's joke during the Korean War. A Chinese squad was made up of three hordes and a mob."

Robert Leckie, in *The Wars of America*, vol. II (1968), repeats a rifleman's quip: "I was attacked by two hordes, sir, and I killed them both."

In William B. Hopkins's *One Bugle No Drums* (1986), the gag line is: "Hey! How many Chinese hordes are there in one platoon?"

Here is how the term is discussed in *A Dictionary of Soldier Talk*, by John R. Elting, Dan Cragg, and Ernest Deal (1982):

One or more North Joes or Chicoms. Although the Communists did employ massed infantry assaults at what they considered decisive points, most of their attacks were small-scale affairs, shrewdly directed at the flank or rear of a UN position. It is an ancient axiom, followed by all armies, that it is safer to tell higher headquarters that you were outnumbered than that you were outsmarted.

---

hose down. To shoot down an enemy aircraft.

hot pursuit. The chasing of an enemy aircraft. American pilots were forbidden to cross the Yalu River in hot pursuit of enemy airplanes on their way to bases in Manchuria.

hot war. Police action in Korea, used to differentiate it from the Cold War.

human sea. Enemy troops attacking in waves. In *The United States in the Korean War* (1964), Don Lawson writes: "The North Korean 'Human Sea' attacks were also new to the G.I.'s—new and frightening." See also RED TIDE.

hyakoo. Hurry up; pretty soon. This term, like many other linguistic creations of the war, derives from the Japanese, a fact explained by the amount of time G.I.'s spent in Japan for rest and relaxation.

★ ☆ **I** ☆ ★

I&I. Intercourse and intoxication; a play on **R&R.**

ichiban. The best; from the Japanese *ichiban* ("number one").

idewa [pronounced "ee-dee-wa"]. Come here; from the Japanese. Here is how the term is discussed in *A Dictionary of Soldier Talk* (1984), by John R. Elting, Dan Cragg, and Ernest Deal: "The derivation of the expression is obscure. Most sources regard it as of Korean origin, but no comparable Korean form has been found. In all probability, it is pidgin Japanese, a corruption of o-ide nasai 'come here,' in which nasai has been dropped and the nominative particle wa has (incorrectly) been added in its place."

idiot board. A Korean A-frame pack board used for carrying supplies in areas accessible only on foot or by mules. They were used by South Koreans to provision American troops in the field. According to *A Dictionary of Soldier Talk* (1984), by John R. Elting, Dan Cragg, and Ernest Deal: "Where there is shooting to be done, no squad, platoon, or company commander is going to detail his best and brightest to run up and down the ridge lines carrying resupplies of ammo, food, and water." See also KOREAN FORKLIFT.

Iron Triangle. A daunting defensive area on the central front regarded by U.N. forces as a major North Korean assembly base and industrial complex. It lay between Pyongyang to the north, Chorwon to the west, and Kumhwa to the east.

it only takes one to kill you. A phrase known as the "rifleman's creed"; a reference to the fact that it made no difference if you were killed by a sniper or by an artillery shell.

★ ☆ **J** ☆ ★

jaypee / J.P. Jet propulsion, as opposed to conventional propeller power (as in, "That plane's on jaypee").

jerkoff lotion. Jergen's hand lotion. Soldiers often requested this product from home to relieve cracking and soreness from the bitter cold. Clearly, it also found other uses.

jet ace. A jet fighter pilot with five or more enemy kills. The first was James Jabara, a World War II ace.

jet-jeep. The XH-26 helicopter.

jet job. A jet aircraft.

jet jockey. A jet fighter pilot.

jettie. A jet engine.

jetwash. The violent air behind a jet airplane; the backwash from a jet engine.

juice. Jet fuel.

jump sack. A parachute.

★ ☆ **K** ☆ ★

KATUSA. Korean Augmentation to the U.S. Army. The term referred, individually and collectively, to the South Koreans integrated into American Army units. In some rifle squads, half the troops were KATUSA.

Here is how the term is discussed in *A Dictionary of Soldier Talk* (1984), by John R. Elting, Dan Cragg, and Ernest Deal:

> Originally, in 1950, as a desperation measure, thousands of Korean civilians, ignorant of military life and the English language, were hastily drafted into understrength American units. Many of them were refugees, half-starved and sick. Generally, they could be used only for work details. This term has since been used for the assignment of Republic of Korea (ROK) soldiers to selected American units to serve as fillers and to receive American military training.

K-day. The first day of hostilities in the war.

Kim. See **Hey, Kim.**

kimchi. (1) A sauerkrautlike Korean dish made of Chinese cabbage, chili peppers, garlic, and occasional other ingredients, salted and fermented in its own juices. Usually eaten raw, it is a staple at Korean meals. Like sauerkraut, it emits a foul odor while fermenting, but the kimchi made during winter is milder and its aroma less offensive to American nostrils than that made during the warmer months. American soldiers generally did not like kimchi, but it has become a popular item in Chinese and Korean restaurants in the United States. Richard Herman, Jr., gives this impromptu review of the dish in a letter: "It has to be smelled to be believed—like miles downwind—and tasted to be truly appreciated. It kills all intestinal parasites,

cleans the plaque off your teeth and substantially cuts down on the use of toilet paper."

(2) By extension, anything Korean (as in, "kimchi dog," "kimchi taxi," and "kimchi fart").

(3) Anything of inferior quality; used synonymously with "shit" (see also DEEP KIMCHI).

kiss my ass good-bye. An alternative interpretation of KMAG (Korean Military Advisory Group). During the early part of the war American KMAG advisors assigned to South Korean troops felt endangered by the South Koreans' poor performance.

KMAG [pronounced "kay-mag"]. See KISS MY ASS GOOD-BYE.

Korean forklift. A wooden A-frame device worn in knapsack fashion. In *Soldier Talk* (1982), Frank A. Hailey reports that Koreans were said to carry objects weighing up to a half ton on one of these packs. See also IDIOT BOARD.

Korean prayer book. An American mail-order catalogue (because the items for sale suggested a degree of comfort and luxury that one could only pray for).

Korean sauerkraut. See KIMCHI.

★ ☆ **L** ☆ ★

lamplighter. A twin-engined C-47 transport airplane used to light up areas for night operations.

land of . . . A construction used in many expressions to refer to the U.S. In

Soldier Talk (1982), Frank Hailey discusses the construction:

"Land of . . ." were the key words which prefixed the hundreds of phrases coined by our soldiers in Korea to describe their homeland. A few of the most commonly heard were: "Land of the multi-colored 'jeeps' (civilian automobiles), "Land of the Big PX" (any large mail order house or department store), "Land of the two-storied Quonset Huts" (civilian apartment buildings), "Land of the off-the-floor-beds" (as opposed to the sleeping mats most Orientals prefer), and the most popular of all, "Land of the Big Round Eyes" (although our soldiers found the dark, almond-shaped eyes of the Korean ladies beautiful and enticing, those GIs not of Oriental extraction longed for the big round eyes of their wives and girlfriends back home).

During the occupation of Germany after World War II, in a phrase discussed in *A Dictionary of Soldier Talk* (1984), by John R. Elting, Dan Cragg, and Ernest Deal: "*Land of the Round Doorknob*. The United States, so called because doorknobs in this country are usually round, while in Europe, especially Germany (where this expression originated), the doorknobs are usually shaped like handles."

layout. A forward observer who hides in a camouflaged hole to observe the enemy.

leap off. To take off in an airplane.

line crosser. A soldier who crosses the M.L.R. looking for prisoners. In *One Very Hot Day* (1967), David Halberstam describes a man who had been a line crosser in Korea: "He had worked for a time filtering back and forth across lines, working on prisoner-snatching, a job as-

signed to him because when the call went out for volunteers his battalion commander had not liked him, had viewed him as expendable and had volunteered him."

line jumper. A North Korean or Chinese communist spy who manages to cross U.N. lines.

Little Chicago. Tongduch'on-ni, South Korea. Here is how it is discussed in *A Dictionary of Soldier Talk* (1984), by John R. Elting, Dan Cragg, and Ernest Deal:

A town north of Seoul, just behind the US I Corps zone. Principal inhabitants: widows and orphans left by the North Korean attempt to "liberate" South Korea in 1950. Principal occupations: prostitution, begging, souvenir peddling, theft. Principal public institutions: orphanages and relief missions supported by US troops.

little friends. South Koreans; a derisive reference to their size.

little R. Recreation. The BIG R was rotation home.

Luke the Gook. A North Korean soldier. The term was sometimes also applied to Chinese communist soldiers, though they were more commonly called "Old Joe Chink." See also GOOK.

Luke the Gook's castle. An enemy fortification.

★ ☆ **M** ☆ ★

mama-san. A madam in a brothel. The term is a combination of the English "mama" and the Japanese suffix -san and means, literally, "boss mother." The suffix was added to many English and pidgin words, in imitation of Japanese use. See also PAPA-SAN.

Marine Corps Rules for Success. "Get a receipt for it, shoot the shit and never volunteer," according to William B. Hopkins in *One Bugle No Drums* (1986).

MASH. Mobile Army Surgical Hospital. The term is defined in *The New Military and Naval Dictionary* (1951), by Frank Gaynor: "A mobile hospital unit, organized and operated for early surgical treatment of non-transportable casualties." This type of mobile unit was later renamed "MUST" (Medical Unit Self-Contained Transportation). As *M*A*S*H*, written with asterisks, the term was the title of a movie and an extremely popular and long-lived TV series. However, the unit depicted in the TV show bore little resemblance to the real thing. The success of the TV series led to a series of books with such titles as *M*A*S*H Goes to Maine*.

megook. A U.S. soldier (as referred to by Koreans). *Polyglot's Lexicon: 1943–1966* (1973), by Kenneth Versand, lists the term, as do other sources. In Marcy Reifer's *Dictionary of New Words* (1955), the term is listed as "megock" but given the same meaning. Neither source suggests the origin of the word.

menticide. A synonym for BRAINWASHING. A May 5, 1952, article in *Life* contained this passage: "This process is known as 'brain-washing.' The new Western word is menticide. No one hides it.

Newspapers report its progress. The Communists boast about it."

The term is defined in *Polyglot's Lexicon: 1943–1966* (1973), by Kenneth Versand: "The gradual destruction of a man's mind, through psychiatric or other means, to the point where he will accept an ideology formerly loathsome to him."

Mickey Mouse boots. Heavy rubber boots that made soldiers' feet sweat and, consequently, freeze. They were so-called, according to David H. Hackworth in *About Face* (1989), "for the striking resemblance to those worn by Walt Disney's famous rodent."

MiG Alley. The airspace over a chain of North Korean valleys where Soviet-made MiG-15 jet fighters based in Manchuria often intercepted U.S. planes attacking North Korea from the south. The MiG-15 (one of a series of Soviet jet fighters named after their designers, A. I. Mikoyan and M. I. Gurevich) was first used in the war in 1950. The term "MiG Alley" appeared in many wartime headlines— for example, "Inside MiG Alley" (*Life*, December 10, 1951) and "Fresh from MiG Alley" (*This Week*, March 16, 1952).

mind sweeping. An alternative term for BRAINWASHING; a feeble play on "minesweeping."

Mister Truman's war. The Korean War (as referred to by those who felt that President Harry S Truman had decided to pursue the war for domestic political purposes).

M.L.R. Main line of resistance (i.e., the front). Martin Russ discusses the term in

The Last Parallel (1957): "The front, or front lines, are rarely referred to as such. MLR is used instead. It stands for 'main line of resistance.' In our case, the MLR is a deep trench, from five to seven feet in depth, running along the ridgeline of the hill mass occupied by our platoon."

moose. A girlfriend. It is a corruption of the Japanese word for "woman." In *Korea: The Untold Story of the War* (1982), Joseph C. Goulden quotes a G.I. on his lack of interest in the war and his definite interest in the comforts of Japan: "I just want to get back to Japan to my little Sasebo Sadie. I have been shacked up there now for more than two years with the prettiest little moose you ever did see."

mother fucker. An oath expressing deep contempt. According to Stuart Berg Flexner in *I Hear America Talking* (1976), this term "first achieved wide use during the Korean War." Interestingly, *Webster's Ninth New Collegiate Dictionary* indicates that this term does not show up in print until 1959.

move on. To BUG OUT.

★ ☆ N ☆ ★

new war. The period after November 25, 1950, when U.S. troops launched a major offensive toward the Yalu River and were met by Chinese communist troops. General G. E. Stratemeyer, describing the beginning of the new war to a congressional committee, said that U.N. forces were moving ahead unopposed, "But then, lo and behold, the whole mountainside turned out to be Chinese."

North Joe. A North Korean.

no sweat. No trouble; I can handle it.

number 1. The best. Less commonly, "number 10" was used to mean "the worst," with intermediate numbers indicating gradations.

★ ☆ O ☆ ★

oil king. A Navy petty officer in charge of fuel oil storage.

Old Fu. Chinese communist troops. The term derives from the insidious fictional character Fu Manchu. In *Soldier Talk* (1982), Frank A. Hailey writes that it was used in lines like, "There goes Old Fu back across the old Yalu."

Old Joe Chink. A Chinese communist; "chink" is a traditional derogatory name for Chinese people.

"Old soldiers never die, they just fade away." A statement made by General Douglas MacArthur at a joint session of Congress on April 19, 1951. He had been relieved of his command by President Harry S Truman and had come to Congress to defend his beliefs and bid farewell to public service. The phrase is from an old song, and reaction to MacArthur's use of it ranged from adulation to mockery. Joke lines based on the statement included, "Old fishermen never die, they just smell that way," "Old gardeners never die, they just spade away," "Old songwriters never die, they just decompose," and "Old lawyers never die, they just lose their appeal."

On your horse, amigo? How are you? This was an American parody of a friendly Korean greeting, *annyong hasipnika.*

Operation Big Switch. The final exchange of P.O.W.'s in August and September 1953, in which 70,000 North Koreans and 6,000 Chinese were exchanged for 4,800 U.N. troops and 8,000 South Koreans.

Operation Killer. The code name of the main U.N. offensive in Korea.

Operation Little Switch. The April 1953 exchange of 6,000 communist prisoners for 700 U.N. prisoners.

Operation Strangle. The code name for the largely unsuccessful attempt to cut off enemy rail and supply lines. It began in August 1951 and lasted for ten months.

Operation Yo-Yo. The battle for Wosan. The name was given to the operation by the Marines who were left sailing back and forth as the harbor was cleared of mines. By the time the Marines were able to land, Bob Hope and a U.S.O. troupe had arrived. The G.I.'s who had done the fighting thus had an excuse to write a new verse to the Marine Corps hymn, which they sang for the Marines as they landed:

> Those tough and fighting Gyrenes
>   Wherever they may go,
> They're always bringing up the rear
>   Behind Bob Hope and the U.S.O.

★ ☆ **P** ☆ ★

panic button. Anything that precipitates an exaggerated response to an emergency. The term was widely used during the war; it derives from the control buttons or switches used in emergencies, which were known as panic buttons. See also PUSH THE PANIC BUTTON.

panic rack. An ejection seat in an airplane. Although the devices appeared at the end of World War II, they first saw real action in Korea. The term "rack" is used in the sense of a bed or cot.

papa-san. Boss man.

papasan stick. Any of various sorts of walking sticks used by elderly men.

peon. (1) Anyone not in an airborne unit, especially ordinary infantry. (2) An airborne-unit private or private first class. The word is Spanish for "peasant."

pimple. A small hill.

ping-pong war. See YO-YO WAR.

pipe. A jet airplane (because of its tubular fuselage).

pipe jockey. A jet fighter pilot.

play it cool. Take it easy; relax.

plumber. A "square" (i.e., someone not "hip" or "cool"). In a report from Seoul, reporter Marvin Stone used the word "square" and got this response from an unnamed soldier: "A square? Man, what kind of talk is that? These days if you're not with it you're a plumber."

police action. A term used to characterize the allied response to the North Korean invasion of South Korea. The conflict could not be called a war by the U.S. because Congress never declared it to be one. The term was used both as a straight description and, mockingly, as a bitter euphemism for the cruel and bloody war.

The term was not an official one. It was approved by President Harry S Truman on June 27, 1950, at his first press conference after the war began. According to Hugh Rawson, in *Dictionary of Euphemisms and Other Doubletalk* (1981), Truman was asked by a reporter if "it would be correct . . . to call this a police action under the United Nations?" Truman replied, "Yes, that is exactly what it amounts to." This led to an immediate spate of headlines—for example, "Truman Calls Intervention a 'Police Action.'"

pongo honcho. A person who passes gas frequently and noisily; from the Korean *pongu* ("gas") and *honcho* ("boss").

Pork Chop Hill. A hill where a particularly savage battle was fought. The hill was named for its peculiar shape. In 1959, a movie about the battle came out, starring Gregory Peck and titled *Pork Chop Hill.* Some of the grimmest fighting of the war took place at sites with names like Old Baldy, Siberia Hill, Stalin Hill, No Name, Bunker Hill, T-bone Hill, and Capitol Hill.

presento. Give me; from a Korean term.

prick-6. The PRC-6 walkie-talkie radio. PRC stands for nothing; it is a letter code.

The PRC-6 was supplemented by the PRC-10 in the 1960s, and both were replaced by the PRC-25 during the Vietnam War.

psy war. Psychological warfare.

pull a Hank Snow. To BUG OUT. The reference is to "BUGOUT BOOGIE."

pull combat time. To serve in combat.

push the panic button. To lose composure under pressure. In this war, this term was often linked with BUG OUT, because bugging out would often ensue when the panic button was pushed. Ironically, as "push the panic button" passed into civilian use it came to stand for doing a job quickly and efficiently, as in meeting a business emergency. Harold Wentworth and Stuart Berg Flexner, in *Dictionary of American Slang* (1960), call it "a term associated with Madison Avenue."

★ ☆ **Q** ☆ ★

quad / quad-fifty. Four .50-caliber machine guns on a single mount. "One of the quads is firing right now, a wicked racket," writes Martin Russ in *The Last Parallel* (1957). Quads first appeared in World War II, but seemed to have a special importance in Korea.

★ ☆ **R** ☆ ★

Rambling ROKs. South Korean ground units. See also ROK.

R&R. Rest and relaxation, rest and recreation, rest and recuperation, rest and recovery, or rest and rehabilitation (i.e., a period of relief from the combat zone—as in, "ten days' R&R in Tokyo").

According to *A Dictionary of Soldier Talk* (1984), by John R. Elting, Dan Cragg, and Ernest Deal, it was unofficially interpreted as, "Rape and Restitution or Rape and Ruin." R&R usually consisted of a five-day leave period for combat soldiers after six months in Korea. Elting, Cragg, and Deal note:

> Frequently the soldier returned twice as tired as before he left, but without his previous thousand-yard stare. . . .
> It was during the initial phase of this activity that serious consideration was given to issuing a special Close Combat Badge to all MPs serving in Japan. However, things soon more or less quieted down.

readjust the lines. To retreat; to BUG OUT.

real estate. Territory (lost or gained).

re-Americanization. Reeducation in the basics of American culture. The process was applied to returning P.O.W.'s, among others.

Red tide. Masses of North Korean troops. The term was popularized by the legendary *New York Times* journalist Homer Bigart, who wrote of a "Red tide" of North Korean soldiers closing in on American troops "silently and relentlessly, the faces of the communist infantrymen showing neither fear nor elation."

reservist mess. The situation under which reservists who were veterans of World War II were called back into action, while members of the National Guard were not. This violated an understanding that men who had served in World War II would be called back only in case of an all-out war, not for a POLICE ACTION.

The reservist mess was part of the larger "mess in Washington." In 1952, an article in *U.S. News and World Report* claimed there were no less than fifteen elements to the mess, including the "MacArthur mess" (his desire to fight to victory got him fired), the "housing mess" (large-scale cheating of World War II veterans through the overappraisal of substandard housing), and the "China mess" (a country the U.S. had liberated from the Japanese, but that was now fighting Americans in Korea).

ride the pipe. To pilot a jet aircraft after the engine dies. "Pipe" is slang for the plane itself and acknowledges the point that a plane with dead engines flies like a pipe.

ridge cottage. A bunker in the craggy demilitarized zone.

Ridgway shuffle. A characteristic way in which paratroopers move to an aircraft's exit hatch. It was described by Korean veteran Frank A. Hailey in *Soldier Talk* (1982): "The shuffling movement of the feet which paratroopers use as they move forward to the exit hatch of an aircraft in flight during an airborne exercise. Keeping both feet on the passageway of the aircraft helps the individual maintain proper body balance, especially under heavy combat load." The allusion is to General Matthew B.

Ridgway, who commanded airborne troops in Korea before becoming the overall American commander during the war.

rocket ripple. A barrage of small Marine surface-to-surface rockets. Martin Russ, in *The Last Parallel* (1957), describes such a barrage: "It may be ridiculous to call any barrage beautiful, but if one doesn't think about it too hard, a barrage is beautiful—to watch; especially a rocket ripple. It is the most violent barrage of them all: 144 rockets are released within seconds; they pass overhead almost in formation, and land with a tremendous overlapping of explosions."

ROK. Republic of Korea. It became a friendly term of address for South Korean troops. The troops pronounced it "rock," while many civilians in the U.S. said "rook."

rotatee. An American soldier on rotation leave away from the war zone.

rove. To fire mortar rounds in no set pattern—one here, one there.

Russian Wolfhounds. The 27th Infantry Regiment. "Russian" in this name does not refer to the people, but to the breed of dog, also known as the Borzoi. See also HAWAIIAN MAFIA and WOLFHOUNDS.

★ ☆ **S** ☆ ★

SAM. Surface-to-air missile.

scrounger. One adept at acquiring food and other goods. In *Marine at War* (1961), Russell Davis points out that a Marine scrounger "is a highly experienced artist and not a mere thief." He adds that the scrounger's idea is that "everything is basically government property, and the government belongs to its citizens. As a citizen in good standing, the scrounger feels entitled to anything he can move, from an orange to a bulldozer or a cargo plane." See also SCROUNGE, under World War I and under World War II.

second balloon. A second lieutenant.

seesaw war. See YO-YO WAR.

semper fi. The Marine Corps motto, "semper fidelis" ("always faithful"). Sometimes the full motto came to be used as an expletive, as explained in *One Bugle No Drums* (1986), by William B. Hopkins: ". . . when one Marine complains about his lack that another possesses, he is usually answered by the cynical version of the motto, meaning, 'Fuck you, man, I got mine.'" This comes up in the context of an incident in which one group of Marines has obtained furlined parkas and another has not. When the men without parkas complain, they are answered with, "Semper Fidelis, ole buddy boy!"

shaver. A particularly diabolical booby trap used by South Korean infiltrators among enemy troops. They would take one wheel off an enemy supply cart and attach a bomb and a trip wire to the cart. When a group of men would lift the cart to replace the wheel the bomb would go off. As reported in Joseph C. Goulden's *Korea: The Untold Story of the War* (1982), it was named "for the effect it had on one's head."

shook. A reaction to combat in Korea. James Brady writes about the term in his memoir *The Coldest War* (1990):

> We were beginning to learn a new word for someone who'd had a bad scare or was losing his nerve. We said he was "shook." English majors such as me wondered why it wasn't "shaky" or "shaken" or something grammatical, but it was always "shook," and you knew what it meant. It had little to do with the old World War "shell shocked." That was another, very precisely defined thing that came from being too close to an incoming shell. "Shook" was nerves in general, and once you had a man who was really "shook" you tried to get rid of him because he was no good to you anymore.

The following dialogue is from Milt Caniff's "Steve Canyon" comic strip for March 16, 1956:

> "In World War One they called what you've got 'shell shock'!"
> "We called it 'combat fatigue' in W.W. Two."
> "In Korea we said a man was 'shook.'"
> "But I guess you're probably just plain nuts."

See also CRACK UP.

silver bullet. An antiaircraft shell that hits precisely on target. The fictional western hero the Lone Ranger—a user of silver bullets—was still in his heyday during the war.

skoshi. Small (in Korean pidgin). It was used by U.N. troops to refer to small children or small amounts—e.g., "skoshi bit," "just a skosh," and "skoshi-timer" (a short-timer).

This observation is from *A Dictionary of Soldier Talk* (1984), by John R. Elting, Dan Cragg, and Ernest Deal:

> Many Japanese loanwords are found in Korean Pidgin English, either imported by the Americans from Japan during and after the Korean War or picked up by the Koreans themselves during the lengthy Japanese occupation of their country. Succeeding generations of GIs have perpetuated expressions like sukoshi, thus proving groundless the fear . . . that the Bamboo English of the occupation of Japan would eventually die out.

The term arrived in the States as "skosh" and came into its own in an ad for blue jeans that featured "a skosh more room" for the postadolescent customer.

slant. An Asian person whose eyes are perceived by westerners as slanting; a racist slur.

slicky boy. A thief; a con man. This pidgin term was used by the Koreans and U.N. forces alike.

snapping-in. Rifle practice.

snooperscope / sniperscope. An infrared receiver, which creates visible images from otherwise invisible infrared radiation.

snorkel sub. A submarine equipped with air intake and exhaust tubes that extend above the water, allowing it to remain submerged for long periods.

sound power. A simple but effective telephone system used in combat areas.

speed burner. A jet aircraft.

spider hole. A sniper's lair in a cave.

squirt / squirt job. A jet aircraft.

static front. The relatively unmoving front line in the cold, bare-boned hills of Korea.

sukoshi. See **skoshi**.

swamp buggy. An amphibious tank.

sweat it out. To wait anxiously while a situation develops.

sweeten. To improve.

★ ☆ **T** ☆ ★

task force. A sometimes motley assortment of ground units. In *Korea: The Untold Story of the War* (1982), Joseph C. Goulden describes "an inexperienced and unenthusiastic band of youngsters, grandiosely titled Task Force Smith, charged with blunting the driving advance of the entire North Korean Army." The term is usually used to refer to a large group of warships.

T-bone Hill. A hill that was the site of a bloody battle; named for its shape.

Teague Sue. A certain Korean woman. She is described by Frank A. Hailey in *Soldier Talk* (1982): "An overendowed Korean lady who treated United Nations soldiers kindly during the Korean Conflict."

teddy bear suit. Winter outerwear worn by tank crews.

tiger. An aggressive pilot.

toksan. A large amount; plenty. According to *A Dictionary of Soldier Talk* (1984), by John R. Elting, Dan Cragg, and Ernest Deal: "The term is widely used in Korea and Okinawa today and has spread throughout the Army and Air Force."

tombi. A cigarette; an Americanization of the Korean word.

touchdown. The landing of the first assault wave in an amphibious operation.

triple jet ace. A jet fighter pilot who shoots down three enemy aircraft in one day. Captain Joseph McConnell, who accomplished the feat on May 18, 1953, was the only one to earn the accolade.

Truman's folly. See MISTER TRUMAN'S WAR.

★ ☆ **U** ☆ ★

upso. There isn't any. This comment by Marvin Stone, writing from Seoul, appeared in the San Francisco *Examiner* of June 2, 1957: "The 'snafus' of World War II have their counterparts, and out of clear skies came new words like 'upso' which today means 'there isn't any.'"

UTA. Up to the ass (i.e., an abundance). In *One Bugle No Drums* (1986), William B. Hopkins says that GOOK and "UTA" were "the most frequently used expressions in conversation."

★ ☆ **V** ☆ ★

Van Fleet load. Massive artillery fire. The expression alludes to U.N. commander Van Fleet, who when ordering a counterattack had said, "We must expend steel and fire, not men. I want so many artillery shells that a man can step from one to another."

★ ☆ **W** ☆ ★

war dogs of capitalism. The Marines (as characterized by the North Koreans and Chinese communists).

war of nerves. Psychological warfare.

war we can't win. The Korean War. A famous line quotes a G.I. insisting that "we can't win, we can't lose, we can't quit."

wet roadblock. The Yalu River (which U.N. forces were forbidden to cross in pursuit of North Korean or Chinese communist troops).

whirlybird. A helicopter.

windmill. A helicopter.

Wolfhounds. The 27th Infantry Regiment. At night on the front lines, the men of this unit would howl loudly to let the North Koreans know who was there. The unit was also called the RUSSIAN WOLFHOUNDS and the HAWAIIAN MAFIA.

word, the. The latest rumor.

World War 2½. The Korean War. The term was used to describe the war and underscore its severity. It was meant to contrast with the term POLICE ACTION, which was still being used after tens of

thousands of Americans had died in Korea. In 1951, after communist China entered the fray, the term "World War III" was brought up as a possibility.

wrong war. A possible all-out war with China. General Omar Bradley stated that it would be "the wrong war, at the wrong place, at the wrong time, against the wrong enemy."

★ ☆ **Y** ☆ ★

yak. An aircraft. This was one of the first bits of slang associated with the war. As early as July 12, 1950, Robert C. Ruark wrote in his syndicated column: "A yak in this war will be an airplane." The name derived from the North Korean YAK-9 jet fighter. In fact the first U.S. "kill" of the war was a YAK-9 shot down by a Navy fighter on July 3, 1950.

yak pack. A KOREAN FORKLIFT, but alluding to the pack animal.

yellow legs. The Marines (as described by the enemy forces).

yo-bo. The Korean Service Corps, responsible for moving supplies.

yo-bo train. A supply column.

yo-yo war. The Korean War. The term alludes to the way the war was fought. As Ralph Reppert put it in an article in the Baltimore Sun of June 24, 1951:

Yo-yo war is exactly what it implies—advance, retreat, advance, retreat and so on. Early in the campaign such tactics were called ping pong war, seesaw war and other names, but none of those terms caught on. Then somebody described the course of battle as yo-yo war or yo-yo'ing it. After that, for the average GI, the Korean type of warfare had a permanent title.

★ ☆ **Z** ☆ ★

zombie job. A night patrol.

zorch. Excellent.

Sources and Acknowledgments

★

Berry, Lester V. and Melvin Van Den Bark. *The American Thesaurus of Slang.* 2d ed. New York: Thomas Y. Crowell Co., 1952. (The first edition of this book was published during World War II, and the second while the Korean War was being fought. Despite major additions and revision the book has very few examples of Korean War slang.)

Boyle, Hal. "A Primer on 'World War 2½.'" *San Francisco Call-Bulletin* (October 3, 1952).

Brady, James. *The Coldest War.* New York: Orion Books, 1990.

Elting, Col. John R., Cragg, Sgt. Maj. Dan, and Sgt. 1c Ernest Deal. *A Dictionary of Soldier Talk.* New York: Scribner's, 1984. (This dictionary contains a number of excellent entries that relate directly to the Korean War.)

Flexner, Stuart Berg. *I Hear America Talking.* New York: Von Nostrand, 1976. (This book gives good attention to the Korean War, and the chapter entitled "The Korean Conflict" is an invaluable source.)

Gaynor, Frank. *The New Military and Naval Dictionary.* New York: Philosophical Library, 1951. (Though weak on slang, this appears to be the only dictionary of military terms with the "feel" of the Korean War to it. It may be the only dictionary of contemporary military terms to cover *homing* [as in missiles] and *pigeoneer* ["an individual trained in and charged with the breeding, care, training, etc., of homing pigeons"].)

Goulden, Joseph C. *Korea: The Untold Story of the War.* New York: Times Books, 1982.

Hackworth, Col. David H., and Julie Sherman. *About Face.* New York: Simon and Schuster, 1989.

Hailey, 1st Sgt. Frank A. *Soldier Talk.* Braintree, Mass.: D. Irving & Co., 1982.

Heflin, Woodford Agee. *The United States Air Force Dictionary.* Washington, D.C.: Air University Press, 1956.

Hopkins, William B. *One Bugle No Drums.* New York: Avon Books, 1986.

Lawson, Don. *The United States in the Korean War.* New York: Scholastic Books, 1964.

Leckie, Robert. *The Wars of America*, Vol. 2. New York: Bantam Books, 1968.

Reifer, Mary. *Dictionary of New Words.* New York: Philosophical Library, 1955.

Reppert, Ralph. "Them's Fighting Words." *Baltimore Sun* (June 24, 1951). (An extraordinarily good report on the war slang while the War was still a going concern.)

Ruark, Robert C. "War Language." *San Francisco News* (July 12, 1950).

Russ, Martin. *The Last Parallel.* New York: Zebra Books, original copyright 1957.

Stone, Marvin. "Natives Fractured by Jargon of GI Joes." *San Francisco Examiner* (June 2, 1957).

Tuckman, Robert. "GI Talk in Korea." *Baltimore Sun* (June 7, 1953).

Versand, Kenneth. *Polyglot's Lexicon: 1943–1966.* New York: Links Books, 1973.

Frank Hailey and Joe Goulden provided much-appreciated additional help. Key bits of information were found in the Tamony Collection and the Enoch Pratt Free Library in Baltimore.

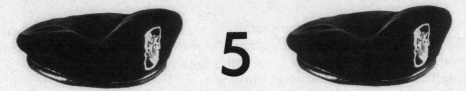

5

VIETNAM VOCAB.

★

Out of the Jungles of Southeast Asia

★

Many of the words and terms of the war are by now so completely
debunked and abused that if they were not so laden with tragedy they
would be funny. Among them "pacification," "light at the end of the
tunnel," "body count," "free-fire zone," "hearts and minds of the people,"
. . . "kill ratio," . . . "search and destroy."
—Paul Dickson, *The New York Times*, April 15, 1972

The patois of the Vietnam experience infiltrated the American consciousness
slowly, for more than a decade, on a Ho Chi Minh trail of the mind.
—Martin F. Nolan, the Boston *Globe*, July 18, 1982

During the war in Vietnam, especially during the early days, it was not
unusual for soldiers to use terms the Army had acquired elsewhere at another
time. Early in the conflict an Associated Press reporter noted, for instance,
that the troops were using such terms as the Japanese *ichiban* ("number one";
"the best"), the Korean *idiwash* ("come here"), and the German *Bierstube*
("beer hall"), picked up during the period of occupation after World War II.

This is how it has always been. Soldiers bring the terminology of one fight
or period of occupation to the next and then embellish it with new terms
until it takes on the flavor of that war. "The war in South Vietnam is producing
its own vocabulary," wrote Jack Langguth in *The New York Times* for September
20, 1964: "Among the Americans stationed here, World War II's argot has
long since faded away. Even Korea's glossary sounds dated."

The war did indeed produce a totally new slang—brutal, direct, and geared to high-tech jungle warfare with a rock 'n' roll beat backed up by the throb of chopper engines. The war also had a totally new result—an American defeat. The costs of the war were enormous, in lives, dollars, and dissent. If the slang seems loaded with raw frustration and bitter cynicism, it figures.

★ ☆ A ☆ ★

ace of spades. A playing card that the Vietnamese interpreted as a symbol of death. American and South Vietnamese soldiers placed the card on enemy dead to scare the living. According to Linda Reinberg in *In the Field: The Language of the Vietnam War* (1991): "United States playing card manufacturers sent packages of the ace of spades to the troops in Vietnam to be used just for this purpose."

acting jack. An acting noncommissioned officer.

agency, the. The Central Intelligence Agency (C.I.A.).

Agent Orange. One of a number of defoliants that were designated by a color-coded bar on the container. Others included Agent White and Agent Purple. Eleven million gallons of Orange were sprayed in Vietnam between 1965 and 1970. It was later shown to cause a variety of serious illnesses.

a-gunner. An assistant gunner.

air. Air power.

Air America. An airline operated by the Central Intelligence Agency. Its origins dated back to the World War II era.

airborn copulation. I don't give a flying fuck.

air cav. The Air Cavalry, the helicopter-borne infantry.

airmobile. Movement of personnel and equipment by helicopter.

air-to-mud. Bombing or gunnery from an aircraft against surface targets; a play on the official term "air-to-ground."

Alcatraz. A high-security prison near Hanoi where some American prisoners were held.

Alcoholics Anonymous. The 82nd Airborne Division. The nickname was inspired by the two A's on the unit's shoulder patch. Other such nicknames included "Almost Airborne," "All-Afro," and "All American."

all the way. The goal of an officer who wanted to rise as high as possible in his military career.

Alpha Hotel. An asshole (i.e., an objectionable person).

Alpha Sierra. Air support.

ambush academy. Courses in jungle warfare, guerrilla warfare, etc.

Americal Division. The 23rd Infantry Division. Because of its role in the 1968 My Lai massacre, the Americal was given such names as "Americally," "Ameri-kill," and "Atrocical." It was also called the "Metrecal Division sponsored by General Foods," possibly a blend of "American" and "calorie."

AMF. Adios (or aloha) motherfucker (i.e., good-bye). A long-running television ad for "The Greaseman," a Washington, D.C., radio personality, ended with "The Grease" waving and yelling, "AMF."

ammo humper. An artilleryman; any GRUNT carrying ammunition.

angel. A false radar image.

animal, the. A device that detonates a dozen or more antipersonnel mines at the same time, letting loose a "hailstorm of 14,000 steel balls."

animals of the Army. The Army Rangers.

ankle express. On foot.

ape. A member of the Air Police; from the initials.

applesauce enema. Mild criticism. The term is defined in *A Dictionary of Soldier Talk* (1984), by John R. Elting, Dan Cragg, and Ernest Deal: "To give a chewing out (the enema) to a subordinate, but to do it so tactfully and gently that he goes away feeling better for the experience."

Arizona Territory. The region south of Da Nang, known for Viet Cong ambushes (hence the reference to the Old West).

armpit sauce. Nuoc mam, a fermented fish sauce central to the Vietnamese diet and noxious to many Americans in the country.

Army brat. A child of an Army officer.

artie. Artillery.

Arvin. (1) A South Vietnamese soldier; from the initialism A.R.V.N. (Army of the Republic of Vietnam). An alternative name was "Marvin Arvin." (2) The South Vietnamese Army.

as loud. Heroin smoked with tobacco (because tobacco was not "as loud"—i.e., smelly—as marijuana).

ass and trash mission. Troop and cargo transport by aircraft (as opposed to combat or rescue work).

AWOL bag. A small piece of black luggage popular with the troops in the war. Its name suggests something small enough to use when going AWOL.

★ ☆ **B** ☆ ★

baby shit. Mustard.

bad paper. An other-than-honorable discharge.

banana clip. A slightly curved ammunition clip designed to hold thirty rounds.

banana smoke. A yellowish cloud from a smoke grenade.

band-aid. A medical corpsman.

B&B. Booze and broads; a play on R&R.

bandit. An enemy aircraft.

B.A.R. Browning Automatic Rifle. See under World War II.

bare-ass. Barracks.

baseball. A round hand grenade about two and a half inches in diameter.

basic. Basic training; boot camp.

B.C. Body count.

beans and dicks. The beans and hot dogs in a C-RATION (see under World War II).

beans and motherfuckers. The lima beans and ham in a C-RATION (see under World War II).

bear. A copilot in the backseat of a two-person jet aircraft. The term is explained in T. E. Cruise's *Wings of Gold III: The Hot Pilots* (1989): "That's what the pilots call their backseaters in Vietnam, bears, as in trained bears."

beehive round. A shotgun shell that discharges forty to fifty small darts. The darts spin and kill "like nails with fins," according to Mark Baker in *Nam* (1981).

believer. A dead soldier (usually, an enemy soldier).

bends and motherfuckers. Squat and thrust drill exercises.

Betty Crocker. A serviceman assigned to Saigon (i.e., one who is safe behind a desk, assuming an almost domestic role).

big belly. The bomb-carrying compartment in the B-52 bomber.

big boy. An artillery piece.

big bullet. The radar-guided Sparrow air-to-air missile.

Big Charlie. The CH-47 helicopter; also known as the JOLLY GREEN GIANT. An immense vehicle, it could carry as many as twenty-six troops. The name "Charlie" was doubtlessly suggested by the "CH" designation.

big P.X. in the sky. Death.

Big Red One. The 1st Infantry Division; also known as the "Bloody One."

big shotgun. The 106-mm recoilless rifle used to fire antipersonnel canister ammunition.

big top. A large open tent of the size used by circuses.

big 20. An Army career of twenty years (the point at which one can retire with pay).

bird. An aircraft (but usually reserved for helicopters).

bird colonel. A full colonel; from the eagle insignia.

birdfarm. An aircraft carrier.

birdland. Quarters for senior officers (because bird colonels live there).

bird shit. Paratroopers (because they fall from the sky).

black hats. (1) The communist enemy. (2) Drill instructors. (3) Special units, wearing black baseball caps, sent in to clear and manage landing zones; also known as "pathfinders."

black magic. The M-16 rifle (because it was made of black plastic and steel).

blade time. (1) The time a helicopter is in the air. (2) The time for which a unit has helicopter support.

blood. A black soldier.

blood stripe. A promotion to N.C.O. in the field because of a casualty (i.e., because of spilled blood).

blood wings. A paratrooper's first set of wings; so-called because of the demands of jump training.

Bloody One. The 1st Infantry Division (because of the red number one on its shoulder patch); also known as the "Big Red One."

blooper man. The squad member responsible for the M-79 grenade launcher, which was known as the "blooper" because it lobbed grenades out to three hundred meters.

blow away. To kill.

blow smoke. To confuse; to cover up.

blow Z's. To sleep (in the manner of a cartoon character who emits a string of Z's).

blue / blue feature. A body of water; from the color used for water on maps.

blue balls–type situation. A frustrating situation; from "blue balls" (acute male sexual frustration, leading to painful testicles). In T. E. Cruise's *Wings of Gold III: The Hot Pilots* (1989), a pilot is asked what the phrase means, and he replies: "Well, there, nephew, meaning I've got an ammo drum jam-packed with rounds hanging low beneath my cannon, and I'm feeling frisky and light now that those bombs are away."

Blue Max. The Congressional Medal of Honor; from its blue field and for a German air medal nicknamed the Blue Max.

blues. An AIRMOBILE company.

Blue Trees. Protective reaction strikes; a code name. These strikes are defined in Robert K. Wilcox's *Scream of Eagles* (1990) as "controversial attempts to start a fight."

boat people. Refugees fleeing Vietnam by boat after the 1975 U.S. withdrawal.

body bag. A zippered bag in which bodies or body parts are put for shipment; also known as a "rubber bag." See also HUMAN REMAINS POUCH, under the Gulf War.

bogey. An enemy aircraft (actual or suspected).

bolo. A soldier who flunks his rifle qualifications. In *Korea: The Untold Story of the War* (1982), Joseph C. Goulden reports: "As punishment at Fort Chaffee, Arkansas, circa May-July, 1956, such a cluck was given a 'bolo,' a crude Southern scythe, and put to work cutting grass on the entire firing range." See also BOLO SQUAD, under the Spanish-American War era.

bomb pocket. A target so attractive that it was bombed regardless of the cost.

bom-de-bom. Ba Muoi Ba beer.

boobies. Booby traps.

boo-coo. Many; from the French *beaucoup*.

boom-boom. Sex.

boom-boom girl. A prostitute.

boom-boom house. A whorehouse.

boomer. An operator who refuels airplanes in midair with a telescoping refueling boom.

boonie rat / boonierat. A soldier who has spent a lot of time in the field.

boonies. The jungle. The term is derived from BOONDOCKS, first used by U.S. troops in the Philippines following the Spanish-American War.

boot. (1) A soldier just out of boot camp. (2) New; untested. In *A Rumor of War* (1977), Philip Caputo writes: "I was alliteratively known as the 'boot brownbar,' slang for second lieutenant."

bottlecap colonel. A lieutenant colonel; from the insignia, which looks like the tinfoil on a bottlecap.

bouncing betty. A land mine that, when triggered, pops up waist-high and sprays shrapnel. See also under the Gulf War.

bowl. A pipe for smoking marijuana.

box. A target zone about five eighths of a mile wide and two miles long.

brace. An exaggerated position of attention. In *The Boo*, a novel about the Citadel, a military school, Pat Conroy describes plebes bracing: "Their chins are tucked in, their shoulders thrown back, and their backs are rigidly straight."

break down. To disassemble (as a rifle).

break starch. To put on a fresh set of heavily starched fatigues.

brew. (1) Coffee. (2) Beer.

bring heat. To fire; to shoot.

bring smoke. To attack; to call in an air strike.

bring the max. To kill.

brown bar. A second lieutenant; from the insignia of a single gold bar.

brown-shoe army. The Army prior to September 1, 1956, when a change was made from brown to black shoes. The existing shoes had to be dyed, so over the following Labor Day weekend everything was awash in black gook.

bubble. The two-man Ott-13 Sioux helicopter.

buckle. To fistfight.

Buddha grass. Drugs mixed with tobacco and smoked.

bullshit bomber. An airplane used to drop propaganda leaflets while broadcasting psychological warfare tapes over loudspeakers.

bullshit frolics. Another name for the FIVE O'CLOCK FOLLIES.

Bumfuck. An apocryphal place where no one wants to be assigned. In Vietnam, the spelling was sometimes given a local spin: "Bhum Fuck" or "Bum Fuk." In *Ghouls* (1971), a character says: "After that I went to Aberdeen Proving Grounds and you went to Bumfuck, Saudi Arabia."

bum's roll. A light pack—dry socks, a jungle blanket, a set of fatigues, C-rations—used in jungle warfare. The pack was reminiscent of those carried by hoboes.

bunker buster. A satchel charge composed of C-4 explosive and a short-fuse detonation cord.

Bureau, the. The Navy Bureau of Personnel.

burp. A Marine (especially to an infantryman).

bush. (1) The jungle; the BOONIES. (2) Ambush.

bushmasters. Units skilled in jungle operations.

bust. To reduce in rank.

bust caps. To fire rapidly (especially an M-16 rifle). In *Nam* (1981), Mark Baker says that the term is "probably derived from the paper percussion caps used in toy guns." See also CAP.

bust chops. (1) To give someone a hard time (as in, "The C.O. was really busting my chops"). (2) To give one's all (as in, "I really busted my chops getting it done before dark").

Butcher Brigade. The 11th Infantry Brigade, after the My Lai massacre.

butter bar. A second lieutenant; from the insignia of a single gold bar.

buy it / buy the farm. To die; to be killed.

★ ☆ **C** ☆ ★

cammies. Camouflaged apparel.

camo. Camouflage.

C&C / C&C bird. Command-and-control helicopter.

canker mechanic. A medic; so-called because of his role in dealing with boils, hemorrhoids, canker sores, and other non–combat-related medical problems.

cannon cocker. A soldier whose area of specialty is artillery. A character in Philip Caputo's *A Rumor of War* (1977) is described as a "cannon-cockin' Texas shitkicker."

cap. To shoot; from the cap-gun-like sound of the M-16 rifle.

Care package. A package of goodies (candy, cookies, etc.) from home; from the charitable organization CARE (Cooperative for American Relief Abroad), which sends packages to the needy overseas.

Cav. Air cavalry.

caydet. A military academy student.

C.F.B. Clear as a fucking bell.

chairborne. Said of a military bureaucrat or paper pusher; a play on "airborne."

Charlie. The Vietcong; short for "victor charlie" (i.e., "V.C." in alphabet code). Other names for the enemy in South Vietnam included "Mr. Charles," "Mr. Charlie," and "Chuck." In *Word of Honor* (1985), by Nelson DeMille, one character asks another if the word GOOK refers to the enemy, civilians, or both? Here is the reply: "'Gooks' could be both. Slants and slopes were civilians. Dinks could be both. It depended a lot on where you were and what you was doing. Charlie was always the enemy."

charlie tango. Control tower (in alphabet code).

cheap Charlie. A skinflint.

cherry. (1) A new man in a unit. (2) New; inexperienced; virginal. The term "cherry" has long been slang for the female hymen.

cherry unit. A unit that has not seen combat.

chicken guts. The looped braid on officers' dress uniforms.

chicken plate. Personal armor (e.g., the kind that helicopter pilots wear across their chest and groin).

chickenhawk. Nickname for a young Army helicopter pilot.

Chicom. (1) Chinese communist (see under the Korean War). (2) A North Vietnamese hand grenade.

chopper. A helicopter.

chow. Food. See under the Civil War.

chuck. A white person. "A term applied by black marines to identify white individuals," according to James Webb in *Fields of Fire* (1978), who adds that it was often used derogatorily. It is very likely that this term is a variation on "Mr. Charlie," a term blacks use for whites in civilian life.

C.I.B. Combat Infantryman's Badge. "Probably the most sought-after medal of the Vietnam War. If you didn't have one of these you were not combat tested," says a man who was there for more than five years. See also under the Gulf War.

Cinderella liberty. A period of leave that ends at midnight.

civil serpent. A civil servant (especially one who works with the uniformed military).

claymore. A type of directional antipersonnel mine carried by infantrymen.

clerks 'n' jerks. Support staff in noncombat areas.

click / klick. (1) A kilometer. (2) A short distance.

cluster fuck. Mass confusion; a SNAFU (see under World War II).

clutch belt. A cartridge belt worn by Marines.

C.O. Commanding officer.

Coasties. Members of the Coast Guard.

cock. To ready a helicopter or other aircraft for instant takeoff (as one would cock a pistol).

combat ineffective. Wounded or killed.

commfu. Completely monumental military fuck-up.

commo. Communications (especially radio).

company, the. The Central Intelligence Agency (C.I.A.).

Coney Island. The Marine base at Khe Sanh (because of the number of lights visible at night).

Cong. The Vietcong.

connex. A large metal box used for shipping and storage.

contact. Firing or being fired upon; engaging the enemy in combat.

contour. Flight at treetop level (i.e., following the ground's contour).

cots. Apricots. During the Vietnam War a superstition developed among Marine tank crews that apricots—contained in some rations—brought bad luck.

country club. The headquarters area at Long Binh, South Vietnam (to men in the front lines).

cramper. A "tiger cage," or a small cell used to break a prisoner's psychological defenses. The cell was so small that a prisoner couldn't sit up, lie down, or kneel properly.

crapper. A latrine.

C-rats / Cs. C-RATIONS. See under World War II.

Creep. The AC-119 aircraft.

crispy critters. (1) Burn victims. (2) Enemy troops undergoing a napalm strike or flamethrower attack.

Crotch, the. The Marine Corps. The term is often used in lines like this one from Philip Caputo's *A Rumor of War* (1977): "We're in the Corps, P.J., The Crotch. Semper fi and fuck your buddy."

crow. An electronic warfare officer. Electronic warfare people call themselves "old crows."

crunchie. Ground infantryman; probably because soldiers' feet make a crunching noise while marching, especially on gravel.

cumulo granite. A mountain hidden by cloud cover.

cunt cap. See under World War II.

C.Y.A. Cover your ass.

cyclo [pronounced "sick-low"]. A motorized version of a rickshaw, common in Saigon.

★ ☆ **D** ☆ ★

daily-daily. Dapsone antimalaria pills (because they were taken daily).

day the eagle shits, the. Payday. The eagle is the federal government. See EA-GLE DAY, under World War II.

debrief. To get an oral report about an event (i.e., a reconnaissance mission or an engagement with the enemy).

deep serious. A very bad situation (e.g., being overrun).

deros. Date eligible to return from overseas; date of expected return from overseas. In *Everything We Had* (1981), Al Santoli called it "the sweetest word in the military language."

deuce and a half. A two-and-a-half-ton medium cargo truck.

dew. Marijuana.

dich [pronounced "dick"]. Dead; from the Vietnamese word. It was one of the terms used for enemy killed (as in, "We have twenty dead dichs here").

diddy-bop. To walk with a bounce and a strut.

di di. To run; from the Vietnamese *di di mau* ("get out of the way"; "hurry").

dinger. A marksman. In *Khe Sanh: Siege in the Clouds* (1989), Eric Hammel writes: "The crew felt it had earned the bragging rights as 'Best Dingers' in the battery. They got no argument."

dink. An Asian person; a slur. Gregory R. Clark, in *Words of the Vietnam War* (1990), points out this was originally a Vietnamese name for Americans, meaning "hairy men from the jungle."

dinky dau. To be crazy or off the wall; from the Vietnamese *dien cai dau* ("crazy"; "ridiculous").

dirty officer. A duty officer.

D.M.Z. Demilitarized zone. In Vietnam, the D.M.Z. was five miles wide and positioned along the 17th parallel.

doc. A medical corpsman.

dog tags. Identification tags.

do mal / doo-mommie. Motherfucker; from a colloquial Vietnamese term.

domino theory. The belief that if the U.S. allowed Vietnam to fall to the communists, then Thailand, Laos, Cambodia, and perhaps even the Philippines would follow.

double. To turn someone into a double agent. In *Khe Sanh: Siege in the Clouds* (1989), Eric Hammel writes about a defector who was a Moscow-trained agent: "We 'doubled' him immediately, and the take was astonishing."

double-hatted. Holding two jobs.

double veteran. A man who has sex with a woman and then kills her.

D.O.W. Died of wounds.

downtown. Hanoi, North Vietnam. Attacking the city was known as "going downtown."

Dow shalt not kill. Motto worn on bright orange T-shirts as a protest against Vietnam veterans' exposure to AGENT ORANGE. The allusion is to Dow Chemical Company, which was a leading supplier of war-related chemicals, including napalm. The slogan had been used earlier by protesters opposing the use of napalm.

dragon ship. See PUFF THE MAGIC DRAGON.

Dragon's Jaw. The Thanh Hoa Railroad Bridge, south of Hanoi, North Vietnam. It got its nickname, according to Robert K. Wilcox in *Scream of Eagles* (1990), because of its "near invincibility."

dream sheet. An official form on which servicemen indicate their preference for their next location and job.

D-ring. A D-shaped metal snap ring used to hold gear together.

dung lai. Stop; halt. This is said to have been one of the first Vietnamese terms learned by American servicemen in Vietnam.

dust. To kill.

dust off. (1) A medevac (medical evaluation) helicopter. (2) To be lifted out by a medevac helicopter. Both meanings derive from the radio call used to summon the first medevac helicopters deployed in Vietnam.

★ ☆ **E** ☆ ★

Eat the apple, fuck the Corps. A Marine expression of anger; a play on "Corps" and "apple core."

eight. A master sergeant; from the pay grade, E-8.

elephants' graveyard. Boston Naval District Headquarters, which was the last posting for Navy officers during the Vietnam War era. The allusion is to the legend that elephants go to a special place to die.

E-nothing. One at the bottom (i.e., an imaginary pay grade below that of a recruit, E-1).

E-tool. An entrenching tool carried by infantrymen.

evak'd. Evacuated.

★ ☆ F ☆ ★

farang. A foreigner.

Farm Gate. The code name for Detachment 2-A, the first U.S. Air Force unit to go into combat in Vietnam. As Neil Sheehan points out in *A Bright Shining Lie* (1988), the expression is gallows humor, a play on "buy the farm" (to die).

fart sack. A bedroll.

fat. Said of a unit that is over its authorized strength.

fat city. (1) The Military Assistance Command, Vietnam (MACV). (2) To be in good shape.

fat-rat. Describing an easy job outside of combat areas.

fatty-gews / fatykes. Fatigues.

field first. A sergeant who runs a company when the first sergeant is absent.

field-grade night. A night during which there is enough light for pilots to see features on the ground.

50-cal. A 50-caliber M-2 HMG Browning Heavy Machine Gun.

51-cal. A type of heavy machine gun used by the enemy.

Fightertown. Miramar Naval Air Station, near San Diego, California. This was home base for all West Coast fighter squadrons during the war.

Find the bastards and pile on. The motto of the 11th Armored Cavalry Regiment when under the command of George S. Patton III, son of the famous World War II general.

finger charge. A finger-sized explosive charge used in booby traps.

fireball. To concentrate a great deal of artillery fire in one area.

fire base. An artillery base.

firefight. An exchange of fire with the enemy.

firefly. A team of three helicopters: two gunships and one equipped with a searchlight or arc lights.

fire in the hole. Explosives to be detonated deliberately (e.g., a satchel charge in a suspected enemy HIDEY-HOLE).

first john. A first lieutenant.

first pig. A first sergeant.

five o'clock follies. The daily briefing held in Saigon for reporters covering the war. Although frequently satirized as self-serving chest thumpings, these sessions were generally frank and factual. In *The New York Times* of February 4, 1991, R. W. Apple compared it to the daily briefing given in Riyadh, Saudi Arabia, during the Gulf War: "In the view of the correspondents who reported from Vietnam, it is considerably less useful than the much-satirized 'Five O'Clock Follies,' the daily briefing in Saigon, because far fewer facts are made available."

flag. To mark a person's military records; to freeze a promotion or transfer.

flaky. In a state of mental disarray (e.g., DINKY DAU).

fleshette. An antipersonnel round that disperses dart-shaped nails that rip flesh. This action is described in A. D. Horne's *The Wounded Generation: America After Vietnam* (1981): "The fleshette-round erupted just up the hill, its centerpoint in back of Smitty. Nine-thousand dart-shaped nails saturated that portion of the field, filled the ditch, and drove Smitty and Speed lifeless against the streambed."

flying butterknife. A patch worn by paratroopers, showing a winged bayonet.

flying eavesdropper. The Navy's EC-121 aircraft, a radar and communications center.

Flying Horsemen. The 1st Air Cavalry. There is a horse silhouette on its patch.

flying telephone pole. A surface-to-air missile; from its size and shape.

F.N.G. Fucking new guy.

Fort . . . . Many Army forts were given derogatory nicknames. In *In the Field: The Language of the Vietnam War* (1991), Linda Reinberg lists a number of them: Fort Fucker—Fort Rucker, Alabama; Fort Lost in the Woods—Fort Leonard Wood, Missouri; Fort Piss—Fort Bliss, Texas; Fort Pricks—Fort Dix, New Jersey; Fort Puke—Fort Polk, Louisiana; Fort Screw Us—Fort Louis, Washington; Fort Smell—Fort Sill, Arkansas; Fort Turd—Fort Ord, California; Fort Useless—Fort Eustis, Virginia.

four-deuce. A 4.2-inch mortar.

fourteen. (1) The M-14 rifle. (2) The Grumman F-14 Tomcat aircraft.

fox. To fire; from the former alphabet code for "F" (the new code word is "foxtrot"). A pilot says "fox one" to report that he has fired his first missile. "Fox two" means that an infrared missile has been fired; "fox three" means that a machine gun or cannon is being fired, and the unofficial "fox four" is what pilots jokingly refer to as a midair collision.

frag. (1) A fragmentation grenade. (2) To explode a fragmentation grenade; to wound or kill with a grenade. (3) To kill or wound one's superior officer; from the fact that a fragmentation grenade was often the weapon of choice.

freak. Frequency (i.e., a radio broadcasting frequency).

freedom bird. An airplane returning soldiers to the U.S. at the end of their tour of duty.

free fire zone. An area in which permission was not required prior to firing on targets.

friendlies. Military and civilian personnel on one's own side.

friendly fire. Fire accidentally directed at troops on one's own side. *Friendly Fire* was the name of a powerful 1979 made-for-television movie about a woman named Peg Mullen (played by Carol Burnett) who with the help of her husband attempted to find out the truth about their son's death in Vietnam. The movie popularized the term but it began with the book *Friendly Fire* (1976), by C. D. B. Bryan, on which the movie was based. See also under the Gulf War.

frog hair. A very small distance (as in, "Lay that two frog hairs to the right").

fruit salad. Two or more rows of campaign ribbons.

F.T.A. Fuck the Army.

Fuck it. / Fuck it. Don't mean nothin'. / Fuck it. Don't mean nothin'. Drive on. A phrase that soldiers utter repeatedly as a means of comforting themselves. It is described as "the mantra of the infantry" in John M. Del Vecchio's *The 13th Valley* (1982).

fucked up. (1) To be killed or wounded. (2) To be drunk or on drugs. (3) As in earlier conflicts, to do something stupid.

fugazi. Fucked up; screwed up. This odd euphemism began in the Marine Corps.

full bird. A colonel; from the eagle insignia.

full bull. A full colonel.

funny money. See MONOPOLY MONEY.

funny papers. Topographic maps (because of their comic book colors).

★ ☆ G ☆ ★

Gainesburgers. Canned ground-beef patties in gravy; from the name of a popular brand of dog food.

garritrooper. A soldier in a safe, comfortable location. The term was coined late in World War II by cartoonist and writer Bill Mauldin to describe a soldier who was "too far forward to wear ties and too far back to get shot." The term survived and gained special currency in Vietnam in the early days of the war. Researcher Charles D. Poe has noted, "On Barry Sadler's album of Vietnam songs [*Ballads of the Green Berets*] there is one entitled 'Garet Trooper' and the song's lyrics suggest that Sadler had in mind pretty much the same kind of soldier that Mauldin was describing."

get short. To approach the end of one's tour of duty (usually, when one has less than six and a half months to go—i.e., the halfway point of a normal thirteen-month tour).

get some. To kill the enemy.

get the hell out of Dodge. To move out of a dangerous position; from the Western movie idea that a good way to avoid getting shot was to get out of Dodge City. During the course of the war Dodge City came to be several places—for instance, it was Hanoi to pilots attacking that city, and to the Marines it was any place where many firefights occurred. See also BOOGIE OUT OF DODGE, under the Gulf War.

ghosting. Goldbricking.

G.I.B. Guy in back (i.e., the copilot/weapons officer in the F-4, F-100, and F-105 aircraft). The G.I.B.'s primary mission in Vietnam was to operate electronic weapons, detection, and targeting systems.

G.I.-proof. Said of weapons basic enough to resist jamming and other problems encountered when GRUNTS are given sophisticated weapons.

glad bag. A BODY BAG; a play on the name of a brand of plastic bags.

go green / go hot. To take a weapon off safe (i.e., get it ready to fire).

golden B.B. / golden bullet. A bullet that fortuitously hits a soldier or an aircraft. Aviators realized that it took only one small lucky bullet to shoot down an enormous airplane. See also under the Gulf War.

gomers. The North Vietnamese.

gook. See under the Spanish-American War era, World War II, and the Korean War. In this war, of course, the term was mainly applied to the Vietnamese people.

Gooney Bird. The C-47 cargo aircraft.

"Goooooooood morning, Vietnam!" Armed Forces radio call by Adrian Cronauer beginning in 1965. It became the title of a 1987 film starring Robin Williams, who played a Cronauer-like character.

Go to Hell. Go Dau Ha, South Vietnam.

goya. Get off your ass.

grab ass. To have fun.

gravel. A type of mine used by allied forces. It is described by William C. Anderson, in *Bat 21* (1980), as "a little Marquis de Sade touch introduced in the Vietnam War." He goes on to explain:

> A tiny innocent-looking explosive about the size of a lemon, it was a mine released in large numbers from low-flying aircraft. Dropped in a frozen state, it hit the ground and, upon thawing, armed itself and sent out a web of feelers in all directions, like the tentacles of an octopus. Brushing one of the feelers might not prove fatal, but the explosion could neatly separate a person from an arm or leg. Further refinements to the tiny mine sometimes included its camouflage in the form of dog feces, a form employed with considerable success in keeping invaders off the Ho Chi Minh trail.

grease. To kill. "Brother or not," says a character in Alfred Coppel's *Apocalypse Brigade* (1981), "you come out now or we grease you on the spot."

greased. Killed in action.

green. (1) Safe (e.g., a green **L.Z.** would be a safe landing zone). (2) Paper money.

green apple. The knob that is used to get oxygen flowing in an aircraft.

green bait. A reenlistment bonus.

green beanies. The Army's Special Forces units; from their green berets. The term was not appreciated by the members of the Special Forces themselves.

green machine, the. (1) The Army, especially its bureaucracy. (2) By extension, the Veterans Administration after the war.

groundpounder. (1) A non-pilot (usually, an infantryman). (2) Sometimes, one with a desk job.

G.R. point. Graves registration point (i.e., a place on bases in Vietnam where dead soldiers were identified, embalmed, and shipped home).

grunt. (1) An infantryman. (2) A Marine rifleman. According to Gregory R. Clark, in *Words of the Vietnam War* (1990): "The combat infantryman got the nickname 'grunt' because as legend goes, it was an indication of his I.Q." See also under the Gulf War.

GUMP check. The standard preflight check of gas, undercarriage, mixture, and prop.

gun bunny. An artilleryman.

gunny / guns. A Marine gunnery sergeant.

gunship. An armed helicopter.

gyrene. A Marine. See under World War II.

★ ☆ **H** ☆ ★

hack. To endure; to cope.

hand frag. A fragmentation grenade that is thrown rather than fired with a launcher.

H&I. Harassment and interdiction (a tactic in which random artillery fire is used to deny areas to the enemy).

Hanoi Florsheims. Footwear favored by the Vietcong and North Vietnamese troops. They were made from used automobile tires.

Hanoi Hilton. Hoa Lo Prison, near Hanoi, North Vietnam. In 1992 this structure where American fliers were tortured and interrogated was demolished to make room for an office complex and, ironically, a 200-room luxury hotel. See also HILTON.

hard rice. Munitions given to friendly tribesmen.

hard-stripe sergeant. A nonspecialist N.C.O. with E-5 or E-6 chevron insignia. Mark Baker notes in *Nam* (1981): "Others of the same rank without the stripes were little more than PFCs."

hash mark. A diagonal uniform stripe—or "slash," from which "hash" may derive—signifying four years of military service.

hassle. To fight.

head man. A soldier who practiced decapitation. Here is a passage from Myra MacPherson's *Long Time Passing* (1984): "I was a head man. Cut a man's head off with an ax. I cut off twenty-one heads. We sold 'em to doctors and sech as that."

heart. A Purple Heart, the medal that signifies a combat wound. In *Fields of Fire* (1978), James Webb reported on the "three heart rule" which was in effect in Vietnam. It stated that any Marine wounded three times during one tour of duty was immediately removed from the combat zone.

heavy. A high-ranking officer. In *The Grunts (1976)*, Charles R. Anderson quotes one of the grunts: "Them fucking heavies back in their air-conditioned bunkers at Quang Tri just sit there drinking beer and throwing darts at the map. That's how they decide where we're going, Studly."

hell-hole. (1) An observation hole in the floor of the CH-53 helicopter occupied by a crew chief and a door gunner. (2) An area under the mast of a helicopter where the craft's transmission and hydraulics are enclosed with the aid of a hell-hole cover.

hidey-hole. Any hole scratched into the ground or into the brow of a hill where a soldier can take refuge.

high-angle hell. Mortar fire.

higher-higher. The commanders: the high command.

hill fights. A series of brutal battles that lasted for more than two weeks in April 1967 and involved Hill 881 and Hill 861. Eric Hammel reports in *Khe Sanh: Siege in the Clouds (1989)*, "The first and cruelest struggle at Khe Sanh, the 'Hill Fights' began."

Hilton. A name given to places totally unlike a Hilton Hotel. When Bob Hope returned from Vietnam in 1967, he noted: "Every broken down hut, hootch or quonset hut is called the Chu Lai Hilton, or the Hilton East or the Hilton something." The most infamous Hilton was the HANOI HILTON, a prison in which many American P.O.W.'s were held. There was a 1987 film starring Michael Moriarty entitled *The Hanoi Hilton*.

hitch. A period of enlistment.

hobo. A homing bomb. The first one used, in May 1973, knocked out a bridge north of Hanoi that had resisted other attempts to destroy it.

Ho Chi Minh sandals. Sandals fashioned from used automobile tires.

hog. (1) The A-10 (Thunderbolt II) aircraft; also known as the "warthog." (2) A helicopter gunship of the UH (Huey) series.

hogjaws. A special blade attached to bulldozers, used to clear landing zones; also known as a "Rome plow."

Hog-60. The M-60 machine gun. According to Jack Hawkins, in *Chopper One #2: Tunnel Warriors (1987)*: "A door gunner's best friend was his hatch M-60 which many gunnies took to calling Hog-60's, though the old timers complained that a hog was a gunship and not just a small piece of the gunship's armament; but the younger hot dogs refused to listen to what they considered 'lifers' so the term 'Hog-60' stuck."

home-front sniper. A Vietnam veteran who opposed the U.S. government's version of the war. One soldier is quoted in

A. D. Horne's *The Wounded Generation: America After Vietnam* (1981): "When we came back and we spoke and we gave testimony to what we'd experienced and what the reality of Vietnam was, as opposed to the crock of shit the politicians and the media were generating about what the reality of it was, we got infiltrated, we got called 'home front snipers,' and it was allowed to continue through '73 when every one of us that were there, that were in the real fighting capacities, knew that it was going down the tube."

homesteader. A soldier who stays in one assignment for a long time.

honcho. (1) A chief; a boss. (2) A tough, aggressive pilot.

hooch. A tent.

hoochgirl. A young Vietnamese woman working for American military personnel as a maid.

hoofprint. A sandal print made by an enemy soldier.

horse pill. A large antimalarial pill taken weekly by some troops in the field.

hose down / hosepipe. To shoot with an automatic weapon.

hot. Hostile. A hot area is one occupied by the enemy.

hot bunk. A bed occupied by two or more soldiers in succession. The previous occupant leaves the bed warm with body heat for the new occupant.

hotel alpha. To haul ass (i.e., to move quickly); from alphabet code.

hot fueling. Taking on fuel as fast as it is burned, so that a plane in a state of readiness is topped off when it leaves the ground.

hot L.Z. A landing zone under fire.

hots. Hot meals.

hot skinny. New information (usually based on rumor and usually about something important).

hourglass. A funnel point for trucks just south of Haiphong, North Vietnam. It was a target for American bombs.

house mouse. A small soldier used to explore underground tunnels built by the Vietcong.

Howard Johnson. A fire base built with future occupancy in mind.

Howdy Doody. A chemical spray that made those hit with it stiffen up and jerk about; from the television puppet Howdy Doody.

H.Q. Headquarters.

Huey. A UH-1 series utility helicopter. One reporter described it as a combination of "shuttle bus, supply truck, ambulance and weapon of war."

Hummer. The E-2 Hawkeye early-warning aircraft. Its twin propellers made a humming sound.

hump. (1) To march; to hike; by extension, to move faster. "Humping the boonies" meant trying to get deeper into the jungle. (2) An infantryman; a GRUNT. (3) Rotation of twenty-five percent or more of a unit within a thirty-day period; also known as a "rotational hump."

This is a term which has changed its military meaning. Researcher Charles D. Poe reports, "In World War II pilots used the term hump to refer to the terrain between China and India [the high eastern Himalayas] but in the Vietnam War this word was used by infantrymen to describe walking under the heavy weight of their equipment."

hundred and worst. The 101st Airborne Division.

hurtin'. Injured; dead. A 1964 Associated Press dispatch from Vietnam notes that in one case the term was used to mean "that a man's head had been blown off by a howitzer shell."

★ ☆ **I** ☆ ★

I&I. Intercourse and intoxication; a play on R&R.

I.C. Innocent civilian.

Igloo White. The plan to seed the Ho Chi Minh trail with electronic sensors linked to cluster bombs and antipersonnel mines, to form a lethal barrier.

illum. An illumination flare.

immersion foot. TRENCH FOOT. See under World War I.

incoming / incoming mail. Hostile artillery fire.

in contact. Under attack by the enemy.

in-country. A country outside the U.S. to which one is assigned. During the Vietnam war it meant being in Vietnam: "After R&R in Bangkok, I was back in-country." *In Country* was the name of a 1989 film, starring Bruce Willis, about the war.

Indian country. Unsecured territory. In *Fire in the Lake* (1972), Frances FitzGerald writes: "In Vietnam American officers liked to call the area outside GVN [Government of Vietnam] control 'Indian country.' It was a joke, of course, no more than a figure of speech, but it put the Vietnam War into a definite historical and mythological perspective."

ink blot. The theory that hundreds of thousands of men had to spread out like an ink blot (alternatively, like an "oil slick") to ensure that "pacification" was taking hold.

Irish pennant. A loose thread, strap, etc.

★ ☆ **J** ☆ ★

jacket. One's official service record.

jack shit. (1) An idiot. (2) A second lieutenant. Presumably, both of these come from the line "He don't know shit" or "He don't know jack shit."

Jacob's ladder. A rope ladder dropped from a helicopter; from the biblical story of Jacob, who had a dream of a ladder leading to heaven.

Jesus nut. The nut holding the bolt that holds the rotor blade to a helicopter.

john. A lieutenant; hence, FIRST JOHN and SECOND JOHN.

John Wayne. (1) To act heroically. (2) A soldier who "acts it up" for the media, especially the camera. Legend had it that old sergeants told their men: "There are two ways to do anything—the right way and the John Wayne way."

John Wayne cookies. The nearly inedible biscuits in every C-ration box.

John Wayne High School. The Army's Special Warfare School at Fort Bragg; from John Wayne's role in the movie *The Green Berets* (1968).

John Wayne rifle. The .45-caliber service pistol. This term was explained in Charles Mohr's June 20, 1968, *New York Times* review of the Wayne movie *The Green Berets*: "A .45 caliber service pistol—which almost nobody can shoot accurately—is called a 'John Wayne rifle' in Vietnam because in the movies the Duke could knock down a running man at 300 yards with one."

Jolly Green Giant. The CH-47 double-rotor helicopter, able to carry up to twenty-six troops; also known as a "log."

juicer. A boozer (as opposed to a "head," or marijuana user).

jungle boots. Canvas footwear designed like traditional combat boots. The canvas dries easily, while leather would rot in the jungle.

jungle rule, the. "Always be quiet."

jungle utilities. Lightweight fatigues.

junior birdman. A young pilot with no combat experience.

junk on the bunk. One's field equipment laid out on one's bunk for inspection.

★ ☆ **K** ☆ ★

kaserne. A military base; from the German for "camp."

K-Bar. A military combat knife used by the Marines.

khaki tit. The Army. A regular Army person is said to suck the khaki tit.

Khe Sanh shuffle. A slouching run of not more than fifty meters without finding cover. The allusion is to the long, relentless siege at Khe Sanh.

K.I.A. Killed in action.

kick. A dishonorable discharge.

kick-out. Supplies kicked out of a helicopter to troops on the ground.

kill. A downed enemy aircraft.

killer team. A unit that roams around searching for the enemy.

kill-fire. A burst of gunfire so effective that it leaves nobody to return fire. Such action is described in James Mills's *Underground Empire* (1986): "And there's dust and smoke everywhere. And . . . all the noise to silence. Except for groans and moans. That's what they call a kill-fire. Because when you do it right there's nobody left and there's no return fire. It's a kill-fire."

killing box. A target zone. See BOX.

Kit Carson. A Vietcong who changes sides, usually for money. The allusion is to the use made by frontiersman Kit Carson of friendly Indians as scouts.

klick. See CLICK.

K.P. KITCHEN POLICE. See under World War I.

K.Y.P.I.Y.P. Keep your pecker in your pants; a long-established motto in the fight against venereal disease.

★ ☆ **L** ☆ ★

laager. A defensive perimeter.

Land of the 24-hour generator. Vietnam (where power outages were common).

lay chilly. To lie still (i.e., to "freeze").

L.B.J. Long Binh jail; a play on the initials of President Lyndon Baines Johnson. The actual name of the prison was Long Binh stockade, but most soldiers changed the last word to accommodate the word play.

Leatherneck Square. A northern area of South Vietnam where Marines worked, defined by Dong Ha, Quang Tri, Hue, Cam Lo, and the D.M.Z.

legos / legs. A unit that is neither airborne nor mechanized.

lick. A mistake.

lifer. A career military person.

lifer juice. Coffee.

lightning-bug mission. A mission involving a Huey helicopter loaded with a large number of illuminating flares.

liquid cork. Diarrhea medicine.

little people. The enemy.

L.L.D.B. Lousy little dirty bastards (i.e., the Vietnamese special forces).

loach. A light observation helicopter, or LOH.

log. The CH-47 double-rotor helicopter; also known as the "Jolly Green Giant."

long tom. The long-range .155-mm artillery piece.

louie. A lieutenant.

lower than whaleshit. (1) At the bottom (in terms of rank or status). (2) Very depressed.

L.P. (1) Listening post (i.e., a forward position for observing the enemy, manned by two or three soldiers). (2) Landing platform (an amphibious piece of equipment used in beach landings).

lurp. Special ration of food packaged for those on long-range patrol. Officially called the Long-Range Patrol Ration, which was developed by the Army's Natick Laboratories. Lurp is semi-acronym for Long Range Patrol Ration.

Lurp: The Consensus

The lurp is a remarkably lightweight, compact ration that can be flexibly packaged because it has no cans. Its major item is one of eight precooked, freeze-dried entrees (such as chicken stew or beef hash) that can be turned into a hot meal with the addition of hot water. But it can also be eaten cold with cold water or dry "as is" like popcorn. The lurp also comes with a sweet, cereal or a fruitcake bar, coffee, cream, sugar, toilet paper, matches, and a plastic spoon. It was found to be "highly acceptable" by men who lived on them for as long as ten days at a time. Former G.I.'s commonly write to the developer of the ration, Natick Laboratories, attempting to buy some for use on camping trips. (Freeze-dried foods very like those in the lurp have begun to show up in catalogues and stores selling to campers and backpackers.)

---

lurps. Long-range reconnaissance patrols.

L.Z. Landing zone. Mark Baker describes L.Z.'s in *Nam* (1981): "usually a small clearing secured temporarily for the landing of resupply helicopters. Some become more permanent and eventually become base camps."

★ ☆ **M** ☆ ★

MACV [pronounced "mac-vee"]. Military Assistance Command, Vietnam; the command center for Americans in Vietnam.

mad minute / mad moment. A brief period of intense automatic rifle or machine gun fire. The new and improved weapons used in Vietnam made it possible to fire many more rounds per second than in previous wars. All the weapons around a U.S. base would be fired at once to kill as many infiltrators and snipers as possible. The radio call for a mad minute was MIKE-MIKE.

mad monkeys. The staff of the MACV.

Maggie's drawers. (1) A red flag displayed from the target pit on a rifle range when a shot has completely missed the target. (2) A miss.

Marvin Arvin / Marvin de Arvin. See ARVIN.

maverick. A stolen or misappropriated government vehicle.

McNamara's folly. The F-111 jet aircraft (because, among other things, of its many cost overruns); named for its greatest supporter, Secretary of Defense Robert S. McNamara.

McNamara's line. A barrier across the D.M.Z., composed of electronic sensors and antipersonnel weapons. It was named for Secretary of Defense Robert S. McNamara. Al Santoli described it in *To*

Bear Any Burden (1985): "It was a joke, about seven hundred meters wide and thirteen miles long. Barren, it looked like something out of a World War I movie."

McNamara's war. The Vietnam War (because so much of the buildup of U.S. forces in Vietnam occurred while Robert S. McNamara, a key supporter of the war, was secretary of defense).

mechanical. Ambush weaponry triggered remotely by the enemy (e.g., mines, flares, etc.).

mechanized ambush. An ambush employing high-tech booby traps.

medevac. Medical evacuation (i.e., a quick helicopter trip to medical help). In *Fields of Fire* (1978), James Webb distinguishes between various levels of medevac: "Emergency medevacs were those near death. Priority evacs were those seriously wounded and unable to ambulate. Routines were ambulatory or dead. All Vietnamese casualties were routine."
The term long ago passed into civilian use. Medevac helicopters are used by state police and other organizations for medical emergencies.

mere gook rule. The idea that a crime isn't a crime if it is committed against a Vietnamese (a "mere gook").

mess kit repair battalion. A mythical unit to which goofs and BOLOS are sent.

MiG country. An area defended by Soviet MiG jet aircraft.

mike-mike. (1) A millimeter. (2) Any of the automatic weapons fired from heli-copter gunships (.20-mm guns, .762-mm guns, etc.). (3) A radio call initiating a MAD MINUTE or indicating that one is in progress.

military power. The maximum power for an aircraft without using after-burners.

million-dollar wound / million-dollar zap. A noncrippling wound that is serious enough to warrant return to the U.S.

miracle rice. A special strain of rice—designated "IR8"—that the U.S. introduced to Vietnam in 1970–1971. It came close to doubling the average rice output per acre.

missing link. A second lieutenant (seen as prehuman).

M.L.R. Main line of resistance (i.e., the front line). Often used with bravado: "I've got more time on the M.L.R. than the REMF has in-country."

M-1 pencil. Any technique used to cheat or to beat the system. Originally, the term referred to a pencil used to make holes the size of an M-1 bullet in a target to improve one's score on the rifle range. In *About Face* (1989), David H. Hackworth writes: "M-1 penciling had long ago left the . . . range and become synonymous—Army wide—with cheating in all the little ways."

Mongolian ghost trap. A radar reflector used by downed airmen to signal their position. In *Phantom Over Vietnam* (1984), John Trotti says that the device is "so intricate that by the time the crewman gets it erected, he has either been rescued or died of exposure."

Monopoly money. Military payment certificates issued in lieu of cash in Vietnam; an allusion to the fake money used in the popular board game.

monster. (1) The AN/PRC-77 radio (because of its considerable bulk and weight). (2) The Phantom aircraft (which has been said to resemble a prehistoric reptile).

moonshine. An aircraft carrying flares.

M.O.P. Missing on purpose (as opposed to the involuntary status M.I.A. [missing in action]). It is another way of saying A.W.O.L. (see under the Civil War, World War I, and World War II).

mop up. See under World War II.

mortie. A mortar.

most ricky tick. Immediately; right now. This was a bit of pidgin picked up by the Marines in Okinawa.

motherfucker. An all-purpose oath. In *About Face* (1989), David H. Hackworth writes of the use of the term in Southeast Asia: "In the Airborne, the term 'motherfucker,' unless spoken harshly, was among the highest terms of endearment." It was ubiquitous in Vietnam.

mother-in-law. A BOGEY; from the notion of a mother-in-law as a pest.

mousetrapped. Caught in an ambush.

Mr. Charlie. (1) The enemy. (2) White people; a term used by blacks.

M.R.E. Meal Ready to Eat; a field ration that replaced the C-RATION (see under World War II) and E-ration. See also under the Gulf War.

Mr. No-shoulders. A snake. In Vietnam, snakes were common.

Mr. Refrigerator. American ambassador Ellsworth Bunker (because of his perceived coldness).

Mr. Zippo. A G.I. operating a flamethrower.

mule. A small motorized platform used to carry arms, and sometimes supplies and troops; also known as a "mechanical mule" and a "tug." In Philip Caputo's *A Rumor of War* (1977), it is described as "a heavy-weapons carrier that looked nothing like a mule but rather resembled an oversized toy wagon."

mummy sack. A **body bag.**

mush. To lose airspeed (i.e., for an aircraft to feel like it is flying through mush).

mustang. An officer who has come up through the ranks; an officer who has been given a battlefield promotion.

mystery meat. Meat served at mess that lacks clear identity.

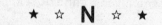

Naked Fanny. Nakon Phanom air base, in Thailand.

Nam. Vietnam.

nap of the earth. Flight as close to the earth's surface as possible.

N.C.O. Noncommissioned officer. The term was often reinterpreted as "no chance outside."

newby / newfer. A replacement person (i.e., a new boy).

nipple palm. The nipa palm, which grows in Vietnam.

No-clap Medal. A good conduct medal; from the belief that one will be given the medal if one avoids acquiring a sexually transmitted disease, such as the clap. An old saw states that enlisted men get the clap while their officers come down with nonspecific urethritis (the technical name for the clap).

NOD. Night observation device.

No days like that! Not likely to happen.

no-fire area. An area occupied by friendly forces.

non-hostile. Accidental. The term is used to characterize wounds or deaths that are not caused by the enemy.

November Foxtrot Whiskey. No fucking way; from alphabet code.

nugget. New. The term is used for a man on his first tour of duty, such as a "nugget pilot" or a "nugget replacement."

nylon. A parachute. In this war, parachutes were no longer made of silk.

★ ☆ O ☆ ★

O-club. Officers' club.

o-dark-thirty. Very early in the morning; from the twenty-four-hour system of military timekeeping in which the early morning hours start with zero—e.g., one A.M. is 0100 (stated as "o-one-hundred hours").

officer material. Not officer material; a goof-off.

O.J. A perfectly rolled marijuana cigarette soaked in an opium solution.

Old Shaky. The ancient C-124 aircraft.

one-digit midget. A person with less than ten days left to serve in Vietnam or in the Army (i.e., a real SHORT-TIMER).

on the line. In combat; on the front lines.

ontos. A 106-mm recoilless rifle carrier.

O.P. Outpost.

ossifer. An officer.

other war, the. The highly touted pacification program in Vietnam.

outgoing / outgoing mail. Friendly artillery fire.

outside, the. Civilian life.

outstanding / out-fucking-standing. An expression of mock enthusiasm for anything from the excellent to the barely acceptable.

over-two. More than two thirds of the way through a normal enlistment of three years.

★ ☆ **P** ☆ ★

P. Piaster (the unit of currency in South Vietnam).

paddy foot. Same as TRENCH FOOT (see under World War I).

palm. Napalm.

Papa Sierra. A platoon sergeant (in alphabet code).

P.B.I. Poor bloody infantry.

penny nickel nickel. The 155-mm howitzer (described in terms of coinage).

Pentagon East. A sprawling, low office complex at Tan Son Nhut air base, airconditioned and outfitted for four thousand officers and enlisted staff.

peter pilot. A copilot.

p.f.c. Private first class. It was also used for the often-desired status of "private fucking civilian."

P.I. Political influence; political interest. A private whose father was a member of Congress might find the initials "P.I." on his service jacket.

pick up brass. To leave; to move out. The expression comes from the rifle range, where soldiers are required to pick up their brass shell casings when they are done.

ping. To criticize.

Pinkville. An area northeast of Quang Ngai, South Vietnam; from the fact that its high population density caused it to appear red on Army maps.

piss tube. A rocket casing stuck in the ground and used as a urinal.

pocket leave. To take one's leave without leaving the post or base; probably so-called because the leave papers stay in the soldier's pocket.

pogue. A rear-echelon military person; used derogatorily. See also under World War II and the Gulf War.

point / point man. The forward man on patrol or on a combat mission. His purpose was to draw enemy fire and allow the main body of soldiers to attack.

police. To clean up.

pop. To shoot; to kill.

pop smoke. To ignite and throw a smoke grenade as a signal to incoming aircraft.

pos. Position.

prang. To land a helicopter roughly.

prick-25. The AN/PRC-25 field radio.

professional copilot. A terrible pilot.

Psychedelic Cookie. The 9th Infantry Division; from the octofoil design of its shoulder patch.

psywar. Psychological warfare.

P.T. Physical training.

ptomaine domain / ptomaine palace. A mess hall.

pucker factor. A measure of intense fear (i.e., the degree to which a soldier's anus tightens up). See also under the Gulf War.

Puff. Popular forces; Montagnards.

Puff the Magic Dragon. A C-47, DC-3, AC-130, or other aircraft armed as a gunship—or dragon ship—with 7.62-mm machine guns or similar rapid-fire weapons used in support of ground troops; from the title of a popular song of the period, sung by Peter, Paul, and Mary.

puke. A rookie.

Puking Buzzards. The 101st Airborne Division; from the screaming eagle on its patch.

pull rank. To exercise the power of one's position or rank.

pull the pin. To leave; from the rapid exit one makes after pulling the pin on a hand grenade.

purple vision. Night vision; from the color seen in night vision scopes.

puss guts. Members of the American Legion and the Veterans of Foreign Wars who gather in meeting halls and drink beer.

Puzzle Heart. The MACV (Military Assistance Command Vietnam) headquarters restaurant.

P.X. Post exchange.

P.X. hero. A soldier who bought medals at a P.X. rather than earning them.

P.Z. Pickup zone.

quartermaster property. Dead (because burial is a job of the Quartermaster Corps).

que lam. A peasant (from the Vietnamese); used derogatorily.

rabbit. A white American soldier; a term used by some black soldiers.

rack. A cot; a bed.

rack in / rack out. To go to bed.

rack time. Sleep.

rail. A first lieutenant; from the single silver bar insignia.

Ranch Hand. An allusion to defoliation. A Ranch Hand airplane was a C-123 outfitted with gigantic defoliant-filled tanks. The Ranch Hand pilots' motto, according to Edwin Corley in *Siege* (1969), was "Only you can prevent forest fires."

R&R. Rest and relaxation; rest and recuperation. R&R was a three- to seven-day vacation from combat zones.

Rat, the. Phanrat, South Vietnam.

ratchet. To escalate the war a small amount. The term was used by Secretary of Defense Robert S. McNamara.

rat fuck. (1) RF's (i.e., South Vietnamese "reaction forces"). (2) A mission or operation that is doomed from the beginning.

ration drawer. A person who collects (i.e., draws) food, pay, and benefits without working for them.

ration of shit. A hard time.

read. To hear or understand a radio transmission.

real world. See WORLD, THE.

rear-echelon motherfucker. An expression of contempt for enlisted men and officers assigned to noncombat areas. *Crisis in Command* (1978), by Richard A. Gabriel and Paul L. Savage, provides this insight into the term: "Often the individual infantryman would spend days in the field in search of the enemy only to witness upon his return large numbers of clean-shaven and starch-fatigued officers going about their business in their secure environments. The troops developed a series of terms for these officers, the most derisive of which was 'rear-echelon mother-fucker.'" See also REMF.

reckless rifle. A recoilless rifle.

recon. Reconnaissance.

red cunt hair. A very small distance (as in, "That is one red cunt hair out of alignment.").

red L.Z. A landing zone under hostile fire.

red phone. A telephone reserved for the direst of emergencies.

reefer. (1) A refrigerator; a refrigerated vehicle. (2) A marijuana cigarette.

REMF. Rear-echelon motherfucker (i.e., a base camp support soldier). In John M. Del Vecchio's *The 13th Valley* (1982), a man expresses himself redundantly by saying, "and I do my job better than any mother-fucking REMF." See also REAR-ECHELON MOTHERFUCKER.

repple-depple. A replacement depot—the casual camp where incoming soldiers (replacements) are processed. This term first came into play in World War II, but was used so commonly in Vietnam that its strongest association is with this war.

Rice Krispie mission. A mission to set fire to enemy rice fields. The term is defined in *The Heart of a Man: A Naval Pilot's Vietnam* (1973), by Frank C. Elkins: "One of our mission flights will be to set the VC rice fields on fire (we hear that they are short on food for the first time). These operations are appropriately called 'Rice Krispie' missions. Cute, eh?"

riff. To let go before retirement; from "reduction in force." Riffing has been said to be the Army's way of controlling its reserve officer corps population.

rifle. An infantryman. An ancestor to this term is BAYONET (see under the Civil War).

ring-knocker. Any military academy graduate.

rip cords. Loose threads from the cord that is pulled to open a parachute.

roach wagon. A mobile canteen or snack bar.

rock and roll. (1) To put a weapon on full automatic fire. (2) Automatic weapon fire.

rocker. Any of the lower stripes on an N.C.O.'s insignia, which look like the rockers that would be found on a rocking horse. For instance, a master sergeant (or E-8) wears three stripes and three rockers.

rocket city. A base under constant rocket fire.

roll out. To get up.

Roman candled. Said of a parachute whose silk has rolled and twisted around itself (i.e., looking like the white tube of a Roman candle).

Rome plow. A bulldozer with a mammoth blade for clearing jungle (manufactured by the Rome Company, of Georgia).

rotate. To return to the U.S. after a period overseas.

round eye. A non-Asian person (i.e., one whose eyes are not perceived as slanting by westerners).

ruck. A rucksack; a pack.

Ruff Puff. Regional Forces (R.F.) and Popular Forces (P.F.) of the South Vietnamese military.

★ ☆ **S** ☆ ★

sack. (1) A bed. (2) To totally destroy an enemy area.

sack in / sack out. To go to bed.

Sadeye. The Mark 5 Universal Weapons Dispenser, which releases antipersonnel bomblets.

Saigon cowboy. An inappropriately dressed soldier in a noncombat area. The type is described by David H. Hackworth in *About Face* (1989): "a breed of rear-echelon soldiers so called for their latest and greatest, dressed to the hilt warrior look that they took no closer to the combat zone than absolutely necessary."

Saigon tea. Colored water drunk by Vietnamese bar girls, which soldiers paid for as if it were an expensive, exotic cocktail.

salty dog. A piece of equipment lost as the result of enemy action.

Same mud, same blood. A saying that described the good race relations that often characterized combat zones.

S&D. Search and destroy.

sandpaper. Government-issue toilet paper.

sap charge. An explosive.

sapper. (1) An infiltrator. (2) A North Vietnamese or Vietcong commando.

sarge. Sergeant.

Scared Horse. The 11th Armored Cavalry Regiment; so-called because of the rearing horse on its shoulder patch.

school solution. A solution taught at a military training school, such as Fort Benning. School solutions were not highly regarded. In *Delta Force* (1983), by Charlie A. Beckwith and Donald Knox, there is a story about a fake tombstone placed outside a Ranger briefing shack, bearing this verse:

> Here lies the bones
> Of Ranger Jones,
> A graduate of this institution;
> He died last night
> in his first fire fight,
> using the school solution.
> Therefore, be flexible!

scope head. A radarman (because he is always looking at a radar scope).

scrambled eggs. The gold embellishment on the hat visors of senior officers.

seagull. A pilot who does not like to fly. The term is explained by Robert K. Wilcox in *Scream of Eagles* (1990): "you have to throw a rock to get them to fly."

search-and-destroy mission. An operation aimed at killing enemy soldiers but not at holding the ground afterward.

second balloon. A second lieutenant.

second john. A second lieutenant.

see the elephant. To be in combat. See **elephant, the,** under the Civil War.

service benes. Privileges (e.g., P.X. privileges); "benes" is short for "benefits."

sewer trout. Fish served at mess.

shake-and-bake. (1) A sergeant without much time in the service (e.g., a graduate of an N.C.O. training school). In *Army Blue* (1989), by Lucian K. Truscott IV, this explanation for the term's origin is given: "Sergeants who came from the NCO school were also known as 'shake-and-bakes,' after a television commercial for a product that promised something equally, improbably instantaneous, like fried chicken from the oven." The term was sometimes applied to graduates of officers candidate school, who got their commissions after three months. (2) To be led out.

shaped charge. An explosive whose energy is focused in one direction.

shavetail. A new lieutenant. This old term dates back to a time when the Army used mules. New mules had their tails shaved so that their handlers could distinguish them from the trained mules. See also under the Spanish-American War era and under World War I.

shithook. The CH-47 Chinook helicopter; a play on "Chinook" and a critique of the helicopter's slowness.

shit on a shingle. Chipped or creamed beef on toast. See s.o.s., under World War II.

shoot and scoot. An artillery firing technique in which a unit is moved quickly after firing to avoid return fire.

short-arm inspection. An inspection for venereal disease.

short-stick / short-timer's stick. A stick used to keep track of one's enlistment period. In *Charlie Company* (1983), by Peter Goldman and Tony Fuller, short-sticks are identified as "the chunky batons that grunts would carry and notch day by day when their time in country was running out."

Here is another description, from Mark Baker's *Nam* (1981): "[W]hen a soldier had approximately two months remaining of his tour in Vietnam, he might take a long stick and notch it for each of his remaining days in-country. As each day passed he would cut another notch in the stick until on his rotation day he was left with only a small stub."

Although there was some metaphorical use of this term, it usually referred to a real stick, whose owner would display it as evidence that he was "short."

short-timer. One whose tour of duty or period of enlistment is nearing an end. Such a person was sometimes said to be "short."

shotgun envelope. A manila envelope for interoffice mail. It is punched with holes (so that it is easy to see if anything remains in the envelope), as if shot with a shotgun.

silo sitter. A soldier assigned to a missile site.

single-digit fidget. A nervous condition afflicting those with less than ten days remaining in their tour of duty.

single-digit midget. A soldier with less than ten days remaining in his tour of duty.

sitmap. A situation map (i.e., a map showing the dispositions of friendly and enemy forces).

sitrep. A situation report.

S.I.W. Self-inflicted wound.

skag. Heroin.

skate. An easy accomplishment; a period of ease. In *The 13th Valley* (1982), John M. Del Vecchio writes: "Normally resupply day was a skate, a day the command cut the boonierats some slack."

sky out. To flee; to leave suddenly.

sky pilot. A chaplain.

slackman. Second man behind the point man on patrol.

slant. See under the Korean War.

slick. (1) A helicopter without rockets or other external armament (used to carry troops and supplies). (2) A helicopter that lands on runners rather than on wheels. (3) A helicopter.

slicksleeve. Private: E-1.

S.L.J.O. Shitty little job officer.

slop chute. An on-post beer hall for enlisted men not of N.C.O. rank. The reference is to the chute in farmyards filled with food for hogs.

slope. An Asian person; a racist slur. The allusion is to the slope of the forehead.

smadge. Sergeant major.

smart bomb. A bomb with remarkable accuracy, guided by a laser beam or a TV camera.

smash. Supersonic speed; from the sound and shock of breaking the sound barrier.

SMASH. Southeast Asia Multisensor Armament for Huey; a passive infrared and moving-target-indicator fire-control system for use by day or night.

Smokey Bear. A drill sergeant; from the "smokey-bear hat," like the hat worn by Smokey Bear, the Agriculture Department's cartoon spokesman against forest fires.

Smokey the Bear. A flare-dropping or smoke-laying aircraft. The name came not only from the smoke generated, but also from the resemblance of a smoke generator on a helicopter to Smokey Bear's hat.

snake. The AH-1G Cobra attack helicopter.

snake eater. An Army Special Forces soldier (i.e., a Green Beret); so-called because the Green Berets on patrol allegedly ate snakes.

snatch. A capture; a rescue (i.e., an operation in which live subjects are brought back). A squad specializing in such operations goes on "snatch patrol."

snoop 'n' poop. Search and destroy.

snowdrop. A member of the Air Force Security Police; from their white helmet.

snuffy. A recruit; a low-ranking individual. The term may allude to the hapless Snuffy Smith of the funny papers.

S.O.L. Shit out of luck.

S.O.P. Standard operating procedure; standing operational procedure.

Sorry about that. A response to any bit of ill-fortune, from the trivial to the tragic.

S.O.S. (1) Squadron officers' school. (2) Same old shit. (3) Chipped or creamed beef on toast; see under World War II.

space cadet. A young show-off pilot.

Spad. An A-1 Skyraider (a propeller-driven airplane). It was based on a design that was so old that, to quote T. E. Cruise's *Wings of Gold III: The Hot Pilots* (1989), "it reminded the jet jockeys of the famous Spad biplane fighter of World War I."

spec. Specialist.

special feces. Special Forces.

spider hole. A camouflaged enemy firing position; a sniper's lair in a cave.

spin. A "separation program number" (S.P.N.), any of 446 coded reasons why a soldier could be discharged with other than an unmodified honorable discharge. For instance, there is a spin for bed-wetting and another for immaturity. Discharge papers without the taint of a spin were "spin-free."

spit and polish. Impressive outward appearance; from the fact that mixing water (or spit) with shoe polish makes the polish go on better.

spoon. A part of a hand grenade. Releasing the spoon causes the grenade to explode. Philip Caputo uses the term in *A Rumor of War* (1977): "He tried to throw a grenade at them, but his hand slipped off the spoon. The grenade went off and blew the sentry in half."

squared away. Prepared; ready for action. The expression derives from the military practice of packing one's clothing in a locker with geometric regularity.

stack pencils. To kill time.

stand down. To rest. A military unit stands down when it ceases all operations except security.

stand tall. (1) To come to attention. (2) To be ready.

starch. Plastic explosive.

stateside. The U.S.

steel pot. The M-1 helmet (a steel helmet with a fiber liner).

stewburner. A cook.

stick. A group of paratroopers.

sticks. Pants.

stitched. Killed (presumably, because the dead person has been filled with holes, as if stitched).

STRAC / strac. (1) Strategic Army Command; Strategic Army Corps. (2) Soldier trained and ready around the clock (i.e., a soldier who is smart, sharp, and well prepared). In *Charlie Company* (1983), by Peter Goldman and Tony Fuller, the term is called "the Army honorific for a Class A soldier."

straphanger. A useless person (i.e., one who is just along for the ride).

strawberry jam. Gasoline or napalm. As Jack Hawkins writes in *Chopper One #2: Tunnel Warriors* (1987), it was "whatever the flamethrowing tanks were carrying this week."

Street Without Joy. South Vietnam's Highway 1; from the French name, La Rue sans Joie.

strike. To barhop (as if making a series of air strikes).

stroke it. To back off.

stupid. Said of a missile that has lost its target (i.e., that has stopped being "smart"). In *Scream of Eagles* (1990), Robert K. Wilcox writes of a Sparrow missile that "went stupid," which, he adds, was "similar (although at much faster speeds) to World War II searchlights losing enemy bombers in a night raid."

sub-gunny. Substitute door gunner.

SWAG. Scientific wild-assed guess.

sweep. A search-and-destroy mission.

sweet. Good (as in "sweet radio signal" and "sweet radar lock").

swinging dick. A male soldier.

swinging man trap. A particularly vicious booby trap.

★ ☆ **T** ☆ ★

tac air. Tactical air support.

T.A.D. Temporary active duty.

tail chase. To play follow-the-leader with jet fighters.

take fire. To be shot at.

take hits. To receive fire (e.g., a ship might take hits).

tanker / tankerman / tankman. A soldier in a tank unit.

T.D.Y. Temporary duty.

tee-tee. Very small or little.

television war. The Vietnam War (because it showed the face of war to people sitting in their living rooms).

tent peg. A stupid or worthless soldier.

terr. Terrorist.

Thirty-Three. A brand of Vietnamese beer manufactured under French license. According to Frank Snepp, in *Decent Interval* (1977), "its most distinctive quality was its formaldehyde-like preservative which packed a wallop that equaled or surpassed that of Carolina white lightning. As the GIs used to say, it killed you and pickled you in one stroke."

30-year man. A career Army man (i.e., a LIFER—one who stays in the Army for a full thirty years).

Thud. The F-105 Thunderbird aircraft.

Thule coolie. A soldier on duty in Thule, Greenland; a play on the cold climate of Greenland.

thumper. (1) A squad member who carries an M-79 grenade launcher, also known as a *thumper man.* (2) The M-79 grenade launcher. The term derives from the characteristic sound of the launcher.

thunder road. South Vietnam's Highway 13.

thunder run. A movement of armored columns along a road or trail with the vehicles firing alternately to the two sides.

ticket-punching. The process of meeting the routine requirements for promotion, by officers seeking advancement. In *About Face* (1989), David H. Hackworth writes: "So it had a name, I thought: ticket punching—the syndrome that had me chasing down that elusive degree."

tiger stripes / tiger suit. Camouflaged tropical fatigues marked with brown and black stripes.

tight. (1) Close, like good friends. (2) Performing well (said of equipment).

Tin City. A complex of metal barracks at Guam's Andersen Air Force Base.

titi. A small quantity.

toad sticker. A bayonet.

T.O.E. [not pronounced "toe"]. Table of organization and equipment. This was a document listing the type of equipment and personnel a unit was supposed to have.

toe popper. A small mine that detonates when stepped on.

Tomb. Colonel Toon, said to be North Vietnam's leading fighter pilot.

top. A top sergeant (the highest-ranking N.C.O. in a company or battalion).

tour 365. Year-long tour in Vietnam.

tracer. A round of ammunition treated so that it will glow or smoke when fired, so that its flight can be followed.

track / tracks. (1) An armored personnel carrier. (2) Any vehicle equipped with treads.

trained killer. A soldier. The term was usually applied ironically to boys who seemed to be anything but killers.

trash hauler. A transport pilot not involved in combat.

treadhead. A soldier whose specialty is armored vehicles employing treads. A character in Harold Coyle's *Team Yankee* (1987) says: "Shit, don't they teach you treadheads anything at Fort Knox?"

trial by urine. Testing for drugs by urinalysis.

tripwire. (1) A booby trap. (2) An unlucky soldier (i.e., with a knack for stumbling upon booby traps).

tripwire vet. A Vietnam veteran who dealt with the stress of having served in a difficult and unpopular war by living in the deep woods in North America. The headline for an Associated Press article in the Washington *Post* of December 31, 1983, read: "State Seeks 'Tripwire' Vets Hiding in the Wild."

troop. A soldier.

tube steak. A hot dog.

tunnel rat. A soldier who searches enemy tunnels (often, with little more than a flashlight).

turnaround. On an aircraft carrier, the time in port between cruises.

turret-head. An arguer; one who is always spouting off.

turtles. New replacements; so-called because they take so long to arrive.

twink. (1) A rookie second lieutenant. (2) A new recruit.

two hots and a Charlie. Two hot meals and a C-ration.

★ ☆ **U** ☆ ★

ultimate weapon. An infantryman.

unass. To get up quickly from a sitting position.

unbloused. Having one's pants not tucked into one's boot tops.

uncle / uncle sucker / uncle sugar. Uncle Sam (i.e., the U.S. government).

Uncle Charlie. The Vietcong. The term is used in Al Santoli's *To Bear Any Burden* (1985): "We controlled the daytime, but the night belonged to Uncle Charlie." See also CHARLIE.

unload. To accelerate.

up North. Common way of referring to North Vietnam.

use up. To kill.

utilities. Marine combat fatigues.

V.C. Vietcong. The term was applied to the North Vietnamese forces as well as to the Vietcong.

V.C. land. An area controlled by the Vietcong.

vengeance patrol. A group of American soldiers who would seek revenge after suffering losses. In *Dispatches* (1977), Michael Herr tells of "entire squads wiped out (their mutilated bodies would so enrage marines that they would run out 'vengeance patrols' that often ended the same way)."

Victor / Victor Charlie. The Vietcong; from alphabet code.

Vietnamization. The process of giving responsibility for fighting the war back to the South Vietnamese. Another version of this notion was Richard Nixon's "de-Americanization . . . with all deliberate speed." Vietnamization was also Nixon's idea.

Vietnam syndrome. An expression of the postwar public feeling about the unpopular, costly, prolonged, and unsuccessful American involvement in Vietnam. The term reappeared during the Persian Gulf crisis when, on March 1, 1991, President George Bush said, "By God, we've kicked the Vietnam syndrome once and for all."

ville. A village; from the French. In Mark Baker's *Nam* (1981), a ville is said to be "any location from a small town of several hundred inhabitants to a few thatched huts in a clearing."

void vicious. (1) Hostile jungle area. (2) The final approach to a hot landing zone.

★ ☆ **W** ☆ ★

wait-a-minute bush. A thorny bush native to Vietnam. David H. Hackworth, in *About Face* (1989), writes that it "could hold a trooper as tenaciously as a strand of barbed wire."

wake-up. The last day of one's tour; as in "ten days and a wake-up."

walk in the sun. Troop movement without risk of combat.

warm body. A soldier.

Warthog. The A-10 aircraft (also called the Thunderbolt II).

waste. To kill (i.e., to throw away a life). This term appears to derive from street gang slang, in which "lay waste" meant to defeat.

wasted. Dead.

water-walker. One who has achieved perfection (i.e., one who can do the impossible).

wax / wax someone's ass. To kill.

web gear. A canvas belt and shoulder straps used for packing equipment and ammunition.

wet read. To study a reconnaissance photo while it is still wet from processing.

WETSU [pronounced "wet-soo"]. We eat this shit up. This acronym takes aim at the petty, tedious routines of military life.

WHAM. Winning the hearts and minds (of the people). This was often officially stated as a parallel goal with winning the war.

whispering death. The F-111 aircraft (as characterized by the North Vietnamese). This interesting term was also applied to the Navy F-4 Corsair in World War II and the M-1 Abrams tank in the Persian Gulf War.

white bird. A light observation helicopter.

white mice. The South Vietnamese police; so-called because of their size and their bright, lightweight uniforms, featuring white gloves and helmets.

white sidewalls / whitewalls. A military haircut (because the hair is clipped so close to the sides of the head that the white of the scalp shows through).

W.I.A. Wounded in action.

wild goose. A mercenary.

Wild Weasel. The F-105 Thunderchief aircraft with a modified fuselage to accommodate a second man.

willy peter / willie pete. White phosphorus.

willy-peter bag. A bag for white phosphorus. It is described in Philip Caputo's *A Rumor of War* (1977): "They did not find enough of him to fill a willy-peter bag, a waterproof sack a little larger than a shopping bag."

WIMP. Weak Incompetent Malingering Pussy according to those insisting this was an acronym during the war.

wire. The perimeter around a base, where trip wires set off booby traps.

wire hanger. A soldier so far out of the combat zone that he can enjoy the luxury of hanging his clothes on hangers.

wood line. A row of trees at the edge of a rice paddy or a field.

word one. Talk. The expression is usually used in the negative, as in, "I didn't get a chance to say word one."

World, the. The U.S.; home. Sometimes the term was "the real world."

W.P. White phosphorus.

★ ☆ **X** ☆ ★

xin loi. "Sorry about that" or "goodbye" delivered in Vietnamese.

X.O. Executive officer (the second in command).

★ ☆ **Y** ☆ ★

Yards. Montagnards (a mountain people of Vietnam).

yellow on rice. The Vietnamese point of view.

yobo. Lover; from the Korean. The term is usually applied to a girlfriend.

yo-yo. A vertical aerial combat maneuver.

★ ☆ **Z** ☆ ★

Z, the. The demilitarized zone; from **D.M.Z.**

zap. To kill; to wound; to destroy.

zebra. An N.C.O. in the higher grades (E-6 to E-9). The term alludes to the number of insignia stripes on the sleeves.

zero-dark-thirty. Very early in the morning. See **O-DARK-THIRTY**.

Z.I. Zone of the interior. This was a nickname for the U.S.

zip. A Vietnamese person; a slur.

zipperhead. A Vietcong or North Vietnamese soldier (i.e., any enemy).

Zippo. A flamethrower; from the brand of cigarette lighters.

Zippo job / Zippo mission / Zippo raid. A search-and-destroy mission in which villages are set afire. The allusion is to Zippo cigarette lighters.

Zippo squad. A squad that conducts a ZIPPO JOB.

zot. Zero; nothing; a loser.

zulu. A casualty report.

Sources and Acknowledgments

★

American advisers to this chapter have been Charles D. Poe of Houston, Texas, military-slang expert Frank Hailey, Russell Mott, Charles Moss, and Joseph C. Goulden. Mr. Poe has supplied hundreds of references from fiction and nonfiction of the Vietnam period to put the terms in context. Author Richard Herman helped with terms in this and the next two chapters.

Books about Vietnam with useful glossaries include Mark Baker's *Nam* (Berkley Books, 1981); Stanley W. Beesley's *The Heartland Remembers* (University of Oklahoma Press, 1987), John M. Del Vecchio's *The 13th Valley* (Bantam, 1982); Bernard Edelman's *Dear America: Letters Home From Vietnam* (Pocket Books, 1985); Jack Hawkins's *Chopper 1: #2 Tunnel Warriors* (Ivy Books, 1987); Eric Helm's *The Scorpion Squad #2: The Nhu Sky Sting* (Pinnacle Books, 1984) *Iron Triangle* (Worldwide Library, 1988) and *P.O.W.* (Worldwide Library, 1986); Al Santoli's *Everything We Had* (Ballantine Books, 1981); Wallace Terry's *Bloods* (Ballantine, 1984); Lynda Van Devanter's *Home Before Morning* (Beaufort Books, 1983); and James Webb's *Fields of Fire* (Bantam, 1978).

Two important early dictionaries are Frank A. Hailey's *Soldier Talk* (Irving Publishing Co., 1982) and *A Dictionary of Soldier Talk* by Col. John R. Elting, Sgt. Maj. Dan Cragg, and Sgt. Ernest Deal (Charles Scribner's, 1984). Two major works that are recent are Linda Reinberg's *In the Field: The Language of the Vietnam War* (Facts on File, 1991) and Gregory R. Clark's *Words of the Vietnam War* (Jefferson, N.C.: McFarland and Co., 1990).

Other books with good linguistic insight include William C. Anderson's *Bat 21* (Bantam, 1980); Philip Caputo's *A Rumor of War* (Ballantine, 1977); Harold Coyle's *Team Yankee* (Berkley, 1987); Col. David H. Hackworth's *About Face* (with Julie Sherman, Simon and Schuster, 1989); Eric Hammel's *Khe Sanh: Siege in the Clouds* (1989); Richard Harman, Jr.'s *The Warbirds* (Avon, 1989); Myra MacPherson's *Long Time Passing* (Signet, 1984); Dennis J. Marvicsin and Jerold A. Greenfield's *Maverick* (G. P. Putnam's Sons, 1990); Shelby L. Stanton's *The Rise and Fall of an American Army* (Dell, 1985); and John Trotti's *Phantom Over Vietnam* (Berkley, 1984).

6

A GULF GLOSSARY

★

Grains of "Sandspeak" from the War That Was on Every Channel

★

Some of it is new. Some of it is old. But an ofttimes bewildering wartime vocabulary is evolving in the desert of Saudi Arabia . . . Even veterans of military service just 20 or 30 years ago find they are woefully out of date on terminology and slang.
—Jeffrey Ulbrich, in the Columbia *Missourian*, January 21, 1991

It was a short and decisive war with its own feel and spirit. It was marked by technological derring-do and by success in the air, on the sea, and on the ground. Above all, it was unsullied by significant numbers of allied deaths.

The Gulf War also produced a body of slang and other terminology that was documented at every turn. The recording of this new lingo—a "Persian patois," as one writer dubbed it—was significantly aided and abetted by the relatively long period during which a corps of close to a thousand reporters waited with the troops for the ground war to begin. There were just so many things that one could report on during this long eve of war, and one of those things was the language of the conflict.

Some complained that the combat was made to sound like a bloodless bureaucratic exercise rather than a war, and some of the new official jargon tended to validate that judgment. The person sent out to tell a family of the death of a son or daughter was called a "casualty assistance coordinator," a bullet hole in a human being became a "ballistically induced aperture in the subcutaneous environment," the destruction of Iraqi antiaircraft weaponry was referred to as "suppressing assets," and then there was the politically correct "cultural bonding officer" who was nothing more than a person whose job it was to prevent G.I.'s from offending their Saudi hosts.

One writer suggested that if the famous World War II message, "Sighted sub, sank same," had been translated for this war it would have been, "Locked onto asset, visited, acquired." An editorial cartoonist for the Boston *Globe* drew a "Gulf War Word Quiz," in which one was to match phrases in one column ("pounding positions," "softening up," "collateral damage," "saturation strikes," and "carpet bombing") with their correct meanings in another column. All of the correct meanings read, "killing."

Editorializing in *The New York Times*, Eric Zicklin made the point that is made in every war: that what we do and what the enemy does are described in very different ways—for instance, "that a 'war crime' is a bare knuckled beating but that dropping loads of explosives on a nation's capital is called a 'sortie'" and "that 'collateral damage' means civilians in the enemy's country die while terrorist attacks are when civilians in an allied country die."

Columnist Clarence Page, writing in the Washington *Times* for December 5, 1991, makes the point that the colorized jargon of the military had become "more colorful than ever" in this conflict. After pointing out that bombing runs had been called "servicing the site" or "visiting a site," he writes: "During these visits 'hard' and 'soft' targets, otherwise known as buildings and human beings, were 'degraded,' 'neutralized,' 'attrited,' 'suppressed,' 'eliminated,' 'cleansed,' 'sanitized,' 'impacted,' 'decapitated' and 'taken out.'" He adds that these things were likely to occur during a "healthy day of bombing."

On top of all of this were new issues of sexism and correctness. Jamie Ann Conway, an Army captain, in a February 18, 1991, letter to *The New York Times* strongly disagreed with that newspaper's "continued use of the term 'servicemen.'"

While the slang terms that emerged from this theater in the sand may have lacked political correctness, for the most part they also lacked the bitterness and anger of Vietnam. Here is what this conflict sounded like.

★ ☆ A ☆ ★

A.A.F. Allied air forces.

Abdul. An Arab male. This term dates from at least World War I, when it was used by British troops generically for a Turkish soldier.

A.C.M. Air combat maneuvering (i.e., maneuvers made to put a fighter plane in firing position).

adopt-a-pilot. The urge experienced by ground troops to cheer for aviators, who would presumably soften up the resistance to a ground invasion.

A.F.V. Armored fighting vehicle. This is essentially a tank with tires rather than treads, used to haul Marines into battle.

air-breathing. Jet-propelled. The jet-powered Tomahawk missile was often described as "air-breathing." The term contrasts with "internal combustion."

AirLand warfare. A tactical doctrine created in the 1970s (and which, as *The New York Times* notes, "the Army eccentrically persists in spelling as one word") that first came into play in this conflict. It calls for concentrating the heaviest fire on an enemy's rear lines, to cripple tanks, artillery, and armored vehicles before they can come into play.

airplane driver. A pilot.

airwing Alpo. A field ration that includes corned beef hash and meatballs with barbecue sauce; from the name of a popular brand of dog food.

ALICE. All-purpose lightweight individual carrying equipment (a medium-sized backpack with a frame).

all-terrain vehicle. Any rental vehicle used by a Gulf War journalist.

Amazing Grace. Army cavalry's 63-ton tank.

angels. Altitude (e.g., "Angels 25" refers to an aircraft flying at 25,000 feet). See also under the Cold War.

Antichrist, the. Defense Secretary Dick Cheney (as characterized by reservists, after he increased the call-up of reserve forces).

any sailor / any soldier. The addressee on a large number of letters forwarded to servicemen in the war zone. Not all the letters were as striking as one from a "Georgetta," of Rockville, Indiana, which arrived on the battleship *Wisconsin* and was reported on in the Washington *Times:* "I couldn't understand why my husband was doing drugs and did not want to go home all the time. I thought I could solve it by throwing gas and a match on him. He didn't die, but he has to live the rest of his life with the scars. . . . That is how I know that Jesus is real."

Elisabeth Hickey, who wrote the report on this remarkable pen pal, concluded her article with this line: "The sailors now believe this is proof that one should not answer letters from women with inmate numbers on their return address."

area denial weapon. A cluster bomb that creates great damage in a confined area, thus denying its use to the enemy.

artichoke suit. The brown and green "woodland" B.D.U. (work and combat uniform).

arty. Artillery. See also DIVARTY.

ashtray. The desert; because ashtrays in hotels and military institutions are filled with sand.

A.T. Antitank (i.e., any antitank weapon).

attrit. To reduce the number of troops in a military force, as a result of hostilities or by any other means. The term derives from the noun "attrition."

The verb was first noted by a 1961 issue of *American Speech*, after being spotted in an Air Force publication. It was used during the Vietnam War, as in this line from an unnamed American official, quoted in *Time* of August 28, 1972: "If we can attrit the population base of the Viet Cong, it will accelerate the process of degrading the VC." In televised briefings attendant to this war, Lieutenant General Thomas Kelly, operations director for the Joint Chiefs of Staff, used the word often.

The very sound of the verb was enough to touch off editorial comment, such as this by Charles E. Claffey in the Boston *Globe* for January 29, 1991: "To the purist, attrit registers as discordantly as a Spike Jones recording. Nonetheless, its increasing usage in war-related news stories in the print media and on television and radio broadcasts is lending it semantic legitimacy. Language is nothing if not accommodating."

★ ☆ **B** ☆ ★

BACK drill. A mnemonic device for reminding potential P.O.W.'s of the four "don'ts" of capitivity: "B" is for "bowing" (don't do it in public); "A" is for "air" (no on-air broadcasts); "C" is for "crimes" (never admit to any); and "K" is for "kiss" (don't kiss your captors good-bye).

Baghdad Betty. An "Iraqi female disc jockey who became a favorite among the troops" (according to E. M. Flanagan, Jr., writing in the November 1991 *Army* magazine).

Baghdad boil. Leishmaniasis (a skin disease transmitted by sandflies).

Baghdad Buffoon. Saddam Hussein.

bandit. An enemy aircraft.

bang out. To eject oneself from an aircraft.

battle winner. See DEADLY DOZEN.

B.C.D. Bad conduct discharge (facetiously renamed "big chicken dinner").

B.C.D.'s. Birth-control devices; a facetious name for military-issue spectacles, which were deemed so ugly as to discourage potential mates. They were also known as "B.C.G.'s" (birth-control glasses).

B.D.A. Bomb damage assessment.

B.D.U.'s. Battle dress utility (or "battle dress uniform"). This is a soldier's war and work clothes; they were formerly known as fatigues.

beach. The desert; fighting terrain (i.e., the BOONDOCKS; see under the Spanish-American War era).

Beagle. The F-15E jet fighter.

Bear, the. General H. Norman Schwarz-kopf (the U.S. commander); is also known as "Stormin' Norman."

Bedrock. A gigantic U.S. tent city in Saudi Arabia; from the name of cartoon character Fred Flintstone's home town. The mess tent was known as "Dino's Diner"; from Dino, the Flintstones' pet dinosaur.

big blue 82. The BLU-82 (a 12,540-pound bomb that created tremendous blast overpressure); also called "daisy cutter."

big chicken dinner. See B.C.D.

big red. The brutal desert sun (as in, "Me and big red don't get along real well").

Big Six in the Sky. God. See SIX.

bimp. A Soviet-made infantry fighting vehicle; from its official designation, "B.M.P."

black hole, the. The complex of underground rooms under Saudi air force headquarters in Riyadh where allied personnel analyzed and selected targets.

blooper. A 40-mm grenade launcher; the soldier detailed to fire it. The term

derives from the distinctive sound that the weapon makes when fired.

blowboat. A hovercraft (e.g., the LACV-30 [large air-cushion vehicle]).

blower. An afterburner in a jet engine.

blue on blue. Fire accidentally directed at troops on one's own side. The term stems from NATO exercises, where the opposing forces were "blue" and "red." It is another term for FRIENDLY FIRE.

B.M.O. Black moving object (i.e., a black-robed Saudi woman with her face veiled by the traditional black *abeyah*).

B.M.P. See **bimp.**

B/N. A bomber/navigator (i.e., the person who sits next to or behind the pilot in a two-seater aircraft).

Bob. (1) A Bedouin; an Iraqi. (2) Saudi (an adjective, as in, "Bob car, Bob clothes and the like," according to *Army* magazine).

boghammers. Small gunboat.

bogus. The reality of the war zone (as in, "This place is bogus"). Perhaps the term represents a modern incarnation of the assertion, "War is hell."

bolo badge. A Purple Heart (the medal awarded to soldiers wounded in combat). The term was most likely to be applied when the wound was, in the words used in a *New York Times* dispatch, "foolishly acquired." See also BOLO, under the Vietnam War.

boloed. Destroyed; killed.

bone dome. A Kevlar helmet. This high-tech helmet became standard equipment during this conflict.

boogie out of Dodge. To move out of a dangerous position. This quote from a Marine captain appeared in the Boston *Globe*: "We move in quick, hit hard and then boogie out of Dodge. By the time he hits back, we ain't there." See also GET THE HELL OUT OF DODGE, under the Vietnam War.

boot-top—level morale. The low morale of the Iraqis awaiting battle in their desert bunkers.

bouncing betty. A shrapnel-filled mine that pops up a few feet out of the sand and then explodes. An article in the February 9, 1991, Witchita *Eagle* had this comment on the mine: "A Marine officer said they reduced their victims to 'a red mist in the air.'"

The bouncing betty can also be fired from howitzers. It hits the ground, jumps into the air, and explodes at stomach level.

bovine scatology. Bullshit (as rephrased by the U.S. commander, General H. Norman Schwarzkopf).

box out. To exclude; from the defensive maneuver of boxing out in basketball, in which one positions oneself in front of another player when jockeying for position.

BUFF. Big ugly fat fucker (i.e., the B-52 bomber). A number of war glossaries in family newspapers reported that this stood for "big ugly fat fellow." An oft-quoted line on this veteran aircraft was: "The most accurate weapon we have— its bombs always hit the ground." It also prompted this riddle:

Q: What was the last number in Saddam Hussein's bingo game?

A: B-52.

bull. A bull's-eye when bombing a target; see also SHACK.

bullet-stopper. A Marine; a Navy term.

bunkering. Searching Iraqi bunkers for goods and war souvenirs.

★ ☆ C ☆ ★

Cadillac. The M-1 Abrams tank.

camel meat. An unappetizing entree.

camel spider. A tarantula.

camies. Camouflaged clothing.

cank. See C.N.X.

cannon cocker. An artilleryman.

carpet bombing. Intensive bombing of a limited area, usually by B-52's (i.e., laying a wall-to-wall carpet of high explosives). On January 27, 1991, General H. Norman Schwarzkopf denied knowledge of this term ("I don't know what it means," he said), because it connoted indiscriminate bombing. As William Safire noted in his language column in *The New York Times Magazine* for February

3, 1991: "Reporters like the term carpet bombing, a dysphemism for 'bombing in a close pattern to destroy a large area rather than specific targets.' (A *dysphemism*, obviously, is the opposite of a euphemism.)"

The term can be traced back to the end of World War II, when it referred to saturation bombing used to clear the area for advancing ground troops. In the Vietnam War, it was called "rolling thunder."

cell. A group of bombers, usually consisting of three planes.

check six. Looking directly behind to make sure an enemy aircraft is not following; a reference to the "o'clock" system that pilots use to indicate direction. Twelve o'clock is directly in front, and six o'clock is directly behind.

cheese. To curry favor with a superior.

cheese dick. A person who curries favor with superiors; also called a "cheeser."

chem lights. Six-inch-long plastic tubes that glow in the dark by means of a chemical reaction.

chocolate chips / chocolate chip cookie / chocolate chip suit. A desert camouflage uniform; from the randomly distributed chocolaty brown spots on a tan background, giving the uniform a strong resemblance to baked cookies from home.

chu-hoi. Enemy troops who surrender. The term is defined in New York *Newsday* for March 7, 1991: "In the gulf con-flict, GIs have used this phrase frequently in regard to the thousands of Iraqi soldiers who have surrendered in Kuwait and Iraq. It's Vietnamese for 'surrender' and was picked up by U.S. troops during that war."

C.I.B. Combat Infantryman's Badge. The blue medal is given to Army infantrymen who come under fire. It is much prized; as Harry Levins noted in the St. Louis *Post-Dispatch* of January 27, 1991: "non-infantrymen tend to sulk because the rules exclude them from getting one." See also under the Vietnam War.

CINC [pronounced "sink"]. Commander in chief.

CINCENT [pronounced "sink-ent"]. Commander in Chief Central Command. This term was used by the troops to refer to General H. Norman Schwarzkopf.

C.N.N. complex. A condition resulting from watching too much of the twenty-four-hour war coverage. The term was created by a psychologist, who applied it to families with loved ones in the gulf. It comes from the initialism for the Cable News Network, which provided much of the war coverage for Americans and many others worldwide.

C.N.X. Cancel (in military code). Troops pronounced the term "cank"; there was much talk of the war being "canked."

coaxe. Coaxial (i.e., a secondary weapon configured to fire along with a main weapon). The coaxial is usually a machine gun matched with a larger-caliber gun.

"Cold, cold, smoked the bitch." A pilot's report on shooting down an Iraqi airplane.

collateral damage. Civilian casualties (in euphemistic Pentagonese). This term had been in use for many years in discussions of nuclear war, but it came into its own during the daily press briefings in Riyadh, Saudi Arabia, to describe the effects of the allied air war against Iraq.

The term is included in an article by R. W. Apple, Jr., in *The New York Times* of February 4, 1991:

> There are obvious cultural differences ... between the highly disciplined military men, with their odd words and phrases like "attrit" for "wear down" and "collateral damage" for "civilian casualties," and the reporters, who make their living by questioning authority and doubting official pronouncements. To them, Pentagonese is a laughable language.

crank. To start; to get going. The term applies to both machines and humans.

crash-bang. A stun grenade (especially the kind that temporarily blinds as well as incapacitates); also known as a "flash-bang."

C-rat. A field ration (even though the C-ration had been replaced by the M.R.E.). A Marine told a reporter from the Boston *Globe*: "Rock 'n' roll is C-rats for the soul."

crease. To wound (as in, "We just creased him, and all it did was make him mad").

cuff 'em and stuff 'em. A policy of quickly detaining and transporting non-combatants who might get in the way of military operations. Speaking of an area adjoining the Kuwaiti border, a military policeman told a reporter for the Washington *Post*: "No one gets in, not even Bedouins looking for their sheep. If they give us trouble we cuff 'em and stuff 'em."

cultural bonding officer. An officer whose job it was to prevent soldiers from offending their Saudi hosts. Here are two descriptions of this job: "a military Miss Manners" and "a doctor of civil graces assigned to prevent outbreaks of the disease Uglius Americanus among U.S. personnel in the Gulf."

★ ☆ **D** ☆ ★

daisy cutter. See BIG BLUE 82.

dampen down. To slow; to minimize (as in, "dampening down of expectations," often heard in briefings). The term derives from firefighting, where it refers to the process of wetting (dampening) material so that it does not catch fire.

dance of the whales. The maneuvering of oil tankers in the gulf as they line up to form a convoy.

deadly dozen. The Multi-Launched Rocket System (a conventional weapon capable of tearing up an area the size of a dozen football fields). In the Washington *Times* of February 7, 1991, it was called "the most powerful conventional artillery weapon in the world. A single shot from its firing system can destroy city blocks." The weapon was also known as the "battle winner," "grid buster," and "grid square removal service."

Dear John letter. A letter from one's wife or sweetheart informing one that the relationship is over. See also under World War II.

Death Row / Death Row Highway. A long, narrow road south of the Iraqi border from which allied troops staged their invasion and their eventual march into Kuwait. A large number of Iraqis were killed and equipment destroyed in allied air attacks prior to the invasion. The road was also known as "Suicide Road" and M.S.R. DODGE.

decapitating attack. An attack on enemy commanders behind the lines. This leapfrogs the masses of enemy tanks, artillery, and fortified positions that make traditional warfare slow and costly.

deconflict. To ensure that attacking aircraft don't interfere (or conflict) with one another.

degrade. To run down; to pulverize. The term is usually applied to a target.

desert cherry. A new soldier; from the general use of the term "cherry" for a virgin.

Desert Express. A military special-delivery system for parts. The name is based on the assertion that this was "the Federal Express of the Military Airlift Command."

Desert Shield. See OPERATION DESERT SHIELD. The term was also used playfully,

as defined in *Army* magazine: "Anything that protects a soldier from the blowing sand."

Desert Shield bar. A heat-resistant chocolate bar produced by Hershey Foods.

dinkie. A military version of a two-seater dune buggie; also known as an "F.A.V." (Fast Attack Vehicle).

Dino's Diner. See BEDROCK.

D.I.P. Die in place. According to Captain Joseph M. Michael, it means to "defend this position no matter what the cost."

divarty. Division artillery.

Diver. Charles Jaco, a Cable News Network reporter (because of his dives off camera during SCUD missile alerts).

dogs. Feet. One soldier who served in the gulf advised, "Don't do them right and they'll bark at you."

dog someone out. To criticize; to chide.

Dolly Parton. The "Assad Babyle" Iraqi tank (a version of the Soviet T-72 tank); named in honor of the buxom country singer because of its rounded reinforced turret. It was also known as "super Dolly Parton."

do-mode. The condition of being busy or working on solutions; from the modern military proclivity to describe equipment according to its mode of operation.

do-rag. A bandanna or scarf worn over the head and tied at the back, in lieu of regulation headgear.

Double Ugly. The F-4G fighter; also known as "Rhino" and the "Wild Weasel." The aircraft's main mission is to take electronic-warfare countermeasures to blind enemy radar.

down under. A homemade beer created by Australian troops in the gulf; from the nickname for Australia, "Down Under."

dozens, the. A game in which insults are traded, often between troops of different races and ethnic backgrounds. A Washington *Post* article of May 19, 1991, on troops returned from the gulf contained this demonstration of the dozens: "And so 'the dozens' usually begins, with the men of this racially mixed Army platoon blowing off steam and laughing as they lob verbal grenades at each other: redneck, bubba, chink, half-breed, Klan-tucky, grape-ape, or Jheri-Curl-wearin'-Kentucky-Fried-Chicken-eatin' . . . ."

driver. (1) A pilot. (2) A Navy officer who serves as officer of the deck.

dumb bomb. A conventional bomb (i.e., a bomb whose trajectory depends only on gravity). The term was created to distinguish such a bomb from a laser-guided SMART BOMB.

dune goon. An Iraqi soldier fighting in the desert.

★ ☆ E ☆ ★

Eagle. The F-15A, F-15B, F-15C, and F-15D fighters, but not the F-15E, which is known as the "Beagle."

echelons beyond reality. Higher command (the source of orders and directives). The term suggests that higher command was out of touch with reality.

E.C.U. Environmental control unit (i.e., a tent); an Air Force term. This was one of those terms that seemed truly preposterous to outsiders covering the war. "A tent?" asked the Boston *Globe* in a report of January 30, 1991. "No, the Air Force will say, sneering at the plebeian sound of the word. Their alternative, on display in the Arabian desert, is called the 'environmental control unit.' Honest."

In fact, the desert-tan tents came equipped with heat pumps to create air-conditioning in the summer and heat in the winter.

eight-charge. Eighty pounds of black powder trussed in a canvas satchel. This antiarmor howitzer package was used by the Marines.

Electric Jet. The F-16 fighter-bomber; also called the "Fighting Falcon," "Lawn Dart," and "Viper."

el-tee / L-T. Lieutenant; a term of address often used with a hint of the sardonic.

Emerald City. King Khalid Military City, Saudi Arabia; from the Emerald City of Oz in L. Frank Baum's novels for children.

entrenching tool. A shovel. It was often described mockingly in full Pentagonese by the troops: "Tool, entrenching, one each."

E.P.W. Enemy prisoner of war. During the gulf crisis more than one commentator noted that this term was reserved for Iraqi prisoners, while allied prisoners were still known as P.O.W.'s. Eric Schmitt of *The New York Times*, in a report from Riyadh of February 18, 1991, wrote that "E.P.W." was "a term that replaced P.O.W. in the Pentagon lexicon after the Vietnam War to avoid the association with American service members still listed as missing in Southeast Asia."

Escan Village. Quarters for troops stationed in Riyadh. The village was a compound of town houses and high-rises originally built for Bedouins, who refused to live there, preferring the desert. Though the living quarters were bright stucco buildings with marble floors and modern conveniences, soldiers began using the term "Escan Village" ironically, for that which could never be a paradise, despite the amenities.

extract. To recover or pick up (as when a helicopter "extracts" a special operations unit from the desert).

★ ☆ **F** ☆ ★

face-shot. An air-to-air missile fired at an enemy aircraft; also known as "in the lips."

F.A.E. Fuel-air explosive. This terror weapon covers a large area with a combustible liquid and then ignites it; it is a 1990s version of the napalm bomb used in Vietnam. Iraq was believed to have F.A.E.'s, but none were ever employed, although a U.S. version was used, ostensibly to clear minefields. It was seen as an especially horrible weapon in the hands of Iraq, acquiring the moniker "the poor man's nuclear weapon." Here is how it was described in *The New York Times* of January 24, 1991: "Saddam Hussein might be planning to use a . . . horrific weapon, never before employed in combat, known as the fuel air bomb, which spreads a circle of fire."

fangs out. Excited; about to make a kill. The allusion is to a serpent.

fast mover. (1) A high-performance jet aircraft. (2) The M-1 Abrams tank. (3) The Bradley Fighting Vehicle.

F.A.V. Fast Attack Vehicle. See DINKIE.

F.B.W. Fly by wire (i.e., flying by instruments).

feet dry. Describing an aircraft crossing from sea to land; radio code.

feet wet. Describing an aircraft crossing from land to sea; radio code.

Fido. A pet scorpion.

field expedient. Doing what's necessary to get the job done. Captain Joseph W. Michael defined the term: "Generally creating something or performing some task in some non-typical and innovative manner."

Fighting Falcon. The F-16 fighter-bomber; also called the "Electric Jet," "Lawn Dart," and "Viper."

fitter. The Soviet-built SU-22 fighter plane. Like most other NATO weapons nicknames, this one has nothing to do with the characteristics of the weapon.

fizzog. One's face (as in, "Clean your fizzog"). This British military slang was picked up by Americans. It derives from "physiognomy" (the outward appearance of one's face).

flash-bang. See CRASH-BANG.

FLIR. Front-looking infrared. This is a system that fits on the nose of some airplanes and presents a TV-like image to pilots.

flyby. A missile that misses its mark (e.g., a SCUD that falls harmlessly into the Persian Gulf).

force package. A military aircraft armed with a combination of missiles and bombs that represents a significant degree of force, in the language of the Department of Defense. Derided by those who felt it made a lethal weapon sound like a laxative.

for the duration. The period of a soldier's stay in the gulf during the conflict. It replaced DEROS (see under the Vietnam War). As explained in *Newsweek*: "Since the troops are not being rotated, as in Vietnam, there is no DEROS." The phrase was first used during World War I.

fox. A missile fired by an aircraft. "Fox one" means that the first missile fired hit its target; "fox two" means that the second missile fired hit its target; and so forth.

foxtrot. Fuck; fucking; etc. This stand-in for the obscenity is alphabet code for the letter "F."

foxtrot bravo. Fucking bastard; from alphabet code for "F.B."

fratricide. The accidental shooting down of a friendly aircraft. Of course, "fratricide" in standard English is the act of killing. See also MORT THEMSELVES OUT.

freelance. To go out independently in a rented vehicle in hopes of getting interviews and seeing action. The term was applied to journalists unable to get into the official pools created by the Pentagon.

friendly fire. Fire accidentally directed at troops on one's own side. In this war, thirty-nine deaths and seventy-two injuries were attributed to such incidents, proving the adage, "Friendly fire isn't." See also under the Vietnam War.

frog. Free rocket over ground (an Iraqi weapon). A "frog site" was a point from which the Iraqis would launch such a missile.

frogfoot. An Iraqi attack airplane (officially known by its Soviet designation, SU-25). The plane is similar to an American plane, the A-10 Thunderbolt. At the beginning of the conflict, Iraq had about sixty of the aircraft. The term "frogfoot" was originally a NATO designation and had no relationship to the characteristics of the plane.

furball. The frenzy of air combat; a dog-fight.

★ ☆ G ☆ ★

G-day. The day the allies' ground offensive began.

get your gut right. To eat.

ghost rider. A pilot who flew an F-117A Stealth aircraft by night and slept by day.

giant viper. A long explosives-filled hose that explodes mines as it snakes across a mined area.

goat rope. A confused situation (as one would experience trying to rope goats).

go chemical. To be subjected to a chemical attack. The possibility was feared for a number of reasons, including the fact that SCUD missiles could deliver chemical weapons.

golden B.B. / golden bullet. The Soviet antiaircraft doctrine of putting enough ordnance in the air to virtually guarantee some hits. In the gulf conflict the term was used derisively, to characterize the Iraqis' emulation of Soviet anti-aircraft defenses. See also under the Vietnam War.

go MOPP. See MOPP.

gone Elvis. Lost; missing in action. The reference to Elvis Presley derives from the highly publicized and continued "sightings" of Elvis after his death.

go 911. To panic or become terrified; from the 911 emergency telephone number.

GOO. Gulf of Oman (as in, "sailing through the GOO").

good grab. Any delectable native Bedouin food.

good to go. Fit; competent; ready to perform. As reported in a January 31, 1991, article in the Washington Times, "Grunt Slang," by Elisabeth Hickey and Michael Hedges: "Journalists who had spent one too many seasons straddling a chair and punctuating their work with doughnuts and then arrived here wanting to go to the front were considered not 'good to go' by the military."

goofy goggles. Night vision goggles (because they made the wearer look so odd).

gorilla cookie. A cake packed in the M.R.E. field ration.

go sludding. To suffer the effects of chemical warfare. The acronym "slud" stands for "salivates, lachrymates, urinates, defecates."

grease. (1) Food. (2) To kill (as during the Vietnam War). In the gulf, the term was used mostly in the sense of being killed (as in, "Anything you do can get you greased, including doing nothing").

grid square removal service. See DEADLY DOZEN.

ground pounder. An infantryman.

grunt. An infantryman. Harry Levins, in the St. Louis *Post-Dispatch* of January 27, 1991, had this to say about the use of this term in the gulf: "'Grunt' dates from Vietnam; until the desert deployment, it was being shouldered aside by 'mud soldier.' But the desert has little mud."

Not everyone in the gulf earned the title. Just back from the gulf, Captain Joseph W. Michael wrote down these definitions for "grunt":

> Army: combat arms—tankers, artillerymen, and infantry.
> Marine Corps: virtually all.
> The term pertains to the highly developed vocabulary skills of soldiers and Marines, who endure more hardship for less benefit than anyone.

See also under the Vietnam War.

guest. An Iraqi prisoner brought into Saudi Arabia (because they were to be treated as guests of the Saudi government). According to the February 2, 1991, Albuquerque *Tribune*: "For religious and political reasons, the Saudi government does not want to offend other Moslems by treating the Iraqis as prisoners and causing them to lose face."

gulfspeak. Euphemistic language used by officials giving briefings.

gut ripper. An antipersonnel mine or grenade (used by either side) that pops up and explodes at stomach level. Such weapons have been called the "scourge of the infantryman." A U.S. version of a gut ripper is the BOUNCING BETTY.

★ ☆ **H** ☆ ★

hail mary. The secret movement of more than two U.S. corps into western Saudi Arabia to deliver a flanking hammer blow against the Iraqi army. It was successfully executed, with the simultaneous advance of allied troops into Kuwait.

The term derives from the name of a football play and was used by American commander General H. Norman Schwarzkopf as a code phrase. In football, the hail mary is a play in which the quarterback sends all his receivers toward the end zone and throws the ball in their direction, hoping that one of them will catch it and score. In football, it is a desperation play. Oddly, the use of this football term was inappropriate, because Schwarzkopf's strategy was carefully based on a position of strength while the hail mary play in football is an act born of desperation near the end of a game by a team that is behind.

hair on fire. Excited.

hard target. A building or a military installation. A "soft target" is a human being.

hasty. A shallow, quickly dug foxhole; also known as a "run and dive."

hawk. The cold experienced in northern Saudi Arabia in the winter of 1991. One dispatch defined it as "a piercing chill that cuts through the flesh to the bone with a talon-like grip." Paratroopers have long used this term for cold weather, as in Harold Coyle's *Sword*

Point (1988): "As if on cue, the ramp behind Evans began to open, letting in the cold night air, known to paratroopers as 'the Hawk.'"

headache. A journalist.

headquarters pukes. Support staff in noncombat areas.

heat tab. The hot desert sun; more commonly known as "nature's heat tab." The term derives from the heat tablet used to warm beverages.

heavy metal. Heavy artillery; naval guns; etc. The term derives from a form of rock 'n' roll popular among the soldiers in the gulf.

hellacious. Extremely violent. The term was used to describe the occupation of Kuwait and various other combat situations during the war. This civilian slang imported to the gulf by American troops infatuated the British press, as can be seen in this headline: "Marines Die in 'Hellacious' Land Battle."

high speed, low drag. An all-purpose expression of approbation. According to *Time* of February 25, 1991, this was a phrase "indicating that an operation went exactly according to plan." The Washington *Post* of February 9, 1991, defined the phrase: "Paratroopers' term for something impressive." Captain Joseph W. Michael gives the phrase this nononsense definition: "Fast, sexy, and/or real good."

him. Saddam Hussein.

hip shooting. The movement of artillery from position to position, firing at each stop. The term for this U.S. offensive tactic derives from the method of quickly firing a pistol. The practice is also known as "shoot and scoot."

hog. The A-10 aircraft; from WARTHOG.

home plate. The airfield where a flight originated and to which it will return. The term derives from baseball—a batter begins at home plate and scores a run by returning there after a trip around the bases.

Homer. A member of the Iraqi armed forces (either an enlisted man or an officer); apparently, an allusion to the bumbling television cartoon character Homer Simpson.

homes. A friend; from "homeboy." The plural is "homies."

hoo-ah / ooh rah / urah / yeehah. An all-purpose expression of enthusiasm for almost any situation in which the speaker is alive and well. For instance, it was almost invariably used to greet mail call. It was termed "the signature call of the American forces" by the Houston *Post.* The expression was used to great effect by Al Pacino in the 1992 film *The Scent of a Woman.*

hooch. A tent. This usage dates from the Vietnam War.

hoo-yah. The war; combat.

hot turn. See QUICK-TURN BURN.

human remains pouch. A BODY BAG (see under the Vietnam War).

The term was upsetting to some, including Oregon senator Mark O. Hatfield, who felt that the Pentagon was trying to put the war into a tidy little linguistic package. His reaction to the term was quoted in the Boston *Globe* of January 24, 1991: "That ['body bag'] is too messy. That conjures up all the wrong images, of blood and pain and suffering. Now body bags are called human remains pouches. There, America, does that make you feel any better?"

human shield. A hostage taken to a military site to dissuade attacks. This was done by the besieged Iraqi government early in the air war, and it became the main source of American outrage.

humma. Et cetera; whatever.

Hummer. The Hawkeye early-warning aircraft.

humvee / hummer. High-mobility multi-purpose wheeled vehicle (H.M.M.W.V.). The vehicle was the successor to the jeep and the most common military vehicle in the gulf. It was diesel powered and was bigger and faster than the jeep. Don Kirkman, of Scripps-Howard News Service, wrote about the vehicle: "President Bush's Thanksgiving dinner was served on the hood of a Hummer. Bob Hope and his troupe of entertainers bounced from base to base in Hummers. The humble Hummer seems to be in the background of every news clip about troops in the field." Less commonly used as a nickname for the Navy's Hawkeye early-warning aircraft.

hunker down. To cower and dig in (i.e., what the Iraqi army did during the allied bombing); a term of derision. The term made its own news when CBS reporter Bob McKeown reported from Kuwait City during its liberation that he and a band of Marines were hunkered down near the U.S. embassy. Anchor Dan Rather, reporting from Saudi Arabia, jumped in with this line: "I smile when I say U.S. Marines do not 'hunker down.' They may be holding the embassy, but not hunkered down."

★ ☆ **I** ☆ ★

I'll make it happen. An expression of determination to carry out orders. It was a standard response by enlisted troops to their officers and was equivalent to "can do." See also NOT A PROBLEM.

Imminent Thunder. A major amphibious landing exercise staged in Saudi Arabia in November 1990.

incontinent ordnance. Bombs and artillery fire that miss their targets, endangering civilians.

insert. To drop off (as when helicopters hover near the ground and insert special operations units in their desired positions).

intel puke. A member of military intelligence, especially one working far from the front.

in the lips. See FACE-SHOT.

I-rackies. American soldiers' preferred way of identifying those from the nation their British counterparts call "Eer-awk." By the same token, U.S. troops in the gulf talked of Patriot missiles as "Pate-riut missels" while the same two words from a British soldier came out as "Pat-riut miss-aisles."

★ ☆ **J** ☆ ★

janitor. An infantryman; used self-deprecatingly. According to the authors of *The Official Lite History (and Cook-book) of the Gulf War* (1991), the term is "based on the idea that 'police call' is the only infantry skill that can be translated to an equivalent civilian career." A "po-lice call" is an order to clean up, or po-lice, an area.

jarhead. A Marine.

Jedi Knights. A group of young majors who worked on the "fine print" of the combat operations in the gulf. The name was given to them by U.S. commander General H. Norman Schwarzkopf. They were part of a planning hierarchy that also included the WARLORDS. The name derives from the Jedi Knights, who were the elite fighters in George Lukas's *Star Wars* trilogy.

jeep on steroids. The bulky HUMVEE.

JIB. Joint Information Bureau. JIBs were established in major hotels in Saudi cit-ies to give briefings to the press and pro-vide other information.

jib rat / jiblet. A reporter who watched the war on television, from a hotel room;

used almost exclusively to denote those sitting out the war at the Dhahran Inter-national Hotel's JIB.

jihad. A Muslim holy war. The term, often associated with terrorism, was used during the Iraqi invasion of Kuwait.

Joe. A soldier; a contraction of G.I. JOE (see under World War II).

Johnny Weissmuller shower. A shower so cold that it induces a Tarzan-like yell (Weissmuller was one of several actors who played Tarzan in the movies).

J-STARS. Joint surveillance target at-tack radar system (a battlefield recon-naissance aircraft).

juke. To move quickly (e.g., in order to evade enemy fire).

★ ☆ **K** ☆ ★

K-day. January 16, 1991, the day the al-lies began the offensive aimed at the lib-eration of Kuwait.

Kevlar. A K-POT; from the name of the high-tech synthetic fabric of which it is made.

kick butt. To attack with overwhelming power. It was the preferred term of the high command when discussing things like 1,400 sorties a day against Iraq. President George Bush euphemized it further to "kicking a little you-know-what."

kill. To destroy; to put out of action. The term was applied to aircraft, equipment, and weapons (rather than to human beings). As a *Stars and Stripes* reporter put it to a reporter from *The Guardian*: "The gun lobby in the United States is fond of saying that people are not killed by guns but by other people; here, people get to kill guns."

kill box. A rectangle on an aircraft radar screen in which a target is seen blowing up.

killer bee. An attack aircraft; from the name of a species of Africanized bee much discussed in the U.S. at the time of the Gulf War.

killing box. One of the areas into which a target area is divided for the purpose of destroying enemy equipment, vehicles, and buildings.

kill sack. An area of Iraqi obstacles to an allied ground offensive. Kill sacks were described in the Baltimore Sun of January 24, 1991: "Minefields and oil-filled trenches beyond the Saudi-Kuwait border through which U.S. troops would have to move if a ground war begins."

klick. A kilometer.

K-mart. Kuwait.

K-mart parking lot. The tanker anchorage off the port of Khor Fakkan, Kuwait.

K-pot. A Kevlar helmet: a parallel term to STEEL POT (see under the Vietnam War). The K-pot replaced the steel pot as the standard Army helmet.

K.S.A. Kingdom of Saudi Arabia.

K.T.O. Kuwaiti theater of operations.

K.Z. Killing zone (an area where fire can be concentrated to inflict heavy damage on the enemy).

★ ☆ **L** ☆ ★

LANTIRN. Low-altitude navigation and targeting infrared night.

lanyard puller. An artilleryman; a reference to the time when cannons were fired by pulling a lanyard.

larse. Long-range surveillance; a replacement for LURPS (see under the Vietnam War).

lase. To lock a laser beam onto a target.

Lawn Dart. The F-16 fighter-bomber; also called the "Electric Jet," "Fighting Falcon," and "Viper."

L.C. A line crosser (i.e., an enemy soldier who defects).

leather personnel carriers. Boots; mock-Pentagonese. In tune with the Pentagon's penchant for three-letter acronyms, they were often called "L.P.C.'s."

leg. See STRAIGHT-LEG.

leg infantry. The marching infantry, which walks into battle (in contrast to the mechanized infantry, or MECH).

LES. Leave and earnings statement. The LES is an accounting given to each reservist called to active duty; it tells the reservist exactly how much he or she will be paid in base pay and allowances. It was often noted that one's LES showed how much less money one would make in uniform than in civilian life.

lifer juice. Coffee (because it is the favorite beverage of lifers—those who stay in the military until they retire).

life-support area. A military base. This absurd example of Pentagonese was not used by the troops.

lima delta. Line of departure (i.e., the jumping-off point for an attack); alphabet code.

Little Hollywood. An area near the swimming pool at the rear of the Dhahran International Hotel. Television correspondents from four American networks (ABC, CBS, CNN, and NBC) delivered their live reports there. John Kifner of *The New York Times* alluded to the Hollywood aspect of this in his February 9, 1991, article, "War Notebook": "Sometimes the on-camera correspondents wear helmets, flak jackets and goggles, or even chemical suits, while the producer and crew wear T-shirts."

The blue domes visible in the background during reports from Little Hollywood looked otherworldly on television, but they were nothing more than cabanas and storage areas.

lost-and-found badge. An Army name tag; a Marine term.

love boat. A naval vessel on which a significant number of the female sailors become pregnant. The term was specifically applied to the *Acadia*, because thirty-six pregnant crew members had to be transferred out of the war zone. More than half of them became pregnant after the ship got under way for the gulf. The term alludes to a television program, *The Love Boat*, which centered around shipboard romances.

love Scud. The penis (seen as a missile).

L.P.C.'s. Boots. See LEATHER PERSONNEL CARRIERS.

L-T. See EL-TEE.

★ ☆ **M** ☆ ★

make the rubble bounce. To bomb a city heavily; the phrase originated with British forces.

Meal Refusing to Exit / Meal Rejected by Ethiopians / Meal Rejected in Ethiopia. See M.R.E.

meat fleet. A hospital ship or ships.

mech. Mechanized. The mechanized infantry rides into battle (in contrast to the LEG INFANTRY, which walks).

media puke. A journalist.

mick. A minute (as in, "Give me five micks"). The term made a euphonious pairing with "klick" (a kilometer).

military orphans bill. Any of several pieces of proposed legislation to allow military couples with children to ask that one parent be kept out of a war zone.

Despite the name, the bills were meant to prevent orphaning, rather than to provide for military orphans.

minder. A member of the armed forces assigned to help journalists and keep tabs on them.

MOPP. Mission-oriented protective posture (i.e., being dressed in chemical-weapons protective gear, including a gas mask). According to a November 1991 article in *Army:* "To 'go MOPP' is to go to one of the four stages of MOPP. MOPP 4 is full anti-nuclear-biological-chemical gear: rubber gloves and boots, charcoal-lined pants and jacket and the ever-present gas mask."

morality police. Muslims who keep other Muslims in line spiritually by stoning or beating them; a play on "military police."

MORE. Meal, Organizational Ready-to-Eat; a supplement to the M.R.E.

mort themselves out. To fire at each other accidentally (said of friendly aircraft). Damaging or shooting down a friendly plane is FRATRICIDE.

M.O.S. Military occupational specialty (i.e., a soldier's job description).

mother of all battles, the. The ground war to come (according to Saddam Hussein). This "mother of all clichés" became "the first great catch phrase of the 90s," in the words of the Associated Press. It created what *Newsweek* termed "a virtual ocean of bad puns and dopey wordplay." Secretary of Defense Dick Cheney noted that the war had produced "the mother of all retreats," which others termed "the mother of all routs." The Boston *Globe* preferred "the mother-in-law of all battles," and observed that Saddam Hussein had painted himself into "the mother of all corners." Johnny Carson opened with "the mother of all monologues." The Seton Hall basketball team's first Big East championship was "the mother of all victories." When Queen Elizabeth was bitten by one of her pet corgis, it was because she "attempted to interfere with the mother of all dog battles." On February 27, 1991, U.S. commander General H. Norman Schwarzkopf gave "the mother of all briefings," a key press briefing summarizing the results of the war. In March 1991, President George Bush hailed his wife, Barbara, as "the mother of all Bushes."

The original "mother of all battles" was the great Arab victory over the Sassanian Persians in 636 A.D. The Arabic word for "mother" (*umm*) can also mean "ultimate" or "chief."

M.R.E. Meal Ready to Eat. This successor to the C-ration was the standard American field ration of the war. Many of those forced to subsist on the M.R.E. claimed that there were three lies in the name. Columnist Jack Anderson said that M.R.E.'s "have a shelf life of five years and flavor to match."

One popular reinterpretation of "M.R.E." was "Meal Refusing to Exit," reflecting a belief held by many medics and troops in the gulf that the plastic-packed field ration caused constipation. A February 1991 report in the Washington *Times* by Elisabeth Hickey and Michael Hedges contained this comment: "They believe the pouches filled with processed food—guaranteed to last long after every veteran of the Persian Gulf campaign has departed the earth—are filled with chemicals that prevent a bowel movement more than once a week."

Another widely heard translation of "M.R.E." was "Meal Rejected by Ethiopians" (or "Meal Rejected in Ethiopia"), alluding to the extended period of famine in Ethiopia.

Ironically, during the summer of 1991 the Pentagon offered to give away surplus M.R.E.'s from the gulf deployment, and one of the few nations that agreed to take the food was Ethiopia.

At Ease: MRE Food Review

A Knight-Ridder report in the Washington Post for January 3, 1991, noted that the most popular M.R.E.'s were chili macaroni and chicken with rice. The least popular was tuna noodle casserole. A later report (February 25), in the Washington Times, listed these as most popular, in descending order of preference:

1. Spaghetti.
2. Beef stew.
3. Chicken stew.
4. Chicken and rice.
5. Ham slice.

The Washington Times report added: "Of the 'accessories' that come with the grub, the best-liked are candy (M&Ms and caramels), cocoa, and Hershey's new non-melt chocolate bar. The least-liked are applesauce, Kool-Aid and dehydrated fruit."

The Manchester Guardian reported that the going trade rate among the allies in the gulf was one French field meal for three M.R.E.'s.

M.S.R. Dodge. Military Supply Route Dodge (the road south of the Iraqi border where allied troops massed for the ground offensive). "Dodge" appears to be a reference to Dodge City, a metaphor for any place where there is military action. See also DEATH ROW.

mud mover. A bomber pilot; a term used by fighter pilots, who often assert that all the bombers do is move the mud around.

mud soldier. See grunt.

Murphy's Laws for Grunts. Mock "laws" demonstrating that, as far as the GRUNT is concerned, life is unfair and nothing will go according to plan. They derived from the original Murphy's Law: "If anything can go wrong, it will." Anonymously created, they were circulated everywhere in the gulf, thanks to copy machines, faxes, and computer modems.

Similar laws were created during the Vietnam War—for example, "Body count math is 2 VC + 1 NVA + 1 water buffalo = 37 KIA."

At Ease: Murphy's Laws from the Gulf

There were many versions of Murphy's Laws for Grunts. Here's a sample collection culled from various sources, including one adapted from a list on a Pentagon bulletin board and published in the Chicago Tribune by David Evans, the paper's military correspondent:

1. Suppressive fire—won't.
2. Friendly fire—isn't.
3. When in doubt empty your magazine.

4. Never forget that your weapon was made by the lowest bidder.

5. If your attack is going really well, it's an ambush.

6. The enemy diversion you are ignoring is the main attack.

7. If the enemy is in range, so are you.

8. Tracers work both ways.

9. If you take more than your fair share of objectives, you will have more than your fair share to take.

10. All five-second grenade fuses will burn down in three seconds.

11. Anything you do can get you shot, including doing nothing.

12. The important things are always simple.

13. The simple things are always hard.

14. The easy way is always mined.

15. Professional soldiers are always predictable, but the world is full of amateurs.

16. Murphy was a grunt.

17. If it's stupid but works, it ain't stupid.

18. Don't look conspicuous—it draws fire.

19. Never share a foxhole with anyone braver than you are.

20. Try to look unimportant—they may be low on ammo.

21. If you are short of everything except enemy, you are in combat.

22. When you have secured an area, don't forget to tell the enemy.

23. Make it too tough for the enemy to get in, and you can't get out.

24. Never draw fire—it irritates those around you.

25. When both sides are convinced they are about to lose, they are both right.

26. Teamwork is essential—it gives them other people to shoot at.

27. Incoming fire has right of way.

28. No inspection-ready unit has ever passed combat.

29. If at first they don't succeed, they will make you try again.

★ ☆ N ☆ ★

nasty boys, the. A nickname adopted by a number of combat units in the gulf. One such unit was described in *USA Today* for January 21, 1991:

> Bravo Company calls itself "The Nasty Boys." "We like to get it done, get it done quickly, with as much viciousness as we can," said Sgt. Rick Gonzales, 24, of San Antonio. Spec. Daryl Smallwood, 21, of Gainesville, Ga., said his platoon is making up death cards to place on Iraqi soldiers they kill. His card: "Personal Debt Paid." "I got 50. But I know I'll need more."

nature's heat tab. The hot desert sun; from the heat tablet used to warm beverages.

nick. To steal. This common British slang became part of the American vocabulary in the gulf.

night cap. Night combat air patrol.

nine-four. A radio sign-off; a chummier version of the traditional "ten-four."

Ninja woman. An Arab woman veiled in black (like a Ninja fighter).

Nintendo effect / Nintendo war. The war as seen in videotapes of exploding buildings, which made bombing seem like a Nintendo video game.

nittenoid. A petty detail; one who is obsessed with petty details.

no clue. Confused; lost (as in, "He has no clue").

no-hope Pope. A reservist. The name for active duty forces was "people with no lives."

N.O.K. Next of kin.

Not a problem. An expression of determination to carry out orders. It contrasts markedly with an expression such as "Sounds like a personal problem to me," of the Vietnam War era. See also I'LL MAKE IT HAPPEN.

nuclear coffee. A drink prepared by taking the instant coffee, cocoa, creamer, and sugar contained in an **M.R.E.** accessory package and mixing them in a canteen half filled with water.

★ ☆ **O** ☆ ★

OBOGS. On-board oxygen-generating system (the air supply in jet airplanes).

oil. To use oil as a weapon (e.g., to dump it into coastal waters to clog water-purification plants or to use it to inhibit an amphibious landing).

one-eighty out. A wrong answer (i.e., that which is 180 degrees from the truth).

ooh rah. See HOO-AH.

Operation Baby Stork / Operation Baby Storm. Nicknames given to the plans for dealing with a very high birth-rate—triple the average—as a consequence of thousands of soldiers returning from Saudi Arabia in April and May 1991 and getting their mates pregnant (or, in the case of female troops, getting pregnant). Both names are a play on OPERATION DESERT STORM.

Operation Cobra. The code name for the thrust by the 101st Airborne Division in which 15,000 U.S. paratroopers landed behind enemy lines in late February 1991. The paratroopers successfully set up a landing zone for 270 helicopters and thus helped cut off the road linking the front to Baghdad.

Operation Cookie Shield. A nickname for the arrival of an excess number of parcels containing baked goods for the troops. They were well fed, but more in need of letters and news from home.

Operation Desert Con. The scams and hoaxes used to take advantage of the concerns of the families of those in the gulf. These ranged from the sale of overpriced "gift packs" to venal schemes by which families were enticed into making expensive 900-number calls for information on their loved ones.

Operation Desert Shield. The code name for the allied military protection of Saudi Arabia after Iraq's invasion of Kuwait. See also DESERT SHIELD.

Operation Desert Storm. The code name for the conflict itself. Months later many were still using it, because the war lacked a commonly agreed-upon name. Among the names that have been used are the Persian Gulf War, the Gulf War, the Gulf Conflict, and the War with Iraq. See also MOTHER OF ALL BATTLES, THE.

During the war, the television networks had their own names for the event. NBC's was "America at War," while it was "Showdown in the Gulf" on CBS and "War in the Gulf" on CNN and ABC.

Operation Welcome Home. The June 10, 1991, victory celebration in New York City. The "National Victory Celebration" had been held in Washington, D.C., on June 8, 1991.

★ ☆ P ☆ ★

patch guy. A highly experienced fighter pilot; from the patches worn to signify awards, special schooling, and flying experience.

Patriot. (1) A missile used to shoot down incoming Iraqi SCUD missiles. (2) Part of the name of a short-lived but much publicized brand of condom: "Patriot Defense Condoms."

Patriot baiter. A television correspondent (especially one working from LITTLE HOLLYWOOD, who seemed to be in line to be hit by a missile, even a friendly Patriot).

Patriot-to-Scud tally. An indication of the relative effectiveness of the **Scud** and the **Patriot.** It was a way of keeping score.

pencil. A reporter without a camera crew (i.e., a print journalist).

penguins. Air Force ground crews (because they are wingless birds).

people with no lives. Active duty forces (as seen by reservists; see NO-HOPE POPE).

pig. The M-60 machine gun. This is the 7.62-mm weapon that Sylvester Stallone used in the *Rambo* movies.

pizza sheik. A Saudi eatery serving pizza; a play on the names of such American fast-food chains as Burger King and Pizza Hut.

pogue. Anyone who arrived in the gulf after you. See also under the Vietnam War, as well as World War II.

PONTI. Person of no tactical importance (i.e., a journalist). See also PONTS.

PONTS. Person of no tactical significance (i.e., a journalist, or anyone else not in uniform). This British acronym was adopted by the Americans, who added it to their list of pejorative terms for journalists, which included "headache" and "media puke."

pool people. The privileged hundred or so reporters (out of the estimated nine hundred covering the war) who were members of combat pools, enabling them to go into the field to interview and photograph the troops. Those not in the pools, according to one dispatch, "stick around the press center, grumble a lot and rewrite reports faxed in from the front," or they might FREELANCE.

The term "pool" is an established name for the process whereby one or more journalists cover an event for others. In the gulf, a pool was a group of sixteen journalists who, escorted by a military officer, were given a brief look at military operations. The system had few supporters among the press. "Shunting reporters around in noncompetitive 'pools' makes the military the assignment editor of the war, deciding what should or should not be covered," wrote A. M. Rosenthal in *The New*

York Times. He added: "End it: let reporters work independently within security realities."

poor man's defense. The air defense tactic of dividing the sky into squares and having gunners shoot into particular squares, in hopes that attacking aircraft will fly into the fire. The tactic was pioneered by the North Vietnamese and emulated by the Iraqis, both of whom lacked the technical sophistication to target specific planes.

pop. To kill.

prayer patrol. Saudi sound trucks that cruise the streets and call the faithful to prayer five times daily.

prick-77. The AN/PRC-77 field radio.

Provide Comfort. The spring 1991 air operation by which relief supplies were dropped to Kurdish refugee camps in northern Iraq.

P.T. Physical training. The Army administers a P.T. test to every soldier every six months.

pucker factor. A measure of fear (i.e., the degree to which a soldier's anal sphincter tightens up). In this war, the term was applied especially to those operating Patriot missile batteries.

purple suiter. A military person assigned to a joint services command; a play on "green suiter" (a soldier) and "blue suiter" (an airman), both derived from the color of the dress uniform.

★ ☆ Q ☆ ★

Q-8. Kuwait.

quick-turn burn. A rapid refueling and rearming of an aircraft between sorties (usually, without turning off the engine); also known as a "hot turn." It was done within five minutes during the days of multiple air strikes.

★ ☆ R ☆ ★

rag-head. An Arab; a racist slur. This long-established American slang was first used to refer to Hindus or others who wear turbans.

Rambo. (1) Anyone who is more brave than smart. Rambo was the name of the Vietnam veteran portrayed by Sylvester Stallone in a series of extremely violent movies, and the name became associated with military excess during this war. A British soldier told a reporter for the *Times of London:* "I don't want to sound like Rambo, but you have to assume this is the last time the British will ever go to war in such force and quite honestly, peacetime soldiering will never be the same."
(2) An infantryman who carries SAWs (squad automatic weapons). As a reporter for the Houston *Chronicle* put it, they "look so theatrically lethal while draped in ammunition belts they usually inherit the monicker."

Rambo rag. A bandanna or head scarf. The cloths were used as protection against dust and sand, but some commanders banned them because they were seen as symbols of bravado. The movie character Rambo often wore a bandanna.

Rambo stuff. The kind of bravado that undermines discipline. It can lead to revenge-driven behavior and the commission of war crimes. During OPERATION DESERT SHIELD there was a concerted drive to contain and control Rambo stuff.

real soldiers. The subject of sayings created to characterize the average male **grunt.** Lists of "real soldiers" lines circulated widely in the gulf. The sayings were a takeoff on the "real men" lines of the mid-1980s (as in the novelty book title *Real Men Don't Eat Quiche*), which yielded macho boasts like, "Real cops got balls that clang when they walk" (from Joseph Wambaugh's *The Delta Star*).

At Ease: Real Soldier Defined

Here is a selection of "real soldiers" lines:

Real soldiers don't wear zip-up boots.

Real soldiers don't use spray shine.

Real soldiers don't lend money; they borrow it.

Real soldiers don't smoke their own cigarettes.

Real soldiers never use proper radio or telephone procedures.

Real soldiers cuss over the FM radio.

Real soldiers never change their skivvies in the field.

Real soldiers never drink alcoholic beverages unless they are alone or with someone.

Real soldiers never fly MAC [the Military Airlift Command].

Real soldiers hate disco.

Real soldiers love country and western.

Real soldiers refuse to be left back on

rear detachment when their unit deploys to the field.

Real soldiers live beyond their means.

Real soldiers have financial problems.

Real soldiers go to happy hour.

Real soldiers call happy hour "happy hour" and not "attitude adjustment hour."

Real soldiers remain at the bar long after happy hour has ended.

Real soldiers rarely change their socks in the field.

Real soldiers do not allow their official duties to interfere with their social life.

Real soldiers never get hungry; they stay hungry.

Real soldiers have no patience with anyone except command sergeants major.

Real soldiers drink ungodly amounts of coffee.

Real soldiers drink their coffee black and disgustingly bitter.

Real soldiers' favorite song is "Take This Job and Shove It."

Real soldiers laugh during *Love Story.*

Real soldiers cry when E.T. lives.

Real soldiers drink "Jumpin' Jack Flash" [eight ounces of Jack Daniels over one ice cube].

Real soldiers are not slaves to fashion.

Real soldiers don't wear three-piece suits.

Real soldiers don't own three-piece suits.

Real soldiers never shine their civilian shoes.

Real soldiers rarely iron their civilian clothes.

Real soldiers don't part their hair in the middle.

---

ree. A meal; short for M.R.E.

repat. A repatriate (i.e., an American or British oil company employee who escaped from Kuwait or Iraq).

repo. To reposition a weapon for a kill.

retrograde movement. A retreat; a euphemism used by higher command.

Rhino. See DOUBLE UGLY.

Rivet Joint. The RC-135 aircraft used to record enemy communications; a military code name.

rock and roll. To put a weapon on full automatic fire.

rocket scientist. An especially competent person. According to Captain Joseph W. Michael, it was used for "anyone capable of doing more than his or her specific job."

rope-a-dope tactics. Surprise tactics; kamikaze tactics.

rotor head. A helicopter pilot.

rototilling. Carpet bombing enemy territory with strategic bombers.

Rudolf Hess. A mess. This is a rare example of traditional British rhyming slang becoming part of American military slang. "Hess" is used for the simple reason that it rhymes with "mess."

rumint. Rumor intelligence; a play on "humint" (human intelligence), used during the Vietnam War.

rumor control / rumor control central. A mythical "official" source of all rumors.

run and dive. A shallow, quickly dug foxhole; also known as a "hasty."

★ ☆ S ☆ ★

S.A. Saudi Arabia.

Saddam. (1) Bullshit. (2) To lie; to exaggerate.

Saddam Happens! Life is unpredictable and often unpleasant. This motto was based on the "Shit Happens!" bumper sticker of the late 1980s. It seems to have had its origin in a cartoon in the Washington *Times* depicting a tank with a "Saddam Happens!" bumper sticker.

At Ease: Mottoes and Slogans from a Short War

A visitor to West Point in October 1990 observed a giant NO SLACK FOR IRAQ banner (and noted that the cadets were dressed in battle dress in support of their fellow soldiers in the gulf).

The folks at the Orkin Pest Control Company heard that Saddam was terrified of cockroaches, so they designed and shipped to the gulf bumper stickers that featured a roach in a storm coat (a play on "Desert Storm") exhorting the soldiers to BUG THE THUG.

Another bumper sticker alluded to President George Bush's well-advertised dislike of a certain vegetable: SUPPOSE KUWAIT'S MAIN PRODUCT WAS BROCCOLI . . . ?

Still another depicted Saddam as a spider, along with the words IRAQ NOPHOBIA (a play on the term for fear of spiders, "arachnophobia").

Then, of course, there was the T-shirt motto of the war: I INVADED KUWAIT AND ALL I GOT WAS THIS LOUSY T-SHIRT.

Saddam Insane. Saddam Hussein.

Saddamist, the. Saddam Hussein; possibly a play on the riddle, "What did Hussein do to Kuwait? He Saddamized [sodomized] it."

Saddam line. Iraqi fortifications (trenches, mines, etc.) on the Saudi-Kuwaiti border.

Saddam Who's Sane? Saddam Hussein.

Saddamy. Saddam Hussein; a play on "sodomy."

Saddy. Saddam Hussein.

Sammy. Saddam Hussein.

sandbox, the. Saudi Arabia and Kuwait (i.e., their desert terrain).

sandbox express. (1) Any form of desert transportation. (2) Transportation to the gulf region itself.

sanitize. To kill; to purge of life.

Saudi champagne. A fizzy concoction of mineral water, Sprite or 7-Up, and apple juice (i.e., a drink in keeping with the Muslim taboo against alcohol).

Scud. (1) A Soviet-made surface-to-surface ballistic missile. The Iraqis had three versions, with a range of 360 to 1,200 miles, configured to carry conventional or chemical munitions. The official NATO name for the Scud is "SS1," but "Scud" is a long-established NATO code word for the missile. NATO denies giving enemy missiles unflattering or awkward code names, but besides "Scud," NATO code names for Soviet missiles include "Scrag," "Sapwood," and "Spanker." The fact that they all start with the letter "S" indicates that they are surface-to-surface missiles.
(2) To bash someone; to beat someone up (i.e., as if hitting someone with a missile).
(3) An expletive. The term had limited and ephemeral use as a stand-in for "shit."

Scud-a-vision. The Cable News Network (CNN).

Scud Bowl. The King Addul Aziz Naval Air Station. It was described in Army magazine in November 1991 as a barely used soccer stadium north of Port Jubail that had been taken over by the Marines and used as an air base.

Scudbusters. (1) Patriot missiles. (2) The people who designed, built, and controlled Patriot missiles. "In Baltimore, Martin Marietta workers hauled up a big cloth banner saying 'Scudbusters' over their work area," reported the Washington Post in an article on the company that built the missile launcher. Patriots were used as anti-Scud missiles in the gulf, and the name "Scudbusters" is a play on the movie title Ghostbusters.

Scudded. Drunk; from the Scud missile. One trooper, quoted in Army, said of this term: "Ain't no such thing in S.A. [Saudi Arabia]."

Scudinavia. An area in western Iraq from which many Scud missiles were launched. This play on "Scandinavia" was oddly appropriate because many of the Scud launchers were adapted versions of Swedish Saab trucks.

Scud magnet. Dhahran, Saudi Arabia (a Scud target).

Scud puppy. One who mans a Patriot missile battery.

Scud stud. Arthur Kent, an NBC reporter who, with his natural good looks and safari-style outfits and leather jackets, was said to have the greatest sex appeal of all the TV reporters in the gulf. Kent burst upon the scene during a National Football League playoff game, when he dramatically announced a Scud missile attack. He was soon being touted as the war's leading man.

Scud watcher. A journalist.

sebkha. An underground river; from the Arabic. Sebkhas that turn the ground into quagmires that cannot be crossed by tanks lay near the Saudi border and south of Kuwait City. See also WADI.

self-propelled sandbags. Marines (especially those who were dug in at the Kuwaiti border).

Semper Gumby. Always flexible; a play on "Semper Fidelis" (the Marine motto) and Gumby (a rubbery green cartoon character).

Senior Trend. The code name for the F-117 Stealth fighter program.

septics / septic Yanks. U.S. troops. British troops in the gulf devised this bit of Cockney rhyming slang combined with a friendly insult ("Yanks," "tanks," "septic tanks"). It was adopted with some glee by the septics themselves.

service the target. To destroy the enemy. This term and its allies (such as FORCE PACKAGE) "won" the 1991 Doublespeak Award for the Defense Department from the National Conference of Teachers of English.

shack. A bull's-eye when bombing a target; probably from the fact that many targets are buildings. It was also called a "bull."

shake and bake. To employ a mixture of weapons in an air attack.

sham. To shirk; to avoid work. Someone who shams is a "shammer."

SHAW. Shoulder-launched automatic weapon (an improved version of the bazooka).

Shield-107. The Armed Forces Radio station operating in the combat zone; from "Desert Shield" and the modern proclivity for giving radio stations names followed by the frequency or initials, such as Q-107.

shoot and scoot. See HIP SHOOTING.

shooting-gallery phase. That period in Operation Desert Storm when allied aircraft picked off Iraqi field weapons one at a time with little or no opposition. It was an unprecedented move to win superiority on the ground through airpower.

shooting stupid. Uncontrolled antiaircraft fire. The opposite of "smart," as in SMART BOMB.

sideshow. A military action considered strategically unimportant by the allied command.

Silkworm envelope. The Strait of Hormuz (at least, the part of it in range of the Chinese-made Silkworm antiship missiles that Iran had deployed along the coast).

six. A commander; radio code. God is "Big Six in the Sky."

skip bombing. Dropping munitions so that they bounce along the ground or the water and hit the side of a tank or a ship.

sky jockey. A fighter pilot.

SLAM. Stand-off land attack missile. It is launched from an aircraft.

slap and hug. A technique used against Iraqi troops by which they would first be slammed with artillery and then treated to the sound of an aircraft loudspeaker over their bunkers with the friendly voice of an Arabic-speaking soldier asking them to cease resistance.

SLAR. Side-looking airborne radar.

slimed. Hit by chemical weapons; a reference to Bill Murray's line in the movie *Ghostbusters*, "I've been slimed."

SLUD. Salivates, lachrymates, urinates, defecates (i.e., the effects of an attack with chemical weapons).

SLUF. Short little ugly fucker (i.e., the A-7D attack aircraft). See also BUFF.

smart bomb. A bomb with a laser or electrooptical guidance system that gives it a very high degree of accuracy. Smart bombs were used in the waning days of the Vietnam War but came into their own during the Gulf War. Perhaps the best line on the adjective "smart" came from A. Whitney Brown, *Saturday Night Live*'s "cultural commentator," who in discussing the smart bombs used in the gulf said that the military "doesn't want to make them too smart or else they'd have second thoughts about war."

smart decoy. A heat-emitting decoy (e.g., a metal frame and fabric replica of an M-1 tank). Such a decoy attracts heat-seeking enemy missiles while it fools enemy gunners.

smoke 'em. To arrive at one's destination quickly.

snake. The AH-1F Cobra attack helicopter.

snake eater. A Special Forces soldier; also known as a "tree eater." See also under the Vietnam War.

soft target. A human being. A "hard target" is a building or military installation.

sortie. A round-trip mission by a single aircraft (i.e., one mission by one plane equals one sortie; by ten planes, ten sorties). The term (from the French for "departure") has been used for many years in military aviation, but this was the first time it broke into general use. Many thought of it as a construct of this war, and more than a few thought the term being used was "soiree" (allegedly including one major radio personality).

Commenting on the term in the St. Petersburg *Times*, Stephen Koff wrote in early 1991: "Calling it a 'mission' doesn't have the same ring. There's something deliciously sneaky-sounding about the French word—a jet stealing in and then high-tailing it out."

In his *New York Times Magazine* column "On Language" of February 3, 1991, William Safire noted that the first use of "sortie" for an air mission was in a 1918 French book, *En l'Air*.

Southwest Asia. The gulf region. To quote from *Army*: "A term thought up by a DoD staff pogue. It means Middle East or 'Hell,' depending on how you look at it." The term was a pointed reference to Southeast Asia, the venue of the Vietnam War.

spammed. Having been given an unpleasant mission. This British troopers' term derives from Spam, the canned meat whose name is a blend of the words "spiced" and "ham."

speed bumps. Saudi Arabian troops (as if they were simply something to drive over). In *It Doesn't Take a Hero* (1992), Schwarzkopf says that U.S. troops early in the war (when they were few in number and facing large Iraqi forces across the Kuwaiti border) referred to *themselves* as "Iraqi speed bumps" (as if all they could do in the event of an Iraqi attack on Saudi Arabia would be to slow the Iraqis down a little).

splash. A hit against an enemy aircraft (because it splashes in the gulf); a pilot's term.

Spot. A pet scorpion.

Spud. A SCUD. This disparaging term implies that the missile has all of the devastating power of a potato.

Square War, the. The Gulf War (because it was staged from conservative Saudi Arabia, lacking alcohol, drugs, and prostitutes).

squawk. To talk by radio from aircraft to aircraft; from the characteristic radio sound.

squiggles. Arabic writing (especially on highway signs; as in, "It's only twenty kilometers to Squiggles").

SS1. See SCUD.

Stan. Saddam Hussein.

stealth. (1) An aircraft designed to avoid detection on enemy radar. The F-117A was a stealth-equipped jet used in the first raid on Baghdad. (2) To kill.

Stormin' Norman. General H. Norman Schwarzkopf (the U.S. commander); also known as "the Bear."

strack. A soldier with proper bearing and attitude. See use under the Vietnam War.

straight-leg. A nonparatrooper; used derisively. Paratroopers must learn how to land with bent legs to absorb the impact. The term was sometimes shortened to "leg."

strangle. To cut off or switch off equipment (as in strangling a radio).

strike munitions. Bombs (i.e., the munitions used in an air strike).

strip search. To conduct reconnaissance along a straight line between two points of reference; from the term for searching a person who has been stripped naked.

suicide circle. A Saudi traffic circle. "Road accidents have so far claimed the lives of 13 allied soldiers," said *Time* for February 25, 1991.

Suicide Road. See DEATH ROW.

super Dolly Parton. See DOLLY PARTON.

surgical. Precise (as in, "surgical air strike").

Schwarzkrieg. Name given to the 1,000-hour Gulf War air campaign by retired Marine Corps colonel Gerit Feneda and adopted by *Armed Forces Journal* and others.

 ★ ☆ **T** ☆ ★

T / T-rat. A tray ration. These large trays of a single dish were designed for feeding large numbers. They received less than a four-star rating in the gulf.

tag and bag. To mark a corpse and put it into a body bag (as in, "Tag 'em and bag 'em").

take down / take out. To destroy.

take it in the face. To eat.

tally ho. Target in sight (in air combat).

tango uniform. Out of action; unable to perform. The phrase is alphabet code for "TU," which is official code for equipment that is out of order. It was often unofficially applied to an ill or tired soldier.

tankbuster. An antitank weapon (e.g., the A-10 Warthog aircraft). This is one of several post-*Ghostbuster* terms ending in "buster" that appeared in this war, including SCUDBUSTER.

target rich. Said of an area where there were lots of things to shoot at. Iraq and Kuwait were called the "target-rich environment."

thumbprint. Confirmation that a path to a target has been established by laser-guided weapons. A circling plane equipped with a laser points its beam at a target. When the laser defines a clear track for the bomb or missile to follow, the thumbprint has been established. The term derives from the use of a fingerprint (e.g., a thumbprint) in a criminal investigation to establish identity.

tippin'. Acting stupid; also known as TRIPPIN'.

toast. An enemy hit by a bomb (i.e., one who has been burned, or toasted).

toe popper. A small land mine. Despite the cute name, it can take one's leg off up to the knee.

Tomahawk. An unmanned, rocket-launched, jet-propelled ground-hugging cruise missile fired from ships or B-52 bombers. Guided by an onboard computer, it can hit a target as far as eight hundred miles away from the launch point.

Top Gun. General Colin Powell, chairman of the Joint Chiefs of Staff.

total immersion. Nonstop television coverage.

TOW. Tube-launched, optically-tracked, wire-guided missile.

tragic kingdom. Saudi Arabia; a sad, mocking reference to Disney's Magic Kingdom.

trash hauler. Transport aircraft.

T.R. double E. A phrase used in hazing new soldiers. It was explained in *Army* magazine:

> "A way to weed out the pogues from the dust-biters," reported one Desert Storm Marine. A dust-biter would ask the pogue if he ever set up a "T.R. double E"—referring to an antenna—and the pogue would almost always say "Yes." Then the hard-charger would reply, "Stick to pushing papers—there aren't any trees in the desert."

tread head. A tanker; a reference to tank treads.

tree eater. A Special Forces soldier.

triple A. Antiaircraft artillery (as in, "We gave them a lot of triple A"). "Triple A" was known as ACK-ACK in World War II.

trippin'. Acting stupid; a reference to the "trips" of drug use. Also known as TIPPIN'.

tube. A gun tube (specifically, an artillery piece).

tumbleweed. Completely confused.

turkey shoot. A rout. The term was applied to the devastating allied attack on the huge convoy of Iraqi tanks and other military vehicles fleeing Kuwait. It is a direct reference to the slaughter of domestic turkeys, which are defenseless and totally unaware of their fate.

turn 'em and burn 'em. To get airplanes back in the air quickly after a mission. The person in charge of this feat is the crew chief.

A civilian meaning of this phrase was reported in *USA Today* of July 18, 1991: the practice of some high-tech companies of hiring people out of top universities and working them hard while holding out the possibility of granting them lucrative stock options.

★ ☆ **U** ☆ ★

U.A.V. Unmanned aerial vehicle (i.e., a pilotless reconnaissance airplane).

ulu. The middle of nowhere; from a term for the Malayan interior.

unilateral. A reporter who disguises himself as a soldier to get to the front (i.e., one who broke from the pool and its rules).

unit of fire. A standard load of ammunition for one soldier or one weapon.

urah. See HOO-AH.

★ ☆ **V** ☆ ★

vampire. An American sniper who stalks his prey at night.

vertical insertion. Arrival on a battlefield by helicopter.

video canary. A television journalist; an allusion to the birds used by miners to detect the presence of gas.

Viper. The F-16 fighter-bomber; also called the "Electric Jet," "Fighting Falcon," and "Lawn Dart."

★ ☆ **W** ☆ ★

wadi. A dry river gulch; from the Arabic. A wadi can turn very wet very quickly in the desert winter. According to the March 1991 issue of *Airman:* "The Iraqis have set up a defense line behind the wadi that runs along Kuwait's border with Iraq." See also SEBKHA.

Wally World. The Persian Gulf. An Associated Press dispatch of December 19, 1990, on Navy slang in the gulf, reported: "For reasons that remain obscure, the Persian Gulf itself has been dubbed 'Wally World,' a term borrowed from a film starring comedian Chevy Chase."

Warlords. General H. Norman Schwarzkopf's name for his corps commanders.

Warthog. The A-10 Thunderbolt aircraft. This was an affectionate, mocking nickname for the ugly, clumsy-looking beast of American warplanes. It acquired its name from that of a slow-moving tusked pig.

waste. To kill.

weaseling. Operating the F-4G jet fighter (the Wild Weasel), a complex job.

web gear. Tools and pouches carried on web belts, plus the belts themselves.

weenie. Anyone farther to the rear than the speaker.

whale. A tanker in the gulf.

whizo. A weapons systems officer. It is a pronunciation of the initialism, "W.S.O."

W.I.A. Wounded in action.

Wild Weasel. See DOUBLE UGLY.

wingman. The second aircraft in a flight formation. The primary obligation of the wingman, who flies to the side of the leader, is to defend the leader.

woof. To talk without saying anything.

woof, woof. Meaningless talk (like barking).

world, the. Any place except the gulf region. A Houston *Chronicle* report of August 28, 1990, with a dateline of Bedouin One, Saudi Arabia, illustrates: "Here at a remote desert camp that takes its name from the nomadic Bedouin tribes, Marines voraciously question visitors from 'the world' about the latest details of the U.S.-Iraqi standoff."

wrench. A mechanic; in the same sense that a "spoon" is a cook.

W.T.O. Washington theater of operations; an ironic reference to the Pentagon.

★ ☆ **Y** ☆ ★

yeehah. See HOO-AH.

★ ☆ **Z** ☆ ★

zero. None; nothing (said of the outcome of an experience or event).

zoom bag. A flight suit.

zoomy. A pilot (i.e., one who zooms).

zulu / zulu time. Greenwich Mean Time (G.M.T.). The military keeps track of time for all military operations in zulu time, which starts at 0000 and runs to 2359.

This term had been used by the military for many years, but like the term SORTIE, never enjoyed wide popular acceptance. During the Vietnam War, "zulu" was the infamous code word for casualty reports.

Sources and Acknowledgments

★

This book was begun during Operation Desert Shield which presented a perfect opportunity to collect the slang of the war as it was being heard, recorded and reported. Because of the nature of the conflict and its relatively long build-up, there were many journalists who reported on the terminology of the American troops in the Gulf. Quite simply, the language of the GI in the Gulf was a legitimate story for many reporters looking for an angle during Desert Storm.

In order to gather as much of this as I could, I contacted a number of friends and associates—including several on active or reserve duty in the military—and asked them to be my linguistic eyes and ears for the duration. My appeal looked like this:

I WANT YOU!

. . .to help me collect terminology linked to the Gulf War. A few days ago I began assembling and documenting such a collection including:

+ OFFICIAL TERMS.
+ JARGON & SLANG.
+ NAMES.
+ ALLUSIONS.
+ VERBAL PECULIARITIES (euphemism,
oft-repeated quotations, journalese, slogans, images etc.)

Would also love any glossaries, comments on the language of this war, and any other illuminating clippings, etc.

Lest there be any question, I think that there is an important and informative glossary to be created from all of this and I am making an early bid to create an early one. Examples from the early days of this: Republican Guard . . . Triple A . . . Sortie . . . EPW . . . Smart Bomb . . . Dumb Bomb . . . Golden BB . . . Frogs . . . Thumbprint . . . Persian Gulf War . . . Scud . . . Collateral Damage . . . etc.

Sincerely,
Paul Dickson
Linguistic
Recruiter.

The recruits: Russell Ash, Terence Blacker, Bruce O. Boston, Bob Calvert, Don Crinklaw, Isabelle C. Dickson, Douglas E. Evelyn, Mike Feinsilber, Walt Gianchi, Joseph C. Goulden, Bob Greenman, the late Irving Hale, Kelsie Harder, Betty Hartman, Capt. Lawrence P. Lapuh, Dave Matheny, Bill Mead, Capt. Joseph Michael, Herbert H. Paper, Ross Reader, Randy Roberts, Bob Skole, the late Robert C. Snider, Mike Stackpole, Norman D. Stevens, Robert Throckmorton, Steve Teicher, Elaine Viets and Loren K. Weissman.

It should be noted that Capt. Joseph W. Michael of Fort Eustis, Virginia was kind enough to respond to my request (which caught up with him in Saudi Arabia) with a major league memo on the subject after serving in the Gulf.

The newspapers which were used in this quest included these: the Akron *Beacon-Journal*, the Albuquerque *Tribune*, the Baltimore *Sun*, the Boston *Globe*, the Columbia (Mo.) *Daily Tribune*, the Denver *Post*, the Houston *Chronicle*, the Houston *Post*, the *Huntsville News*, the *Times* of London and the *Sunday Times*, the London *Daily Telegraph*, the Los Angeles *Times*, New York *Newsday*, the New York *Post*, the New York *Times*, the Rocky Mountain *News*, the Seattle *Times*, the St. Louis *Post-Dispatch*, the St. Petersburg *Times*, the Washington *Post*, the Washington *Times*, the Witchita *Eagle*. Much material was collected from the three broadcast networks, the Cable News Network, National Public Radio and the Associated Press.

The book which was the first to capture both the official and unofficial language of the Gulf is *The Official Lite History (and Cookbook) of the Gulf War*, and the fullest early magazine attempts were "Before the Battle" by E. M. Flanagan, Jr. in the November, 1991 *Army* magazine and "Miles of Sand and Desert Slang" by Elisabeth Hickey and Michael Hedges which appeared in the February 25, 1991 *Insight* magazine (and which was based on their earlier reports in the Washington *Times*). The special report "Among The New Words" by John and Adele Alego, both of the University of Georgia in Athens, in the Winter 1991 (Vol. 66, Number 4) *American Speech* is a most significant contribution to cataloging the language of the Gulf War; as is a supplement which appears in the Spring 1992 issue, (Vol. 67, Number 1) of the same journal.

DOOMSDAY'S DICTIONARY

★

Verbal Fallout from Nukes, the Cold War (1946–1991), and the Puzzle Palace

★

> To exacerbate or not to exacerbate, that is the dichotomy;
> Whether 'tis more viable vis-à-vis the mind to suffer
> The thrusts and boggles of outrageous escalation,
> Or to take arms against a sea of pragmatism,
> And by opposing, end them. To die, to crunch,
> No more, and by a crunch to say we end
> The xenophobia and the thousand counter-productive dialogues
> That flesh is heir to; 'tis an inhouse ambivalence
> Devoutly to be opted, to die, to sleep . . .
> —"Gobbledygook," by Argus J. Tresideer, in *Military Review* (April 1974)
> [Hamlet's soliloquy rewritten in the jargon of the Pentagon]

The best war slang is collected by veterans, and I could be regarded as a Cold War vet. For starters, in elementary school I was part of a sixth-grade fund-raising drive to sell garden seeds to purchase heavy room window shades that would, we were assured, protect us from atomic bombs. We were pioneers at desk diving and could hit the floor instinctively when the teacher yelled, "Drop and cover!"

I got my Army draft notice just after the Berlin Wall went up, but instead went into the Navy, where I served on an aircraft carrier that spent most of its days exercising against a known enemy whose electronics-laden trawlers followed us like so many sea gulls. We carried nuclear bombs, which I liked to touch as often as I could—for good luck, of course. We were there for the Cyprus crisis and were at Guantánamo when Fidel Castro turned off the water to the American base. At Guantánamo, I stared eyeball-to-eyeball at a Red Chinese Rambo who guarded the perimeter of the base with a machine gun (but allowed Cuban nationals to come onto the base to cut the grass and tend to the flowers at the officers' club pool).

For several years after leaving the Navy, I wrote about high-technology electronics for *Electronics* magazine and spent a lot of that time writing about big, expensive things with initials for names—like ABM and AWACS—that would come into play if the Cold War got hot.

For most of the war I kept my ear cocked and eyes open for the language that defined it—"it" being the Cold War, the massive military buildup and the ever-present (though now much-diminished) nuclear threat.

Here then is a one-of-a-kind collection of acronyms, code words, strange jargon, and pure slang—a small portion of the many terms peculiar to the cold warrior. If the terms chosen seem to have a slant—an eye to the absurdity of it all; a nuclear nonchalance—so be it. Tough. I was there. The Cold War is over.

★ ☆ **A** ☆ ★

A.A. Air America; air assault; airborne alert; air-to-air; Alcoholics Anonymous; antiaircraft; appliqué armor; approving authority; arrival angle; assembly area; attack assessment. These meanings of what may be the most common—and therefore most confusing—initialism in the modern military vocabulary are from *The Dictionary of Military, Defense Contractor and Troop Slang Acronyms* (1990), by Philip C. Gutzman.

A.B.C. American-British-Canadian; Argentina-Brazil-Colombia (the ABC countries); atomic, biological, and chemical. These meanings are taken from the official Department of Defense Acronym List (1988), which is, as the Washington *Post* termed it, "449 jam-packed pages of Pentagonisms."

absolute dud. "A nuclear weapon which, when launched at or emplaced on a target, fails to explode" (as defined in the *Department of Defense Dictionary* [1991]).

accidental war. An "outlaw" term. The *Department of Defense Dictionary* (1991) says: "Not to be used, use accidental attack."

acey-veecee. The Arms Control Verification Committee (ACVC).

ADCOMSUBORDCOMPHIBSPAC. Administrative Command, Amphibious Forces, Pacific Fleet Subordinate Command. This Navy term is the longest English acronym in captivity (at least, it is the longest of the 45,000 entries in the 1965 edition of the *Acronyms, Initialisms, and Abbreviations Dictionary*). If it ever is bettered, the new champion also will probably come from the Navy, which seems to have a special penchant for creating long acronyms, especially portmanteau, or telescope, words, in which two or more words are joined. Other naval portmanteaus include NAVFORKOR (Naval Forces, Korea) and BUPERS (Bureau of Personnel).

age of moon. A measure of time. It is the official Department of Defense and NATO nomenclature for, "The elapsed time, usually expressed in days, since the last new moon."

aim point. Target in a nuclear attack.

air breathing. Requiring the intake of air—or inhaling—for fuel combustion. The term describes a missile or other airborne delivery system that must remain within the earth's atmosphere.

air support. Bombing. In 1974 an Air Force colonel won a Doublespeak Award from the National Council of Teachers of English for his complaint about reporters writing about a U.S. bombing mission: "You always write it's bombing, bombing, bombing. It's not bombing! It's air support."

ALTAIR. Advanced Research Projects Agency long-range tracking and instrumentation radar. This third-generation acronym from the Pentagon contains two earlier acronyms: ARPA (Advanced Research Projects Agency) and "radar" (radio detection and ranging). Such acronyms embedded within other acronyms are termed "tour de force acronyms" by Kenneth H. Bacon in a 1977 article on the subject in *The Wall Street*

Journal. Bacon used the Army's SCAMPERS as an example: Standard Corps Army MACOM (for Major Army Command) Personnel System.

ALCUM. Nickname for the air-launched cruise missile, derived from the initialism ALCM.

anchored. Am orbiting a visible orbit point; an air-intercept code word.

angels. Aircraft altitude (in thousands of feet); an air-intercept and close air support code word. See also under the Gulf War.

ANGUS. Air National Guard of the United States.

antipersonnel. Designed to kill people. An antipersonnel weapon is meant to destroy people rather than equipment.

apportioning the poverty. Dividing the expected 1990s budget cuts among the branches of the armed forces.

ARISTOTLE. Annual Review and Information Symposium on the Technology of Training and Learning. This Air Force formulation is but one of a number of "classical" acronyms. Others include PLATO (Programmed Logic for Automated Training Operation), ADONIS (Automatic Digital On-line Instrument System), SOCRATES (System for Organizing Content to Review and Teach Educational Subjects), and CASSANDRA (Chromatogram Automatic Soaking, Scanning, and Digital Recording Apparatus).

armstrong. A term indicating responsibility for arming and fusing circuitry; used by the Air Support Radar Team.

atomic cemetery. A burial place for atomic waste; a term of the early 1960s.

atomic itch. An effect of atomic radiation. This new term for the year 1947 was defined by one authority as, "A skin irritation, accompanied by high fever, brought about by radiations from the atomic bomb."

atomic words. See PURR WORDS.

auntie. Anti- (as in, "antimissile missile").

★ ☆ **B** ☆ ★

backchannel. General officers' personal message traffic transmitted by electrical means. The forward channel is reserved for official military business.

Backfire. A Soviet bomber. During the Cold War the Soviets refused to disclose their own names for many of their weapons, so the Western powers had to give them names. Predictably, the names chosen were sometimes less than flattering—like "Backfire," "Forger," and SCUD (see under the Gulf War).

backpack nuke. A nuclear device that can be carried by a single person.

back tell. The transfer of information from a higher to a lower echelon of command (the opposite of the usual path up the chain of command). The term is official NATO nomenclature.

balisage. The marking of a route by a system of dim beacon lights, enabling vehicles to be driven at near daytime speed under blackout conditions. The term derives from the French *baliser* ("to place beacons or markers").

balloon goes up, the. A major war starts. The term is discussed by Nigel Rees, in *Why Do We Say . . . ?* (1987): "It derives from the barrage balloons used during the two world wars to protect targets from air raids. The mere fact that these (or observation) balloons had 'gone up' would signal that some form of action was imminent."

BAMBI. Ballistic missile boost interceptor; a system of rockets capable of homing in on the heat of enemy missiles and colliding with them shortly after they are launched. The system was never actually built, but BAMBI research went on for decades, beginning in the late 1950s. Like INFANT, it's a cute name for a deadly system. "Bambi," the name of an adorable baby deer in a children's book and a Disney movie based on it, has acquired a connotation of supreme innocence.

basic encyclopedia. A list of targets that an enemy might choose to attack. The Department of Defense defines it in official documents: "A compilation of identified installations and physical areas of potential significance as objectives for attack."

battle star. A laser-armed satellite that can incinerate enemy missiles seconds after they are launched. In the late 1970s and early 1980s, battle stars were seen as the A.B.M.'s (anti–ballistic missiles) of the 1990s.

Bay of Pigs, the. Enlisted women's quarters; a derogatory term, from about 1961 to the early 1990s. The references are to the hapless American invasion of Cuba at the Bay of Pigs (April 1961), "pig" as an ugly woman, and "bay" as a living area for troops. As is pointed out in *A Dictionary of Soldier Talk* (1984), by John R. Elting, Dan Cragg, and Ernest Deal: "The term is fast becoming obsolete among today's generation of young soldiers living in coed barracks."

B.C.F. Blind copy furnished. The term is used by Pentagonians protecting themselves. Here is an insider's definition: "A record placed on an Official File Copy that you have sent a copy of the letter to another party and you don't want the addressee to know it."

BEDOC. Beds occupied; an official Army measure of habitation.

bells and whistles. New responsibilities or requirements imposed on a system as it proceeds through development (e.g., more firepower, armor, or radar).

below the zone. Said of the selection of an officer for promotion ahead of his contemporaries; also known as "secondary zone" promotions (in that the officer jumps ahead of those in the primary zone) and "five percent," or "nickel," promotions (because only a small percentage are so selected).

Beltway bandit. A high-priced consultant or consulting firm working for the Department of Defense or other government or military agencies. The name alludes to the Beltway, an interstate highway that encircles Washington, D.C.

bias. The average distance a warhead will land from its target ("ground zero").

big bird. The Keyhole (KH-9) surveillance satellite.

big one. A Soviet test of a missile capable of carrying nuclear warheads.

bingo. (1) I have reached minimal fuel for safe return to base or to designated alternate; a pilot's term. (2) Proceed to alternate airfield or carrier as specified; an air controller's term.

bingo field. An alternate airfield.

bird. (1) A pilotless object in flight (satellites, space probes, and the like). (2) A helicopter.

birdman. A pilot.

black. Relying on illegal concealment; an official intelligence term used in certain phrases (e.g., "living black" and "black border crossing").

black book. Name for book which outlines the president's options in a nuclear war.

black box. A complex piece of equipment that can be installed or replaced as an unopened unit. In 1971 the Senate Military Appropriations Committee determined that some avionic (aviation electronic) black boxes were "twice as costly as gold."

black list. A list of people deemed security risks. The term is defined in the official *Department of Defense Dictionary* (1991): "An official counterintelligence listing of actual or potential enemy collaborators, sympathizers, intelligence suspects, and other persons whose presence menaces the security of friendly forces."

blast. One of the effects of a nuclear explosion. It has been described as an otherworldly wind traveling faster than the speed of sound and killing all who are exposed to it.

bless. To approve an action.

blood chit. A small cloth chart with a picture of an American flag and a statement, in several languages, to the effect that anyone assisting the bearer in reaching safety will be rewarded.

blowoff. The planned separation of a section of a rocket vehicle after it has served its purpose (e.g., an empty fuel tank).

Blue Bark. U.S. military personnel, U.S. citizen civilian employees of the Department of Defense, and the dependents of both categories, who travel in connection with the death of an immediate family member; apparently, an arbitrary code name.

blue top. A press release; from the traditional Department of Defense press release forms, which have blue tops. To blue top something is to put out a press release on it.

BMEWS. Ballistic missile early warning system. The BMEWS network consists of radar systems located at Thule, Greenland; Flyingdales, England; and Clear Air Force Base, Arizona. The network was designed to detect Soviet missile attacks against the U.S., Canada, and Western Europe.

bogey. A flying object that is unidentified but assumed to be enemy.

bogsaat. Bunch of guys sitting around a table; a form of decision making.

boiler plate. Standard verbiage used to describe things that don't change (e.g., budget program elements).

B-1. A U.S. bomber. It was critiqued by Peter J. Ognibene in the April 17, 1976, issue of *Saturday Review:* "a vitamin we need; a $100 million bomber we don't."

bonus damage. Destruction beyond the initial target (e.g., targeting an air base but also destroying a small city). There is a certain cynicism in this use of the word "bonus."

BOOB. Bolt out of the blue (i.e., an unexpected nuclear attack). The term was discussed by Bill Prochnau in the Washington *Post* for April 29, 1982: "This is what they call in the jargon of the nuclear trade, a BOOB attack. . . . No warning. Just whump."

boomer. (1) A submarine armed with ballistic missiles carrying nuclear warheads. (2) A member of the nuclear-powered Navy.

bootleg copy. An unofficial advance working copy of an official document.

brainstorm / brainstorm session. A meeting at which ideas are freely allowed to surface and be discussed, no matter how far out they may be, in the interest of uncovering all possible approaches to (or parameters of) an issue or problem.

Bravo. The code name for a 1954 U.S. hydrogen bomb test.

brilliant pebbles. A defense technology that would employ thousands of small satellites floating in space to home in on incoming enemy missiles and destroy them.

brinksmanship. Going to the brink of war, teetering there, and then coming back. The term was inspired by the diplomacy of John Foster Dulles (who had been described in *Life* as having the ability to walk to the brink) and first used (perhaps created) by Adlai Stevenson in a February 25, 1956, speech in which he said, "We hear the Secretary of State boasting of brinksmanship." (In fact, Dulles did not boast of it.) For his book *Phrase and Word Origins* (1961), Alfred H. Holt wrote to Stevenson and got this reply: "I cannot claim authorship of *brinksmanship*. I am not sure, however, whether I read it or heard it or dreamed it up. . . . I am reasonably sure that I did not invent it."

broken arrow. The Defense Department code name for a major accident involving nuclear weapons. The U.S., according to the Department of Defense, had 32 broken arrows between 1950 and 1980, such as the A-bomb accidentally dropped over Mars Bluff, South Carolina, in 1958. In that incident the bomb's trigger exploded, leaving a deep crater, but a nuclear explosion did not follow.

brown job. An Army person. Marines used this term because of the Army's brown uniform.

buck slip. Optional Form 41, Routing and Transmittal Slip (a piece of paper attached to a document showing its source and destination). This form is used primarily for simple handwritten communications internal to an office.

bum. (1) A reproduction of a document using copying equipment (i.e., not a legal version). (2) A bag in which classified waste is placed in preparation for destruction; perhaps a short form for "bumfodder," which is a Briticism for both toilet paper and memoranda.

burn a copy. To make a photocopy; probably from photography, in which a print is "burned," or printed on paper.

burned. Said of a clandestine operator who has been exposed to the opposition (especially by surveillance) or whose reliability as a source of information has been compromised.

burn notice. An official statement by an intelligence agency to other intelligence agencies, domestic or foreign, that an individual or group is unreliable.

burnout. The moment when an engine's fuel is used up. In the 1980s, the term came to signify a sudden loss of energy or motivation (e.g., "teacher burnout" and "executive burnout").

burnout velocity. The speed of a rocket or airborne vehicle at the moment it runs out of fuel.

buster. Fly at maximum continuous speed (or power); an air-intercept code word. For all intents and purposes, as explained in *Final Flight* (1989), by Stephen Coonts, it means "hurry, bust your ass." See also GATE.

butcher charts. Large flimsy charts on a chart stand, which are turned vertically, like pages in a pad. The paper used is roughly the same size as the paper used to wrap meat in butcher shops.

button up. To prepare a missile for firing (close the blast door, go to emergency power, etc.).

★ ☆ **C** ☆ ★

Canoe U. The Naval Academy: Annapolis.

catalytic attack. "An attack designed to bring about a war between major powers through the disguised machinations of a third power" (according to the *Department of Defense Dictionary* [1991]).

C-cubed. Communications, command, and control.

chairman, the. The chairman of the Joint Chiefs of Staff.

CHAMPION. Compatible Hardware and Milestone Program for Integrating Organizational Needs; an Air Force program.

CHASE. Cut holes and sink 'em. The acronym is used for a Navy ammunition disposal system of sinking crates of explosives.

cherry jump. One's first parachute jump after graduating from jump school.

chick. A friendly fighter aircraft.

chicken switch. An abort switch or any other control that stops a mission.

chop. Signature. To get approval one must often get the CO's chop. Something signed is said to have been chopped.

Christmas tree. A panel of indicator lights in a control room or cockpit. The name derives from the fact that many of the indicator lights are green (good) or red (bad). A "green board" indicates that all is in order.

chuff. For a rocket to burn intermittently and with an irregular noise; from the traditional term for the sound of escaping steam.

city bargaining. A concept in nuclear war strategy by which a war is controlled after it has begun. The scope of the war is limited by "bargaining"—trading your own cities for your enemy's.

city buster. A tactical nuclear weapon powerful enough to destroy a city. Arms designers use the term, which echoes the block busting of World War II.

CLAIM. Chemical low-altitude missile.

clara. Radar scope is clear of contacts other than those known to be friendly; an air-intercept code word.

clock code position. The position of a target in relation to an aircraft or ship. See O'CLOCK, under World War II.

Clod. The Soviet AN-14 short takeoff and landing (STOL) transport aircraft; the official NATO code name.

clutter. Extraneous echoes on a radar scope, caused by clouds or other atmospheric conditions (as in, "Contact has entered scope clutter").

COCO. Contractor-owned, contractor-operated (e.g., a factory owned and operated by a private firm performing a service, under contract, for the government). See also **GOGO.**

cocooning. The spraying or coating of aircraft or other equipment with a substance (e.g., a plastic) to form a cocoonlike seal against the effects of the atmosphere; official NATO nomenclature.

cod. Carrier onboard delivery (i.e., an airplane that delivers mail and other supplies to an aircraft carrier).

code 3. A high-ranking official. As explained by former Assistant Secretary of Defense John G. Kester in his February 1982 article on Pentagonese in the *Washingtonian*, the term is "used in messages to designate rank of an expected visitor, as in 'I have a Code 3 on board.' Code 1

is the president; Code 6s are too common to mention."

code war. "A state of international tension wherein political, economic, technological, sociological, psychological, paramilitary, and military measures short of overt armed conflict involving regular military forces are employed to achieve national objectives" (according to the *Department of Defense Dictionary* [1991]).

code word. More secret than top secret. At this level of secrecy a document is coded "code word."

COED. Computer-operated electronic display.

COIN. Counterinsurgency.

Cold War. The state of antagonism and military preparedness that marked the relationship between the United States and its NATO allies and the Soviet Union and the Warsaw Pact nations between 1946 and 1991. The war ended with the collapse of the Soviet Union.

The term was created in 1946 by Herbert Bayard Swope. He mentioned it to Bernard M. Baruch, who began using it in 1947 and helped make it famous in an October 24, 1948, statement to the Senate War Investigating Committee. Many have attributed the phrase to Baruch, but he was scrupulous in giving credit to Swope. Baruch said that he kept the term on ice until 1947. In his 1948 Senate statement, he said: "Although the war is over, we are in the midst of a cold war which is getting warmer." The term was also used by Walter Lippmann as the title of a 1947 book.

collateral damage. Civilian damage from a nuclear strike. In the Gulf War, it was applied to any unintended war damage.

COMSERFORSOPACSUBCOM. Commander, Service Force, South Pacific Subordinate Command; a Navy term.

CONELRAD. Control of electromagnetic radiation; a system of "planned confusion" to prevent enemy bombers from locating U.S. cities by homing in on A.M. radio stations. The system came into being in 1953.

cookie. An easy opponent for a fighter pilot. In *Sweetwater Gunslinger 201* (1983), William H. LaBarge talks of Libyan pilots as "Khadafy's Cookies" or "the Colonel's Cookies," "because we've eaten them up every time they come at us."

countdown. A count backwards (e.g., from ten to one) to the start of something (e.g., a weapons test, nuclear blast, or missile firing).

counterforce strike. An attack aimed at an adversary's military capability (especially, his strategic military capability).

countervalue strike. An attack aimed at an opponent's cities or industries.

country buster. A very powerful nuclear weapon; a play on BLOCKBUSTER (see under World War II). It is larger than a CITY BUSTER.

covered voice. An encrypted voice transmission. "Covered" means "disguised," as in espionage activity.

cow. A junior at West Point.

cowboys and cossacks. The cat-and-mouse game played for many years by U.S. and Soviet submarines; a play on the game of "cowboys and Indians." In Mark Joseph's *To Kill the Potemkin* (1986), the game is called "practice for World War III."

crash. Top priority.

crawlerway. A heavily reinforced road built for transporting space vehicles on gargantuan treaded crawler tractors.

crib. An underground trench for the disposal of nuclear waste. Cribs allow the waste to seep into the ground. A report from the General Accounting Office in the late 1970s reported that more than 31 million gallons of radioactive waste had been dumped into cribs between 1956 and 1958 alone. The code name of one of the most dangerous leakers is "crib Z-9," in Hanford, Washington.

critical mass. The minimum amount of fissionable material capable of supporting a chain reaction under precisely specified conditions.

C.R.P. Crisis relocation planning; sometimes pronounced "crap." It is a civil defense scheme created in the 1970s to get as many people as possible more than ten miles away from the site of a nuclear explosion before it occurs. Under C.R.P., people head for smaller towns called "host areas." C.R.P. for Washington, D.C., for example, called for people whose license plates end in an even number to leave first and for those whose plates end in an odd number to wait for the evens to get out of town.

cryppie. A cryptologist.

cubed out. Filled to capacity.

culture. Man-made features of the terrain. Says the *Department of Defense Dictionary* (1991): "Included are such items as roads, buildings, and canals; boundary lines, and, in a broad sense, all names and legends on a map."

cut and paste. To reorganize the basic elements of a document (e.g., the paragraphs). Sometimes, this literally means cutting up the document and pasting it together in the new version.

★ ☆ **D** ☆ ★

DASTARD. Destroyer antisubmarine transportable array detector.

Dave's Dream. The B-29 that dropped the atomic bomb nicknamed Gilda on Bikini Island.

d-cubed. A "drop dead decision" to abandon a particular weapons system.

death sand. Radioactive earth. Around 1950, it was seen as having potential use as a weapon.

decapitate. To disrupt an opponent's chain of command by killing its leaders.

decay. Loss of energy.

deep space. Outer space beyond the orbit of Pluto (i.e., outside the solar system).

dense pack. A cluster of intercontinental ballistic missiles in protected silos.

DEW Line. The Distant Early Warning radar system, which began to be dismantled in 1991.

DIAIAPPR [pronounced "diaper"]. Defense Intelligence Agency intelligence appraisal.

dingbats. Panamanian strongman Manuel Noriega's brutal Dignity Battalions. The term was used during the U.S. invasion of Panama in 1989.

dirty battlefield. A combat zone obscured by smoke and dust. The term is used in discussions of smart weapons, which depend on lasers and electronic sensors that may not work well in such an environment.

DISCO. Defense Industrial Security Clearance Office.

D.O.E. (1) Death of Earth. A "D.O.E. reaction" is armageddon, or doomsday. (2) Department of Energy.

dog-and-pony show. A formal presentation aimed at gathering support. Visuals (usually projected on a screen), handouts, and large graphs are essential to a true dog-and-pony show. Sometimes the term is used to refer to a simple briefing.

doolie. An Air Force Academy cadet.

doomsday plane. See KNEECAP.

door bundle. A package that is pushed out of the door of an aircraft in flight. A door bundle is normally followed by parachutists.

down gripe. A problem with an aircraft of such severity that it cannot fly. An UP GRIPE can wait until after the next flight is over. The term is based on the ancient "gripe" (a complaint).

downwinders. People living downwind of nuclear facilities or test areas. An organization called the Hanford Downwinders was formed to investigate the health risks of the Hanford nuclear plant near Richland, Washington.

drone. An unmanned aircraft; from the older sense of the term meaning a drudge or a parasitic loafer.

drop. A fuel tank that hangs under the wing or belly of an aircraft and that can be jettisoned when it is empty.

dry run. A practice; a rehearsal.

duck. Trouble headed your way; an air-intercept code word.

dud. See ABSOLUTE DUD, DWARF DUD, and FLARE DUD.

DUMB. Deep underground mountain basing; a Department of Defense acronym for missile siting.

dwarf dud. "A nuclear weapon that, when launched at or emplaced on a target, fails to provide a yield within a reasonable range of that which could be anticipated with normal operation of the weapon. This constitutes a dud only in a relative sense." This is an official Department of Defense definition.

Dyna-Soar. A manned hypersonic vehicle boosted into orbit by a rocket; it would then descend until it bounced off the upper atmosphere and finally land at its destination. Also known as the X-20, this very ambitious project of the late 1950s and early 1960s was canceled in 1963 because it was proving to be too expensive and because it did not fulfill military requirements (in other words, there was no military use for it). "Dyna-Soar" was a contraction of "dynamic-soaring."

★ ☆ **E** ☆ ★

Eagle Claw. The code name for the disastrous 1980 U.S. military operation to free the American hostages in Iran.

Early Bird. A compilation of military-related news clippings distributed early each morning for the edification of those who work at the Pentagon. It is prepared by the News Clipping and Analysis Service of the Department of Defense. There is also a Late Bird.

Earnest Will. The code name for the 1987 U.S. escort of Kuwaiti oil tankers in the Persian Gulf.

EGADS. Electronic ground automatic destruct system; the system that sends a signal to destroy a missile in flight. The "egads button" is the switch used to send the signal.

ejecta. Debris thrown up by the explosion of a missile; from the term for the matter ejected from a volcano.

Eldorado Canyon. The code name for the 1986 U.S. bombing of Libya.

emasculation. The destruction of a missile force by nuclear attack. This term helped critic Nigel Calder, in *Nuclear Nightmares* (1979), conclude: "Missiles are all but pornographic as phallic symbols."

empty hole. A site from which a missile has been fired. The concept is as important to nuclear planning as empty squares are to checkers: Assume that country X dispatches missiles aimed at country Y's offensive missile silos. Meanwhile country Y figures out what is afoot and launches its missiles in retaliation. The laugh is on X, which is now in the process of destroying empty holes. Planners try to avoid targeting empty holes.

E-Ring. The outermost ring of offices in the Pentagon. The third-floor E-Ring is where the offices of key officials are located and is the grandest of the corridors in the Pentagon, where one can actually see daylight. It is reserved for the likes of the Secretary of Defense and the Joint Chiefs of Staff.

escalate. To intensify; to wage a wider war. In 1966 the national commander of the Veterans of Foreign Wars, Andy Borg, called for a "big and fast step-up of the U.S. war effort in Vietnam." UPI's Dick West termed that statement a "horrible blunder" because, as every hawk and dove knew, you don't "step up" a war, you "escalate" it.

"Escalation agility" is the ease with which one can ESCALATE.

event. A nuclear explosion.

event 1000. An incident in which men are trapped in a submarine stranded on the bottom, and search and rescue operations are to be initiated.

exfiltration. The removal of personnel or units from areas under enemy control (i.e., the opposite of "infiltration").

★ ☆ **F** ☆ ★

faces and spaces. Personnel and available positions.

faded. Contact has disappeared from reporting station's scope, and any position information given is estimated; an air-intercept code word.

FAGTRANS. First available government transportation; a term used in military transportation orders.

family gram. A newsletter sent by commanders of Navy vessels to the families of crew members. Family grams are commonly sent when a ship is on a long cruise.

famished. Have you any instructions for me? (i.e., "I am famished for instructions"); an air-intercept code word.

Fat Albert. A wide-bodied jumbo jet; from the Fat Albert character created by comedian Bill Cosby.

Fat Man. The 22-kiloton atomic bomb dropped on Nagasaki, Japan, in 1945.

feasless. Without feasibility.

F.E.B.A. Forward edge of the battlefield.

ferret. An aircraft, ship, or land vehicle especially equipped for the detection, location, recording, and analyzing of electromagnetic radiation. The term comes from the verb "to ferret" ("to search out"), originally with the aid of the animal of the same name.

fifth service. The civilian Pentagon bureaucracy. It is said to have an agenda of its own, which sometimes is different than that of the armed services.

firebreak. Name for the barrier that separates the use of conventional weapons from nuclear weapons in a conflict.

first strike. A surprise nuclear attack. A first strike would be meant to establish tremendous nuclear superiority by destroying a large proportion of the other side's arsenal.

fish. A torpedo (no matter how sophisticated).

flag plot. A naval command center. The term comes from the fact that a naval officer above the rank of captain is allowed to fly a flag showing his or her rank—hence the term "flag officer."

flare dud. A nuclear weapon that, when launched at a target, detonates with the anticipated yield but at an altitude appreciably greater than intended. This is not a dud insofar as yield is concerned, but it is a dud with respect to the effects on the target and the normal operation of the weapon.

flash nudet. U.S. military code for the detonation of a nuclear weapon.

flash-to-bang time. The time from light first being observed until the sound of a nuclear detonation is heard.

fly by wire. To fly entirely by electronic signals (wires), rather than by mechanical links.

FOBS. Fractional orbital bombardment system; a long-range ICBM (intercontinental ballistic missile) system tested by the Soviet Union from 1967 to 1971. Missiles targeting the U.S. would have flown over the South Pole rather than the North Pole, thus avoiding the BMEWS.

football. The black briefcase carried by a presidential military aide when the President is out of the White House. It contains the nuclear-weapons release codes and attack option plans.

footprint. (1) The space taken up by an aircraft after it has landed. (2) The area of destruction caused by a nuclear weapon.

Fort Fumble / Fort Futility. The Pentagon.

fourth medium. War in space. The first three martial media are land, sea, and air.

fox away. Missile has fired or been released from aircraft; an air-intercept code word.

fratricide. The destruction of one or more incoming warheads by the detonation of its companions. The term is used in discussions of **MIRVs** (multiple independently targeted reentry vehicles).

freak. Frequency; an air-intercept word for radio frequency in megacycles.

freddie. A controlling unit; an air-intercept code word.

free lance. Self-control of aircraft is being employed; an air-intercept code word.

fubb. Fouled (or fucked) up beyond belief.

fumtu. Fouled (or fucked) up more than usual.

FUNT. French underground nuclear test.

★ ☆ **G** ☆ ★

gadget. Radar. The Department of Defense uses color words to indicate the degree to which radar is being jammed:
"gadget green"—Clear of jamming.
"gadget amber"—Sector partially jammed.
"gadget red"—Sector completely jammed.

Gamma Goat. An updated jeep built by Ling-Temco-Vought (at a development cost of $439 million).

G answer. Antigravity. As James W. Canan notes in *The Superwarriors* (1975), a vehicle capable of defying gravity "would make Model T's of present day rockets and mockeries of Mach-3 fighters." At the time of Canan's book, there was a widespread worry that the Soviets were close to the "G answer."

garnishing. Material applied to an object for camouflage.

gate. Fly at maximum possible speed (or power); an air-intercept code word. See also BUSTER.

G.C.D. General and complete disarmament; a term that first emerged from arms control talks in the 1960s.

general war. All-out war (i.e., when all the buttons are pushed).

gertrude. An underwater telephone, used for communication between submarines.

ghost. An imperfect sonar image.

G.I.B. Guy in back (i.e., the person sitting in the backseat in a two-seater aircraft); also known as a "pitter," because the backseat of the aircraft is known as the "pit."

gigaton. An explosive power equal to a billion tons of T.N.T.; a measure of the destructive power of nuclear weapons.

Gitmo. Guantánamo Beach, Cuba (specifically, the U.S. Navy base there).

GIUK. Greenland, Iceland, United Kingdom. The region is a key point of congestion in the Atlantic for submarines.

GLCM [pronounced "glick-em"]. Ground-launched cruise missile.

GLONASS. Global navigation satellite system.

GOGO. Government-owned, government-operated. See also **COCO.**

go-juice. Jet fuel.

golden arches. Nuclear slang for attacking nuclear missile paths as they are over the North Pole.

Golden Pheasant. The code name for the deployment of 3,200 troops to Honduras in 1988.

goldie lock. Ground controller has electronic control of an aircraft (i.e., it is "locked on"). The term is peculiar to air support radar operations.

Gold Room. The room in the Pentagon where the Joint Chiefs of Staff meet; so-called because of the color of its drapes and carpets. It is also known as "the Tank."

go nuclear. To develop and deploy nuclear weapons.

go or no-go. The decision to launch or not to launch a space vehicle.

grand slam. All enemy aircraft originally sighted are shot down. The term derives from baseball and contract bridge.

gray propaganda. Propaganda that does not identify its source.

graze. In artillery and naval gunfire support, an observation that a burst occurred on impact.

ground zero. (1) The point at which a nuclear weapon makes its impact. The term is officially defined in a recent Joint Chiefs of Staff glossary: "The point on the surface of the earth at, or vertically below or above, the center of a planned or actual nuclear detonation." (2) A snack bar in the center of the courtyard in the middle of the Pentagon; an allusion to the fact that it would be the prime target in a missile exchange.

guns or butter. Describing the debate over military expenditures versus expenditures for domestic programs. In the 1960s, the phrase was tied to the question of paying for the Vietnam War and nuclear missiles or paying for the War on Poverty. The phrase was popularized in 1938 with the publication of R. H. Bruce Lockhart's *Guns or Butter*, which contained this quote on its title page: "Guns will make us powerful; butter will only make us fat." The quote was attributed to German field marshal Hermann Goering.

Gut, the. A rough-and-tumble section of Naples, Italy; the name was used by generations of American sailors. It may be a clipped form of "gutbucket."

gut issue. The single most important consideration.

★ ☆ **H** ☆ ★

HADES. Hypersonic air data entry system.

HAIR. High-accuracy-instrumentation radar.

hair trigger. Describing the condition in which both superpowers are poised and ready for a nuclear attack.

hang fire. To have an undesirable delay in the functioning of a firing system.

happy to glad. To make minor non-substantive corrections to a document.

hard. Protected. A hard target is one that has been covered with earth and concrete.

hardbody. Slang for a nuclear missile streaking toward its target after it has been identified by a defensive system.

hard kill. The destruction of a target in such a way as to produce physical evidence of its demise. A videotape of a building exploding, for example, would be evidence of a hard kill.

hardstand. (1) A paved area where vehicles are parked. (2) An open ground area having a prepared surface and used for the storage of material.

HAVOC. The Soviet MI-28 antitank attack helicopter; the official NATO code name.

HAWK. Homing-all-the-way killer; a missile. "HIP" stands for "HAWK Improvement Program."

he. (1) The enemy. This is one of the surest ways to distinguish the military mind from the public mind: the public says "they"; the Pentagon says "he." Here is an example from a report on the Vietnam War: "I don't believe the enemy has any great capability to assume any general offensive in the near future. He has been hurt and hurt badly. He is tired." (2) The President of the United States.

heads up. (1) Enemy got through; look out. (2) I am not in position to engage target. In both meanings, this is an air-intercept code phrase.

heavy bead. The biggest of the big-ticket items in the annual Pentagon budget; from the self-mocking notion that the budget is loaded with beads and trinkets.

heavy drop. The delivery of heavy supplies and equipment by parachute.

HELLFIRE. Helicopter-launched fire-and-forget missile.

holiday. An unintentional omission in imagery coverage of an area.

homebodies. American missile combat officers. Nigel Calder, in *Nuclear Nightmares* (1979), says they are so-called "because the missile men must not mind too much being posted with their families for a couple of years to the sparsely populated districts where missiles are planted."

Honest John. A type of missile. According to an October 19, 1975, Los Angeles *Times* article on missile naming, it was named either for a bartender in Juárez, Mexico, or for James L. McDaniel, who was director of the Missile Research and Engineering Laboratories at the Missile Command, in Huntsville, Alabama.

horror story. A public disclosure of the outrageous prices paid by government for parts (e.g., $9,609 for a simple wrench and $900 for a plastic cup).

horseholder. A person who serves as an aide or in some other capacity (e.g., military assistant) in direct support of a general officer or senior civilian; from the sense in which a gentleman would have his horse held during mounting and dismounting.

hot biscuit. A promising research program.

hot line. The open telex line between the White House and the Kremlin. It is not a telephone, as often depicted.

humint. Human intelligence (i.e., intelligence information gathered directly by a human being, as opposed to information gathered electronically). See also SIGINT.

hummer. (1) A missile (i.e., a humdinger). (2) The Hawkeye E-2 early warning aircraft.

★ ☆ | ☆ ★

icing. The accumulation of ice on an aircraft.

Idealist. The U-2 aircraft.

idiot blocks. Lines at the end of a staff document that give a decision maker space to indicate his or her choice by using a check mark.

igloo space. An area in an earth-covered structure of concrete and/or steel designed for the storage of ammunition and explosives.

I go. I am remaining on my patrol (or mission); an air-intercept code phrase. See also I STAY.

Indians. Staff members. Their bosses are "chiefs."

INFANT. Iroquois night fighter and night tracker; a Vietnam-era weapons system produced for the Army by Hughes Aircraft. INFANT, like BAMBI, is an innocent name for a fearsome reality. It flies in the face of Winston Churchill's dictum that things military should have military names and that he would never send British troops off to fight in something called Operation Begonia.

I stay. I am remaining on my patrol (or mission); an air-intercept code phrase. See also I GO.

it. A ship. In deference to the genderless society, the Department of Defense ruled in 1979 that a ship would be an "it" and not a "she" and that it would be "crewed" and not "manned."

At the same time the shipboard "mess" was officially renamed "enlisted dining facilities," the "galley" of yore became a "kitchen," and the "brig" became a "correctional facility."

In 1984, a good year to lash out against such things, then–Secretary of the Navy John F. Lehman, Jr., condemned "the bureaucratization of naval language" and ordered all naval facilities to return to traditional use by January 1, 1985. Halls were once again "passageways" and toilets again became "heads."

★ ☆ **J** ☆ ★

jacfu. Joint American-communist fuckup; a Cold War variation on the JACFU of World War II.

jam. To interfere with. Electronic jamming is the purposeful impairing of an enemy's electronic systems.

JEEP. Joint Emergency Evacuation Plan; the plan for a select group of military leaders to get out of Washington, D.C., in a hurry before a nuclear attack.

jiggle. To maneuver an aircraft (diving, turning, etc.) so as to break a radar lock by the enemy.

Jo. A female soldier (as in, "G.I. Jo").

judy. I have contact and am taking over the interception; an air-intercept code word.

Julie. The system that activates the Navy's sonar buoys. James W. Canan reported in *The Superwarriors* (1978) that it had been named Julie "after a Philadelphia stripteaser who had a reputation for turning passive boys into active boys."

JUMPS. Joint Uniform Military Pay System.

Jumpseat. The code name for any of the National Security Agency communications intelligence (COMINT) satellites stationed in geosynchronous orbit to intercept Soviet communications relayed via satellites. According to *The Language of Defense* (1990), by Mark M. Eiler: "The first Jumpseat satellite was launched in March 1971. The classified prime contractor for Jumpseat satellites is believed to be either Hughes Aircraft or TRW."

Just Cause. The code name for the December 1989 U.S. military invasion of Panama.

★ ☆ **K** ☆ ★

kill-jam. To impair the ability of an enemy aircraft's electronics and communications while a second plane comes in for the kill.

kneecap. The E-4B jet aircraft that sits ready to take the President out of Washington, D.C., in the event of an enemy missile attack. The plane is designated the National Emergency Airborne Command Post (NEACP), and "kneecap" is a pronunciation of the acronym. The official code word for the plane is "Nightwatch," and it is often referred to as the "doomsday plane," because its use is envisioned only in case of nuclear war.

★ ☆ **L** ☆ ★

Langley. The Central Intelligence Agency, which is based in Langley, Virginia.

laughing third. A country that is able to persuade two nuclear powers to annihilate each other. The term dates from the early days of strategic nuclear planning.

lazy. Equipment indicated at standby; an air-intercept code word.

Lazy Dog. The MK-44 missile cluster bomb. After being dropped from an aircraft, it dispenses 10,000 small bomb-shaped iron missiles. It is an antipersonnel weapon of the first order.

leprosy effect. The taint imposed on everything associated with a failed program.

liner. Fly at speed giving maximum cruising range; an air-intercept code word.

liver patch / liver pad. The Army Staff Identification Badge (ASIB). "Authorization to wear the badge normally is granted to officers and warrant officers at the Headquarters, Department of the Army," says the 1986 *Staff Officer's Handbook.*

L.N.O. Limited nuclear option; the use of tactical nuclear weapons instead of conventional weapons.

Looking Glass. The code name for the EC-135 aircraft commanded by a U.S. Air Force general on a 24-hour-a-day basis. The general has authority over all Strategic Air Command forces in the event that primary underground command centers are destroyed in a nuclear war.

low-dollar-value item. A budget item that normally requires considerably less management effort than others.

low grazing. Describing a missile that comes in at a low angle. In a December 24, 1982, article in the Washington *Post* on nuclear language, George C. Wilson notes that SEQUENTIAL DUMPING is a means of getting low-grazing Soviet missiles to skip off a target "like flat stones skittering across a pond."

LOX. (1) Liquid oxygen. (2) To load liquid oxygen into the fuel tanks of a missile or space vehicle.

★ ☆ **M** ☆ ★

MAD. Mutual assured destruction; the theory that neither superpower will attack the other because retaliation would be fatal. Mutual destruction of two nations was and is a profoundly disturbing notion, even to nuclear planners, and the irony of the acronym has never been seen as anything but accurate. (As could be predicted in the acronym age, there is more than one military meaning of "MAD." It also stands for "magnetic airborne detection" and "magnetic anomaly detection," to name just two others.)

MADDAM. Multiplexed analog to digital, digital to analog multiplexed; a Coast Guard computer system term.

man-eater. Aircraft (e.g., the A-7) with engines that can easily suck a man into their intake. The term is used on aircraft carriers, where such accidents are a problem.

man portable. Capable of being carried by one man; official NATO nomenclature.

many. Eight or more aircraft (generally, enough for a raid); an air-intercept term.

maritime strategy. A plan for destroying the Soviet navy by aggressive fleet action.

mark mark. A command from a ground controller for an aircraft to release its bombs.

mark one eyeball. Human sight (described as first-generation military equipment). This term came into play during the moon landings, which were helped considerably by the mark one eyeball.

Mark 1 Mod Zero. The earliest or most basic version or model of something (usually, a weapon). An infantryman with no special skills is a Mark 1, Mod Zero Soldier. In Richard Marcinko's *Rogue Warrior* (1992), the author refers to himself as a Mark 1, Mod Zero sailor.

married failure. A moored mine lying on the seabed and connected to its sinker, from which it has failed to release owing to a defective mechanism.

MaRV. Maneuverable reentry vehicle; a type of warhead.

megacorpse. A million dead people; a nuclear-age word. This term first appeared in print in 1957, the same year OVERKILL came into being.

megadeath. A million dead.

meltdown. The situation in which a nuclear reactor goes out of control and the core melts. In *500 Years of New Words* (1983), William Sherk notes that "meltdown" appeared in print as early as 1975 as nuclear slang, but "lost its quotation marks and became a full-fledged member of the English language in March, 1979 when an accident at the nuclear power plant on Three Mile Island, near Harrisburg, Pennsylvania led to the leakage of dangerous radioactivity, and created the possibility of a meltdown."

M.F.R. Memorandum for record; a written memo recalling what went on at a given meeting.

middleman. Very high frequency or ultrahigh frequency radio relay equipment; an air-intercept code word.

milicrat. Military bureaucrat.

mini-nuke. A neutron bomb (a small fusion bomb whose lethality comes from radiation rather than blast force and heat).

MIRV. Multiple independently targeted reentry vehicle.

mirved. Armed with a MIRV.

mixed bag. A collection of naval mines of various types, firing systems, sensitivities, arming delays, etc.

MOMCOMS. Man-on-the-move communications system.

MOOSEMUSS. Maneuver, objective, offensive, surprise, economy of force, mass, unity of command, simplicity, security

(Karl von Clausewitz's nine basic principles of war). Clausewitz (1780–1831) was a noted authority on military science.

MOPOT. Mobile psychological operations transmitter; a facility for broadcasting psychological warfare programming.

Muenster. The code name for an atomic blast on January 3, 1976, in the Nevada desert. It was one of a series of bomb tests named for cheeses, which began with "Edam" on April 4, 1975. According to "Nuclear Devices Set Off an Explosion of Names" (1983), by Harry Jaffee, other atomic test series have been named after "golfing terms ('Backswing,' on May 14, 1964), mixed drinks ('Daiquiri,' September 23, 1966) and parts of sailboats ('Rudder,' December 28, 1976)."

music. Electronic jamming; an air-intercept code word.

★ ☆ **N** ☆ ★

nabu. Nonadjusting ball-up. This is a contemporary addition to military screw-up acronyms of the SNAFU and FUBAR school of catastrophe (see under World War II).

narrow yellow. OCSA Form 159, Referral Slip. Used in assigning routine actions to others, it is a narrow yellow form that may have been named after the pop song "Mellow Yellow."

N.B.C. Nuclear, chemical, and biological warfare.

NCAP. See NIGHTCAP.

NEACP. See KNEECAP.

near space. Near the earth.

nightcap. Night combat air patrol; a pronunciation of the acronym, "NCAP."

Nimrod Dancer. The code name for the American deployment of two thousand troops to Panama. The name made little sense, and the Pentagon admitted that it had been picked by a computer.

Noah's Ark Plan. A concept in civil defense in which only the young and healthy would be evacuated in anticipation of a nuclear attack, while the old and sick would be left behind. Never put into place, it was at one time proposed for Los Angeles.

no first use. The strategic policy of announcing that one will not be the first to use nuclear weapons in a war. Neither the U.S. nor the Soviet Union ever proclaimed a "no first use" policy.

nonlethal military assistance. Assistance to another country in building roads, railroads, and airstrips for military use, but not supplying actual weapons or ammunition.

nonseller. A proposal that probably will not be approved. See also WON'T WASH.

no-op. An aircraft planned for and designed but never built and operated.

nth country. The next country to acquire nuclear capabilities. Until France joined the nuclear club some years ago, the equivalent term was the "4th country problem," because only three countries (the U.S., the Soviet Union, and China) then had the bomb.

nuc. A crew member on a nuclear submarine.

NUC. Naval Underseas Command.

nucint. Nuclear intelligence (i.e., intelligence information derived from the collection and analysis of radiation and other such effects).

nuclear buddy system. Name for the system of safeguards which presumably makes it impossible for a single person to start a nuclear attack.

nuclear winter. The possible climatic effects of an all-out nuclear war. Some scientists believe that the smoke, haze, and debris produced by multiple nuclear explosions could blot out the earth's sunlight for weeks or months and cause a profoundly disastrous drop in the planet's average surface temperature.

nuke. (1) The inner core of a nuclear weapon. (2) A nuclear weapon. The term made its debut on February 1, 1959, in a *New York Times Magazine* article: "Soon there may be 5-inch nuclear shells and portable Davy Crockett 'nukes' for the infantryman." (3) A nuclear-powered submarine. (4) To attack with nuclear weapons. William Sherk, in *500 Years of New Words* (1978), reports that the first use of the verb was in a July 11, 1970, *Look* magazine article in which the possibility of "nuking" China was broached.

NUTS. Nuclear utilization targeting strategy; a nuclear strategy based on the idea that military targets, and not population centers, should be destroyed in a nuclear exchange. It is summarized in *The Language of Defense* (1990), by Mark M. Eiler: "that nuclear weapons can be employed in limited wars that do not escalate into a full-scale nuclear exchange." Clearly, "NUTS" is as crazy as **MAD.**

★ ☆ O ☆ ★

o'club. Officers' club.

offload. To unload.

onload. To load.

on the deck. At minimum altitude.

ops-to-ops. From one operations officer to another; a Navy term.

oranges. Weather; an air-intercept code word. If the oranges are "sour," the weather is unsuitable for the aircraft's mission, while "sweet" oranges indicate that the weather is suitable for the mission.

overkill. More nuclear destructive ability than called for. It was usually put in terms of the number of times that the U.S. and the Soviet Union would have been able to destroy each other. Overkill estimates of the 1970s ranged from "17 times over" to "100 times over."

over-the-shoulder bombing. "A special case of . . . bombing where the bomb is released past the vertical in order that the bomb may be thrown back to the target" (according to the *Department of Defense Dictionary* [1991]).

★ ☆ **P** ☆ ★

padding. "Extraneous text added to a message for the purpose of concealing its beginning, ending, or length." This definition appears in Department of Defense glossaries.

palace guard. The highest echelon of Air Force officers; the generals.

pancake. I wish to land; an air-intercept code word. The reason may be specified (e.g., "Pancake ammo" means "I wish to land because I am out of ammo"; "Pancake fuel" means "I wish to land because I am out of fuel").

panopo. Pacific to Atlantic via the North Pole. This acronym is used as a title for those who have made the trip by submarine.

paradrop. Delivery by parachute of personnel or cargo.

parrot. Identification as "friend or foe" using transponder equipment (the IFF). "Strangle parrot" is an order to shut off one's IFF unit. "Parrot" alludes to the sound of radio equipment.

PAWS. Phased-array warning system.

Pax / Pax River. The Navy Air Test Center at Patuxent River, Maryland.

Peacekeeper. The MX missile. The name was cited (c. 1984) by those fascinated by euphemisms to show that Orwellian Newspeak had become a reality.

pecked line. A symbol consisting of a line broken at regular intervals (i.e., as if it had been pecked by a bird).

pen aids. Penetration aids; missiles that act as decoys to cause the other side to expend defensive missiles.

Pentagonese. The language of the Pentagon.

Pentagonian. One who works in the Pentagon.

Parade Rest—A Few Thoughts on Pentagonese

Writing in *National Journal*, David C. Morrison had this to say: "Perhaps no institution has twisted the mother tongue more systematically . . . than the Defense Department. Not only do Defense officials tend towards a particularly leaden bureaucratic patois, often called 'Pentagonese,' but military secrecy requirements also generate a dense thicket of evasive phrasing and arcane code words."

The term "Pentagonese" is wryly defined in *A Dictionary of Soldier Talk* (1984), by John R. Elting, Dan Cragg, and Ernest Deal: "A peculiar artificial language developed by the aborigines of the Puzzle Palace for the express purpose of confusing the troops. It is extremely difficult to translate into English."

But perhaps the best definition came from the late Charles McCabe of the San Francisco *Chronicle*: "a non-lingo in which murder can be made to mean salvation." There was a time during the darker days of the Vietnam War when the Pentagon created terms to make the adventure sound like a Boy Scout hike. The thirty-four dollars given to families of South Vietnamese civilians killed by mistake was officially called a "condolence award," and gross bombing errors were seldom termed anything more incriminating than "navigation errors," "misdirections," or "technical errors." Defoliants that could kill plants fifteen miles from where they were dropped were termed "weed killers" ("the same as you buy in the hardware store at home," said an American official in 1966). Phrases like "routine improvement of visibility in jungle areas" and "resources control" gave defoliation the sound of a conservation effort.

Pentagoose Noose. The *Pentagram News*, a newsletter distributed within the building.

pepper report. An ammunition report; a Navy term.

Perdue missile. A device created to fire dead chickens at 700 miles per hour at grounded aircraft to test cockpit canopies, to ensure they don't shatter when they hit birds in flight. The allusion is to Frank Perdue, who advertises his chickens on television.

permissive link. An element that must be completed or supplied before a nuclear weapon can be armed and fired. The permissive link can be anything from a key to a coded radio signal.

physics package. A thermonuclear bomb. After a Senate debate on the limitation of "physics packages," a letter to the Washington *Post* asked: "Does anyone not think or not care to think that these 'packages' are in fact bombs?"

piffy-ab. The President's Foreign Intelligence Advisory Board (P.F.I.A.B.).

pigeon. The magnetic bearing and distance of base (or other unit indicated) from you is (a certain number of) degrees/miles; an air-intercept code word.

pip. A radar signal; probably derived from "blip."

plank owner. A member of a ship's original crew (i.e., one who trod its deck timbers, or planks, when still new).

plutonium wine. An illegal drink created on nuclear submarines.

pocket war. A brief war.

pod. A detachable compartment of a spacecraft.

pogo. Switch to communications channel number preceding "pogo." If unable to establish communications, switch to channel number following "pogo." Neither this air-intercept code word nor the NASA acronym POGO (Polar Orbiting Geophysical Observatory) seem to have anything to do with the cartoon possum Pogo, created by the late Walt Kelly.

popeye. In clouds or area of reduced visibility; an air-intercept code word.

porkchop. A Navy supply officer. According to The Random House Dictionary of the English Language, "porkchop" is a traditional metaphor for a "livelihood, especially one acquired with little effort."

post-attack economy. The American economy, if any, that would exist after a nuclear war. Several plans exist for such a world, including one created by the RAND Corporation in the late 1960s, which says that post-attack America would be better off without the old and feeble: "The easiest way to implement a morally repugnant but socially beneficial policy is by inaction. Under stress, the managers of post-attack society would most likely resolve their problems by not making any special provisions for the elderly, the insane and the chronically ill."

POT. Portable outdoor toilet.

Potemkin site. A dummy Soviet surface-to-air missile site. In *The Superwarriors* (1978), James W. Canan describes a period in the 1970s when the U.S. had identified more than eight hundred such sites, "complete with fake launchers, radar, revetments, and vehicles." As Canan reminds us, the sites were named for G. A. Potemkin, the eighteenth-century architect of false-front villages used to deceive Catherine the Great on her visit to the Ukraine and the Crimea in 1767.

PRAM. Productivity, Reliability, Availability and Maintainability; an Air Force office.

Praying Mantis. The code name for the 1988 retaliatory attack in which the U.S. destroyed or sank six Iranian naval vessels and two oil platforms.

preach to the choir. To propose an idea to those who already agree with it (rather than trying to persuade those who disagree).

prematured. Said of a torpedo that explodes long before it gets to its target.

product. Plutonium to be used in a nuclear weapon. It is not to be confused with the "device" (the bomb itself).

program. Almost anything. More than thirty years ago Senator Stephen Young defined a Pentagon program as any assignment that took more than one phone call to complete.

pronto. As quickly as possible.

pump up. To brief someone until he or she is fully informed. The term is frequently used in relation to staff briefings, where the individuals doing the briefing may represent several different organizations. Representatives of the other organizations involved "pump up" the briefer in their areas of interest.

punch. You should very soon be obtaining a contact on the aircraft that is being intercepted; an air-intercept code word.

purple suiter. A military officer working in a Department of Defense position (e.g., in the Office of the Secretary of Defense). Army officers serving in that office receive periodic update briefings on what the Army is doing, and this is sometimes referred to as the "regreening process."

purr words. Euphemistic and "cleaned up" terms used in discussions of atomic warfare. An article by Blossom Grayer Feinstein in *Word Study* of February 1965 contains this indictment:

> A study of the words that are being used in connection with atomic warfare and atomic activity may reveal attitudes of the press that are otherwise hidden from public view. What semanticists have called purr words are actually being used in articles that are apparently objective. Look at "an optimistic picture of progress towards making the hydrogen bomb," "enriched uranium plants," "unintended war," "perfection of atomic device for exploding hydrogen bombs." If one were ignorant of the subject matter, it would be easy to feel hopeful with optimistic and progress; proud with enriched and perfection; innocent with unintended.
>
> In contrast to these purr words for atomic bomb activity, snarl words were used in an article on an A-Bomb Protest Rally. Even though Bertrand Russell spoke at that rally, and even though its theme was the total destruction involved in atomic warfare, the article used terms like: scuffles, motley crowd, snarling traffic, minor brawls, springboards of aggression, antibomb zealots. Once again, without a careful acquaintance with the subject matter involved, one might easily associate ugliness, aggressiveness, undue anger, uncivilized activity, and a general "lower-class" atmosphere with meetings where atomic warfare is described.

push the button. To launch a nuclear attack.

push time. The moment a pilot begins his descent to an aircraft carrier. As this is the toughest moment in carrier operations, "push" probably derives from "push comes to shove."

Puzzle Factory / Puzzle Palace. (1) The Pentagon. (2) The National Security Agency.

★ ☆ Q ☆ ★

q-message. A classified message relating to navigational dangers, navigational aids, mined areas, and searched or swept channels.

quarantine. A blockade. The term arose when John F. Kennedy spoke of "quarantining" Cuba during the Cuban missile crisis.

quiet sun. The condition of the sun when it is relatively free of sunspots and other factors that interfere with radio transmission.

★ ☆ R ☆ ★

rainout. Radioactive material in the atmosphere brought down by precipitation.

ratline. (1) An organized effort for moving personnel and/or material by clandestine means across a denied area or border. (2) A line used to secure a ship to its mooring; from the idea that rats will use such a line to get on and off a ship. Sometimes, the lines carry metal collars to prevent such traffic.

razor blades. A scrapped ship; presumably, from the idea that the ship has been converted into razor blades.

recce / reccy. Reconnaissance (as in, "recce photos").

reclama. A request to duly constituted authority to reconsider a decision.

redout. The blinding of infrared detectors due to high levels of infrared radiation produced in the upper atmosphere by a nuclear explosion. The term derives from "blackout."

reefer. (1) A refrigerator. (2) A motor vehicle, railroad freight car, ship, aircraft, or other conveyance so constructed and insulated as to protect commodities from either heat or cold.

retool. To do something over.

retro. A braking rocket (retro-rocket) on a spacecraft.

revolving door. The process whereby military officials leave the Pentagon for jobs with defense contractors.

ripe. Said of a naval mine that is armed (i.e., it is ready for the picking).

Rock, the. The Alternate National Command Center (a deep-underground installation near Camp David, Maryland, where three thousand top officials could be housed for more than a month). It lies under tons of mountain granite and is entered through two tunnels.

romper. A ship that has moved more than ten nautical miles ahead of its convoy and is unable to rejoin it.

R2D2. The Navy's close-in-system Gatling gun; from its shape, which resembles that of R2D2, a robot in George Lucas's *Star Wars* films. (It has been reported that Lucas came up with the name while working on *Star Wars*, after seeing a box of edited film of *American Graffiti* labeled "Reel 2, Dialogue 2.")

rubber duckie. An inflatable rubber boat towed behind a ship to confuse radar-guided missiles.

Rube Goldberg. Any extremely complex or farfetched nuclear weapon. The name is that of a cartoonist whose specialty was zany, oddball mechanical contraptions.

rug rank. A high rank (i.e., the rank of an officer who rates a rug on his or her floor).

R.V. Reentry vehicle; the cone-shaped package that carries a nuclear warhead to its target.

★ ☆ **S** ☆ ★

SACEUR. Supreme Allied Commander Europe.

salted weapon. A "dirty" nuclear weapon (i.e., one that has been "salted" with high-radiation "extras"). The term is officially defined in the *Department of Defense Dictionary* (1991): "A nuclear weapon which has, in addition to its normal components, certain elements or isotopes which capture neutrons at the time of the explosion and produce radioactive products over and above the usual radioactive weapon debris."

saltnik. One favoring the various Strategic Arms Limitation Treaties (SALT).

sanitize. To edit out; to censor.

sapfu. Surpassing all previous foul-ups (or fuck-ups).

saunter. Fly at best endurable speed; an air-intercept code word.

scare book. A periodic report formerly issued by the secretary of defense and entitled *Soviet Military Power*. It is so-called because of its tendency to magnify Soviet military strength. Scare books were usually released to coincide with the Pentagon budget request.

scenario dependent. Dependent on a chain of events.

scram. I am about to open fire. Friendly units get clear of indicated contact, bogey, or area. This air-intercept code word may be combined with an indication of the proper direction of withdrawal, and the type of fire may also be indicated (e.g., "Scram proximity," meaning "I am about to open fire with proximity-fused ammunition"; "Scram mushroom," meaning "I am about to fire a special weapon").

scramble. To take off in a hurry; an Air Force term.

scrub. To cancel a mission; to back out of a mission. The term may come from the act of rubbing—or scrubbing—one's mission off a blackboard.

search and destroy. Destroy and then search; pure Pentagonese.

Secdef. Secretary of defense. The Washington *Post* reported in 1988 that there was a sign in the top man's military airplane—on the door of his private cabin—that read "Secdef and Mrs. Carlucci."

second strike. A retaliatory attack (i.e., following a "FIRST STRIKE").

secure. Term used to underscore the assertion that the various branches of the services speak a different language as attested to by this anonymous statement which was being passed around the Pentagon in 1993:

> One reason the Military Services have trouble coordinating joint operations is that they don't speak the same language. For example: If you tell Navy personnel to "secure a building," they will turn off the lights and lock the doors. The Army will occupy the building so that no one can enter. The Marines will assault the building, capture it, and defend it with suppressive fire and close combat. The Air Force, on the other hand, will take out a three-year lease with an option to purchase.

selected. Promoted. To be "deselected" is to be demoted.

selected out. To be let go; to be fired.

sequential dumping. The unloading of tons of rocks on top of missile silos.

shadower. A seaborne observer maintaining contact with an object. Shadowing may be carried out either overtly or covertly.

shelf life. Period of time during which a nuclear weapon can remain effective without being exploded.

Sherwood Forest. A missile room on a submarine; because the densely packed missile tubes resemble enormous tree trunks.

short fuse. A close deadline, or **suspense.**

shotgun. The simultaneous distribution of a document to several offices.

shotgun guy. An Air Force officer used as an escort pilot for such jobs as flying diplomats to high-level conferences. In 1990 the Washington *Post* referred to shotgun guys as "top-of-the-cloud escorts." In the Old West, a man would "ride shotgun" next to the driver of a stagecoach.

sick. Equipment indicated is operating at reduced efficiency; an air-intercept code word.

sick paint. A radar image caused by the radar signal reflected from an object.

sigint. Signal intelligence (i.e., intelligence gathered electronically rather than by spies). See also HUMINT.

sign off on. To sign or initial; to pass along.

silent service. The submarine service. According to I. J. Galantin, in *Take Her Deep!* (1987), the name was "bestowed by a long-forgotten reporter, or some ingrained idea about classified information to which other branches of our armed forces were less sensitive."

SINS. Situational inertial navigation system.

SIOP. Single Integrated Operational Plan; a plan for nuclear war. Peace has been described as a "benign pre-SIOP environment."

sitrep. Situation report.

Skunk Works. The Lockheed research-and-development operation where the SR-71 and U-2 spy planes were developed. The term is now used more generally. Here is how it is defined in *The Language of Defense* (1990), by Mark M. Eiler: "A separate program management operation established outside the normal defense acquisition process because of the high security classification of the work being performed by the contractor. Examples of such programs include development of the B-2 stealth bomber and the SR-71 strategic reconnaissance aircraft." The term was taken from the late Al Capp's *Li'l Abner* comic strip; illicit Kickapoo Joy Juice was made in Big Barnsmell's Skonk Works.

SLCM [pronounced "slick-em"]. Sea-launched cruise missile.

slew time. The time needed for a weapon to aim at a new target after firing at a previous one.

SLOB. Satellite low-orbit bombardment.

slow flyer. Cruise missile which is slow and low-flying.

SNORT. Supersonic Naval Ordnance Research Track. Nothing to sniff at, this administrative project was running along at a cost of $1 million a year in the 1980s.

snowbird. An interim assignment.

soft. Vulnerable; not protected from nuclear attack (e.g., a city). "Soft targets" are people, while "soft bases" are missile installations that are vulnerable to enemy attack.

sortie. A nuclear missile (to the crew operating missile sites). The term is also used by pilots (see under the Gulf War).

southside basing. The nestling of U.S. missiles against the southern side of high western mesas to protect the missiles from Soviet missiles coming over the North Pole.

SOW. Statement of work.

spasm war. All-out war. The term is taboo at the Pentagon.

Spearhead. The 3rd Armored Division, which spent thirty-seven years keeping an eye on the Iron Curtain from its base in Germany. It officially came home on January 17, 1992. It was Elvis Presley's old unit.

special weapons. Nuclear arms.

splashdown. The landing of a space vehicle in the ocean.

splashed. Enemy aircraft shot down; an air-intercept code word. Followed by number and type, this term was given much play during the Gulf War.

spoof. (1) To deceive the controllers of an enemy military satellite by making them think that the satellite needs control when it does not. When an improper correction is made, the satellite is lost or disoriented, or it uses up much of its fuel. (2) To deceive a pilot by using electronics or confusing tactics.

spoofer. A contact employing electronic or tactical deception measures (i.e., one that is deceiving, or SPOOFING); an air-intercept code word.

spook. A friendly counterintelligence person who inspects offices at night for possible security violations.

square one. The first step in a process.

squib. A small pyrotechnic device that may be used to fire the igniter in a rocket or for some similar purpose.

state chicken. I am at a fuel state requiring recovery, tanker service, or diversion to an airfield; an air-intercept code phrase.

state lamb. I do not have enough fuel for an intercept plus reserve required for carrier recovery (i.e., one is as helpless as a lamb); an air-intercept code phrase.

state tiger. I have sufficient fuel to complete my mission as assigned; an air-intercept code phrase.

stick. A number of paratroopers who jump from the door of an aircraft during one run over a drop zone.

The Stick. The *U.S.S. Theodore Roosevelt*, because of T.R.'s motto "walk softly and carry a big stick."

stick shaker. An alerting device used to indicate that an airplane may stall soon.

stovepipe. An organization aligned vertically and specializing in one functional area (e.g., logistics, finance and accounting, or personnel training). The term also applies to informal vertical communications from one action officer to another.

strangle. To switch off equipment.

straphanger. A person at a briefing or on a trip whose presence is not required.

stratospheric drip. Fallout.

straw man. A weak argument advanced as a basis for discussion. In the form of a document, it is sometimes referred to as a "think piece" and is usually the forerunner of a more well thought out document.

strike. An attack. According to Nigel Calder, in *Nuclear Nightmares* (1979), in Europe this term means a nuclear attack, while Americans use the term for a conventional attack also (as in, "air strike"). This discrepancy was especially disconcerting to European planners during the Vietnam War, when virtually everything the Americans did was called a strike.

strip search. See under the Gulf War.

sucker. A nuclear missile.

suitcase warfare. Warfare with small, powerful, highly portable weapons. A discussion of the term appears in a report by an insurance industry think tank: "It is conceivable that an object the size of a suitcase, and carried as inconspicuously, could contain any of several substances which could destroy whole structures and even whole cities."

surviving spouse. A widow or widower; a Department of Defense term. The official term for the cash settlement a surviving spouse is given is "death gratuity," which sounds like a tip you give an undertaker.

suspense. The time allowed to complete an action. See also SHORT FUSE.

SWAG. Scientific Wild-Ass Guess—as one might be prone to making in military situations.

sweet. (1) Workable. In *The Weapons Culture* (1968), Ralph E. Lapp speaks of the H-bomb becoming "technologically sweet." (2) Generally good. In *Flight of the Intruder* (1986), Stephen Coonts applies the term to aviation: "The bombardier reported to the ship that the tanker was 'sweet,' that is, it could transfer fuel, so the spare tanker on deck would not be needed."

★ ☆ **T** ☆ ★

TACAMO. Take charge and move out. The Navy's E-6A TACAMO aircraft would be used to communicate with ballistic missile submarines during a nuclear war.

tacnuk. Tactical nuclear weapon.

Tailhook. Name for a fraternal organization of Navy and Marine aviators taking its name from the device on the underside of an aircraft that grabs the wire that slows the plane down on landing. The 1991 Tailhook convention was a lurid affair characterized by sexual excess and acts of harassment.

Tailhook Terms

The investigations in the wake of the 1991 Tailhook Convention yielded a tawdry slang of its own:

ball walking. striding about with one testicle exposed.

decks afoul. Call announcing a woman too ugly to attack.

decks awash. Call announcing fair game.

sharking. Butt biting.

zapping. Slapping squadron emblems on parts of women's anatomy.

tally ho. Target visually sighted; a military aviation code word. Officially, the *Department of Defense Dictionary* (1991) adds: "This should be followed by initial contact report as soon as possible. The sighting should be amplified if possible (e.g., 'tally ho pounce,' or 'tally ho heads up')."

tank. A housing facility for a submarine and its innumerable spare parts.

Tank, the. The room in the Pentagon where the Joint Chiefs of Staff meet; also known as the GOLD ROOM.

tape. The chain of command; from "red tape" and the similarity between a tape and a chain.

terminal leave. Unused vacation time left over at the end of an enlistment.

thermal radiation. Heat radiation from a nuclear explosion. At the source, temperatures are equivalent to those at the center of the sun.

think tank. An organization dedicated to research on policy issues, including national security. Important think tanks in the arena of military studies include the RAND Corporation and the Institute for Defense Analyses.

threat fan. The area vulnerable to an enemy missile that could take a number of possible paths.

threat tube. The path of an incoming enemy missile (as in, "The threat tube was narrow").

three-humped camel. The chaotic result of the joint work of the three armed services.

three pointer. An aircraft landing in which the three sets of wheels all touch down at the same time; a good landing.

three p's. Pay, promotion, and pension. These are said to be the obsession of all Pentagonians.

throw-weight. "The combined weight that a ballistic nuclear missile can lift into flight for a given distance. Throw-weight determines the size and numbers of warheads, decoys, and penetration aids that a missile can carry" (according to *The Language of Defense* [1990], by Mark M. Eiler).

tied on. The aircraft indicated is in formation with me (i.e., tied to the formation); an air-intercept code word.

tight. Said of military electronics that are working fine, either alone or in tandem.

tinman. An aluminum space suit.

Tomcat. The F-14 jet fighter.

tooth-to-tail ratio. Combat power in comparison to support (noncombat) base.

Top Gun. The Navy's Fighter Weapons School, located at the naval air station in Miramar, California.

top line. The maximum dollar amount that the Department of Defense, a service branch, or other military unit has to spend. This is, of course, the opposite end of the spectrum from the well-known "bottom line."

total nuclear war. All-out war. It says under this entry in the *Department of Defense Dictionary* (1991): "Not to be used. See general war." This squeamishness about total war reaches a peak in the official *Dictionary of United States Army Terms*, which shies away from defining not only a "total nuclear war" but also "general war," "nuclear war," and "war."

touchdown. The landing of a manned or unmanned spacecraft.

TRADOC. Training and Doctrine Command (U.S. Army).

Triad. The three elements of the U.S. nuclear response—submarines, land-based missiles, and long-range bombers.

Trinity. The code name for the first test of an atomic bomb, at Los Alamos, New Mexico, in 1945. It was given this name by J. Robert Oppenheimer, who tried to explain why he named it in a 1962 letter to General Leslie R. Groves:

> There is no rational answer to your question about the code name Trinity. . . . Why I chose the name is not clear, but I know what thoughts were in mind. There is a poem of John Donne, written just before his death, which I know and love. From it a quotation:
>> As West and East
>> In all flatt Maps—and I am one—are one,
>> So death doth touch the Resurrection.
> . . . That still does not make a Trinity; but in another, better known devotional poem Donne opens, "Batter my heart, three person'd God;—." Beyond this I have no clues whatever.

tube. See THREAT TUBE.

two-man rule. A method for preventing the accidental or improper use of nuclear weapons by requiring the joint activity of two people. Its official definition is: "A system designed to prohibit access by an individual to nuclear weapons and certain designated components by requiring the presence at all times of at least two authorized persons each capable of detecting incorrect or unauthorized procedures with respect to the task to be performed."

two-way street. The policy of buying arms from and selling arms to friendly nations.

2 x policy. The policy of massive retaliation to a nuclear attack.

★ ☆ U ☆ ★

U-bomb. In 1955 this weapon was announced, and never heard from again. It was said to combine the "best" features of the A-bomb and the H-bomb.

unk-unks. Unknown unknowns; factors considered in deciding on new weapons systems. "Things we not only don't know about, but don't even know we don't know about," is how John G. Kester defined them in his article "How to Speak Pentagonese," in *The Washingtonian* of February 1982. The term is used by military planners, whose unk-unks usually pertain to what enemy military planners are planning.

unobtanium. A substance or piece of hardware that is desired but not obtainable. This term was created in the early days of the space race and was adopted by the military. It is a parody based on the "-ium" of, e.g., uranium.

up gripe. A problem with an aircraft that does not prevent it from flying. The term is defined by Stephen Coonts in *Final Flight* (1988) as a "nuisance problem that could wait until the bird was down for another problem or a planned maintenance inspection before it was repaired or 'worked off.'" See also DOWN GRIPE.

Urgent Fury. The code name for the 1983 invasion of Grenada.

uti possidetis. The principle that states that a nation owns the territory it holds at the end of a war.

UTTAS [pronounced "utahs"]. Utility tactical transport aircraft system; a helicopter.

★ ☆ V ☆ ★

very high. An altitude of more than fifty thousand feet.

very low. An altitude below five hundred feet.

vote. To turn the switch that activates and fires a nuclear missile. More than one person must vote—usually four, and all at the same time—to perform such an act.

vulture's row. Position high up on an aircraft carrier's superstructure where senior officers observe flight operations.

★ ☆ W ☆ ★

waist bubble. The waist, or middeck, catapult control cab on Nimitz-class aircraft carriers.

walks on water. Miraculous; perfect. Officers talk of gaining walks on water fitness reports.

WANAP. Washington National Airport.

wargasm. The condition of total havoc that occurs when all the nuclear buttons get pushed. The term is an ironic play on "orgasm." See also SPASM WAR.

War Room. Term actually used by those who work there to describe the White House military communications center; officially called the Situation Room.

weaponeer. A person who prepares a nuclear weapon for action.

weapons system. A weapon. At some point it became unfashionable to call a weapon a weapon; even the simplest tool of combat became a system.

weps. Weapons (as in the "weps elevator" on an aircraft carrier).

what luck? What are the results of the assigned mission?; an air-intercept code phrase.

what state? Report amount of fuel, ammunition, and oxygen remaining; an air-intercept code phrase.

what's up? Is anything the matter?; an air-intercept code phrase.

whiz kid. A systems analyst or senior staff member of the Department of Defense staff; a derogatory term since the early Vietnam War era.

wild card. A major unforeseen development. A nuclear holocaust, the total collapse of civilization in its present form, a worldwide totalitarian state, and an extraterrestrial invasion are all wild cards.

wild geese. Mercenaries.

Wimex. Worldwide Military Command and Control System; the master alerting system for nuclear war. The term is a pronunciation of the acronym, "WWMCCS."

window. (1) A gap; an opening. A "window of vulnerability" is a defensive gap that would allow an enemy to make a first strike. (2) The period during which it is possible and/or economical to begin a space mission.

WINE. Warning and indications in Europe; a system to warn of an approaching attack. It is not to be confused with WINK (warning in Korea) or WISE (warning indicators system Europe).

wiring diagram. An organizational chart (because of its resemblance to an electrical wiring diagram, with all of its lines and boxes).

won't wash. Having little chance of favorable consideration; unworkable. See also NONSELLER.

wooden bomb. A weapon that is completely reliable, has an infinite shelf life, and requires no special handling, storage, or surveillance. It is a concept, not a reality.

woompher bomb. A weapon resulting from a technological breakthrough of such magnitude that the country that made it would have a decisive strategic advantage.

wordsmith. To rewrite a document by smoothing out the wording without changing the substance.

★ ☆ Y ☆ ★

Yankee White. An extremely high level of clearance. It deems an individual "unquestionably loyal to the United States."

yardbird. A shipyard worker.

yellow cake. Uranium concentrates used in nuclear weapons.

yellow stuff. Small tractors, earthmovers, etc., used in military operations. In civilian life, these vehicles are usually yellow.

★ ☆ Z ☆ ★

Z-bomb. A mythical bomb of such power that exploding it would "end it all." The term was used in the 1950s, and a stripper of that period, Lolinda Raquel, billed herself as "Margo The Mexican Z-Bomb 'The Absolute End.'"

zero-g. The state of weightlessness (i.e., when there is zero gravity).

Z-gram. A memo or order in the terse, direct style pioneered by Admiral Elmo Zumwalt during his tenure as Chief of Naval Operations.

zip fuel. High-energy jet fuel.

zippers. Dawn and dusk combat air patrol.

Sources

★

Calder, Nigel. *Nuclear Nightmares.* New York: Viking, 1979.

Canan, James W. *The Superwarriors.* New York: Weybright and Talley, 1978.

Dickson, Paul. *The Electronic Battlefield.* Indiana University Press, Bloomington, 1976.

Jaffe, Harry. "Nuclear Devices Set Off an Explosion of Names." A 1983 dispatch from Network News, Inc.

Joint Chiefs of Staff. *Department of Defense Dictionary of Military and Associated Terms* (Joint Pub 1-02). Washington, D.C.: Department of Defense, December 1, 1989.

Lambdin, William. *Doublespeak Dictionary.* New York: Pinnacle Books, 1979.

Lapp, Ralph E. *The Weapons Culture.* New York: Norton, 1968.

Molenhoff, Clark R. *The Pentagon.* New York: G. P. Putnam's Sons, 1967.

"Nukespeak: Of War and SIOP." *MacLean's* (December 5, 1983).

Pringle, Peter, and William Aiken. *S.I.O.P.: The Secret U.S. Plan for Nuclear War.* New York: W. W. Norton, 1983.

Shafritz, Jay M. *Words on War.* New York: Prentice Hall, 1990.

Sheehan, Neil. *The Arnheiter Affair.* New York: Random House, 1971.

Sherk, William. *500 Years of New Words.* New York: Doubleday, 1983.

Semler, Eric, James Benjamin and Adam Gross. *The Language of Nuclear War.* New York: Harper & Row: 1987.

Tsouras, Peter, and Bruce W. and Susan W. Watson. *The United States Army: A Dictionary.* New York: Garland Publishing, 1991.

Wilson, Andrew. *The Bomb and the Computer.* New York: Delacorte, 1968.

Zuckerman, Ed. "Hiding from the Bomb—Again." *Harper's* (August 1979).

Index of Defined Words and Phrases